Elements
of
COBOL Web
Programming

with
Micro Focus
Net Express

Wilson Price

Object-Z Systems, Inc
Orinda, CA

Object-Z Publishing
Orinda, California

Object-Z Publishing
Orinda, California

Elements of Cobol Web Programming
with Micro Focus Net Express

Cover design by Kevin Mykal Long

Production/printing by Norcal Printing, San Francisico

9876543

Email author at: wprice@objectz.com

For information about other Object-Z activities and publications:
www.objectz.com

Order Information:
Elements of Cobol Web Programming with Micro Focus Net Express
ISBN 0-9655945-1-3 (**without** Micro Focus Net Express, University Edition)
ISBN 0-9655945-2-1 (**with** Micro Focus Net Express, University Edition)

Object-Z Publishing
At the time of this printing
we are in the process of relocating.
Check our Web site www.objectz.com
for address and phone numbers.

To Jean

Contents Summary

Chapter

0	Getting Started	2
1	The Net Express Interactive Development Environment	10
2	The World Wide Web	26
3	A Basic Net Express Web Example	50
4	Working with the CGI Program	74
5	Making Selections	98
6	Building Applications from Legacy Code	138
7	Processing Cobol Tables	164
8	Hyperlinks and Other Good Stuff	190
9	More Complex Applications	217
10	Maintaining State	238
11	File and Database Processing	280

Appendix

Data Files and Subprograms	326

Index

Index	350

Detailed Table of Contents

Chapter 0 Getting Started

The Example Applications CD 4
  Folder (Subdirectory) Contents 4
  Folders for Examples and Assignments 4
  Loading Files From the Examples CD 4
  Net Express Skeleton Files 5
Conventions Used in this Book 5
  Use of Fonts 5

Menu Sequence 6
Cobol Program Listings 6
Project Markers 6
Updating Your Copy of Net Express 6
  The Need for Software Updates 6
  Accessing Micro Focus Web Sync 6
Deploying Applications 9

Chapter 1 The Net Express Interactive Development Environment.

The Interactive Development Environment:
  First Look 12
Net Express Projects 12
A Sample Project... 12
Starting the IDE 13
The Net Express Toolbar 15
File Access 16
Building and Running the Application 17

Handling Program Errors 18
  Correcting Compiler Errors 18
  Stepping Through a Program for Debugging 19
  Using Breakpoints for Debugging 20
Free Format 22
Changing the Look and Feel of the IDE 24
Summing Up 25
Coming Up 25

Chapter 2 The World Wide Web

Basic Web Principles 28
  The Client/Server Concept 28
  The Emergence of the World Wide Web 29
  Basic Terminology 30
The Web and Commerce 31
  Intranets 31
  Extranets 31
  The Web and Client Server 31
  The Web and Net Express 32
How Does the Web Work? 32
  Internet Addressing 32
  Protocol 32
  The URL 33
Dissecting the URL 33
  Host Computer 33
  Path 34
A Library Inquiry Application 34
The Basics of HTML.. 37

Tags: The Code of HTML 37
Controlling Lines of Output 38
Document Structure Tags 39
The HTML Script's Header 39
The HTML Script's Body 40
  Headings 40
  The Input Tag 40
  The Form Tag 41
Behind the Scenes 41
  Handling Data.. 41
  The Output Page 42
  The Common Gateway Interface (CGI) 42
The Cobol CGI 43
  The External-Form Clause 43
  Accept and Display 45
  Overall Relationships 46
Summing Up 48
Coming Up 49

Chapter 3 A Basic Net Express Web Example

Folders for Projects 52
Generating a Web Application 53
  Creating the Project 53
  A Naming Convention 54
  Creating a New Form 54
  The Form Designer Screen 56
Building the Input Page 57
  Text Entries 57
  Some Tips on Inserting Controls 59
  The Input Text Control 60
  About Selecting Names 62
  Completing the Input Form 62
Building the Output Page 63
  The Server-Side Text Control 63
  Building the Output Page 63
Creating the CGI Program 64

The Results of Your Endeavor 66
  The Project Screen 66
  The Net Express Operating Environment 66
  Running the Application 67
  Terminating a Run 68
Improving the Appearance of Screen Displays 69
  Using the Format Tool Bar 69
  Setting Style Attributes 69
  Using the Input Text to Display Output 71
  The Horizontal Rule 71
Summing Up 72
  Project Summary 72
  General Summary 72
Coming Up 73
Assignment 73

Chapter 4 Working with the CGI Program

The Generated CGI Program 76
  Four Components 76
  The CPF Copy File 76
  The CPY and CPV Copy Files 78
Overall Execution of the CGI Program 78
  Handling Input from the Form 78
  User Application Code 79
  Handling Output to the Page 79
  Embedded HTML 79
Displaying a Patron Name 79
  Modifying the Output Form 79
  Inserting Code in the CGI Program 80
Other Features 83
  Displaying Copy Files in the Program 83
  No Program Looping 83
Enhancing the Output 83
  Required Displays 83
  About Cloning an Application 84
  Duplicating the Input Page 85

Duplicating and Modifying the Output Page 85
Duplicating the CGI 87
Changes to the CGI Program 88
Calling a Subprogram from the CGI—Lib04 88
  The Subprogram LIB-SUB0 88
  Modifying the CGI 89
  Adding the Subprogram to the Project 89
Accessing Data From a File—Lib05 90
  An Indexed File Processing Subprogram 90
  Modifications to the CGI Program 91
  Replacing Lib-sub0 With Lib-sub1 92
  About the File-Accessing Subprograms 92
  Don't Forget Your Cobol 92
Summing Up 94
  Project Summary 94
  General Summary 94
Coming Up 95
Assignments 95

Chapter 5 Making Selections

A Typical Web Selection Screen 100
Check Boxes 101
  Creating Checkboxes 101
  Setting Properties 103
Radio Buttons 105
  What are Radio Buttons? 105
  Creating a Screen With Radio Buttons 105
  Be Consistent With Existing
      Cobol Applications 107
  Resulting CGI Code 107
Using Multiple Radio Button Groups 109
  The Three Groups of Figure 5-1 109
  An Output Page 110
  Grouping Screen Controls 110
  Aligning Screen Controls 111
  Justifying Text 112
  The CGI Program 112
The Reset Button 115
The Table Control 115
  Project Proj0502—Using a Table 115
  Table Characteristics 115
  Entering Column Headings 117
  Entering Radio Buttons 118

Other Table Features 119
The Select Control 120
  About the Select 120
  Creating a Select Control 121
  Other Properties 124
  On The CGI Side 125
Multiple Selection 125
  Creating the Input Page 126
  Creating the Output Page 127
  The CGI Program 128
  Trial Runs 129
Using Color in the Display Form 129
  A Simple Example 129
  Creating the Output Form 130
The CGI 133
  Searching a String 133
  Inserting Your Code into the CGI 133
Comments About Different Browsers 135
Summing Up 135
  Project Summary 135
  General Summary 135
Coming Up 136
Assignment 136

Chapter 6 Building Applications from Legacy Code

A File-Accessing Program 140
The Patron File 140
The Subprogram Lib-sub2.cbl 140
The Stateless Nature of the Web 141
A Basic Subprogram Application—Proj0601 142
Incorporating the Subprogram
into the Application 142
The Output Form Lib06-OUT. 144
CGI Code—Lib06.cbl 145
Manipulating Subprogram Input for
Display—Proj0602 146
The Output Page Lib07-OUT 146
CGI Code—Lib07.cbl 146
Creating Applications With Form Express............ 147
About the Application Wizard 147
Create the Application Project 148

Create the Application 149
Modifying the HTML Pages 152
The Input Page 152
The Output Page 153
The CGI 155
Using Disabled Edit to Display Data 156
Placing Form Express in its Proper Context 156
Data Validation 157
Built-In JavaScript Data Validation Functions .. 157
Designating Data Validation 158
Summing Up 161
Project Summary 161
General Summary 161
Coming Up 162
Assignment 163

Chapter 7 Processing Cobol Tables

Multiple-File Data Access.................................. 166
A Conventional Cobol Screen Display 166
The Data Files 166
The Subprogram Lib-sub3 167
Textarea Control Display 167
Displaying a List of Books 167
The Output Form—Lib09-OUT 170
The CGI Program 171
Using the Table Control 172
Using the HTML Display Text Control 172
Creating the HTML Table—Lib10-OUT 173
CGI Code 177

Managing Repeating Data—Lib12 178
Handling Subscripted Cobol Data Items 178
Features of the Lib12 CGI 178
The Output Page Lib12-OUT 182
Using Form Express to Generate Table Output 184
Creating the Application 185
The End Result 185
Summing Up 187
Project Summary 187
General Summary 187
Coming Up 188
Assignment 188

Chapter 8 Hyperlinks and Other Good Stuff

Web Administration for Solo 192
Web Shares 192
Creating a New Web Share 193
Adding Images to HTML Forms 195
About Graphics in the Web 195
Inserting an Image Into Lib12 195
The Input Image Control 197
Project Border 197
Including an Input Image Control in a Form 199
CGI Code for Handling Input Image 200
Providing for Repetition 201
Using a Text Control as a Hyperlink 201
A Graphic as a Hyperlink 203
Defining Events 204
What is an Event? 204
The Script Assistant 204

Displaying Help 205
Event Handler Code—JavaScript 208
Modifying Properties with Event Handlers 208
Duplicating Data... 208
JavaScript Code for Duplicating Data Items 209
Creating the Event Handler 210
More on Setting the Value 211
Setting Check Boxes and Radio Button 212
Using an Input Button to Transfer Control........... 213
A Word of Caution 213
Summing Up 214
Project Summary 214
General Summary 214
Coming Up 214
Assignment 215

Chapter 9 More Complex Applications

One Form for Input and Output 218
Asymmetric and Symmetric Programs 218
Features of Proj0901 218
Creating the Application 219
Creating the CGI 221
CGI Code 221
Finish-Up Tasks 224
Multiple Output Forms 226
The Nature of the Project 226
The CGI Program 228

Multiple Actions—Two Submit Buttons 229
Project Input and Output 229
About the Subprogram Book-sub.cbl 230
The Input Form and Multiple Submit Buttons 232
Selecting Names For Form Items 232
The Generated CGI Program 233
Summing Up 235
Project Summary 235
General Summary 235
Coming Up 236
Assignment 236

Chapter 10 Maintaining State

Techniques for Maintaining State 240
   Scenarios Requiring State Maintenance 240
   Three State-Maintenance Mechanisms 240
   Considerations 241
Controlling Repetition With a Hidden Input 241
   Overview of the Application 241
   Inserting a Hidden Input Control 242
   Creating the CGI programs 243
   CGI Code 244
   Some Other Observations 244
Restricting Data Access With a
   Hidden Input Control 245
   About this Example 245
   The Input Password Control 246
   CGI Code 247
Multiple Screen Input 247
   The Order Processing Example 247
   Project Hidden03 249
   The Application's CGI programs 250
   A Form With Hidden Input controls 250
Using a Cookie in the Form-Letter Order System . 251
   About This Example 251
   Inserting a Cookie into a Form 252
   Cookie Data Preparation by the CGI 253
   Retrieving Cookie Data 255

Using a Cookie to Store an Access Code 258
   The Project Proj1005 Pages 258
   The Project's CGI Programs 259
Maintaining State Across Browser Sessions 259
   Persistent Cookies 259
   Setting a Cookie Expiration Date 262
   Accessing Cookie Data with the Accept 263
Maintaining State Using a Server-Side File 264
   The Micro Focus Sstate.cbl Subprogram 264
   Preserving Name/Address Data Within a
   Browser Session 265
   The CGI Programs 266
   Building the Project 268
Using a Cookie with a Server-Side File 269
   State Preservation Between Sessions 269
   Component Diagram—Proj1008 271
   CGI Code—Project 1008 272
   Removing Aged Server-Side Records 272
Summing Up 274
   Project Summary 274
   General Summary 275
   Summarizing the Sstate Subprogram
   Entry Points 276
Coming Up 278
Assignment 278

Chapter 11 File and Database Processing

Components of the Patron File-Maintenance
   Projects 282
   About the Patron File 282
   Patron File-Access Subprograms 283
   Copy Files 284
Adding Records to the Patron File 284
   The Project Screens 284
   The CGI 286
One Page for Input and Output 287
   Features of Proj1102 287
   CGI Considerations 288
   The Project's Event Handlers 290
Record Maintenance—Pat03 290
   About the Pat03 Project 290
   The HTML Page Pat03U-DIS 293
   The CGI Programs 293
Accessing a Relational Database
   from NetExpress 294
   Relational Databases and SQL 294
   Setting Up to Use ESQL in
   NetExpress Programs 297
First Look at OpenESQL Assistant 299
   Starting Point 299
   Host Variables 300
   Creating a Simple Query 300
   Basic Nature of the SQL Select 302
   Establishing Search Critera 302

Inserting ESQL into the CGI 304
   The Query Code 304
   Connect and Disconnect 305
   Inserting Working-Storage Code 306
   SQL Compiler Directive 307
   The CGI Program with Embedded SQL 307
Required User-Inserted Code 309
   Input Code 309
   Output Code 309
Linking Tables and Accessing Multiple Rows. 309
Joining Two Tables 309
   The SQL Cursor 310
   The Need for Two Queries 311
Creating the Queries 311
   Generating the Query for Patron Data............. 311
   Generating the Query for Book Data 312
   Inserting Auxiliary Code into the CGI 314
   User-Inserted Code 315
Using the Application Wizard for an
   SQL Database 317
   Using the Application Sql03 317
   Creating an SQL Application 318
   Modifying and Expanding a
   Wizard-Built SQL Application. 320
Summing Up 322
   Project Summary 322
   General Summary 323
Assignment 324

Appendix Data Files and Subprograms

About the Data Files 328
   Files in the NE-Data Folder 328
   Using the Data Files 329
Example Applications Files 330

Data Files 330
Subprograms 332
Assignment Files 341
   Data Files 341
   Subprograms 343

Preface

Introduction

You're a Cobol programmer. You know your organization's Cobol legacy applications, replete with ISAM files, inside and out. An hour ago you left a meeting with your manager who declared "Jean/Gene" (your preference) "we *must* bring our applications to the Web." Now what? You and those in your programming group are Cobol programmers. Your knowledge of the Web revolves around email and the Alta Vista search facility. Panic sets in! Do we need to retrain in Java or C++ (shudder) or Visual Basic? How will you survive without the great file handling and data manipulation capabilities of Cobol? The answer to the first question is a resounding "NO" because you don't need to survive *without* Cobol: the answer *is* in Cobol. Indeed, features from Cobol vendors include capabilities for the Cobol programmer to bring legacy applications to the Web, all the while working with Cobol. In fact, that's the subject of this book: creating Web applications with Cobol using Micro Focus Net Express.

Intended Audience

This book covers the basics of using Micro Focus Net Express to create Web applications utilizing Cobol. Note the word "basics." There are Web features of Net Express that I do not cover—for instance, creating applications using ActiveX. But overall, topics of this book will give you a solid foundation in the vast potential for Cobol on the Web. In that respect, the book becomes a must for any Cobol programmer who wants to keep pace with the profound effect the World Wide Web is having on all areas of computing. Prerequisites for its use are (1) a first Cobol course, or (2) Cobol programming experience. Be aware that this is not a book on Web site design—that topic is best left to other books, some of which cover it well.

Example Applications

Examples in this book are organized as projects, consistent with the Micro Focus technique for designating applications. A project is simply a grouping of programs needed for a given application (the project file itself is effectively a directory for the project). The Examples CD included with this book contains 43 projects, each illustrating one or more new topics. Loading and using the CD are described in Chapter 0, *Getting Started*. In almost all cases, you should run an application before reading the text descriptions.

Web Site Help

Look on our Web site `www.objectz.com` for: an errata list for this book, tips on using Net Express, and work-arounds for problem areas. From the home page, click on the Object-Z Publishing icon then the book title "Elements of COBOL Web Programming." You will see a Tips/Help link.

Project Icons

For your convenience, the starting point of each project description in this book is marked by a project icon identifying the project folder and the project name. For instance, the icon to the left would indicate project the project Lib01 stored in the Proj0301 folder.

Micro Focus Net Express

This is a hands-on book. As such, you need a copy of Micro Focus Net Express available in two versions: the full version and the University Edition. If your copy of the book does not included Net Express, University Edition, you can order it from MERANT Micro Focus, Mountain View, California.

COBOL versus Cobol

We all know that COBOL is an acronym for COmmon Business Oriented Language. Consequently, we use uppercase for all letters. However, within a book, I've found that several instances of the uppercase COBOL tend to leap out at me thereby distracting my focus from the particular topic at hand. Consequently, I use Cobol, not COBOL, throughout this book.

Acknowledgements

A text book is never the product of a single person's thoughts and ideas. We all learn and build from others. I'm no exception. During three decades of writing, I have many to thank for their input. This project has been long and difficult as so many of the concepts were new to me. The following technical people at Micro Focus provided much needed support as Net Express evolved from Version 2.0 to Version 3.0 and as I learned the "ins and outs" of Web programming.

Ian Archbell	Chris Hatton
Simon Ellis	Chris Lee
Derek Gardner	Steve Mondeaux
Drew Hannah	Simon Wray

Wayne Rippin, Net Express product manager, provided essential support without which many aspects of this project would have been impossible. Paul Halpern, director of the academic program at Merant, did a terrific job of acting as a "point man" in smoothing out bumps along the way and providing ongoing support. Efforts of Jo Ruta's students at Chattannoga State Community College in identifying errors in a "final" manuscript version were greatly appreciated. Steve Guynes (University of North Texas) did a terrific job of identifying errors in the first printing as well as making solid suggestions for improvements. (Thank Steve for a rewrite of the Chapter 6 assignments.) Participants in workshops for college teachers (sponsored by Object-Z Systems and Merant/Micro Focus under the name "Cobol University") contributed immensely to the finished product. Those individuals (participants in the early workshops), listed on the following page, and others who contributed have my sincerest thanks.

Ken Arseneau
Dawson College, Canada

Madeline Baugher
Southwestern Oklahoma State

Barbara Brannen
Sarasota County School Bd.

Margaret Brown
Dawson College, Canada

Marlene Camper
Manchester Community Tech. College

Evan Coulston
Central Queensland University, Australia

Tom Craig
Systems & Programming Consultants

Adesina Fadairo
Medgar Evers

Larry Fagan
Dawson College, Canada

Roy Foreman
Purdue University, Calumet

Kenneth Fougere
Bryant College

Melvin Franz
Central Missouri State University

Elaine Heitner
Dawson College, Canada

Harris Jacobs
Lake County Schools

Carole Lamontagne
College de Sherbrooke, Canada

David Laverell
Calvin College

Michael Lifzka
Kishwaukee College

Mark Long
DeVry Institute

Terry Mackie
Central Freight Lines, Waco, TX

Caroline Marchand
Dawson College, Canada

Mayur Mehta
Southwest Texas State University

Ed Moody
Quinnipiac College

George Morgan
Southwest Texas State University

Roosevelt Mowete
Medgar Evers

Corrine Ohayon
Dawson College, Canada

Verale Phillips
Cincinnati State

Patricia Rausch
Leesburg, FL

Herb Rebhun
University of Houston, Downtown

Cindy Riemenschneider
University of Arkansas

Cathy Steed
Central Freight Lines, Waco, TX

James Struell
Central Missouri State University

Ann Studwell
Northern Illinois University

Christian Vaudry
CEGEP de St-Laurent, Canada

Kenneth Weeks
University of Wisconsin, Superior

Sharon White
Carolina A&T State Univ.

Bill Wiley
Taylor University

Elements
of
COBOL Web
Programming

with
Micro Focus
Net Express

Getting Started

Chapter Contents

The Example Applications CD 4
  Folder (Subdirectory) Contents 4
  Folders for Examples and Assignments 4
  Loading Files From the Examples CD 4
  Net Express Skeleton Files 5
Conventions Used in this Book 5
  Use of Fonts 5
  Menu Sequence 6
  Cobol Program Listings 6
  Project Markers 6
Updating Your Copy of Net Express 6
  The Need for Software Updates 6
  Accessing Micro Focus Web Sync 6
Deploying Applications 9

Chapter

0

Chapter Introduction

This chapter includes the usual "preliminaries" that you need to get started with the Net Express examples of this book. Following are the primary topics of this chapter.

- Contents of the Examples CD included with this book.
- Suggested subdirectory usage.
- Loading files from the Examples CD.
- Basic conventions used in this book.
- Using the Micro Focus WebSync capability for updating your copy of Net Express.

The Example Applications CD

Folder (Subdirectory) Contents

The Example Applications CD included with this book contains the folder
Elements-CWP. In turn, **Elements-CWP** contains the following folders:

- **NE-Examples**: Contains project folders. Each of these folders includes
  components of a single example project.
- **NE-Data**: Contains indexed data files used by examples and required for
  assignments.
- **NE-Progs**: Contains Cobol subprograms used by examples and required for
  assignments.
- **NE-Images**: Contains image files for graphics and background in Web-screen
  displays.
- **NE-Utils**: Contains miscellaneous programs that I used in creating and
  testing files and subprograms. For instance, Ord-cvt.cbl creates a new indexed
  file pair for the Order file.

As you work with examples and prepare your own applications, you will probably
need to look at listings of data files and Cobol subprograms—see the Appendix.

Folders for Examples and Assignments

To provide the simplest working environment, each of this book's example projects
is stored in a separate folder within the **NE-Examples** folder. A naming convention
is used to relate the folder to the book's chapter describing the application. For
instance, the folder **Proj0402** pertains to Chapter 4's Example 2.

For your own assignments, I suggest you use the same technique. For instance,
you might create the folder **My-Assgns**. Then for each assignment, create a folder
within **My-Assgns**, for instance, **Assgn0301** for Chapter 3's Assignment 1 (3-1).
This is a convenient means for keeping everything straight and for providing portability if you must hand in diskettes with completed assignments. This will become
clear when you start working with Net Express in Chapter 3.

Examples of this book are illustrated with tutorials that step you through the
process of recreating example applications. For this activity, I suggest you create
still another folder, for instance, **My-Examples**. Within that folder, you can create
folders for individual projects, thereby mimicking the **NE-Examples** folder.

Loading Files From the Examples CD

Although you can load the Examples CD contents into any drive or subdirectory,
you will find life much easier if you load to drive C according to the following
instructions.

1. Bring up Windows Explorer and display the CD directory. You will see the
   single folder **Elements-CWP**.
2. Copy this folder (not just its contents, but the entire folder) to your C: drive.

3. Double-click on the file **fix-attr.bat**. This runs a DOS batch program to turn the ReadOnly attribute off (carried over from the CD). If you don't do this, you will not have Net Express access to the examples.

The Examples CD contains a number of subprograms, some used by the example applications and others that you will use in completing assignments. Most of the subprograms process data files. To that end, they include Select clauses identifying the data files containing record descriptions with paths as follows.

```
C:\Elements-CWP\NE-Data
```

If you must load onto a drive other than the root directory of drive C then you must change the above path entries (for Select and Copy statements) in the subprograms stored in the folder **Elements-CWP\NE-Progs**.

Also, be aware that copying the files from the CD brings the read-only attribute with them. The batch file of load Step 3 turns that attribute off. If you put the files in some other drive or folder, you will need to reset the ReadOnly attribute yourself. Inspect **fix-attr.bat** to see how to do this.

Net Express Skeleton Files

When you load Net Express (*not* included on the Example Applications CD of this book), you will find within your main Net Express folder, the folder **base\bin**. One of many files in this folder, **CGI.skl**, is a skeleton (template) file that Net Express uses in generating Web-ready Cobol programs for your applications. This file contains many lines of comments and commented code for different scenarios. As a consequence, you end up looking at many lines not relevant to your application. To avoid that problem in using this book, I have included on the Examples CD the following two skeleton files from which unneeded code has been removed from **CGI.skl**.

CGI-min.skl   Used by most examples in this book.
CGI-nibi.skl   Used by some examples in Chapters 9 and 11.

If, as I suggest, you intend to use them, copy them into the **NetExpress\base\bin** folder. Then from Windows Explorer right-click each, click Properties, and turn the ReadOnly attribute off.

Conventions Used in this Book

Use of Fonts

In addition to the basic type fonts used in this text, two additional fonts are utilized to depict Cobol code and screen display items.

```
Move this-field to that-field
```

This is a fixed-pitch font in which all program listings and example Cobol code is displayed.

Project from an existing application

This is a proportional font similar to that used by Net Express menu items and other screen displays.

Menu Sequence

From your experience with Windows, you know that the environment is one of click this, click that, and so on. For instance, to create a new Net Express project you click the File entry in the menu bar, the New entry in the resulting drop-down menu list, and the Project icon in the resulting popup menu. That menu sequence is depicted in this book as "click File/New/Project."

Cobol Program Listings

Programming books in which example programs span several pages have always been one of my pet peeves. To that end I have (1) kept lines of code short so that code can be listed in two columns within a page and (2) omitted sections of program code that are not relevant to the topic being discussed. As a consequence, no program listings in this book span two or more pages.

Project Markers

For your convenience, each example project described in this book is marked with an identifying icon in the outside margin of the page (marking the beginning of the discussion on the project). For instance, the application Lib01 stored in the folder Proj0301 would be indicated by the marker to the left.

Proj0301
Lib01

Updating Your Copy of Net Express

The Need for Software Updates

Most software packages that we use contain massive amounts of code. A direct consequence of such a mass with its ensuing complexity (no matter how carefully designed) is *bugs*. It is impossible for any company to make a complicated system of software available that is free of bugs (some companies do better than others). Most companies provide updates (commonly called patches), available through the Internet, that you can download to correct bugs detected after the product has shipped and you've installed it in your computer. Micro Focus is no exception, providing update service through their **WebSync**.

Accessing Micro Focus WebSync

Micro Focus provides each owner of Net Express access to WebSync via Net Express itself. To log on to WebSync, click Help on the Net Express menu bar and from the drop-down menu, click WebSync. If you are logging on for the first time you will need to fill out an information form. Do so and you will be in business. In using WebSync, you will follow a procedure something like the following. Note that most

Figure 1. WebSync menu screen.

Web sites are in a constant state of revision. The screens you see here were those in use at the time this book was in preparation. Undoubtedly what you see will be different, but the overall look should be much the same.

1. Once connected, you will see a general selection-oriented screen—for instance, look at Figure 1.
2. Click Download as you want access to the downloadable Net Express upgrades.
3. The next screen should look something like Figure 2.

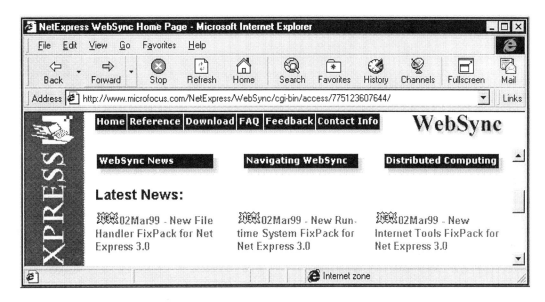

Figure 2. Software option screen.

Micro Focus provides two categories of software updates: (1) fixes (patches) that correct bugs and (2) updates that include new features added to Net Express. You can look at both but most of what you need will likely be in the fixes category.

4. Click FixPacks and you will see a screen that looks like Figure 3 listing the update packs available. (When you access WebSync you will probably see more than the four packs listed in Figure 3.)

Each entry in the first column of the table identifies an exe file, a self extracting zip file that will install the upgrades on your system. Each contains updates to one individual component of Net Express. The third entry entitled "Internet Tools FixPack" is the latest update as of the publication date of this book. Look at others and if any sound relevant to your needs, click more (in the Description column) for a detailed description. If you find a pack that you need, then proceed as follows.

5. Click Installation Instructions; read the displayed instructions (you may want to print them).
6. Click on the desired package, in this case, ITL3setup.exe.

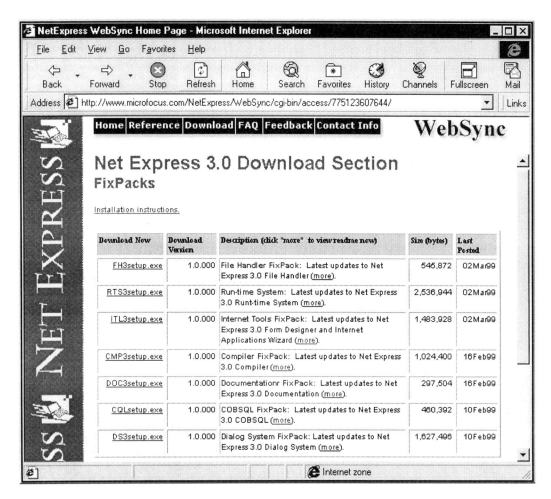

Figure 3. Download Section screen.

You will see a window that gives you the option of running the update directly or of downloading to one of your folders from which you can run it at your convenience. When you do run, updates will be installed automatically; the fix's readme file will also be installed on you computer.

Deploying Applications

This book describes means by which you can build and test Web applications totally within your computer via a simulated server. Ultimately, applications must be **deployed (published)** to a real server and made ready for use. This book focuses on using Net Express to create and test applications. For details on deploying applications to the Web, refer to the Internet Applications online manual included with every copy of Net Express. You can access the online manuals as follows.

Operating from Net Express.

1. Click Help
2. Click Help Topics
3. Enter online books for the search word.
    The highlight should be positioned on Online books.
4. From the Links to Online books list, select Internet Applications. Click the same topic if a second screen appears. This action will open your browser and bring up the book Internet Applications.

Operating from Windows.

1. Click Start/Programs.
2. From the ensuing program list, click Micro Focus Net Express.
3. From the popup menu, click Net Express Online books.
4. Click Internet Applications.

You want want the following:

*   Chapter 12 Deploying Your Application
*   Appendix B Deploying and Debugging Examples.

I suggest you print these out for handy reference.

The Net Express Interactive Development Environment

Chapter Contents

The Interactive Development Environment: First Look 12
Net Express Projects 12
A Sample Project 12
Starting the IDE 13
The Net Express Toolbar 15
File Access 16
Building and Running the Application 17
Handling Program Errors 18
Correcting Compiler Errors 18
Stepping Through a Program for Debugging 19
Using Breakpoints for Debugging 20
Free Format 22
Changing the Look and Feel of the IDE 24
Summing Up 25
Coming Up 25

Chapter

1

Chapter Introduction

This chapter introduces you to the basic features of the Micro Focus Interactive Development Environment (IDE), a working environment that integrates all the tools you need for writing, editing, compiling, and running Cobol programs. From this chapter you will learn about the following

- The nature of IDE projects.
- Starting the IDE and accessing an application (project).
- Building a project (compiling the programs comprising the project).
- Running a project.
- Debugging programs using built-in assistance tools such as breakpoints and direct interaction with the program during execution.
- Changing the look and feel of the IDE.

In the spirit of getting on with it, some of us tend toward the philosophy "if all else fails, read the instructions." So if you slipped into that mentality and skipped the preceding chapter entitled "Getting Started" stop now and go back to it.

The Interactive Development Environment: First Look

Net Express Projects

The Net Express Integrated Development Environment (IDE) is a working environment that integrates all the tools you need for writing, editing, compiling, and running Cobol programs. Typically, a Cobol application will consist of a main program and numerous subprograms. Similarly, a Web application will consist of Web pages (screen displays) and one or more Cobol programs and subprograms. One of the characteristics of the IDE is that it allows you to identify components of an application as belonging to a **project**. For each project you designate under the IDE, a special project file is created. (Its file extension is .APP, for **application file**.) This project file is somewhat of a directory to the programs comprising project. One advantage of the project concept is that it provides you simple means of keeping track of Web pages, programs, and subprograms that make up an application. Another very significant advantage is that the project file maintains information regarding whether or not changes have been made to any of the program components. At any time, you can request Net Express to rebuild a project and it will recompile all programs that have changed since the last rebuild. If the project is a Web application, it also rebuilds appropriate linkages between components.

A Sample Project

The best way to learn about the IDE and Net Express is to use them, so let's do just that. In this sample session, you will do the following.

- Start the Net Express
- Load a project
- Rebuild the project (compile the programs of the project)
- Run the program
- End the process

The first project is a vanilla-flavored Cobol indexed file application. It consists of the following program and subprogram pair.

LIB-CAL1.CBL   The main, or calling, program provides user interaction. The user is requested to enter the patron number of a library patron. The number is passed to a subprogram. Returned data includes the patron's name and address, and a list of books checked out to the patron.

LIB-SUB3.CBL   Given the patron number from the calling program, the
                      called subprogram searches appropriate files for the desired
                      patron data. All file processing is done in this subprogram.

If you look at the subprogram, do not be concerned that the files are opened each
time the subprogram is called. This will become meaningful in the context of Web
programming.

Starting the IDE

You start Net Express by clicking on

Windows Start/Programs/Micro Focus Net Express/Net Express

If you are using Net Express for the first time
(and have not yet registered it), you will see an
announcement screen indicating the number of
days remaining for use of the product. Click on
Continue. (Note: There is no such restriction with
Net Express, University Edition.) A second
screen will welcome you; click on Continue again.

> In descriptions that follow,
> you will see instructions
> such as "click on Animate/
> Run." This means to click
> on the menu item Animate
> and then click on Run in
> the ensuing popup menu.

You will then see the Net Express window of
Figure 1-1. If you or someone else has worked
with Net Express, your screen will include a
window like Figure 1-2 identifying the project

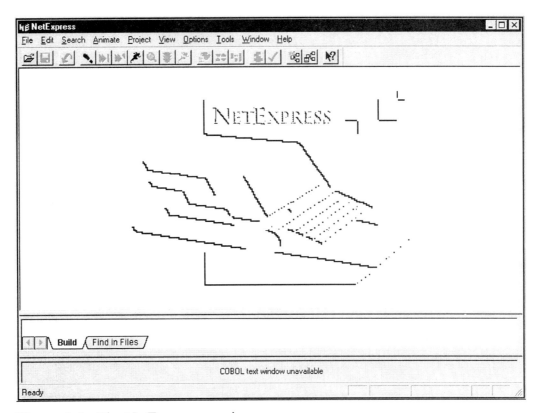

Figure 1-1. The NetExpress opening screen.

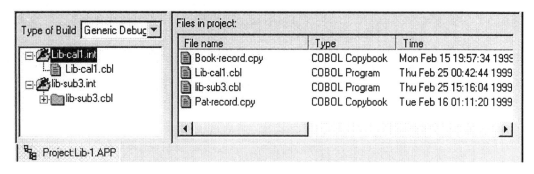

Figure 1-2. The NetExpress project window.

that was open when Net Express was previously shut down. If so, then close it by clicking File/Close or by clicking on the close button ⊠ of the project pane title bar. (Be careful not to close Net Express.)

Note that the following examples operate from the folder **C:\Elements-CWP\NE-examples** described in the *Getting Started* chapter of this book. If you have your files in some other folder, you will need to tell Net Express at the appropriate time.

1. From the Net Express main screen, click on File/Open thus producing an Open window that looks like Figure 1-3. If this is the first time Net Express has been run since being installed, the window contents will be as shown here. Otherwise, the window will display contents of the previously used folder.
2. The application you want is stored in the **Proj0101** folder of **NE-examples.** Make it the active folder by expanding the Look-in box and selecting it. The Open window will then look something like Figure 1-4.
3. Notice the icons preceding each file name.

    📋   Indicates a program.

    ⚎   Indicates a project.

Open the project Lib-1.APP by double-clicking its icon or by highlighting it and clicking Open.

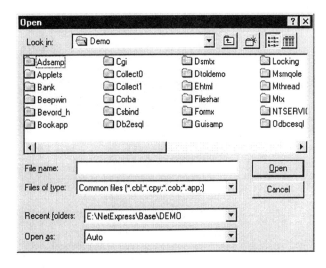

Figure 1-3.
The project Open window.

Figure 1-4.
Opening the Lib-1 project.

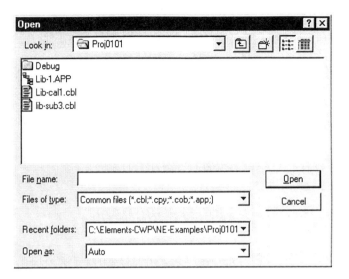

You are presented with the project window of Figure 1-5 listing the files in the project. Be aware that files need not exist to be listed in the project. This list merely serves as a guide to the IDE when you request that the program files be compiled through a rebuild operation. In the left pane of this window you see a tree view indicating a hierarchy. The .CBL files are Cobol source code files; the .INT files are the corresponding executable files in a special Micro Focus intermediate code. The .INT files will be created when you compile the programs.

The right pane is a list of all files in the project—it not limited to program files. (If you do not see all the details shown in Figure 1-5, expand the right border.) Right click on this pane and you will see a popup menu. Ensure that the Show only source files selection box does not contain a check. If it does, click on it to delete the check. Otherwise, this pane will list only program files (files that can be compiled).

The Net Express Toolbar

Now look at the tool bar shown here in Figure 1-6. There are five buttons you will use during your first look at the IDE: Step, Run, Rebuild, Compile, and Context-sensitive Help.

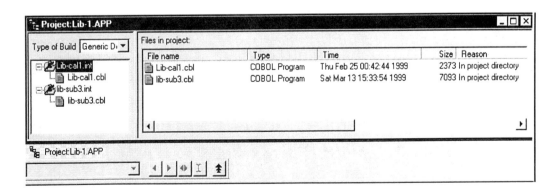

Figure 1-5. The Lib01 project.

Figure 1-6. The NetExpress toolbar.

The Context-sensitive Help button exhibits the standard Windows features. That is, click on it and a question mark is attached to your mouse pointer. Then click on any element of your screen and a help window is displayed.

The Rebuild button causes Net Express to rebuild all parts of the current project that have changed, including files that are dependent upon changed files. This includes compiling Cobol programs. This button can be activated only when the color of the bricks is red; if grayed, it is inactive (standard Windows convention).

The Compile button allows you to compile the single program that is displayed in a program window. It is only active when displayed in red.

The Run button (solid-black icon on the left, not the grayed one on the right) allows you to run a program.

The Step button allows you to step through a program, source statement by source statement. You will see how useful this is for debugging.

File Access

The subprogram **Lib-sub3.cbl,** used in this application processes two files. The Select clauses contain a path to the folder **C:\Elements-CWP\NE-data**. If you loaded into a different drive or different folders, you will need to change the paths accordingly. Make changes by doing the following.

1. Double click on the file name LIB-SUB3.CBL in the right-hand pane of the project window. This opens an edit window and displays the source program.
2. Look at the line following the first Select statement; it is:

    ```
    "C:\Elements-CWP\NE-data\patron.di"
    ```

    If you have stored your data files in some other folder, you must make the appropriate change. Be aware that, Net Express Web applications require a full path *even when the data files are in the same folder as the program files.*
3. Make the same change to the second Select statement.
4. When finished, click File/Save to save the changes.
5. Close the edit window.

Building and Running the Application

Now let's build the project (compile both the calling program and the called subprogram).

1. Move the mouse pointer to the Rebuild button ⛁ and hold it there for a moment—you will see the tool tip "Rebuild Project" displayed. Click on this button to compile both programs. Alternately, you could click Project/Rebuild from the bar menu. As the compilation takes place, you will see the following lines in the lower pane of the Net Express screen.

```
Starting rebuild
Rebuilding          Lib-call.cbl
Rebuilding          Lib-sub3.cbl
Rebuild complete
```

Be aware that if one of the files in the project's file list is highlighted, only that file will be rebuilt.

2. Now you can run the program so click on the Run button 🏃 (alternately, click Animate/Run from the bar menu). You will see the popup menu of Figure 1-7; it identifies the particular program of this project at which execution is to begin (Lib-call located in the DEBUG directory created by the rebuild operation).

3. Click on OK and the program is run displaying an interaction screen with the following prompt.

```
Enter patron number>
```

Note: You may need to enlarge the interactive pane at the botttom of your screen (it should be dark with light printing) and scroll to the top.

4. The data file contains records for patron numbers ranging from 001 to 024. Click anywhere in the interactive window to get a cursor, then type a room number and press Enter. (You may need to expand the interactive screen to see the entire output.)

5. Repeat or terminate as you desire.

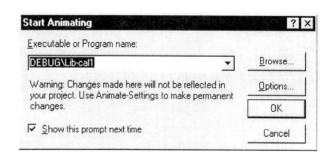

Figure 1-7.
Starting program execution.

```
Rebuilding          Lib-cal2.cbl
C:\Elements-CWP\NE-Examples\Proj0102\Lib-cal2.cbl(52,24):  *  12-S Operand BOOK-POINTER is not declared
C:\Elements-CWP\NE-Examples\Proj0102\Lib-cal2.cbl(55,32):  *  12-S Operand BOOK-POINTER is not declared
C:\Elements-CWP\NE-Examples\Proj0102\Lib-cal2.cbl(60,3):  *  564-S A scope-delimiter did not have a matching verb a
Rebuild complete with errors
```

Figure 1-8. Error messages.

Handling Program Errors

Correcting Compiler Errors

The folder NE-Examples includes the project Lib02; it is identical to Lib01 except the calling program includes a compiler error. Let's see what this looks like when you rebuild the project. You will be working from the Net Express window, so if you have any other windows open, close them.

1. Click File/Open.
2. From the resulting open screen (such as that of Figure 1-4) switch to the Proj0102 folder. Then select and open the project Lib-2.app.
3. Click the Rebuild Project icon ⁑ on the tool bar. The lower pane of your Net Express screen will look like Figure 1-8. You may need to resize this pane in order to see all of the diagnostics.
4. Double-click on the first diagnostic and the edit window of Figure 1-9 is opened. Notice that statements the compiler finds in error are marked with a red X on the left. Furthermore, the data name book-pointer is enclosed in a broken-line box. This is identifies the statement corresponding to the error message on which you clicked. Furthermore, the box indicates the element the compiler believes to be incorrect
5. Click View/Next/Syntax Error and the box indicator is moved to the next error— you may need to do this twice the first time.
6. For any of the errors, position the mouse pointer on the red X. After a few moments, you will see a brief message identifying the error. This is especially

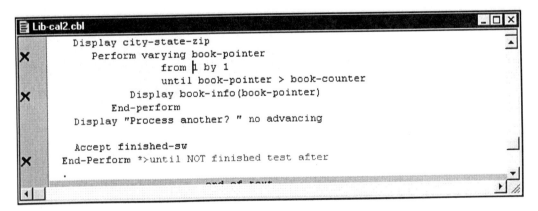

Figure 1-9. Compiler error flags.

convenient if your program has a large number of errors and you do not see all the error messages in the pane at the bottom of the Net Express screen.

7. You know from Cobol that a "data-item not declared" message means you have an inconsistency between the definition in the Data Division and usage in the Procedure Division. So scroll up to the first entry following the Working-Storage Section header and you will see the data item is defined as book-pntr. Change it to book-pointer.

8. Rebuild the project. If your change was correct, you will see the message Rebuild complete with no error messages.

9. You can close the edit window and run the program. It is now identical to the corresponding program of Lib01 so it will execute the same as that project.

Stepping Through a Program for Debugging

Occasionally you will encounter a program bug that simply defies all attempts to find it. The Animator component of the IDE gives you a graphical means to trace execution of your code and examine data values. If you've not already terminated the preceding run, do so now; then do the following.

1. Click on the Step button ✎ (alternately, click Animate/Step from the bar menu).
2. Click OK from the popup menu of Figure 1-7. Your screen will look like Figure 1-10.
3. The statement highlighted in red is the next program statement to be executed. Click on the Step button again and you will see the highlight moved to the first Display statement. Click again and you should see the interaction window displayed. Expand or contract windows as needed.
4. Click the Step button two more times to execute the Accept statement. You will see the program statement highlight disappear and the interaction screen cursor appear.
5. Type the patron number 001 and press Enter. The highlight will return to the Call statement; the Accept statement has been executed thereby causing a value to be entered into the data item in-patron-number.
6. You can check the value stored in any data item by double-clicking on that data item. To illustrate, double-click anywhere in the name in-patron-number (it can be in either the Accept statement or the Call statement). The resulting popup window of Figure 1-11 displays the selected data-name and its current

Figure 1-10. Beginning execution in the Step mode.

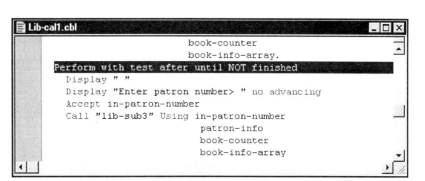

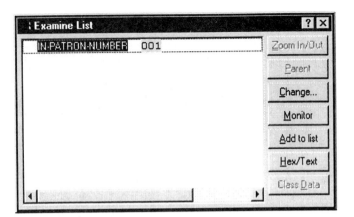

Figure 1-11.
Data item display.

value. To monitor it throughout the debug process, click the Monitor button and a small window showing only the data item will replace the window of Figure 1-11. Then double-click on the data item patron-name (you will find it in the Display statement following the Call). As the program has not yet obtained patron data, the display is blank. Click on Monitor for this data item as well.

7. Assume you have no need to step through the subprogram. You can skip step-by-step execution by clicking the Run Through button located to the right of the Step button. (For more details on how this works, click on it with context-sensitive Help.) Click on the Run Through button ▮▶▮.

8. The statement highlight moves to the If statement following the Call statement. Since the Call has returned a value in the data item patron-name, the patron's name is shown in the monitoring box.

9. The IDE provides you a means by which you can position the cursor on a data item thereby causing Net Express to automatically display its value. To try this, click the Options selection on the main bar menu. Then click Animate and you will see a popup menu in which the Show tool tips box will probably not include a check. If not, click it to insert a check. Then click OK.

10. Now move your mouse pointer to any data item of the program. After a moment, a small display will appear automatically showing the value stored in that data item. If you find this convenient, then leave this option as is; if not, remove the check you set in the preceding Step 9.

11. If you reach a point where you no longer need to step through program (presumably you've found the bug), you can switch to normal execution by clicking the Run button. However, if you want to terminate execution immediately, click Animate/Stop Animating. Do so, then close all windows left open from this execution.

Using Breakpoints for Debugging

With a large program, stepping through statements can be a very time consuming process. You can avoid that problem by using **breakpoints.** To illustrate, assume that a counter in the subprogram that counts the number of books checked out by a user returns an incorrect result to the calling program. You simply cannot find the bug, so you want to observe the counter's value during execution of the subprogram. For this, you will set four break points in the subprogram: one where the counter is initialized and the others where it is incremented. When the program is run, execution halts thereby allowing you to inspect the contents of data items and continue by either stepping or resuming normal operation. Let's try this with the current project. If you don't still have the Proj0102 project open in the Net Express screen, then open it.

1. Double-click on the LIB-SUB3.CBL entry in the right pane of the project window. This opens a window listing the program source file.
2. Scroll down to the 200-process-user-request paragraph. Move the cursor to the second of the following Move statements (the fourth statement in this paragraph).

   ```
   Move 0 to book-counter
   Move ls-in-patron-number to pr-patron-number
   ```

   Note that you want execution to stop *after* the initializing Move statement so that you can inspect the contents of book-counter.
3. Click Animate/Breakpoint. From the ensuing popup menu you see several options. Toggle allows you to set and clear breakpoints. Notice that you can perform this function with the F9 key (which is more convenient than the menu sequence). Toggle and you will see a red stop sign displayed in the left margin indicating a breakpoint on this statement. Use F9 to toggle the breakpoint off (to see how this feature works); then toggle it back on.
4. Next, you must set three breakpoints in the 820-read-book-records module: one following each occurrence of the statement that adds 1 to book-counter and, one at the end of the paragraph. So set breakpoints on the following three statements.

   ```
   Perform 400-set-up-book-info-line (second statement after not invalid key)
   Perform 400-set-up-book-info-line (second statement after the If)
   End-Read *>Book-File
   ```

5. These will allow you to observe the value stored in the data item book-counter (a) when it is initialized, (b) when it is incremented, and (c) when the read loop is terminated.
6. Close the program window and run the application.
7. At the application prompt, enter a patron number of 001 and press Enter. If you've set the breakpoints properly, execution stops on the statement

   ```
   Move ls-in-patron-number to pr-patron-number
   ```

8. Examine the value in book-counter by double clicking on the data name in the preceding statement and you will see that its value is indeed zero. Click on Monitor so you can observe its value as execution progresses.
9. Click the Run button to resume execution. The next breakpoint follows the first Add statement. The displayed value for book-counter should now be 01.
10. Repeat this process and observe the displayed value for book-counter as it changes. Eventually, the count reaches 07 and the program displays the books checked out to the patron. Notice that there are seven of them.

11. When you've satisfied yourself, select Animate/Stop animating to terminate this session.
12. When you are finished with a debugging session, you will usually want to clear all of your breakpoints. Do this by selecting Animate/Breakpoint/Clear all in program. If you have breakpoints in other programs of a project that you want cleared, then click Clear all in project.
13. You are finished with this session so click Animate/Stop Animating.

Free Format

Your main focus in this book is learning to create Web applications. To that end, you will not be writing much Cobol code. However, you may want to inspect Cobol subprograms in the NE-Progs folder. Before doing that, you should be aware of a feature of the next standard that will bring joy to the hearts of most Cobol programmers: **free format**. (It is used in this book's programs and subprograms.) You are no longer locked into the A- and B-margins and column 72. With free format, you position statements anywhere you want on the line. So you can use indenting to clarify structure without restriction. To illustrate these principles, look at the free format version of LIB-CAL1.CBL shown in Figure 1-12. Notice the following features of this example.

1. Code begins in column 1.
2. Although not evident in this example, a source statement can extend beyond column 72.
3. With free format, you can no longer use an asterisk in column 7 to indicate a comment line. Instead, the *> combination, entered at any position, indicates a comment.
4. The *> combination also allows you to enter inline comments. If a statement is followed by this comment indicator, the remainder of the line is treated as a comment (ignored by the compiler).

If you are wondering how long a source line can be with free format, hold your breath. The new standard allows for lines of up to 250 columns.

Because of the vast amount of fixed format code in existence, free format is not automatic. You need to include a compiler directive indicating that your program uses free format. The Micro Focus versions of the directive are:

```
$set sourceformat "free"    for free format
or
$set sourceformat "fixed"  for fixed format
```

As fixed format is the default option, you must be certain to begin the directive in column 7. Within a program, you can switch between free and fixed format by using the appropriate version of the above $set directive.

```
                    $set sourceformat "free"
         *>************************************************
         *> Library Application
         *> W. Price  9/28/97                   LIB-CAL1.CBL
         *> This program calls the subprogram LIB-SUB3.
         *> The input parameter is a patron number
         *> The returning parameters are:
         *>   Name and address information
         *>   A count of the number of books checked out
         *>   An array containing book information
         *> Data is accessed from two files: the indexed
         *> file patron file and the indexed book file.
         *> All file processing is done in the subprogram.
         *>************************************************

         Identification Division.
          Program-id. Library-Caller.

         Data Division.
          Working-Storage Section.
           01  book-pointer              pic 9(02).
           01  in-patron-number          pic X(03).
           01  finished-sw               pic X(01).
               88  finished              value "Y" "y".
           01  patron-info.
               05  patron-name           pic X(23).
               05  street-address        pic X(20).
               05  city-state-zip        pic X(30).
           01  book-counter              pic 9(02).
           01  book-info-array.
               05  book-info             occurs 10 times.
                   10  bi-book-id        pic X(04).
                   10  bi-book-title     pic X(25).
                   10  bi-book-author    pic X(13).
                   10  bi-due-date       pic X(10).

         Procedure Division Using in-patron-number
                                   patron-info
                                   book-counter
                                   book-info-array.
          Perform with test after until NOT finished
           Display " "
           Display "Enter patron number> " no advancing
           Accept in-patron-number
           Call "lib-sub3" Using in-patron-number
                                   patron-info
                                   book-counter
                                   book-info-array

           Display patron-name
           Display street-address
           Display city-state-zip
            Perform varying book-pointer
                     from 1 by 1
                         until book-pointer > book-counter
                     Display book-info(book-pointer)
            End-perform
           Display "Process another? " no advancing

           Accept finished-sw
          End-Perform *>until NOT finished test after
          .
```

Figure 1-12. Illustrating free format.

Changing the Look and Feel of the IDE

The IDE includes a variety of options that that allow you to change the appearance of the environment. For this, click Options on the bar menu and from the resulting pull-down menu of Figure 1-13 click on Customize to see a set of tabs.

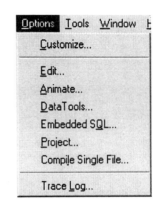

Select the Colors tab and you will see color palletes. Click on the different items of the upper-left pane to observe the color assigned to each element. Notice that you can set both the foreground color (the letters) and the background color. The screen appearance is shown in the Sample Text box.

Figure 1-13. Options.

Next, look at the Fonts tab and you will see that you can select the font in which your different screens are displayed (the default is 10-point Courier). Click on the Change button to see your options.

For editing source programs, the IDE uses margins of 7 and 72, corresponding to the standard Cobol source code columns. As Micro Focus allows free format, you are no longer constrained to Cobol's A and B areas. If you use free format, you should change the margin settings. Do this by clicking the Edit entry of Figure 1-13's Options menu. Then from the Profile tab, change the left margin to 0 and the right margin to some reasonably large number, for instance, 100.

With the default settings, if you hold the left mouse button down and drag on a source code line, the entire line is selected. If you don't like that, you can change the IDE to select only that portion over which you drag the mouse. From the Options/Edit/ Blocks tab, click the radio button entitled Select column blocks then click Apply.

If you have words that you commonly misspell (for instance, you type Preform rather then Perform) you can set the IDE to its auto correction mode. You change this under the Autofix tab. Click on it and you will see the If I type this/Change it to this columns. Delete any entries that do not fit your needs, then enter yours. Don't forget to place a check mark in the check box adjacent to Monitor my typing.

This concludes your brief introduction to the IDE. As you have probably noticed, there are numerous other features to make life easier for you. You can explore them by trying them and by referring to context-sensitive help.

Summing Up

This chapter has described the basic features of the Micro Focus Interactive Development Environment (IDE).

The IDE is a working environment that integrates all the tools you need for writing, editing, compiling, and running Cobol programs.

One of the characteristics of the IDE is that it allows you to identify components of an application as belonging to a **project**. For each project you designate under the IDE, a special project file is created. (Its file extension is .APP, for **application file**.)

Coming Up

Chapter 2 provides you a basic insight to the Internet and the World Wide Web. You will be introduced to terms/concepts including client-server, browser, URL, common gateway interface (CGI) program, and hypertext markup language (HTML).

The World Wide Web

Chapter Contents

Basic Web Principles 28
    The Client/Server Concept 28
    The Emergence of the World Wide Web 29
    Basic Terminology 30
The Web and Commerce 31
    Intranets 31
    Extranets 31
    The Web and Client Server 31
    The Web and Net Express 32
How Does the Web Work? 32
    Internet Addressing 32
    Protocol 32
    The URL 33
Dissecting the URL 33
    Host Computer 33
    Path 34
A Library Inquiry Application 34
The Basics of HTML 37
    Tags: The Code of HTML 37
    Controlling Lines of Output 38
    Document Structure Tags 39
    The HTML Script's Header 39
The HTML Script's Body 40
    Headings 40
    The Input Tag 40
    The Form Tag 41
Behind the Scenes 41
    Handling Data 41
    The Output Page 42
    The Common Gateway Interface (CGI) 42
The Cobol CGI 43
    The External-Form Clause 43
    Accept and Display 45
    Overall Relationships 46
Summing Up 48
Coming Up 49

Chapter

2

Chapter Introduction

The objective of this chapter is to give you an overall idea of the environment in which you will be working: the World-Wide Web. From this chapter, you will learn about the following.

- The client/server concept.
- The basic nature of the Web.
- The Internet, intranets, and extranets.
- Internet addressing (Internet Protocol—IP)
- HyperText Transfer Protocol (HTTP).
- The Web's Universal Resource Locator (URL).
- HyperText Markup Language (HTML), the language of the Web.
- The server-side program, the program on a Web server that performs required actions of an application.
- How Net Express allows you to create server-side programs using Cobol.
- The basic syntax of the Accept and Display used in conjunction with reading and writing Web pages.
- Embedding HTML code within a Cobol program.

Basic Web Principles

The Client/Server Concept

Pick up most any magazine about the Internet and you will probably find an article or two that refers to "client/server." Although the client/server concept is basic to the Internet and **World Wide Web** (www), it is hardly unique to that application. First, let's define some terms. Much of what we do today is based on **cooperative computing**, a model in which two or more processes collaborate on actions necessary to complete a single transaction or application. Most commonly, we think of the cooperating processes as residing in different computers, although both processes *can* be on the same computer. Our interest in this book involves a specific type of cooperative computing: client/server. **Client/server** is a data processing architecture in which one or more processes called **servers** provide processing services for other processes called **clients**. For instance, consider the online transaction processing system illustrated in Figure 2-1. Initial processing of transactions received from terminals is handled by the Transaction Control Process (TCP). The TCP communicates with the Database Management System (DBMS) to obtain needed data to complete the transaction. In this respect, the TCP is a *client* requesting a service from a *server*, the DBMS. Note that these two applications can be on the same computer or on different computers.

Figure 2-2 takes this concept one step further. Assume that the terminals communicating with the TCP are smart: that they have processing power of their own. Considering the terminal/TCP pair, the terminal functions as a client and the TCP is now in the role of the server (it provides a service to the terminal).

This client/server relationship is part of the foundation of the **Internet**. Computers communicating with computers everywhere, many functioning as servers and also as clients requesting services of other computers. For the average person, such as you and me, who surf the Internet, our personal computers function as clients to computers throughout the world, providing us access to an entity some refer to as the "**Universal Computer**."

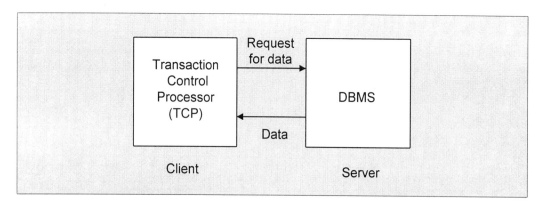

Figure 2-1. A client/server relationship.

The Emergence of the World Wide Web

In what seems like the blink of an eye, the Web has altered the landscape of computing, coaxing islands of stand-alone mainframes, minis, and micros into the "Universal Computer." Rarely has a technology caused such excitement or held such promise. Not since the thrilling early days of the personal computer has our industry seen such a wind of intensity. Yet, the interactivity made possible by the Web is by no means new.

The origins of the Web can be traced to research projects sponsored the U.S. Government in the 1960s and 70s to build a network infrastructure capable of withstanding any number of possible disasters. The result was a loosely coupled network of computers called the **Internet**. The Internet was unique in that it neither had one centralized host nor did it rely on predefined connection paths to move information. The genius of the Internet was that packets of information "found their own way" through the network from source to destination. The result was a network that would continue to function despite the failure of one or more nodes.

Throughout the 1980s and early 1990s the Internet was used primarily by large corporations and universities for e-mail and document transfer. It wasn't until the development of a language called **Hyper Text Markup Language** (**HTML**) and Web browsers that use of the Internet truly exploded. The original intent of HTML, developed by Tim Berners-Lee (a researcher in Switzerland), was to provide a quick and easy way to facilitate information transfer among scientists. The basic idea behind HTML is to insert codes within plain ASCII text that indicate how the text should be displayed. The resulting file is commonly called a **Web page** or a **Web document**. A special **browser** program, resident in the Web client computer (typically your PC) interprets the imbedded codes and displays screens that we are all accustomed to seeing in surfing the Web. The concept is illustrated in Figure 2-3.

The first browser, Mosaic, was an instant success. Users were able to view text and graphics located on other computers by clicking on specially highlighted words or links. The low overhead and simplicity of HTML led to its quick acceptance by Internet users everywhere. The result is what we see today—a simple data transfer protocol, sitting on top of a robust, fault-tolerant network infrastructure: the World Wide Web.

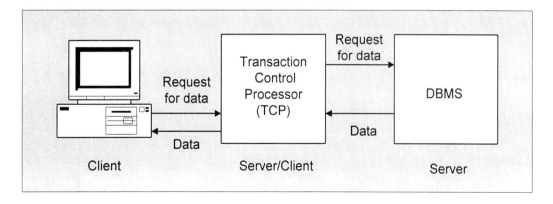

Figure 2-2. Another client/server relationship.

Basic Terminology

Before proceeding, let's be certain of some basic Web terminology.

Client. In the context of the Web, a client is a computer that requests services of another computer.

Server. In the context of the Web, a server is a computer that provides services to a requesting client. A server responds to a client request by sending a Web page.

HTML—HTML HyperText Markup Language. HTML is the most commonly used language for defining Web pages. Imbedded codes within ordinary text describe how information is to be displayed on your screen.

Web Browser. A Web browser is software that interprets HTML codes of a Web page and displays the page on your computer screen. Netscape Navigator and Internet Explorer are the most widely used browsers.

Web Page. A Web page (or **Web Document**) is a text file with embedded HTML code that resides on a Web site for downloading to a Web browser. Web pages commonly contain links to other documents on the Web.

Web Site. A Web site is a computer system maintained by an organization or an individual who makes Web pages available for downloading. Web sites are categorized as commercial, government or educational. You can tell the kind of Web site you are connecting to by examining its extension.

Web Server. A Web server is software running on a Web site that handles communication with Web browsers and returns Web pages to the browser. Also, a Web server can capture information from users and start up other server-resident programs. You will sometimes see the term Web server used in referring to the server hardware (the Web site).

Server-Side Program. A server-side program (or **gateway** program) is application specific software located at the Web site that accepts and handles requests from a Web server on behalf of a user. Net Express includes simple extensions to Cobol making it "Web compatible." This opens the door to accessing corporate databases and legacy Cobol applications from the Web.

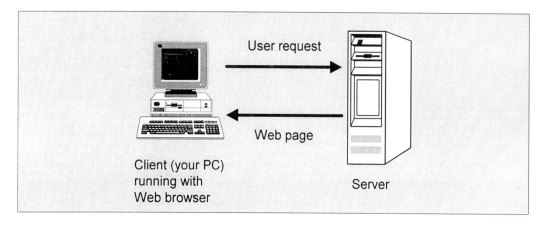

Figure 2-3. The Internet environment.

The Web and Commerce

For many individuals, surfing the Web has become part of everyday life. Corporations are acting to establish a Web presence thereby taking advantage of Web advertising, multimedia and electronic commerce. As a result, the Web has not only changed how we think about information transfer and data lookup but is changing how organizations do business. Two recent extensions of the basic ideas behind the Web are the intranet and extranet.

Intranets

While the Internet has captured media and public attention, internal Internets, or **intranets**, are growing as companies look for new ways to disseminate information and applications within corporations. Through the use of **firewalls**, software that keeps outsiders from accessing company data, intranets are being used for company-wide information distribution, keeping employees up-to-date on everything from corporate leave policies to enterprise-critical planning. Intranets, just like the Internet, use Web browsers sitting on PCs or workstations connected to company servers.

Extranets

Many companies have already developed intranets and are now expanding their reach to include selected sites outside the company. The new network structure known as an **extranet** extends an intranet to include sites integral to enterprise operations. For example, a manufacturing company may want to expand its network to include suppliers of critical goods and materials, making information from those suppliers available to corporate planners. Web connections make this possible, opening up new ways for companies to meet customer needs.

The Web and Client Server

The Web has forced a rethinking of traditional client-server computing. In the 1960s and 1970s, corporate information resources were housed in mainframes that talked to dumb terminals used primarily for data capture and display. As PCs and desktop platforms grew in power, local area networks (LANs) made it possible to partition applications, taking some of the burden off centralized mainframe servers.

The result was a client-server model of computing that distributed processing among powerful clients. Because client platforms required more memory and disk space to carry out their responsibilities, they became known as fat clients, distinguishing them from the earlier generation of dumb or thin clients that served only for display and data entry.

The Web and Net Express

For organizations with Cobol applications and Cobol programmers, the Web opens up a wide range of new options and opportunities. For legacy applications, the Web means that Cobol programs can take on new life by adding Web connections through simple Net Express statements. It also means that Cobol programmers can use Cobol to program the connections between important enterprise applications, data, and the rest of the world. The implication for Cobol is significant. The value of legacy Cobol applications goes up, particularly with the Net Express built-in features for accepting and displaying information on the Web.

Net Express also opens up a new role for Cobol as a language for writing Web server applications. What is more natural for a language that has been the workhorse for mainframe applications for over thirty years? Thus, rather than risking rewrites of existing Cobol applications in new languages, legacy programs can be extended and made Web-ready through built-in Web access languages features of Net Express.

How Does the Web Work?

Internet Addressing

In the same way we have house numbers and Zip codes to designate the address of our home or place of business, each host computer on the Internet has a unique address. Called the **Internet Protocol (IP)** address, it consists of four numbers separated by periods. For instance, the IP address for the Object-Z Systems Web site is 209.196.168.18. Fortunately, we need not deal with the IP address as the Internet allows us to use more familiar forms such as www.objectz.com.

Protocol

A protocol is a set of rules for communication between two entities. For instance, in government, the Department of State maintains a protocol book for how to communicate with dignitaries of foreign countries. At our level as programmers, protocols for computer-to-computer interaction serve a similar purpose: to define the rules for transmitting and receiving data.

The most common protocol on the Web is **HTTP**, the **HyperText Transfer Protocol**. HTTP specifies the rules for communication between a Web browser (client) and a Web server. Although HTTP is the mostly widely used protocol, it is not the only one used on the Internet. Others include FTP (File Transfer Protocol) for transferring data and program files across the Internet, gopher for transferring menus of files, and mailto for e-mail.

The URL

Internet's key to computers accessing computers is the special addressing scheme called the **Universal Resource Locator (URL)**. Computers on the Internet use the URL to make a connection between a Web browser and the target Web server. The URL can also carry information telling a Web server exactly where on its disk to look for a resource of interest.

Each Web site has its own net address which is embedded in a URL. For example, the Object-Z Systems address is www.objectz.com which when embedded in a URL appears as:

```
http://www.objectz.com
```

Typing in the above name at the top of Web browser will take you to the main Object-Z Systems home page. While URLs often correspond to company names, they can be whatever the owner desires.

In addition to connecting to company home pages, URLs can also be used to connect to individual documents stored on a Web server. Clicking on Web page links often takes you to specific documents within subdirectories at Web server locations. By typing in the full URL name and the subdirectory in a Web browser you can go directly to a document without having to navigate links. For example, the URL

```
http://www.objectz.com/Books/ECWP.htm
```

will take you to the page on the Object-Z Systems server that contains a description of this book. (At least it would when this book was written—most Web sites see frequent change.)

Dissecting the URL

URLs are based on the following general format:

protocol://HostComputer/path

The *protocol* is described above. The following sections explain each of the other components.

Host Computer

Following the protocol name and two forward slashes (//), you see the name of the host computer. In the above example, the name www.objectz.com is the host computer, commonly referred to as the **domain name** of the Web server. Domain names can be read from right to left as follows:

`www.objectz.com`

- com indicates that the computer is supported by a commercial organization; following are some common abbreviations supported by the Internet.

edu	Educational insititutions
gov	Government agencies
mil	Military
net	Network centers
org	Organizations difficult to classify

- objectz indicates that the organization's name is Object-Z. While this component of the URL often corresponds to company names, they can be whatever the owner desires.
- www refers to the name of the machine at the organization that is running the Web server software

Path

Any text after the host computer name is interpreted as the path name of the document to be retrieved. In the preceding example, the path is `Books/ECWP.htm` where `Books` is the directory containing the file named `ECWP.htm`. If no path is specified, the http protocol defaults to search for a directory named `public.html` and a file called `index.html`.

A Library Inquiry Application

Let's consider a simple scenario based on an inquiry portion of a library information system. One capability allows a user to enter a library patron number and be presented with a patron information screen. Typical input and output screens are shown in Figure 2-4. Most of us Cobol programmers have written an application of this type. Here you see the results of a program that does the following.

1. Accepts an input patron number.
2. Reads the patron record from a file.
3. Displays the patron information.
4. Repeats if requested.

Typically, the screens of Figure 2-4 would appear from a Web application as shown in Figure 2-5—as you can see, the differences between the pairs of screens is

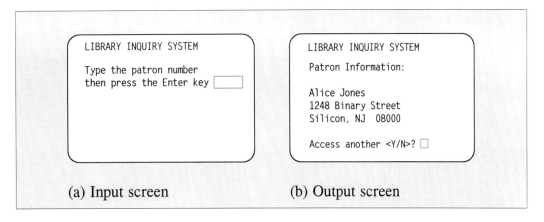

Figure 2-4. A typical screen interaction—Conventional Cobol.

minor. However, the activities taking place behind the scenes in the Web application are considerably different from those of the common Cobol application. To investigate this, consider the environment illustrated in Figure 2-6(a). Remember that a browser (such as Netscape Navigator or Internet Explorer) is running on your PC (the client) and server software is running on the Web site computer. Now look at the sequence of Figure 2-6(b). The screen display of Figure 2-5(a) appears as the result of Step 2 in Figure 2-6(b) and the screen display of Figure 2-5(b) appears as the result of Step 5. That is, the sequence of activities is:

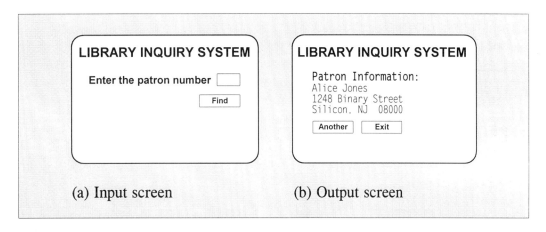

Figure 2-5. A typical screen interaction—Web application.

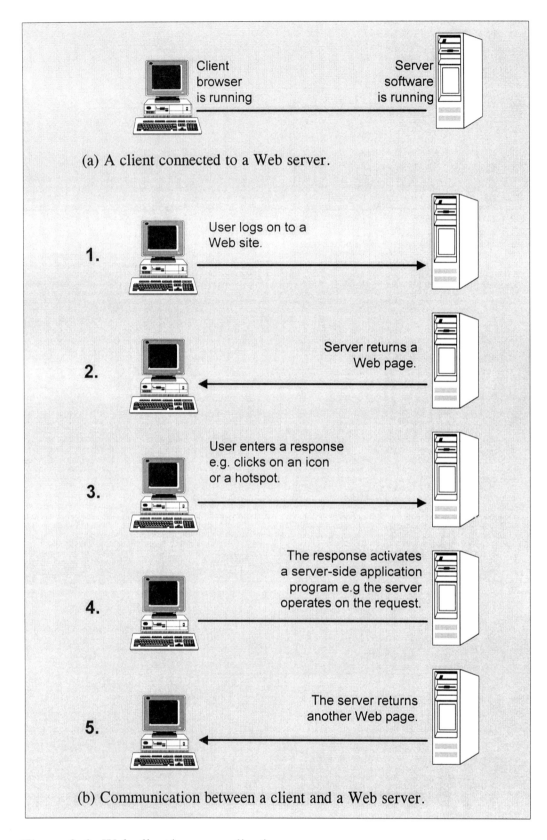

Client
browser
is running

Server
software
is running

(a) A client connected to a Web server.

1. User logs on to a
    Web site.

2. Server returns a
    Web page.

3. User enters a response
    e.g. clicks on an icon
    or a hotspot.

4. The response activates
    a server-side application
    program e.g the server
    operates on the request.

5. The server returns
    another Web page.

(b) Communication between a client and a Web server.

Figure 2-6. Web client/server application.

1. The server sends the Web page to the client's browser.
2. The browser displays the Web page.
3. The browser accepts the input patron number.
4. Data from the Web page (input patron number) is sent to the server.
5. From information received from the browser, the server runs the file-accessing program thereby reading the patron record.
6. The server sends another Web page (that includes patron information) back to the client's browser.
7. The browser displays the patron information.

Each Web page that you see is generated by your browser from a text file containing "instructions" designating what that page is to contain. The most commonly encountered language for defining Web pages is HTML.

The Basics of HTML

Tags: The Code of HTML

As indicated earlier, each Web page stored on a server consists of ordinary text that you want displayed on the screen together with imbedded HTML code indicating how that text should be displayed. For instance, in Figure 2-7 you see a typical browser displayed screen and the HTML script from which it was created. Here you see the following elements in the HTML script.

- The text to be displayed on the screen by the browser; it is highlighted.
- Codes indicating how the text must be displayed
- Identification of "action" boxes (areas where you enter data or click for an action).
- An action command telling the browser what to do when the Find button is clicked.

HTML has codes for headings, input areas, lists, and other components that you've observed when surfing the Web. So the server's action of "returning a Web page" [Steps 2 and 5 of Figure 2-6(b)] is simply one of sending an HTML text file to your browser. Your browser then interprets the "instructions" of the HTML program thereby creating the screen that you see. HTML **tags** designate elements of an HTML program. Tags are key words, enclosed in angle brackets, that designate all the characteristics of a Web page. Some program elements require only a single tag. Other elements are enclosed within a beginning tag and an ending tag. (This is much like Cobol's scope terminators: for example, within IF and END-IF you can enclose one or many statements.)

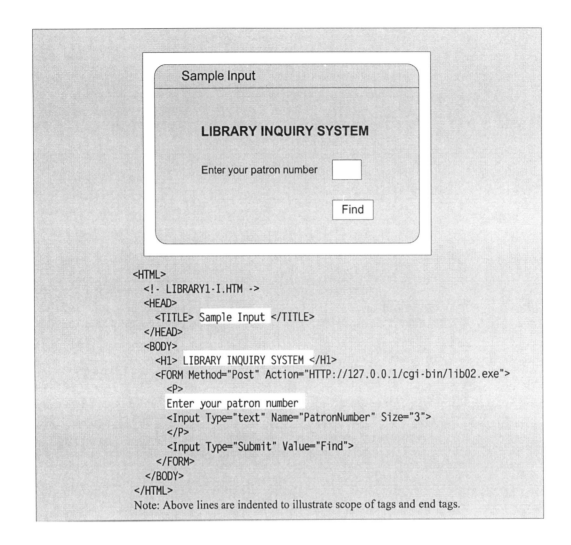

Figure 2-7. A Web page and the corresponding HTML program.

Controlling Lines of Output

The first thing you should recognize is that HTML ignores spaces and carriage returns within the HTML script. For instance, assume you typed the following instruction to the user in your HTML page.

```
A password is required to proceed.
Please enter your password now.
```

The browser would display this as:

```
A password is required to proceed.Please enter your password now.
```

You achieve the desired two-line form by inserting a code to tell the browser to start a new line, that is:

```
Your password is required to proceed.<BR>
Please enter your password now.
```

Here the tag <BR> means "break" and forces a line break in the display.

The paragraph tag <P> </P>, a two part tag, is another way to control lines. It causes the browser to end the current line, insert a blank line, and then display all items between it and the end tag </P> on a single line (in all cases, the end tag of a two-part tag is identical to the begin tag except it includes the / character. For example, consider the following script.

```
<BR>This is the first line
<P>
This will be
displayed
on a single line.
</P>
```

When displayed by the browser, it will appear on the screen as:

```
This is the first line

This will be displayed on a single line.
```

Document Structure Tags

The overall document structure is defined by the following document structure tags.

<HTML>...</HTML> Define the start and end of an HTML program. Each program consists of two main components: the head and the body.

<HEAD>...</HEAD> Define the header of the HTML program.

<BODY>...</BODY> Define the body of the HTML program.

Like any good programming language, HTML provides you the capability for including documentation. If the open angle bracket is followed by an exclamation mark (that is, <!), the entire tag is treated as a comment and is ignored by the browser. Thus, the second line of Figure 2-7's HTML program is a comment.

The HTML Script's Header

The single header entry of this example is the title.

<TITLE>   </TITLE> Contains the heading that will appear on the top border of your browser when the page is displayed.

This example uses the title *Sample Input*, a poor choice for an actual Web page. The title entry should be meaningful to the person viewing the screen and should sum up the content of the document in a concise way. Be aware that the title is utilized when users create a Web browser bookmark to the page. It is also used as the entry when a Web search engine catalogs the site.

Notice that in Figure 2-7, the start tag, title, and end tag are written on a single line. The following would have produced the same result.

```
<TITLE>
Sample Input
</TITLE>
```

The HTML Script's Body

The body portion of an HTML document is defined by the <BODY> and </BODY> tag. You can see in Figure 2-7 that the body comprises almost all of the page definition; you will also see this in pages created by Net Express.

Headings

The first entry you see in Figure 2-7 is the heading entry:

```
<H1>LIBRARY INQUIRY SYSTEM</H1>
```

Ranging from level 1 (<H1>) to level 6 (<H6>), headings allow you to create different sizes of headlines for the particular emphasis you require. Level 1 is the largest heading type size and level 6 is the smallest. Furthermore, the browser places the text enclosed within the heading tag/end-tag on a separate line.

The Input Tag

Next, let's skip to the following paragraph entries of this browser page.

```
<P>
Enter your patron number
<Input Type="text" Name="PatronNumber" Size="3">
</P>
```

Following the text line, you see the <INPUT> tag; it defines the placement and behavior for accepting and sending a form's data item. It has several components; let's examine each.

Type="Text" permits the user to enter a single line of data. Although the word might suggest alphanumeric data, you can enter either alphanumeric or numeric values.

Name="*data name*" where *data-name* (PatronNumber in this example) designates the name of the data item (variable) that will contain data passed to the server. A later example will show the significance of this name.

Size="*n*" where "*n*" (3 in this example) defines the input data item size.

As there is no break tag preceding this input tag (or following the text line above it), the text and the input box are displayed on the same screen line, as you see in Figure 2-7.

The second input tag produces the button you see labeled Find in Figure 2-7.

```
<Input Type="Submit" Value="Find">
```

Type="Submit" places a button on the page for the user to click to send the data to the server.

Value="*label*" where *label* (Find in this example) designates the caption that appears on the button. You can use whatever caption is meaningful for the action to be carried out. Here the intent is to "find" the patron. The programmer could as well have used Get or Locate or any other word.

The Form Tag

The remaining tag to inspect here is:

```
<FORM Method="Post" Action="HTTP://127.0.0.1/cgi-bin/Lib02.exe">
```

This example of the form tag includes two components: Method and Action. Method identifies the method by which data is to be sent from the client to the server. Post causes data name/value pairs to be sent, as you will learn later. Get is another method, but its capabilities are limited. The Action component tells the browser where to send the data and identifies the program on the server that must be run to process the input data. [The URL address you see in this example (HTTP://127.0.0.1/cgi-bin) is the address of the simulated server used by Net Express.]

An HTML page can include more than one form, but only one form can serve as input to a server-side program. So if a page contains, for instance, three forms, then it can have three server-side programs associated with it (one for each form). However, all the examples you will study in this book feature one form per page. In that sense, within this book, form and page are almost synonymous. You will find that occasionally Micro Focus uses the term form when, technically speaking, the reference should be page. In fact, the tool you use to create HTML pages is called Form Designer.

Referring again to Figure 2-7, the rest of the tags in the program are end tags and delimit their corresponding preceding tags.

Behind the Scenes

Handling Data

Let's look again at two of the HTML tags of Figure 2-7.

```
<FORM Method="Post" Action="HTTP://127.0.0.1/cgi-bin/Lib02.exe">
<Input Type="text" Name="PatronNumber" Size="3">
```

As indicated previously, the FORM tag tells your browser where to send the screen's output, and the name of the server-side program to execute upon arrival (in this case, Lib02.exe). The browser assigns the input box of the screen the data name that you've designated in the Name component of the Input tag. The value you type in that box is stored in the data item PatronName. This is much like Cobol where you define and use a data item as follows.

```
10  patron-number     pic X(03).
    .
    .
    .
Accept patron-number
```

Figure 2-8 illustrates what takes place when you enter a value then click on the Find button. For each screen input element, a **name/value** pair is sent to the server (together with the name of the program to be executed).

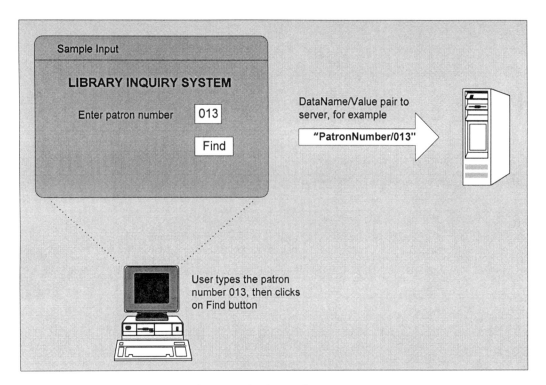

Figure 2-8. Transmission of a name/value pair.

The Output Page

When the server receives the message from your browser, it runs the server-side program designated by your browser. The server-side program accepts the data value (or values), performs its operations, and returns designated results as part of another HTML page. In the library patron example, the returned value is the patron's name, as illustrated in Figure 2-9. In this illustration, the colon preceding the Value field of the HTML code designates that the value stored in f-PatronName must be used, not the literal itself.

The Common Gateway Interface (CGI)

The server-side program for an Internet application communicates with the client through the Web server software of the computer. The interface between a Cobol server-side program and the Web server running it can be any of the following three industry standards.

- Common Gateway Interface (**CGI**)
- Internet Server Application Program Interface (**ISAPI**)
- Netscape Server Application Program Interface (**NSAPI**)

By default, Net Express creates server-side Cobol programs using the CGI standard as it is most widely supported. (Net Express does include simple procedures for converting CGI programs to the other interfaces.) In this book, the server-side programs are referred to as a CGI programs—all of the examples herein are CGI. However, within this book, interpret this as synonymous with server-side program.

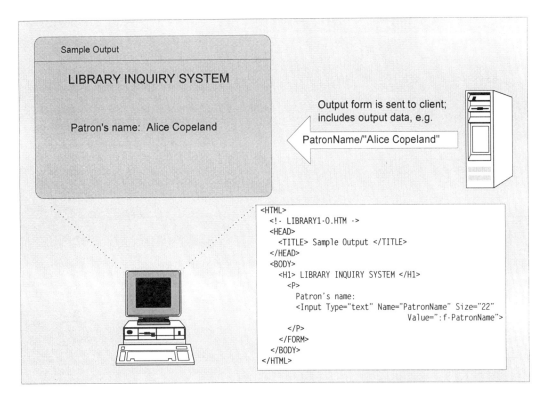

Figure 2-9. An HTML output scenario.

Regardless of what you call it, this program allows information to be passed between Web browsers and Web servers. It is the server-side program that accepts the name/value pair or pairs, performs needed operations, and returns another form to your browser. Net Express lets you write your CGI programs in Cobol via only a few extensions to Standard Cobol, as you can see by inspecting the partial program of Figure 2-10. That's it! You can create a complete CGI program written in Cobol using one new clause, External-Form, and two tried and true Cobol statements: Accept and Display. Before looking at these new elements, remember the execution sequence:

1. The input form accepts your input and transfers control to a CGI program.
2. The CGI program performs its tasks then returns an output form to your browser.
3. The browser displays the output form.

The Cobol CGI

The External-Form Clause

Before getting into the syntax details, simply think of External-form as a data-record definition for HTML forms. Just as you have always defined input and output data records in your Cobol programs, you can now define input and output records for HTML forms using External-form.

```
    Identification Division.
      Program-ID. Lib02.

    Data Division.
      Working-Storage Section.
        01 HtmlInputForm is external-form.
          03 f-PatronNumber    pic x(03)
                               identified by "PatronNumber".
        01 HtmlOutputForm is external-form
                               identified by "lib02-O.htm".
          03 f-PatronName      pic x(22)
                               identified by "PatronName".

    Procedure Division.
      Accept HtmlInputForm

      *>User-written program statements to obtain the patron
      *>name using the f-PatronNumber. This code places the
      *>result in the data item f-PatronName.

      Display HtmlOutputForm
      Stop run

        .
```

Figure 2-10. A simplified CGI program: Lib02.cbl.

General Format

> **data-name is <u>External-Form</u> [<u>Identified by</u> literal-1]**

where

> **data-name** is a named data item
> **External-Form** specifies that an HTML form is being used
> > (permitted only in the Working-Storage Section)
> **Identified by** is a keyword phrase
> **Literal-1** identifies an HTML page, optionally including the drive and path.
> > (for example: `C:\somedirectory\filename.htm`)

Notes:
1. The **Identified by** phrase is not allowed in an input HTML page.
2. An output HTML page must include an **Identified by** phrase.

Let's look at the first 01 entry of Figure 2-10; it identifies the input HTML form.

```
    01  HtmlInputForm is external-form.
```

The data-name `HtmlInputForm` is a conventional Cobol data name (therefore, all Cobol rules for data names apply). The `external-form` phrase indicates that this data-name is associated with an HTML page.

Data elements associated with this input form are defined as elementary items subordinate to this 01, for instance:

```
    03  f-PatronNumber      pic x(03)
                            identified by "PatronNumber".
```

You can think of this as similar to a Select clause in which you relate an external file name to an internal Cobol name. For example, the following Select allows you to refer to the external file `patron.di` by the programmer-defined name `patron-file`.

```
Select patron-file assign to "patron.di"
```

Similarly, the sample 03 associates the programmer-defined Cobol data name `f-PatronNumber` with the HTML input form data item `PatronNumber`. Don't be confused that the names are nearly identical. You could use any name you wish in place of `f-PatronNumber`; Micro Focus uses this as a Net Express standard.

The output form Working-Storage Section entry is similar to the input form entry. However, remember that the CGI program must identify the HTML form that is to be returned to your browser. Consequently, the output form 01 requires the `Identified` by clause as follows.

```
HtmlOutputForm is external-form
                    Identifed by "Lib02-O.htm".
```

Here the `Identified` by clause designates `Lib02-O.htm` as the file containing the output HTML code. When the filename does not include an extension, HTM is assumed. As does the input form 01, the output form 01 includes elementary entries designating the output data items.

Accept and Display

Where external-form provides the capability to define forms for input and output data records, Accept and Display provide the capability to read and write these data records. Notice you use Accept and Display exactly as you've done in the past. The only difference now is that the data names refer to HTML pages. When the user clicks on a Submit button (Find in the library example), the form's Post method sends name/value pair(s) to the CGI program. The Accept statement

```
Accept HtmlInputForm
```

places the input data into the corresponding data items of the external-form record. Actually, the Net Express Accept does a lot of work behind the scenes as the stream of data from the browser is highly encoded. However, the activity is completely transparent to you, the programmer.

Like the Accept, the Display statement does a lot of behind-the-scenes work. It is responsible for packaging the data in an HTTP acceptable format and sending special header data together with the name/value pairs to the requesting client.

Perhaps you are wondering how the server knows where to send the output from the CGI program. The answer to this is that the connection from the browser to the server is, in some ways, like a telephone call. If you receive a call from someone, you don't need to dial his/her number to reply. You simply speak into the phone. The same principle applies to Web transactions. When a browser sends data to a server, it establishes a connection. The connection remains open until the server responds. The server is responsible for keeping track of where to return the HTML form.

Overall Relationships

The relationship between various components of this simple Web example are illustrated in Figure 2-11. Note that the solid arrows represent the sequence of execution: the input HTML page, to the CGI program, to the output HTML page. The broken arrows show relationships between data elements of the HTML pages and the CGI.

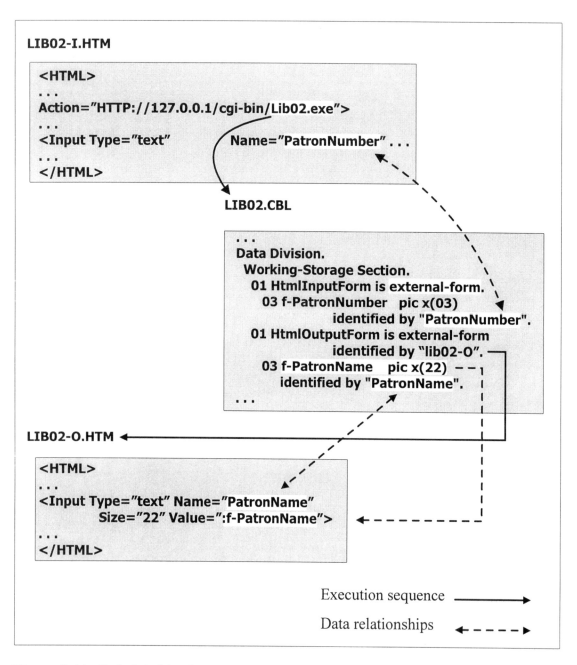

Figure 2-11. Relationships between HTML forms and the CGI program.

Net Express Variations

In the next chapter, your will use Net Express to create HTML pages and generate your CGI program. You will see that the Net Express generated program is different from that of Figure 2-10 in two respects. Although Net Express supports the expanded Display statement, code generated by the Net Express system uses an Exec HTML statement in which HTML code is embedded directly in the Cobol program. This is call **embedded HTML**. Using embedded HTML, separate 01 external-form records are no longer required.

These features are shown in Figure 2-12. Notice that in addition to the differences described above, Net Express creates Cobol names that are identical to the external form data item named (lines 13-15). So that you can work with the more familiar form data names, Net Express inserts Move statements before and after your processing code (lines 19 and 26, in this example). As you will see in the next chapter, Net Express generates all of this code for you; you need only insert your code (as indicated by the comments of lines 22-24).

```
1    Identification Division.
2      Program-ID. Lib02.
3
4    Data Division.
5      Working-Storage Section.
6        01 HtmlForm is external-form.
7          03 f-PatronNumber   pic x(03)
8                              identified by "PatronNumber".
9          03 f-PatronName     pic x(22)
10                             identified by "PatronName".
11
12       *>The following is inserted from a COPY
13       01 data-items-generated-by-NE.
14          03 PatronNumber    pic X(03).
15          03 PatronName      pic X(22).
16
17   Procedure Division.
18     Accept HtmlInputForm
19     Move f-PatronNumber to PatronNumber *> Inserted by NE with
20                              *> a COPY statement
21
22     *>User-written program statements to obtain the patron
23     *>name using the patron number. This code places the
24     *>result in the data item PatronName.
25
26     Move PatronName to f-PatronName *> Inserted by NE with .
27                              *> a COPY statement
28     Exec html
29       <HTML>
30       <!- LIBRARY1-0.HTM ->
31       <HEAD>
32       <TITLE> Sample Output </TITLE>
33       </HEAD>
34       <BODY>
35       <H1> LIBRARY INQUIRY SYSTEM </H1>
36       <P>
37       <H2>
38       Patron's name:
39       <Input Type="text" Name="PatronName" Size="22"
40                          Value=":f-PatronName">
41       </H2>
42       </FORM>
43       </BODY>
44       </HTML>
45     End exec
46     Stop run
47     .
```

Figure 2-12. Some NetExpress variations.

Summing Up

Basic Web terminology introduced in this chapter includes: CGI, client/server, extranet, gateway program, intranet, HTML, URL, Web browser, Web document, Web server, Web site.

The Universal Resource Locator (URL) is the addressing scheme with which we are familiar from surfing the net. For instance, the URL of Object-Z Systems is `http://www.objectz.com`. The `http:` designates HyperText Transfer Protocol; `www` indicates the Web site belonging to `objectz`.

In a Web client/server environment, communication between the Web client (your personal computer) and a Web server is accomplished by passing Web documents (using the HyperText Markup Language—HTML) back and forth.

A browser program on the client computer converts Web documents to the display screens to which we are accustomed in surfing the Web.

An HTML "program" consists of text (and images) to be displayed together with imbedded instructions, in the form of tags, regarding how the text is to be displayed.

The Common Gateway Interface (CGI) program is the application program located on the server to process a user request. The Micro Focus Cobol `External-form` clause extensions to the `Accept` and `Display` statements allow us to write the CGI program in Cobol. The `Exec-HTML` statement provides for embedding output HTML forms directly within the Cobol program.

Coming Up

The basic interface for creating Web applications with Net Express is the Form Designer, which allows you to generate HTML input and output forms. It also produces a CGI program tailored to those forms. You can insert your specific application code into this CGI. The next chapter presents a simple example of creating a new application and building an input form and an output form using a few of the basic HTML elements.

50

A Basic Net Express Web Example

Chapter Contents

Folders for Projects 52
Generating a Web Application 53
   Creating the Project 53
   A Naming Convention 54
   Creating a New Form 54
   The Form Designer Screen 56
Building the Input Page 57
   Text Entries 57
   Some Tips on Inserting Controls 59
   The Text Input Control 60
   About Selecting Names 62
   Completing the Input Form 62
Building the Output Page 63
   The Server-Side Text Control 63
   Building the Output Page 63
Creating the CGI Program 64
The Results of Your Endeavor 66
   The Project Screen 66
   The Net Express Operating Environment 66
   Running the Application 67
   Terminating a Run 68
Improving the Appearance of Screen Displays 69
   Using the Format Tool Bar 69
   Setting Style Attributes 69
   Using the Text Input to Display Output 71
   The Horizontal Rule 71
Summing Up 72
   Project Summary 72
   General Summary 72

Coming Up 73

Assignment 73

Chapter

3

Chapter Introduction

The objective of this chapter is to give you your first experience with creating a Web application using Net Express. The project of this chapter includes an input page, an output page, and a CGI program. From this example, you will learn about the following.

- Creating a project.
- The Form Designer toolbar controls for text display, data input, and text data display.
- The Submit button.
- Creating an HTML page.
- Creating the CGI program.
- Running the application.
- Modifying an HTML page.

A Library Application

A corporate lending library that lends books, periodicals, and videos to employees and contractors is the primary example application used in this book. In the application, a three-digit patron number identifies library patrons. You saw this example in Chapter 2 where a user entered the patron number into an input form and was presented with an output form containing the name of the patron—a relatively simple application. Your first exercise with Net Express is even simpler. You will create the application illustrated by the screens of Figure 3-1. The input screen is shown in Figure 3-1(a) where a user can type a patron number. This sample screen displays three different types of HTML controls you can create.

   a) Descriptive data (equivalent to data defined in a Value clause in Cobol).
   b) An input area (the empty rectangle).
   c) A signal to take an action (the rectangle labeled Accept).

The output page is shown in Figure 3-1(b) where the CGI has responded with a welcome message displaying the input patron number. In generating this application, you will do the following.

- Create the input form (an HTML page).
- Create the output form (an HTML page).
- Generate the CGI program (a Cobol program).

Folders for Projects

Each Web project you create generates a number of files as well as a special folder (named debug). The simplest approach to keeping your work organized is to create a separate folder for each project. For instance, you might consider using the technique employed with examples of this book (as described in the Introduction) in which Chapter 1's second example is stored in the folder Proj0102. For example,

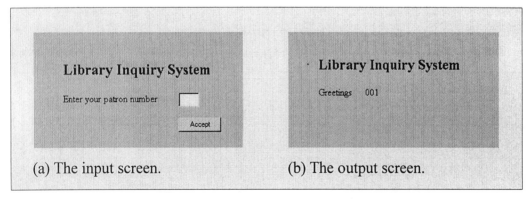

(a) The input screen.   (b) The output screen.

Figure 3-1. Sample Web screens.

consider something like folder Assn0302 for Chapter 3's Assignment 2. If you are using this book in a formal course, using folders in this way simplifies the process of making an individual project disk for turn-in.

All of this book's example projects are stored in the folder **NE-Examples**. For instance, the first example you will look at, Lib01, is stored in the folder **Elements-CWP\NE-Examples\Proj0301**. I suggest that you create your own folder (for instance, **My-Examples**) for creating projects as you step through the tutorials. The following example is based on using that folder.

Generating a Web Application

Creating the Project

You must first bring up Net Express (refer to Chapter 1 for this) and proceed with the following steps.

1. Select File/New. This produces the popup menu of Figure 3-2.
2. From this popup, highlight Project and click on OK; you will see the New Project screen of Figure 3-3.
3. Highlight Empty Project for the project type. Type project name: Lib01.
   For the folder name, type the name of the folder you want to use for this project. If that folder does not exist, Net Express will create it for you. In Figure 3-3, you see the entry C:\My-Examples\Proj0301. Click on Create.

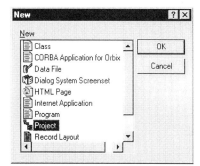

Figure 3-2. The New menu.

4. If you have not already created the folder you entered in the preceding step, Net Express will display a message that the location does not exist. You can click on Yes to create the folder.

Figure 3-3. The project screen.

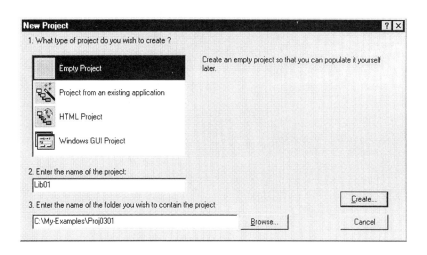

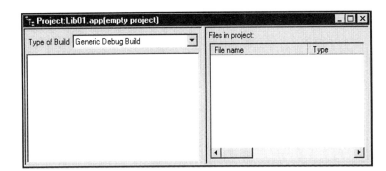

Figure 3-4.
The "empty project"
screen.

Your screen will display the "empty project" window of Figure 3-4. Before creating the HTML pages for this example, let's consider a naming convention.

A Naming Convention

The HTML code for each page you create is stored as a file (actually, two files, as you will learn later). Almost all projects you look at include at least an input page, an output page, and a CGI program. To minimize confusion, a standard naming convention is used in this book in which the project name, Lib01 in this example, serves as the base name. For instance, for the input page you will use the name Lib01-IN, which has the following components.

- Lib signifies the library system.
- If you intend to create more than one version of this application, use a numbering system to distinguish between them. Here, 01 signifies first version of this application.
- -IN signifies an input page file (for instance, Lib01-IN, or Lib-IN if you don't use a version number).

You will name other components as follows.

- -OUT signifies an output page file (for instance, Lib01-OUT, or Lib-OUT if you don't use a version number).
- The CGI program name consists of Lib plus the version number (for instance, Lib01 or Lib if you don't use a version number).

For documentation purposes in this book, suffixes for HTML pages (for instance, -IN and -OUT) will always be in upper-case and will be separated from the rest of the name by hyphens. Suffixes use for CGI programs will always be in lower-case and will never include hyphens.

Note: This completed project, stored in NE-Examples\Proj0301, uses these same names for the project components.

Creating a New Page

To create an empty input page, proceed as follows.

1. Proceeding from Figure 3-4, click File/New.
2. You will again see the popup window of Figure 3-2; this time select HTML Page and click OK.

Figure 3-5.
HTML Page Wizard;
New HTML Form.

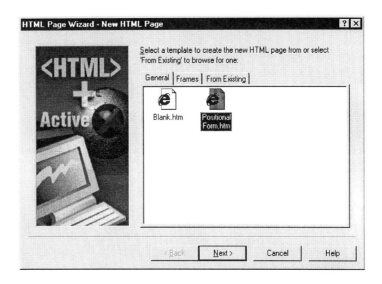

3. From the resulting HTML Page Wizard of Figure 3-5, select Positional Form.htm and click Next.

4. The preceding click produces the screen of Figure 3-6. You must enter the name you want assigned to the form (Net Express displays HTMLPage as the default). Type Lib01-IN.

5. The HTML Output Type gives you two options.
    *   Cross-platform (table output)—the default.
    *   Dynamic HTML positioned (IE4 + only).

    Features of the latter are not supported by many of the browsers in use at the time of writing of this book. Features of the Cross-platform option are common to almost all browsers. You want this option. Click Next.

6. The screen of Figure 3-7 summarizes your choices. It is easy to make a wrong selection when creating a form so get in the habit of checking each of these items. If anything is incorrect, click on Back and make the appropriate corrections. When everything is okay click Finish; after a few moments you will see the screen of Figure 3-8.

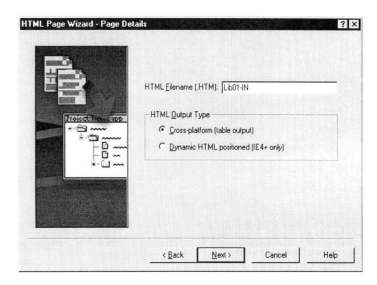

Figure 3-6. HTML
Page Wizard—Form
Details

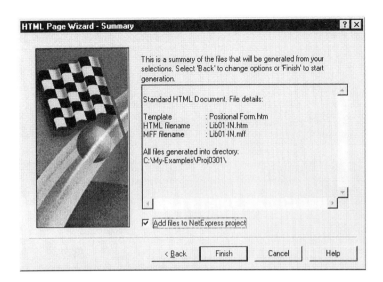

Figure 3-7.
HTML Page
Wizard Summary.

The Form Designer Screen

The Form Designer screen of Figure 3-8 includes the following four panes.

- **Form Designer** pane. The pane with the dotted grid background is where you design your page (you will probably need to enlarge your Lib01-IN.htm pane).
- **Control tree** pane. The pane at the top right shows you all the controls on your HTML page. Whenever you create a positional form, the components shown here are generated automatically. As you add controls (for example, input areas and buttons) you will see them inserted into this tree.

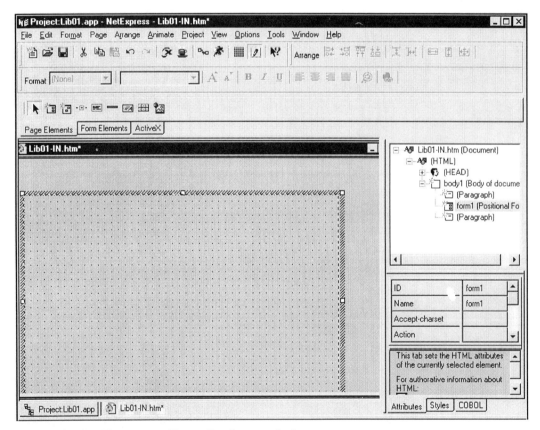

Figure 3-8. The empty Form Designer window.

- **Property list** pane. The pane below the control tree pane shows the properties for the object currently selected in the form design pane. Property names are listed down the left, and the corresponding values down the right. There are three property categories accessible by the three tabs at the bottom: Attributes, Styles, and COBOL.
- **Help** pane. The pane at the bottom right displays help for the property list pane. If you click any field in the property list pane, help for that field appears in the help pane.

Notice in Figure 3-8 that the grid area is bounded by a dotted line and a border containing conventional Windows select handles. Move your cursor (arrow pointer) outside of the grid area but still within the Form Designer window and click. Notice that the grid area is still bounded by a dotted line but the border and selection handles have disappeared. Look at the control tree window and you will see that one of the Paragraph elements is selected. Don't be concerned with these; they are necessary components generated by Net Express.

When you are creating a new page for most of the exercises in this book, you will always be working within the grid area bounded by the dotted lines. If you are not within this area when placing controls, the results will not be what you want. Get back into the grid area either of two ways: place the mouse pointer in the area and click, or click on form1 (Positional Form) in the control tree.

Immediately above the Form Designer window you see three tabs: Page Elements (the default selected tab), Form Elements, and ActiveX. You will be working almost entirely with the Form Elements tab so click on it and you will see the following control toolbar.

The four controls you will use for this exercise are: **ab|**, *Aa*, **Xx**, and ⌗. Referring to the previously stated needs of this application, they allow you to create form controls as follows.

ab|	An input area.
Aa	Descriptive information on the screen.
Xx	An output display area.
⌗	A signal to transfer control to the server.

Building the Input Page

Text Entries

First, let's create the main heading **Library Inquiry System**.

1. Make certain the form is selected, that is, your form must be surrounded by the hashed border and form1 must be selected in the tree window.

2. Click the tool bar's Text icon *Aa* to highlight it.

3. Move the mouse pointer to the approximate place on the design screen you want to place the heading. Click to insert a text field and your screen will look like Figure 3-9. Be aware that this is *not* a drag and drop situation; you simply click on *Aa* (to highlight it), then click where you want the description.

4. If you are not satisfied with its position, you can move it using standard Windows techniques, that is, position the mouse pointer on the control's edge (causing it to change to ✛), left-click, and drag.

5. Click within this control then look carefully and you should see a blinking cursor (vertical line) to the left of the word New. You can edit the existing entry (New Text) in the same way you work with a word processor. Delete this entry either by successively pressing the Delete key or by selecting the entire text and pressing the Delete key.

6. Type in **Library Inquiry System**. When you do this, you will see the line wrap (the word **System** will be on the next line). This occurs because Net Express creates an HTML **span** to encompass all text items. In general, you need not be concerned about this—only be aware that it occurs.

7. To return the form title to a single line, grab the right selection handle and drag the right edge of this span to the right, almost to the right edge of the form. You will need additional area when you increase the type size.

Whenever you are working with the text (have the text cursor active) you will see the text toolbar become active (the elements are no longer grayed out). These are the standard Windows word-processing tools that allow you to manage text.

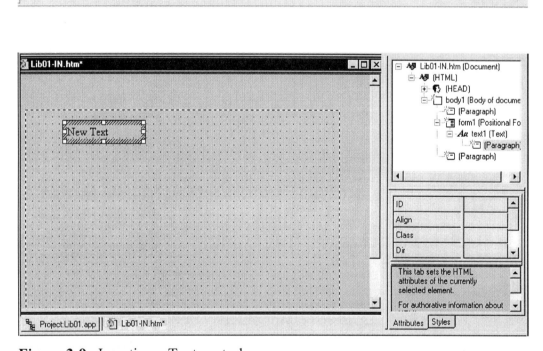

Figure 3-9. Inserting a Text control.

8. Highlight your entry **Library Inquiry System**.
9. Click the icon A and you will see the selected text increase in size. Click this icon twice more to obtain the desired size. When you are finished, your form heading should look like the following.

10. Referring to Figure 3-1, you need another text entry: the instruction to the user "Enter your patron number." Repeat the preceding steps to create this text. Position it just beneath the main heading. Do not change the font size.

Some Tips on Inserting Controls

At this point, your screen should contain the two Text controls: the form heading and the user prompt line. Look at the control-tree window of Figure 3-10 and you will see them identified as *Aa* text1 and *Aa* text2. Subordinate to each, you see a Paragraph entry. Be aware that each text control consists of at least these two components. (The main heading contains an element subordinate to Paragraph; this designates selection of a font other than the default.) For each Text control, Form Designer actually creates an HTML **span** tag and places a paragraph tag within the span. The paragraph provides the area for you to type your description; the span ensures that the browser interpreting the HTML script maintains it exactly as you create it in Form Designer. Selecting a Text control is confusing until you understand what you have. To illustrate, position your mouse pointer below the "Enter your patron number" Text control then slowly move it up to the control and watch it change to the following shapes.

⟲   The mouse pointer.

✛   Indicates you are over the span; clicking here selects the span itself. With this selection, you can move and resize the control.

I   Indicates you are within the paragraph; clicking here places you in the text mode for text entry.

You might find selecting the element a little tricky this way. A sure-fire method to ensure you get what you want is to click on the appropriate element in the control tree pane. For instance, click on *Aa* text1 and you will see the span selected thereby allowing you to move it and change its size. Click on Paragraph and you will be positioned in the span in the text-entry mode.

If you have many Text controls, it is convenient to be able to identify each from its entry in the control-tree pane, not an easy task when they are identified as text1, text2, and so on. You can alleviate this problem by attaching a meaningful name to each as follows.

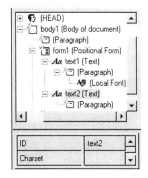

Figure 3-10.
Control-tree window.

1. Select the user-prompt Text control in the control-tree pane, as done at the Figure 3-10. In the properties pane you see the ID default entry text2; you want to change this to something more meaningful.
2. Click on the entry text2 in the ID entry box; delete text2, type QueryLine, then press the Enter key. These panes will then look like Figure 3-11.
3. Alternately, you can right click on the control in the control-tree, select the Set ID option, then edit the entry directly.
4. Change the corresponding description of the other Text control from text1 to something more descriptive.

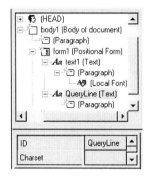

Figure 3-11.
Changing a description.

Be aware that because of the way in which this property is used by other controls, your entry cannot contain spaces nor can it be a Cobol reserved word.

The Text Input Control

Next, you need the Text Input control (to create the area for the user to enter the patron number). Place the mouse pointer on the Text Input icon **ab|** of the toolbar. After a moment the description *Text Input* will appear. Be aware that in HTML *all input is referred to as text*; there is no distinction between alphanumeric and numeric input. Don't confuse this with Cobol and expect to find an equivalent input button for numeric data.

1. Click on **ab|** of the Form Designer toolbar to highlight that button.
2. Place an input control as shown in Figure 3-12.

With the Text Input control selected, you will see a properties pane that looks something like the one shown here in Figure 3-13. Notice that the Attribute tab is the default selection; you are looking at the control's **attributes**. (Your window will

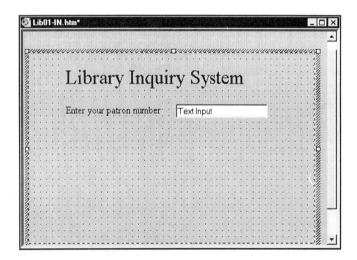

Figure 3-12.
Inserting an
Input Text control.

probably display only a few of these attributes; the scroll
bar provides access to those not displayed.) For now, you
should focus your attention on the following.

- Name This is the data name of the name/value pair
  returned to the server.
- ID As with the Text control, this property designates
  the name you will see in the control tree view
  following the **ab|** icon. From your perspective, it is
  purely informational for this control. A good
  documentation practice is to make this entry
  identical to the Name entry.
- MaxLength This entry specifies the maximum
  number of characters the browser will allow to be
  entered into this control. Here you see a default
  value of 19.
- Size This entry designates the width of the entry
  field (the data entry box size for the screen display)
  in characters. Here you see a default entry of 20.
  You will normally set MaxLength and Size to the same
  value.

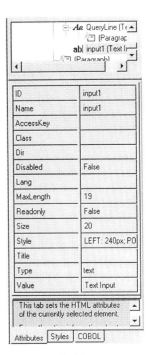

Figure 3-13.
The properties pane.

- Title Specifies a title for the element that the browser displays when the mouse
  pointer is positioned on the control.
- Value If you want the browser to display a default value for this input item,
  you enter that value here. Notice that the default value is Text Input. For most
  applications, you will want this entry blank.

Make the following entries in the properties window of your form. Do this by
clicking in the attribute area of the selected property and typing your entry (in some
cases, over-typing default values).

ID	InPatronNumber
Name	InPatronNumber
MaxLength	3
Size	3
Title	3-digit number
Value	Delete the default entry and leave it blank.

Next you must tell Net Express the type of data item you want generated in the
CGI program. Click the COBOL tab and you will see the default COBOLPicture entry
x(32). If you leave this value unchanged, your CGI program will contain the following entry.

```
03  InPatronNumber   pic x(32).
```

Your entry here can be either an X picture or a 9 picture. You will normally make the
size the same as the MaxLength attribute value. Change this to the following.

```
COBOLPicture x(3)
```

About Selecting Names

As indicated above, the Name entry you make is the data name of the name/value pair returned to the server. To simplify your CGI programming task, the data items created for the Net Express-generated CGI program are assigned the same names as their corresponding HTML names. Thus, you should select names that correspond to those you might be using in existing Cobol programs, or will likely use in Cobol CGI programs you will be writing. Your selection of names is limited by naming rules of Cobol with the added restriction that HTML does not permit hyphens. The technique used in this book is to duplicate the data names used in the Cobol CGI program (whenever appropriate) by omitting the hyphens and by using uppercase as the first letter of each word forming the name. For instance, assume that the patron number field in the Cobol program is in-patron-number. The corresponding HTML name would be InPatronNumber, as you used in this example. As you will learn, you must carefully document names that you use because you are working with multiple components in a Web application.

Completing the Input Form

Finally, you must include a button that sends your request to the server.

1. This is accomplished with the Submit button 🔳 of the toolbar. Highlight it, move to the position of the screen you want it positioned, and click.
2. Change the Value property from Submit Query to Accept so that your screen looks like Figure 3-14. (Actually, you can leave the default value or use whatever caption you feel is clear to the user.)
3. You are now finished with the input form; your screen should contain all the components of the earlier Figure 3-1(a). Click File/Save to save this page. Then click File/Close to close the page.

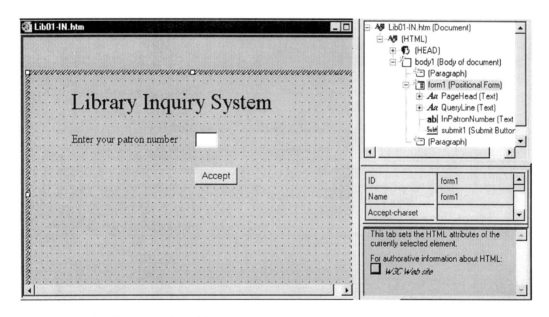

Figure 3-14. The completed input page.

Building the Output Page

The Server-Side Text Control

Remember from Figure 3-1(b) that the input screen accepts a patron number from the keyboard; the output screen displays a greeting echoing back the input patron number. From an Text Input control of the input form, the browser creates an area on the screen into which you can enter data. That data, together with the name assigned to the control is sent to the server as a name value pair. This Text Input control can also be used to return data for display on an output screen. However, for server-produced data to be used solely as output, you will commonly utilize another control: the Server-Side Text control. As it is data from the server, it does not require many of the attributes associated with the Text Input control. For instance, a default value and a maximum number of characters are both meaningless for this control. You will see this when you build the output page

Building the Output Page

To create the output page of Figure 3-1, proceed as follows.

1. From the project screen, click File/New.
2. You will again see the popup window of Figure 3-2; select HTML Page and click OK.
3. From the resulting HTML Page Wizard (Figure 3-5) select Positional Form.htm and click Next.
4. From the next screen (see Figure 3-6), enter the name you want assigned to the form in this case, Lib01-OUT. Select Cross-platform (table output)—the default. Click Next.
5. Check all of your entries on the summary screen. If anything is incorrect, click Back and make the appropriate corrections. When everything is okay click Finish; after a few moments you will see the Form Designer screen.
6. Create the output page [it must look like Figure 3-1(b)] using the preceding techniques for creating the input page, that is, create:
   a. The heading line "Library Inquiry System".
   b. A description line "Greetings"
7. Designate an "output" area for display of the patron's number by highlighting the Server-Side Text button **Xx**; then move to the appropriate position on the screen and click to position it.
8. Change the ID attribute from serversidetext1 to InPatronNumber, the same as the Name attribute of the input form.
9. As this control is to display the three-digit patron number, you can decrease the size of the "box" accordingly. However, before doing that, delete the entry Server-Side Text. Then grab the right selection handle and resize this control to something that will be consistent with the three-digit patron number.
10. Click anywhere outside this control to deselect it and you will see that it nearly disappears from the screen. It is visible in that the dots of the dot matrix

background do not show. So it's a good idea to make some descriptive entry in this box. In this example, type IPN, an abbreviation for InPatronNumber.

11. Click the COBOL tab and change COBOLPicture to x(3), the size of the output patron-number field. If your screen does not display a COBOL tab, you probably have the paragraph element selected. If so, click the **Xx** entry in the control tree to select that control. Your finished screen should look like Figure 3-15.

12. When you've finished creating this page, click File/Save then File/Close.

As you work with more of the form controls, you will find that some attributes have different meanings for different control types. For instance, the Text Input control ID attribute serves primarily as documentation; the Name attribute designates the data name of the name/value pair returned to the server. It also produces a Cobol data item with the same name. On the other hand, the Server-Side Text control does not include the Name attribute. Net Express uses your ID attribute entry as the data item name in the CGI program.

Although using InPatronNumber, the input field in this example, for output is contrived, it provides you with something that is simple to create while serving as a good example for your first look at Net Express.

Creating the CGI Program

You've created both the input and output forms; you must now create the CGI program.

1. Click File/New and select Internet Application.

2. From the resulting Internet Application Wizard, click the Server Program (from Net Express created HTML) radio button. When you do so, the Wizard Input will change to HTML Form(s), as you see in Figure 3-16. Click Next.

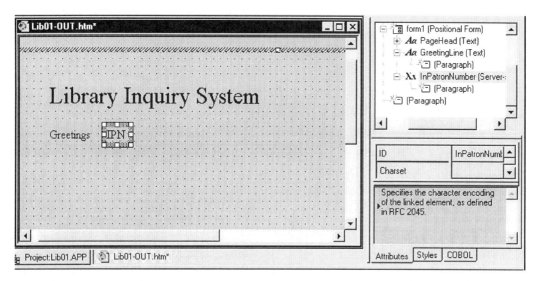

Figure 3-15. The output form.

Figure 3-16.
Designating a
CGI program.

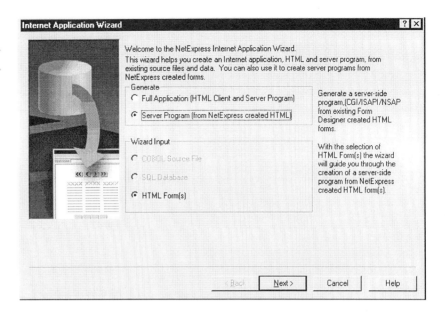

3. The next screen will look something like Figure 3-17. Here you must name the CGI program, optionally designate the CGI code generation template, identify the CGI's input form, and identify the CGI's output page (or pages). For this, make the following changes to your screen.

a) The default Filename entry is mycgi.cbl; change it to Lib01.cbl.

b) If you loaded the alternate CGI skeleton file from the Examples Distribution Medium per the instructions of Chapter 0, you can use it (cgi-min.skl) in place of the default (cgi.skl) for the Generation Template entry. The advantage is that your resulting CGI program is much smaller (and easier to study) because unneeded lines have been removed. To specify this file, click the down button of the Template entry and select cgi-min.skl.

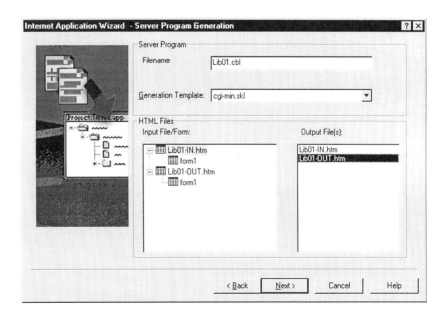

Figure 3-17.
Defining the
CGI features.

     c) Select Lib01-IN.htm for the Input File and Lib01-OUT.htm for the Output File.
         (Refer to the entries of Figure 3-17.)
3. Click Next and you will see a summary screen. *Carefully* check that everything
    is correct, that is, the CGI program name is Lib01.cbl, the input page is Lib01-
    IN.htm, and the output page is Lib01-OUT.htm. If anything is wrong, back up and
    make appropriate corrections. It's a lot of trouble to make corrections once the
    complete project is generated.
4. When everything is correct, click Finish.
5. Net Express will build your project (which will take a while). When finished,
    Net Express returns control to the project screen.

The Results of Your Endeavor

The Project Screen

Your project screen now should look like Figure 3-18. In the pane on the right you
see a list of the files comprising this project. Lib01.cbl is your CGI program; the other
three Lib01 files are source code files that form part of the overall CGI program. You
will look at these later.

    Notice that you have two copies of the input and output HTML form files: mff
and htm. The mff (Micro Focus Form) file contains the information needed to declare
Cobol data items in any server-side program generated from the controls on the
page. For instance, the COBOLPicture property for each HTML control on the page is
stored in this file. The htm file contains the HTML code that produces your display
when your page is sent to a browser.

The Net Express Operating Environment

Before running the application, let's step back and review how a Web application
works. From Chapter 2 you know that you work with the following components.

- A browser operating on your computer (the client)
- A Web server operating on the Web site computer.

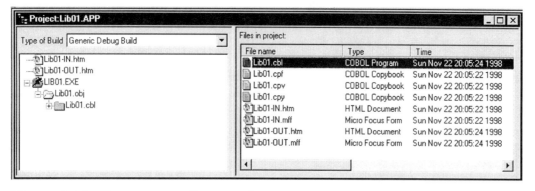

Figure 3-18. Components of your project.

- The HTML input page into which you enter data that is sent to the Web site.
- A CGI program (on the Web server) activated by your input form.
- Another HTML page sent to your computer by the CGI program.

An important feature of Net Express is that you can develop Web applications entirely in a local environment (without going to an outside server). This way you can program and test an application entirely on your own computer before placing it on the Web. Net Express accomplishes this through a special server program called **Solo** (which is included in Net Express). So when you run an application in this mode, the following takes place.

- Net Express starts the Web server software Solo. You know it's running because the Solo icon ⏣ is displayed in the Windows taskbar tray (bottom right of your screen).
- Net Express starts your browser and loads your page.
- You click a submit button on the input form.
- The browser sends the name/value pair(s) from the form together with the name of the CGI program to the server. Because the URL of the form identifies Solo (on your own computer), Solo takes control thereby simulating the server.
- Solo runs your CGI program.
- Your CGI program identifies the output page that is returned by Solo to your browser.

Running the Application

With that brief introduction, let's try running the application.

1. If you've closed this project, then reopen it; your screen will look like Figure 3-18.
2. Click the Rebuild button ⬒ to ensure that all files are properly prepared.
3. Click on the Run button ⚡ of the toolbar (or alternately, select the command sequence Animate/Run). Net Express displays the confirmation screen of Figure 3-19. The box identifies the HTML program that is to begin the process. If yours does not list your input page (Lib01-IN.htm) at the end of the HTTP path, then you made a mistake when constructing the project. The simplest solution at this point is to create a new CGI from Form Designer.
4. Click OK to run. Your browser should bring up the input screen. If you are using Microsoft Internet Explorer 4.0, it will look like Figure 3-20. If you are using another browser, it will be slightly different.

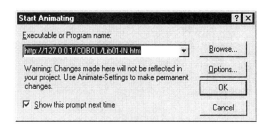

Figure 3-19. Starting a run.

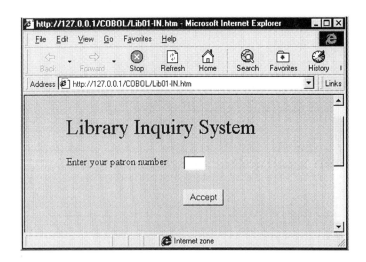

Figure 3-20.
The input page displayed by Internet Explorer.

5. For this simple application, you can enter any value you wish for the patron number, as there is no file lookup involved. Click anywhere in the input box (to ensure the cursor is positioned there) and type a three digit number.

6. Click the Accept button.

The data name/value pair (your input patron number) is sent to the server and acted upon by the CGI program. The CGI program returns the output page thereby yielding the screen created by the page's HTML code—see Figure 3-21.

Terminating a Run

You are finished with this example so you can terminate processing.

1. Close the browser window.

2. The Net Express window is probably minimized. If so, click its button (in the task bar at the bottom of the screen) to return it to view.

3. Click Animate/Stop Animating from the menu bar.

At this point, you can run the application again or you can proceed to make some changes to your pages.

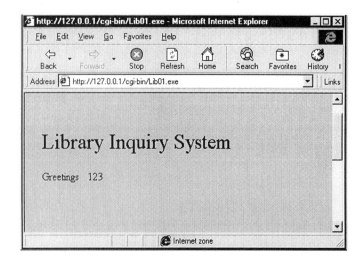

Figure 3-21.
The output page displayed by Internet Explorer.

Improving the Appearance of Screen Displays

Net Express provides a variety of means for you to change the appearance of your browser screen display. To give you an idea of some simple features (that will allow you to "jazz up" your displays), let's modify Lib01-OUT. The overall sequence involves the following steps.

- Bring up Lib01-OUT.htm in the Form Designer screen.
- Make the desired changes.
- Save the page.
- Rebuild the project.

Using the Format Tool Bar

From the project screen of Figure 3-18, double-click Lib01-OUT.htm. Select the "Greetings" control and highlight the entire word. You've already used the following Format toolbar to increase the size of the main heading of this form.

The second box identifies the font type of this item (Times New Roman is the default). Clicking the down arrow expands this list and provides you access to a wide selection of fonts via the conventional Windows form. You can select fonts with or without serifs—a serif is the small cross-stroke at the end of the main character stroke. Try some of them and you will see the word Greetings change. With most fonts, each character uses only as much space as is needed, for instance, the letter M occupies much more space than the letter I. A few fonts allocate the same amount of space for each letter, regardless of its width. The most commonly encountered is Courier.

Notice that you can also change the selected characters to boldface, italics, several heading levels, and other forms. Again, experiment with this to see how it changes the appearance of the word "Greetings."

If you click on the color button a color palate will appear. Select a color, click OK, and observe that the displayed item is shown in your selected color.

Setting Style Properties

Beneath the properties window of your Form Designer display for Lib01-OUT you see the two tabs Attributes and Styles; refer to Figure 3-22. (You also see a COBOL tab if your control selection is Text Input or Server-Side Text.) Let's check out some of its features available to you from the styles properties.

1. In the control-tree window, select body1 (Body of document).
2. Click the Styles tab. The right side of your screen should look like Figure 3-22.

For each control on your screen, whether one containing other controls (such as body1 here) or an individual control (such Paragraph) you will see the list of style properties of Figure 3-22. These allow you to specify styles such as backgrounds, colors, and borders. Let's experiment to observe some of these features.

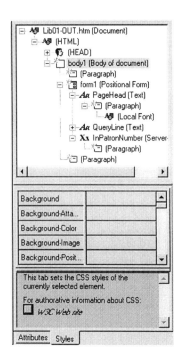

3. With body1 still selected in the control tree, click on Background-Color. In the help window you see the description: Sets the color of the element's background; either choose a named color from the drop-down list, or choose a system or custom color by clicking the right arrow.
4. Click the right-arrow to obtain a color palette.
5. Click a color that appeals to you and click OK. The entire form layout screen changes to the selected color. Notice that the selected color is shown in the properties window.
6. To change the color back to the default, click the down arrow, scroll to the top of the color list, and select the blank entry.

Figure 3-22. Styles.

7. You can change the background color for any control. For instance, select the *Aa* PageHead control.
8. Repeat Steps 3-6 and you will see that only the span area of this heading changes color.

Next, let's take a look at how you can use borders to accentuate portions of your form or the entire form itself.

1. Highlight form1 (Positional Form) in the control tree to select the form itself.
2. Make certain the Styles tab is selected.
3. In the properties window, scroll down and select the Border-Style property. Click the down arrow and you will see a list of border styles.
4. Click any of the border styles that appeals to you. You will see a border around the form.
5. Scroll down and select Border-Width. You can specify the width of the border by typing the following:
   • thin, medium, or thick
   • the width in points (pt), inches (in), centimeters (cm), or pixels (px), for instance, you could enter 6pt (which is 1/12 inch).
6. Scroll up to Border-Color and select a color in the same way you did for the background color.

Be aware that you can place a border around any control on your screen.

The final "goodie" we'll look at is the ability to use a background image obtained from a graphics file. Included in the Proj0301 folder are seven image files: BG01.jpg, BG02.jpg, BG03.jpg, BG04.jpg, BG05.jpg, BG06.jpg, and Eggshell.gif. Let's use Eggshell.gif.

1. In the control-tree window, select body1 (Body of document).
2. Click the Style tab.
3. Select the Background-Image property.
4. Type url(eggshell.gif).
5. If the image displays as a square in the upper-left corner, you must select the Background-Repeat property, expand the list and click Repeat.

You can use these images (or any other in jpg or gif format) with any of your forms. Be aware that you must include the image file in the folder containing your project. In a later chapter, you will learn how to gain access to images in another folder.

Using the Text Input to Display Output

In this example you have seen the Text Input control (**ab|**) used for data input and the Server-Side Text control (**Xx**) used to display the output. Be aware that you could have used the Text Input control to display the patron number on the output screen. However, there is no need to use it in this way unless the output form also serves as input to another CGI. But if you do decide to use it for output (for instance, you might like its appearance), be certain to set either its Readonly or Disabled attribute to True. Otherwise the user can change this value on the screen (even though it is intended only for display). When the application does not include provisions for handling this change (another CGI program), the change will not be recorded by the system. The user will be given no warning that the change has been ignored.

The Horizontal Rule

The Horizontal Bar control allows you to place a horizontal line on your form to serve as a separator, for instance, look at Figure 3-23. You will find this control under the Page Elements tab at the top of your Form Design window. Click it and your control toolbar will change to the following.

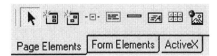

To insert a Horizontal Bar in your screen, highlight the control's icon ▬ then click just below the heading. When the bar is highlighted, you will be able to move it (with the crossing arrows mouse pointer) and change its length (with the double-ended mouse pointer). Experiment with this. When you are finished, you may close this design screen with or without saving the changes you have made.

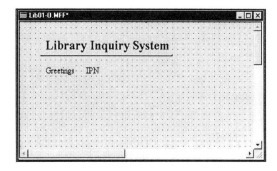

Figure 3-23. Including a horizontal bar.

Summing Up

Project Summary

Proj0301 (Lib01) provides your first look at Net Express generated HTML pages. This example accepts an input data item and echoes it back to the uer.

General Summary

The sample application of this chapter included creating an input page, an output page, and a CGI program.

HTML forms are created from the Form Design screen. Form Design toolbar icons used in this application are:

ab| Creates an Text Input control providing an area for the user to enter input values for transmission to the server.

Aa   Creates a Text control for placing descriptive information on the screen.

Xx   Creates a Server-Side Text control, an output area to display a data item from the server.

Subt   Creates a Submit button to signal the browser to communicate with the server (to take an action).

▬   Creates a horizontal bar on the screen.

Control properties fall in three categories, attributes, styles, and COBOL, each accessible through the corresponding tab to the lower-right of the Form Design screen.

Specific attributes depend upon the control. The Text Input control of this example exhibits several attributes:

- ID: The unique HTML identifier for this control. This property is common to all controls.
- Name: The name of the name/value pair returned to the server. Net Express generates a Cobol data item in the CGI with this name.
- MaxLength: The maximum number of characters that the browser accepts into this item
- Size: The width of the input area displayed by the browser.
- Title: A message displayed by the browser when the mouse pointer is moved to the control.
- Value: The default value displayed by the browser

Styles control the visual display of controls. In this chapter you looked at the following.

- Background-Color: Determines the color of the background area of the control. This can be the entire form, or it can be limited to a single control
- Background-Image: Designates a graphics file to be used as the screen background.
- Background-Repeat: Must be designated if background image is not sufficiently large to cover enter control area.

- Border-Style: Designates that the selected control have a border.
- Border-Color: Determines the color of the border.

Coming Up

You probably feel that your output display is not very exciting. (I'm inclined to agree.) So, in the next chapter you will learn about the structure of the CGI program and how you adapt it to do things that are more interesting.

Assignment

3-1

Create an application that features the input and output screens of Figure 3-24. Use a Text Input control to accept the user's name in the input form (do not display a default entry). The output screen should display the user's name through a Server-SideText control.

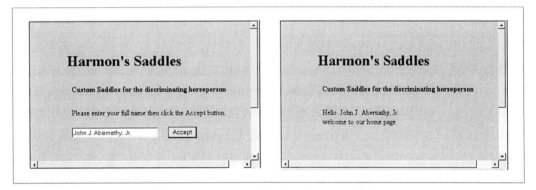

Figure 3-24. Input and output screens for Assignment 3-1.

Working With the CGI Program

Chapter Contents

The Generated CGI Program 76
   Four Components 76
   The CPF Copy File 76
   The CPY and CPV Copy Files 78
Overall Execution of the CGI Program 78
   Handling Input from the Form 78
   User Application Code 79
   Handling Output to the Page 79
   Embedded HTML 79
Displaying a Patron Name 79
   Modifying the Output Form 79
   Inserting Code in the CGI Program 80
Other Features 83
   Displaying Copy Files in the Program 83
   No Program Looping 83
Enhancing the Output 83
   Required Displays 83
   About Cloning an Application 84
   Duplicating the Input Page 85
   Duplicating and Modifying the Output Page 85
   Duplicating the CGI 87
   Changes to the CGI Program 88
Calling a Subprogram from the CGI—Lib04 88
   The Subprogram LIB-SUB0 88
   Modifying the CGI 89
   Adding the Subprogram to the Project 89
Accessing Data From a File—Lib05 90
   An Indexed File Processing Subprogram 90
   Modifications to the CGI Program 91
   Replacing Lib-sub0 With Lib-sub1 92
   About the File-Accessing Subprograms 92
   Don't Forget Your Cobol 92
Summing Up 94
   Project Summary 94
   General Summary 94
Coming Up 95
Assignments 95

Chapter

4

Chapter Introduction

The objective of this chapter is to introduce you to the Cobol CGI program generated by Net Express. Examples of this chapter illustrate basic techniques for modifying the CGI to perform operations required of your specific application. From this chapter you will learn the following

- The nature of the Cobol CGI file and the associated copy files generated by Net Express
- Inserting application code into the CGI.
- Duplicating a project for the purpose of modifying components.
- Modifying an input or output page (HTML).
- Calling a subprogram from a CGI.
- Accessing data from a file with the CGI.

The Generated CGI Program

Four Components

When you created the library Web application in the preceding chapter, Net Express generated four source modules comprising the CGI program:

Lib01.cbl   The Cobol source program. Once created for an application, Net Express leaves it unchanged with subsequent revisions of the related HTML pages. Therefore, you can insert Cobol code pertaining to your application without fear that it will be lost by Net Express.

The following Cobol copy files are rebuilt whenever a change is made to your input or output pages.

Lib01.cpf   Contains HTML Working-Storage Section entries.

Lib01.cpy   Contains Working-Storage data items whose names correspond to data names used in the HTML pages.

Lib01.cpv   Contains Procedure Division code for handling input and output from the HTML pages. Also, includes code to ensure that pic 9 data items contain valid numeric values.

Figure 4-1 lists the source program created using the skeleton cgi-min.skl (see Figure 3-17). For this figure, the copy files have been inserted and are bounded by comment lines with a series of greater-than symbols. Be aware that the line numbers are not part of the program but have been inserted here for convenient reference. Also notice that program code is entered into appropriate Cobol fixed-format columns. The CGI does not use free format. If you used the Net Express skeleton cgi.skl instead of cgi-min.skl, your source program is intimidating as it consists of approximately 200 lines, excluding inserted copy code. However, if you look carefully, you will see that most of the lines are comments with suggested Cobol code for handling different cases. These were removed from the cgi-min.skl file.

The CPF Copy File

The CPF file (Lib01.cpf occupying lines 19-47 in this example) contains the required working-storage external-form definition—lines 19-24. Notice that it includes only one such record, in contrast to the example of Chapter 2. Recall that Chapter 2's sample CGI program included one external-form definition for the input form (received by the Accept statement), and one for the output page (sent by the Display statement). As you will see, Net Express does not use the Display; it uses imbedded HTML, which provides a more powerful capability.

Remember from Chapter 2 that the following statement identifies the data name of the name/value pair from the input form and associates it with the Cobol data item f-InPatronNumber.

```
03  f-InPatronNumber      pic x(3)
        identified by "InPatronNumber".
```

```
  1   IDENTIFICATION DIVISION.                        80
  2       program-id. "Lib01".                        81   convert-input section.
  3                                                    82       *> Convert numeric input values
  4                                                    83       perform input-conversion
  5   ENVIRONMENT DIVISION.                            84       if v-all-ok = 0
  6                                                    85           perform output-form-error-and-stop
  7   configuration section.                           86       end-if
  8   special-names.                                   87       exit.
  9       call-convention 8 is llnk.                   88
 10                                                    89   process-business-logic section.
 11   DATA DIVISION.                                   90       *> Add application business logic here.
 12                                                    91
 13   working-storage section.                         92       exit.
 14                                                    93
 15       *> WARNING: Do not remove this copy statement 94  output-form-error-and-stop section.
 16       *> or modify the contents of the copy file.  95       exec html
 17       copy "Lib01.cpf".                            96           :v-first-bad is a numeric field and
 18       *>>>>>>>>>>>>>>>>>>>>>>>>>>>>>>>>>>>>>>>>>>>> 97           contains an invalid or out of range value
 19       01 HTMLForm is external-form.                98           please enter a valid value
 20           03 f-InPatronNumber        pic x(3)      99       end-exec
 21               identified by "InPatronNumber".     100       exit program
 22           03 f-ssubmit               pic x(60)    101       stop run.
 23               identified by "ssubmit".            102
 24           03 filler                  pic x.       103       *> WARNING: Do not remove this copy statement
 25                                                   104       *> or modify the contents of the copy file.
 26  *>     The following field indicates if input was 105      copy "Lib01.cpv".
 27  *>     received from the Browser                 106       *>>>>>>>>>>>>>>>>>>>>>>>>>>>>>>>>>>>>>>>>>>>>
 28  *>     z"yes" - business logic should be executed 107  Browser-Initialize Section.
 29  *>     z"no" indicates an "initial load" condition 108
 30  *>     (the null terminator is required by JScript) 109      initialize HTMLForm
 31       01 MF-SERVER-EXEC             pic x(4).     110       initialize FormFields
 32                                                   111       exit.
 33  *>     The following fields are reserved for use by 112
 34  *>     numeric conversion routines               113   Input-Conversion Section.
 35       01 MF-NMCNVRT-WS      pic x(4) comp-5.      114
 36       01 MF-NMCNVRT-FMT     pic x(36).            115       if HTMLForm = spaces
 37       01 MF-SEL-INDEX       pic x(4) comp-5.      116           move z"no" to MF-SERVER-EXEC
 38       01 MF-GROUP-COUNT     pic x(4) comp-5.      117       else
 39       01 MF-ROW-INDEX       pic x(4) comp-5.      118           move z"yes" to MF-SERVER-EXEC
 40       01 MF-ROW-ID          pic X(9).             119       end-if
 41       01 f-MF-ROW-INDEX     pic z(10).            120
 42                                                   121       move 1 to v-All-OK
 43       01 HTML-Validation-Flags.                   122       move spaces to v-First-Bad
 44           03 v-First-Bad           pic x(64).    123
 45           03 v-All-OK              pic 9.         124
 46           03 v-InPatronNumber      PIC 9.         125       move 1 to v-InPatronNumber
 47           03 v-ssubmit             PIC 9.         126       move f-InPatronNumber to InPatronNumber
 48       *>>>>>>>>>>>>>>>>>>>>>>>>>>>>>>>>>>>>>>>>>>> 127
 49                                                   128       move 1 to v-ssubmit
 50       *> WARNING: Do not remove this copy statement 129      move f-ssubmit to ssubmit
 51       *> or modify the contents of the copy file. 130
 52       copy "Lib01.cpy".                           131
 53       *>>>>>>>>>>>>>>>>>>>>>>>>>>>>>>>>>>>>>>>>>>> 132  exit.
 54       01 FormFields.                              133
 55           03 InPatronNumber        pic X(3).     134   lib01-out-ini Section.
 56           03 ssubmit               pic x(64).    135       *> lib01-out
 57       *>>>>>>>>>>>>>>>>>>>>>>>>>>>>>>>>>>>>>>>>>>> 136       move "IPN" to f-InPatronNumber
 58                                                   137
 59  *> Enter additional working-storage items here  138       exit.
 60                                                   139
 61   PROCEDURE DIVISION.                             140   lib01-out-cvt Section.
 62                                                   141       *> lib01-out
 63   main section.                                   142       move InPatronNumber to f-InPatronNumber
 64       perform process-form-input-data             143
 65       perform convert-input                       144       exit.
 66       perform process-business-logic              145
 67       perform lib01-out-cvt                       146   lib01-out-out Section.
 68           *> lib01-out                            147       *> lib01-out
 69       perform lib01-out-out                       148
 70           *> lib01-out                            149       exec html
 71       exit program                                150         copy "Lib01-OUT.htm".
 72       stop run.                                   151       end-exec
 73                                                   152
 74   process-form-input-data section.               153       exit.
 75       *> Accept the input from the Browser        154       *>>>>>>>>>>>>>>>>>>>>>>>>>>>>>>>>>>>>>>>>>>>
 76       *> and check for errors
 77       perform browser-initialize
 78       accept htmlform
 79       exit.
```

Figure 4-1. The generated CGI program.

So the action of the Accept statement places the value (from the name/value pair) into f-InPatronNumber.

In addition, you see two other 03 entries. The f-ssubmit data item is derived from the Submit button you selected in building the input form. Do not be concerned that the caption you used for the button was Accept and that you don't see it anywhere in the code. You will learn how these names enter into the overall scheme in a later example.

You can ignore lines 24-47. You will look at a few of them in later chapters; others are used by Net Express for operations you need not worry about.

The CPY and CPV Copy Files

The CPY copy file (Lib01.cpy of lines 54-56 in this example) declares data items with names that correspond to names from your forms. This is really a "convenience factor" to allow you to customize your CGI program using the more familiar names that you selected in creating the input and output pages.

The CPV copy file (Lib01.cpv of lines 107-153 in this example) contains executable code that is unique to this application. Let's consider it in context of the overall procedural code of this example.

Overall Execution of the CGI Program

The basic Net Express generated CGI program can be thought of as carrying out three fundamental actions:

- Handle input from the input form.
- Process user input in accordance with requirements of the application. This is done by code inserted by you, the application programmer.
- Handle output to an output page.

You see this in the following five Perform statements of Figure 4-1.

```
64        perform process-form-input-data
65        perform convert-input
66        perform process-business-logic
67        perform Lib01-0-cvt
69        perform Lib01-0-out
```

Handling Input from the Form

The following occurs when execution begins with main section at line 63, Figure 4-1.

1. Execution of the Perform at line 64 transfers control to the process-form-input-data section (line 74).
2. At line 78 the Accept statement obtains data from the input form.
3. Line 65 transfers control to the convert-input section (line 81).
4. At line 83 control is transferred to the input-conversion section (line 113).
5. For this example, the only statement of interest to us is the Move at line 126,

that is:

```
Move f-InPatronNumber to InPatronNumber
```

It moves the input data item from the HTML definition area into the data item defined for you to use in tailoring this CGI program for the needs of your application. You'll see how you do this in the next example.

For now don't be concerned about other move operations in this section.

User Application Code

After input processing is completed, control is transferred (from line 66) to the `process-business-logic` section (line 89). You insert the code you require for your application here. Your code may look up the patron's name (as you will do in the next example) or it may do other processing.

Handling Output to the Output Page

The output action is essentially the reverse of the input action. First, values from the form field data names (with which you have been working) are moved to the external form (see line 142). Of course, the action is trivial in this case because the same data item is used for both input and output. The output form is sent to the browser using the statement exec `html` (line 149).

Embedded HTML

Net Express uses the `Exec html` statement rather than the extended Display because of its added versatility. Notice the following statements:

```
exec html
  copy "Lib01-OUT.htm".
end-exec
```

You can see that the `Copy` statement causes the output HTML program to be imbedded directly into the Cobol program. This is called **embedded HTML** and is the technique used by Net Express. You need not be concerned with the actual HTML code, as Net Express generates it automatically.

Displaying a Patron Name

Modifying the Output Page

An output screen that merely echoes back the input patron number is not very exciting, so let's modify Lib01 to display the person's name corresponding to the input patron number. [Note: This example is stored as the separate application Lib02 in the Proj0401 folder.]

> Proj0401
> Lib02

1. If you've closed your project Lib01, then open it. From the project screen (see Figure 3-18) double-click Lib01-OUT.htm to bring up Form Designer with this form. Your Form Designer screen will display the output form of Figure 3-15. You must change it to look like Figure 4-2.

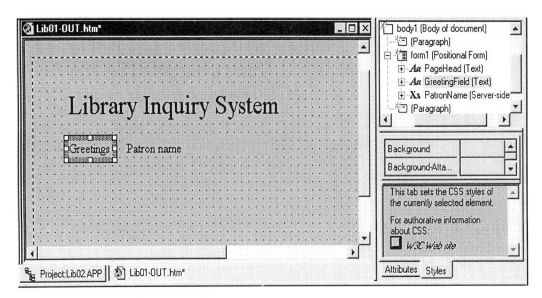

Figure 4-2. The new output form.

2. Select the Server-Side Text control and change its ID entry from InPatronNumber to PatronName. This is the data name you will use in your CGI program.

3. Stretch the width of this control to the right to provide sufficient room for the name.

4. Change the Caption entry from IPN to Patron name. Remember, this serves only to indicate the Server-Side Text control's position on your Form Designer screen.

5. Click the COBOL tab and change COBOLPicture from 3 to 23.

6. Click File/Save.

7. Close the Form Designer window.

8. Click the rebuild icon ≛.

Inserting Code in the CGI Program

This example's CGI program is shown in Figure 4-3 with inserted copy files; let's look at some of its features.

- The Net Express generated form fields now includes PatronName as well as InPatronNumber (line 59).

- Through the input conversion triggered by the Performs at lines 68 and 86, the input patron number is moved from the external-form area to the form field InPatronNumber (line 130).

- Through the output preparation triggered by the Perform at line 70, the output patron name is moved from the form field PatronName to the external form area (line 146).

You must insert code between these input and output actions to obtain the name of the appropriate patron. That code belongs in the process-business-logic section (line 92). For your first simple example, you will insert an Evaluate statement to serve the purpose.

```
 1   IDENTIFICATION DIVISION.                          91
 2       program-id. "Lib01".                          92   process-business-logic section.
 3                                                      93       *> Add application business logic here.
 4                                                      94
 5   ENVIRONMENT DIVISION.                              95       exit.
 6                                                      96
 7   configuration section.                             97   output-form-error-and-stop section.
 8   special-names.                                     98       exec html
 9       call-convention 8 is llnk.                     99           :v-first-bad is a numeric field and
10                                                     100           contains an invalid or out of range value,
11   DATA DIVISION.                                    101           please enter a valid value
12                                                     102       end-exec
13   working-storage section.                          103       exit program
14                                                     104       stop run.
15       *> WARNING: Do not remove this copy statement 105
16       *> or modify the contents of the copy file.   106       *> WARNING: Do not remove this copy statement
17       copy "Lib01.cpf".                             107       *> or modify the contents of the copy file.
18       *>>>>>>>>>>>>>>>>>>>>>>>>>>>>>>>>>>>>>>>>>>>>> 108       copy "Lib01.cpv".
19       01 HTMLForm is external-form.                 109
20          03 f-InPatronNumber      pic x(60)         110       *>>>>>>>>>>>>>>>>>>>>>>>>>>>>>>>>>>>>>>>>>>>>>
21              identified by "InPatronNumber".        111   Browser-Initialize Section.
22          03 f-ssubmit             pic x(60)         112
23              identified by "ssubmit".               113       initialize HTMLForm
24          03 f-PatronName          pic x(32)         114       initialize FormFields
25              identified by "PatronName".            115       exit.
26          03 filler                pic x.            116
27                                                     117   Input-Conversion Section.
                                                       118
52       *> WARNING: Do not remove this copy statement 119       if HTMLForm = spaces
53       *> or modify the contents of the copy file.   120           move z"no" to MF-SERVER-EXEC
54       copy "Lib01.cpy".                             121       else
55       *>>>>>>>>>>>>>>>>>>>>>>>>>>>>>>>>>>>>>>>>>>>>> 122           move z"yes" to MF-SERVER-EXEC
56       01 FormFields.                                123       end-if
57          03 InPatronNumber      pic X(60).          124
58          03 ssubmit             pic x(64).          125       move 1 to v-All-OK
59          03 PatronName          pic x(32).          126       move spaces to v-First-Bad
60       *>>>>>>>>>>>>>>>>>>>>>>>>>>>>>>>>>>>>>>>>>>>>> 127
61                                                     128
62   *> Enter additional working-storage items here    129       move 1 to v-InPatronNumber
63                                                     130       move f-InPatronNumber to InPatronNumber
64   PROCEDURE DIVISION.                               131
65                                                     132       move 1 to v-ssubmit
66   main section.                                     133       move f-ssubmit to ssubmit
67       perform process-form-input-data               134
68       perform convert-input                         135
69       perform process-business-logic                136       exit.
70       perform lib01-out-cvt                         137
71          *> lib01-out                               138   lib01-out-ini Section.
72       perform lib01-out-out                         139       *> lib01-out
73          *> lib01-out                               140       move "Patron name" to f-PatronName
74       exit program                                  141
75       stop run.                                      142       exit.
76                                                     143
77   process-form-input-data section.                  144   lib01-out-cvt Section.
78       *> Accept the input from the Browser          145       *> lib01-out
79       *> and check for errors                       146       move PatronName to f-PatronName
80       perform browser-initialize                    147
81       accept htmlform                               148   exit.
82       exit.                                         149
83                                                     150   lib01-out-out Section.
84   convert-input section.                            151       *> lib01-out
85       *> Convert numeric input values               152
86       perform input-conversion                      153       exec html
87       if v-all-ok = 0                               154         copy "Lib01-OUT.htm".
88           perform output-form-error-and-stop        155       end-exec
89       end-if                                        156
90       exit.                                         157       exit.
```

Figure 4-3. The generated CGI program with copy files.

1. Open the CGI by double-clicking on Lib01.cbl in the right pane of the project screen or with the menu sequence File/Open and selecting the file.
2. Net Express opens a window displaying the CGI source program. Scroll down until you reach the process-business-logic section as shown in Figure 4-4.

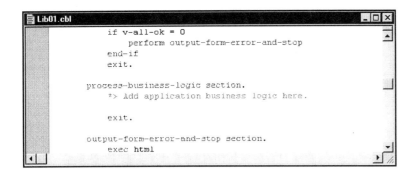

Figure 4-4.
The insertion
point for user
code.

3. Position the cursor on the line above the `Exit` statement and enter the following `Evaluate` statement.

```
Evaluate InPatronNumber
  When "001"
    Move "Orson Karridge" to PatronName
  When "002"
    Move "Sandy Beech" to PatronName
  When "003"
    Move "Bill Board" to PatronName
  When other
    Move "No such patron number" to PatronName
End-evaluate
```

You now have your own business logic inserted into the program.

4. Click on the Compile button ☑. If you made any errors when keying the code, correct them and recompile.

5. Close the program window.

6. Click Rebuild to rebuild the project.

7. Run your application and enter a patron number between 001 and 003 and observe the display.

8. To rerun, click on you browser's Back button ⇐Back .

9. Enter 009 (an entry having no corresponding name) and you will see the error message following the word "Greeting." You'll learn how to generate a more meaningful output form for such an error condition in the next exercise.

10. To terminate, close the browser screen. The browser minimized Net Express so restore it by clicking its icon on your screen's task bar.

11. Click Animate/Stop Animating.

From the project screen you can look at any of the copy files (CPF, CPY, and CPV) simply by double-clicking on their names in the same way you did with the CBL file. However, *do not edit them* as they are rebuilt with each change you make in the project.

Other Features

Displaying Copy Files in the Program

When you are editing the CBL program, sometimes you will find it convenient to see the copy file code expanded (listed within the source code of your program). Other times you may not want that code taking up your screen space. You can toggle the display of copy files from the View menu by clicking Hide All Copyfiles. If the icon adjacent to the Hide All Copyfiles display contains a light border, the copyfiles will not be displayed. Otherwise, this option is deactivated and the copyfiles are displayed. Any program that has been compiled will display copy files in this way. For a program that has not yet been compiled, you can still display a copy file with the following sequence.

1. Position the cursor anywhere on the source code line containing the Copy statement.
2. Click File/Copyfile/Show from the toolbar. You will see the copy file code listed.

No Program Looping

If you ran Chapter 1's example, you were able to repeat for as many patrons as you desired. It is worth noting once again that the CGI program of a Web application does not operate this way. That is, there is no main loop. Control of a Web application progresses as follows.

1. The browser displays a page.
2. The user enters appropriate data and submits the form to the server. This form includes both the name of the CGI program to be run and the input data.
3. The CGI program is run by the server. The CGI gathers data as appropriate and returns it to the client.
4. The CGI program returns a page to the browser then terminates execution.
5. The browser displays the page received from the server.

By clicking the browser's Back button, you repeated the entire process. However, it is important to recognize that the CGI program is loaded and run each time. Again, there is no CGI program main loop of the type to which we Cobol programmers are accustomed.

Enhancing the Output

Required Displays

When an invalid patron number is entered, you see the message:

Greetings   No such patron number

A different look, such as the alternate form to the right in Figure 4-5, is more fitting. To achieve this, you will need to make the following modifications to the preceding project.

- Expand the output form to display both the patron name and the number, and to display either "Greeting" or "Sorry."
- Insert additional code into the CGI to display to handle the no-patron case.

Proj0402
Lib03

Note that this completed application is stored in the Proj0402 folder as Lib03.

About Cloning an Application

Most examples of this book involve modifying a previous example. As Cobol programmers, we know the value of making a backup copy of a program before proceeding to modify it. (It is better to have a vanilla-flavored program that works than an elegant one that doesn't work.) So, to that end it would be convenient to clone an application and make your modifications to the copy. Because of complex interaction between a project's components, the Save-As function (with which you are familiar from Windows applications) is not practical. You may have noticed that the Save As option for both the project and the form screens is grayed out and therefore not available. However, you can achieve much the same result by using a feature of Net Express that allows you to create a new HTML page from an existing one. So let's use that technique to create a new project from your modified version of Lib01. The first step will be creating a new project.

1. Select File/New and click Project.
2. In the New Project screen
      Select Empty Project.
      For the project name enter Lib03.
      For the project folder enter C:\My-Examples\Proj0402.
3. Click Create.
4. If you have not already created this folder, Net Express will ask you if you want to create it. Click Yes. You will be presented with an empty project screen.

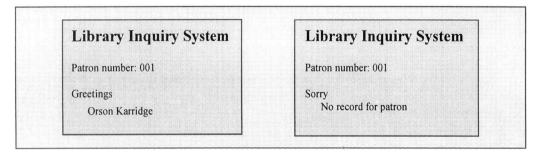

Figure 4-5. Improved output displays.

Duplicating the Input Form

Net Express allows you to create a new page by starting with an existing one thereby essentially providing you a *Save-As* feature not available under the File menu. So let's use this technique to make a copy of Lib01-IN.

1. Select File/New and click HTML Page.
2. From the resulting Wizard screen, click the From Existing tab. Your screen will look like Figure 4-6, except there will be no filename entry.
3. You want this form created from Lib01-IN stored in your Proj0301 folder, so click the Browse button to locate and select it in the usual Windows fashion. Alternately, you can type the following.

   C:\My-Examples\Proj0301\Lib01-IN.htm

4. Click Next.
5. From the ensuing page-details window, for HTML filename, type Lib03-IN then click Next.
6. Check your entries in the Summary window. If any are incorrect, click Back and fix them; if all are all correct, click Finish. Net Express will open your page in Form Designer.
7. Since you will use this page without change, click File/Close.

Duplicating and Modifying the Output Page

To produce the displays of Figure 4-5, you must duplicate your modified Lib01-OUT then change the copy to look like Figure 4-7. By studying the component tree in the upper-right pane, you can see that the following is required in this design.

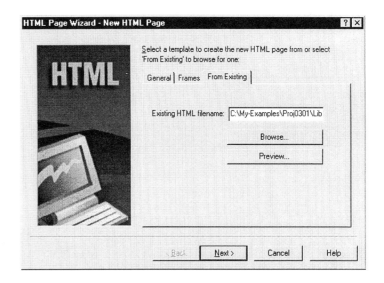

Figure 4-6.
Designating an existing HTML file.

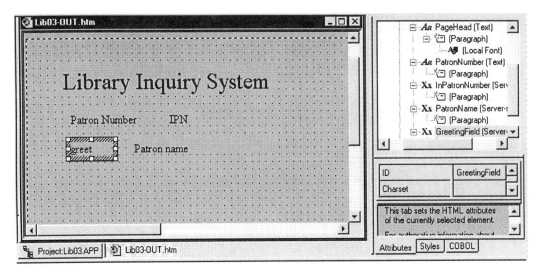

Figure 4-7. The new output screen.

- The patron number is displayed as in Chapter 3's example.
- The greeting field is changed from Text (*Aa*) to Server-Side Text (**Xx**). This allows you to insert code into the CGI program to display either "Greetings" or "Sorry" as shown in Figure 4-6.

For this, proceed as follows.

1. Repeat Steps 1-6 of the preceding input-form creation using the output form -OUT rather than the input form -IN.
2. Delete the Text control (*Aa*) GreetingField (see Figure 4-2) and move the PatronName control down to leave space for the patron number display.
3. Referring to Figure 4-7, insert a Text control (*Aa*) immediately below the heading and change:
   - the description (within the control) from New Text to Patron number.
   - the ID to PatronNumber (or something descriptive).
4. To the right of this control, insert a Server-Side Text (**Xx**) control and change:
   - the ID to InPatronNumber
   - the Caption within the control to IPN (needed only for screen documentation)
   - the COBOLPicture to 3.
5. Insert another Server-Side Text control for the greeting just below the Patron Number entry and change:
   - the ID to GreetingField
   - the Caption within the control to greet (needed only for screen documentation)
   - the COBOLPicture to 9 to accommodate either "Greetings" or "Sorry."
6. Rearrange the controls on your screen to suit your taste.
7. Click File/Save to save the form. If the Server-Side Text controls (greeting and patron name) are too close together, Form Designer will give you a message

that you have overlapping controls and the form cannot be saved as cross platform. If this occurs, click the Cancel button and move the patron-name control to the right. Then try saving again.

Duplicating the CGI

In the previous exercise, you added code to the process-business-logic section of the Lib01.cbl CGI to determine the patron name from the input number. Two minor additions to that code will serve the needs of this example. To that end, it makes sense to duplicate the Lib01.cbl rather than retype the application code. However, look at this program in Figure 4-3 and you will see numerous references to Lib01, for instance, lines 2, 17, 54, and so on.

1. From Windows Explorer, copy Lib01.cbl from your Proj0301 folder to your Proj0402 folder.
2. Change the name of the copy from Lib01.cbl to Lib03.cbl.
3. Open Lib03.cbl in a word processor.
4. Replace occurances of lib01 with lib03. If you do this replacement with confirmation, you will see each entry. You should see 8 replacements. Although you may have counted more occurances in Figure 4-3, many of these are in copy files, not in Lib03.cbl.
5. Save the file and close the word processor.

You can now proceed to build the remaining components of your application under Net Express.

1. Although you already have the CGI program (duplicated from Lib01) you must step through the CGI creation sequence to generate the copy files. Do this by clicking File/New and selecting Internet Application.
2. From the resulting Internet Application Wizard, click the Server Program (from Net Express created HTML) radio button. Click Next.
3. In the next screen (Server Program Generation):
   - Change the default Filename entry to Lib03 (.cbl will be the default extension)
   - Select Lib03-IN.htm for the Input File and Lib03-OUT.htm for the Output File.
4. Click Next and you will see the warning screen of Figure 4-8.
5. Click No as you want to keep the .CBL file and only generate needed copy files.
6. *Carefully* check that all the entries are correct in the ensuing summary screen. If anything is wrong, back up and make appropriate corrections.
7. When everything is correct, click Finish.

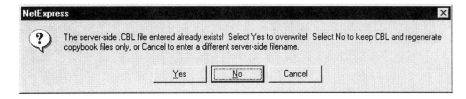

Figure 4-8. Warning screen.

8. Net Express will build your copy files. When finished, Net Express returns control to the project screen.
9. Click the Rebuild button.
10. Run the application to see what your output screen looks like. You will see the patron number but no greeting. You must insert appropriate code into the CGI program.
11. Close your browser window.
12. Maximize Net Express and click Animate/Stop Animating.

Changes to the CGI Program

If you look at the CGI you will see the following form fields defined.

```
01 FormFields.
   03 GreetingField        pic x(9).
   03 InPatronNumber       pic X(3).
   03 ssubmit              pic x(64).
   03 PatronName           pic x(23).
```

Required changes to the CGI program are relatively minimal. Handling the patron name needs no change. The only addition is for the Greeting/Sorry item, which you see in the following code.

```
Move "Greetings" to GreetingField
Evaluate InPatronNumber
   When "001"
     Move "Orson Karridge" to PatronName
   When "002"
     Move "Sandy Beech" to PatronName
   When "003"
     Move "Bill Board" to PatronName
   When other
     Move "No record for patron" to PatronName
     Move "Sorry" to GreetingField
End-evaluate
```

Notice that you need only insert two Move statements into your existing code. When you're finished, compile the program, close the program display screen and run the application. Test it both with valid (001, 002, or 003) and invalid patron numbers to be certain it works correctly.

Calling a Subprogram from the CGI—Lib04

The Subprogram LIB-SUB0

Although you can embed your code directly in the CGI program as in the preceding examples, you'll usually find it more convenient to use a call to a subprogram—perhaps existing legacy code or some modification thereof. (The example that follows is stored in the Proj0403 folder as Lib04.app.) In general, to use a subprogram, you need to know about its parameters. For this example, look at the subprogram Lib-sub0.cbl shown in Figure 4-9 (it is stored in the NE-Progs folder). You see that it requires two parameters:

Proj0403
Lib04

- `in-patron-number`: The input to the subprogram.
- `patron-name`: The output from the subprogram.

Modifying the CGI

With the name accessing code now in a subprogram, you will need to replace the code you've inserted into the `process-business-logic` section of the CGI program with an appropriate subprogram call.

1. If you terminated Net Express, bring it back up and open the project you just completed in the preceding exercise.
2. Open Lib03.cbl either by double clicking on the filename in the upper-right pane, or by clicking File/Open and selecting the file.
3. Scroll down to the `process-business-logic` section.
4. Delete all lines you inserted from the previous exercise (the `Move "Greetings"`... through the `End-evaluate`).
5. In place of the deleted code, type the following.

```
Call "lib-sub0" using InPatronNumber
                      PatronName
If PatronName = low-values
   Move "Sorry" to GreetingField
   Move "No record for patron" to PatronName
Else
   Move "Greetings" to GreetingField
End-if
```

6. Click on the Compile button to compile the program.
7. If you have any compiler errors, you made a typing error so correct it and recompile.
8. Close this program display window.

Adding the Subprogram to the Project

Since this application requires the subprogram Lib-Sub0.cbl, you need to copy it into the folder of your current project (there is a copy in the NE-Progs folder). So make the needed copy using Windows Explorer.

```
1    Identification Division.
2    Program-ID. Lib-Sub0.
3
4    Data Division.
5    Linkage Section.
6    01  in-patron-number        pic X(03).
7    01  patron-name             PIC x(23).
8
9    Procedure Division using in-patron-number
10                             patron-name.
11       Evaluate in-patron-number
12          When "001"
13             Move "Orson Karridge" to patron-name
14          When "002"
15             Move "Sandy Beech" to patron-name
16          When "003"
17             Move "Bill Board" to patron-name
18          When other
19             Move low-values to patron-name
21       End-Evaluate
22
```

Figure 4-9.
A simple subprogram.

Now check the project pane of Net Express and you will see that it does not list the subprogram Lib-sub0.cbl that you are calling from the CGI program. You must add the subprogram to the list and indicate its hierarchy placement manually as follows.

1. Right click anywhere in the blank part of the right pane and you will see the popup menu shown to the right.
2. Click on Add file to source pool.
3. From the resulting list of files, highlight Lib-sub0.cbl and click Add. The file will be added to the list in the right pane.
4. You must now copy this file to the tree structure of the left pane. Do it by selecting it, then dragging it to Lib04.exe of the left pane. Your project screen should then look like Figure 4-10. Notice that the Lib-sub0.obj is subordinate to Lib04.exe.
5. Rebuild the project.
6. Run the program; you should see the same result as you did with the Evaluate statement imbedded in the CGI program

Accessing Data From a File—Lib05

An Indexed File Processing Subprogram

The contrived subprogram of Figure 4-9 gives you an idea of how you incorporate a subprogram into a project. Let's now look at something more realistic: the subprogram of Figure 4-11 to access an indexed file. First, look at the Procedure Division header on the following page.

```
Procedure Division Using in-patron-number
                        patron-info.
```

As before, the input parameter is the patron number. However, the output parameter, patron-info, is a record containing three fields (lines 48-50): the person's name (required by your CGI program) and also address data (not required by this CGI

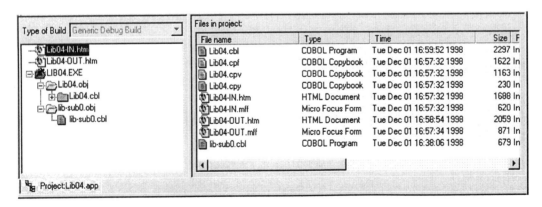

Figure 4-10. Project components with a subprogram.

program). To avoid changing this existing code, your CGI program must contain entries in the Data Division defining an 01 item equivalent to the patron-info field.

You can easily modify the project to use this subprogram by making appropriate changes to the CGI program and by replacing lib-sub0 with lib-sub1. Note that the completed project Lib05.app is stored in the Proj0404 folder.

Modifications to the CGI Program

The completed CGI of Figure 4-12 is reasonably self-explanatory. You see the required Data Division entries at lines 69-72 and the new processing code at lines 104-112. A test is made for low-values (no record for the patron) at line 106.

Replacing Lib-sub0 With Lib-sub1

For this example, you will modify the existing project by replacing Lib-sub0 with Lib-sub1.

```
             $set sourceformat "free"                45  Linkage Section.
 1  *>********************************************    46    01  in-patron-number      pic X(03).
 2  *> Library Application                           47    01  patron-info.
 3  *> W. Price  9/28/98              LIB-SUB1.CBL    48      10  patron-name         pic X(23).
 4  *> This subprogram provides read access to the   49      10  street-address      pic X(20).
 5  *> following indexed file                        50      10  city-state-zip      pic X(28).
 6  *>   PATRON.DI: Indexed by Patron Number; contains 51
 7  *>      patron name, address data and other data. 52  Procedure Division Using in-patron-number
 8  *> Subprogram parameters are:                    53                         patron-info.
 9  *>   in-patron-number  Input key field value for 54
10  *>                     file read.                55    000-Main-module.
11  *>   patron-info       Output patron information. 56      Open Input Patron-File
12  *>********************************************    57      Perform 200-process-user-request
13                                                   58      Close Patron-File
14  Identification Division.                         59      Exit program
15    Program-id. Library-Subprogram.                60      .
16                                                   61    200-process-user-request.
17    Environment Division.                          62      Move spaces to patron-info
18                                                   63      Move in-patron-number to pr-patron-number
19    Input-Output Section.                          64      Perform 800-read-patron-record
20    File-Control.                                  65      If patron-info NOT = low-values
21      Select Patron-File assign to disk            66        Perform 400-setup-patron-output
22        "c:\Elements-CWP\NE-data\patron.di"        67      End-if *>patron-info NOT = low-values
23        organization is indexed                    68      .
24        access is random                           69    400-setup-patron-output.
25        record key is pr-patron-number.            70      Move spaces to patron-name
26                                                   71      String pr-first-name delimited by " "
27  Data Division.                                   72              " "
28    File Section.                                  73              pr-last-name
29    FD  Patron-File.                               74              into patron-name
30    01  patron-record.                             75      Move pr-street-address to street-address
31      10  pr-patron-number   pic x(03).            76      Move spaces to city-state-zip
32      10  pr-first-name      pic X(10).            77      String  pr-city delimited by " "
33      10  pr-last-name       pic X(12).            78              " "
34      10  pr-street-address  pic X(20).            79              pr-state
35      10  pr-city            pic X(14).            80              " "
36      10  pr-state           pic X(02).            81              pr-zip
37      10  pr-zip             pic X(10).            82              into city-state-zip
38      10  pr-privilege-status pic X(01).           83      .
39      10  pr-employee-status pic X(01).            84    800-read-patron-record.
40      10  pr-book-right      pic X(01).            85      Read Patron-File
41      10  pr-periodical-right pic X(01).           86        Invalid key
42      10  pr-video-right     pic X(01).            87          Move low-values to patron-info
43      10                     pic X(20).            88      End-read
44                                                   89      .
```

Figure 4-11. The Lib-sub1.cbl subprogram.

window.

2. From the resulting menu, click on Remove from project. You will need to confirm deleting this file.

3. To add the new subprogram to the project, position the cursor anywhere in the right-hand pane and right-click. Then add Lib-sub1.cbl to the project in the same way you added Lib-sub0.cbl. Don't forget to copy it to the left pane. Then check to ensure that it appears the same way as did Lib-sub0.cbl (refer to Figure 4-10).

About the File-Accessing Subprograms

As described in Chapter 0, the subprogram Lib-sub1.cbl and others included with this book process indexed data files (Patron.di for Lib-sub1). To that end, Lib-sub1 contains a Select clause identifying the file as:

```
C:\Elements-CWP\NE-Data\Patron.di
```

If you loaded the example files into some folder other than this one, then you will need to change the path in the Select clause accordingly. Be aware that Micro Focus implements indexed files with *two* files: the data file itself and an index file with an extension IDX. So for the patron file, you will find Patron.di (the extension chosen by your author) and its index file Patron.idx (the extension assigned by the system). If you move data files around, don't forget the index. You can inspect this files contents as it is listed in the Appendix.

When you are finished, rebuild the project then run the program. You should see the same results as you did with the previous project. (Note: Patron numbers contained in the file range from 001 to 024.)

Don't Forget Your Cobol

It is easy to get caught up in the details of the Web and forget that you are dealing with the same Cobol we've been using all along. In that respect, you could easily combine the greeting and the patron name into a single Server-Side Text field as shown in Figure 4-13. Notice the control GreetingField has a length of 33: 10 for the "Greeting " (including the space) and 23 for the patron name. Of course this would produce the following form fields in the CGI.

```
01 FormFields.
   03 GreetingField            pic x(33).
   03 InPatronNumber           pic X(3).
   03 ssubmit                  pic x(64).
```

Then your CGI code (lines 106-112 in Figure 4-12) would be changed to the following.

```
If patron-name = low-values
  Move "Sorry, no record for patron" to GreetingField
Else
  String "Greetings " patron-name delimited by size
                              into GreetingField
End-if
```

```
1    IDENTIFICATION DIVISION.
2         program-id. "Lib05".
3
4    ENVIRONMENT DIVISION.
5
6    configuration section.
7    special-names.
8         call-convention 8 is llnk.
9
10   DATA DIVISION.
11
12   working-storage section.
13
14        *> WARNING: Do not remove this copy statement
15        *> or modify the contents of the copy file.
16        copy "Lib05.cpf".
17
18   *>>>>>>>>>>>>>>>>>>>>>>>>>>>>>>>>>>>>>>>>>>>>
19        01 HTMLForm is external-form.
20           03 f-GreetingField       pic x(9)
21              identified by "GreetingField".
22           03 f-InPatronNumber      pic x(60)
23              identified by "InPatronNumber".
24           03 f-ssubmit             pic x(60)
25              identified by "ssubmit".
26           03 f-PatronName          pic x(23)
27              identified by "PatronName".
28           03 filler                pic x.


55   *>>>>>>>>>>>>>>>>>>>>>>>>>>>>>>>>>>>>>>>>>>>>
56        *> WARNING: Do not remove this copy statement
57        *> or modify the contents of the copy file.
58        copy "Lib05.cpy".
59
60   *>>>>>>>>>>>>>>>>>>>>>>>>>>>>>>>>>>>>>>>>>>>>
61        01 FormFields.
62           03 GreetingField         pic x(9).
63           03 InPatronNumber        pic X(60).
64           03 ssubmit               pic x(64).
65           03 PatronName            pic x(23).
66   *>>>>>>>>>>>>>>>>>>>>>>>>>>>>>>>>>>>>>>>>>>>>
67
68   *> Enter additional working-storage items here
69   01 patron-info.
70        05 patron-name              pic X(23).
71        05 street-address           pic X(20).
72        05 city-state-zip           pic X(28).
73
74   PROCEDURE DIVISION.
75
76   main section.
77        perform process-form-input-data
78        perform convert-input
79        perform process-business-logic
80        perform lib05-out-cvt
81           *> lib05-out
82        perform lib05-out-out
83           *> lib05-out
84        exit program
85        stop run.
86
87   process-form-input-data section.
88        *> Accept the input from the Browser
89        *> and check for errors
90        perform browser-initialize
91        accept htmlform
92        exit.
93
94   convert-input section.
95        *> Convert numeric input values
96        perform input-conversion
97        if v-all-ok = 0
98           perform output-form-error-and-stop
99        end-if
100       exit.
101
102  process-business-logic section.
103       *> Add application business logic here.
104       Call "lib-sub1" using InPatronNumber
105                            patron-info
106       If patron-info = low-values
107          Move "No record for patron" to PatronName
108          Move "Sorry" to GreetingField
109       Else
110          Move patron-name to PatronName
111          Move "Greetings" to GreetingField
112       End-if
113
114       exit.
115
116  output-form-error-and-stop section.
117       exec html
118          :v-first-bad is a numeric field and
119          contains an invalid or out of range value,
120          please enter a valid value
121       end-exec
122       exit program
123       stop run.
124
125       *> WARNING: Do not remove this copy statement
126       *> or modify the contents of the copy file.
127       copy "Lib05.cpv".
128
129  *>>>>>>>>>>>>>>>>>>>>>>>>>>>>>>>>>>>>>>>>>>>>
130  Browser-Initialize Section.
131
132       initialize HTMLForm
133       initialize FormFields
134  exit.
135
136  Input-Conversion Section.
137
138       if HTMLForm = spaces
139          move z"no" to MF-SERVER-EXEC
140       else
141          move z"yes" to MF-SERVER-EXEC
142       end-if
143
144       move 1 to v-All-OK
145       move spaces to v-First-Bad
146
147       move 1 to v-InPatronNumber
148       move f-InPatronNumber to InPatronNumber
149
150       move 1 to v-ssubmit
151       move f-ssubmit to ssubmit
152
153       exit.
154
155  lib05-out-ini Section.
156       *> lib05-out
157       move "greet" to f-GreetingField
158
159       move "IPN" to f-InPatronNumber
160
161       move "Patron name" to f-PatronName
162
163       exit.
164
165  lib05-out-cvt Section.
166       *> lib05-out
167       move GreetingField to f-GreetingField
168
169       move InPatronNumber to f-InPatronNumber
170
171       move PatronName to f-PatronName
172
173       exit.
174
175  lib05-out-out Section.
176       *> lib05-out
177
178       exec html
179          copy "Lib05-OUT.htm".
180       end-exec
181
182       exit.
183  *>>>>>>>>>>>>>>>>>>>>>>>>>>>>>>>>>>>>>>>>>>>>
```

Figure 4-12. The CGI program Lib05.cbl.

Summing Up

Project Summary

Proj0401 (Lib02.) shows you how to insert simple code into a CGI that accepts a patron number from an input form and displays a patron name from CGI programmer-inserted code.

Proj0402 (Lib03) is variation of Lib02 to improve the output form display.

Proj0403 (Lib04) illustrates CGI programmer-inserted code to access data from a subprogram for display by the output page.

Proj0404 (Lib05) is identical to Lib04 except the subprogram accesses data from an indexed file.

General Summary

When you create a CGI program, Net Express generates four files.
- The program file with an extension CBL. This file contains the skeleton code for CGI processing. You insert your application code in this file. Net Express does not change it when you modify input or output pages.
- Three copy files (extensions CPF, CPY, and CPV). These files contain code that is changed with each modification to an input or an output page. *Do not modify code in these files as it will be lost when you change the input or output pages.*

Modify input and output pages by clicking on the .htm filename in the files list of the project screen.

If you intend to use existing legacy programs in a Web application, incorporate them as subprograms. Then insert code in the CGI program to call the subprogram(s).

If you are calling an existing subprogram from the CGI, you may need to set up data work areas in the CGI Working-Storage section to accommodate parameters of the subprogram.

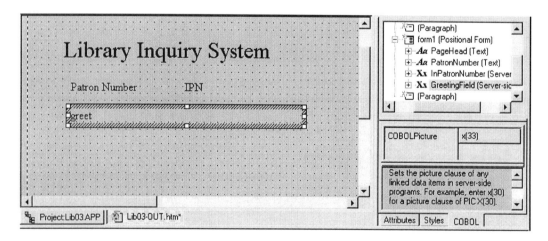

Figure 4-13. An alternate output screen.

Coming Up

This chapter has provided you with a minimum of HTML elements for entering information through your browser screen for transmission to the server. In the next chapter you will learn about the following thereby expanding your input capabilities.

- Check boxes—they provide the capability for accepting yes/no types of responses from a user.
- Radio buttons—they provide the capability for designating a single item from two or more items in a group.
- List selection elements that provide for selection of one or more items from a list.

Assignments

4-1.

This is an expansion of Assignment 3-1. You can either modify 3-1 or create your HTML pages from those of 3-1.

- Change the input form to accept a 4-position customer ID.
- Leave the output form unchanged.
- Insert an Evaluate statement into the CGI program to determine the user's name from the input customer ID. Use the following entries.

Customer ID	Name
1001	Fawn Dew
1002	Adam Zapple
1003	Rob Burr
1004	Xavier Money

4-2

This is an expansion of Assignment 3-1. You can either modify 3-1 or create your HTML pages from those of 3-1.

- Change the input page to accept a 4-position customer ID.
- Leave the output page unchanged.
- Insert a call to the subprogram Cus-sub0.cbl (stored in the NE-Progs folder).

Parameters for this subprogram are:

First parameter: Input; 4-position customer ID.
Second parameter: Output; 23-position customer name

Thus your calling statement would look something like the following.

```
Call "Cus-sub0" using in-cust-ID cust-name
```

4-3

This is an expansion of Assignment 3-1. You can either modify 3-1 or create your HTML pages from those of 3-1.

- Change the input page to accept a 4-position customer ID.
- Leave the output page unchanged.
- Insert a call to the subprogram Cus-sub1.cbl (stored in the NE-Progs folder). This subprogram accesses the indexed data file Customer.di. You will find listings of both in the Appendix.

Subprogram Description.

- Parameters for this subprogram include all fields from the record. However, you can minimize the amount of extraneous code for this assignment by using the following parameters

  First parameter: Input; 4-position customer ID.
  Second parameter: Output group item consisting of
                     23-position customer name.
                     76-position filler (not used).

- Customer IDs range from 1001 to 1020.
- If there is no record for the requested customer ID, the second parameter (customer name) is returned with low-values.

4-4

This is an expansion of Assignment 3-1. You can either modify 3-1 or create your HTML pages from those of 3-1.

- Change the input page to accept a 4-position customer ID.
- Change the output page to include name and address data.
- Insert a call to the subprogram Cus-sub1.cbl (stored in the NE-Assgn folder). This subprogram accesses the indexed data file Customer.di. You will find listings of both in the Appendix.

Subprogram Description.

- Parameters for this subprogram include all fields from the record. However, you can minimize the amount of extraneous code for this assignment by using the following parameters in your Call.

    First parameter: Input; 4-position customer ID.
    Second parameter: Output group item consist of:
        23-position customer name.
        20-position street address.
        28-position city/state/zip.
        28-position filler.

- Customer numbers range from 1001 to 1020.
- If there is no record for the requested customer ID, the second parameter (customer name) is returned with low-values.

Making Selections

Chapter Contents

A Typical Web Selection Screen 100
Check Boxes 101
    Creating Checkboxes 101
    Setting Properties 103
Radio Buttons 105
    What are Radio Buttons? 105
    Creating a Screen With Radio Buttons 105
    Be Consistent With Existing Cobol Applications 107
    Resulting CGI Code 107
Using Multiple Radio Button Groups 109
    The Three Groups of Figure 5-1 109
    An Output Page 110
    Grouping Screen Controls 110
    Aligning Screen Controls 111
    Justifying Text 112
    The CGI Program 112
The Reset Button 115
The Table Control 115
    Project Proj0502—Using a Table 115
    Table Characteristics 115
    Entering Column Headings 117
    Entering Radio Buttons 118
    Other Table Features 119
The Select Control 120
    About the Select 120
    Creating a Select Control 121
    Other Properties 124
    On The CGI Side 125
Multiple Selection 125
    Creating the Input Page 126
    Creating the Output Page 127
    The CGI Program 128
    Trial Runs 129
Using Color in the Display Form 129
    A Simple Example 129
    Creating the Output Form 130
The CGI 133
    Searching a String 133
    Inserting Your Code into the CGI 133
Comments About Different Browsers 135
Summing Up 135
    Project Summary 135
    General Summary 135
Coming Up 136
Assignment **136**

Chapter

5

Chapter Introduction

Everyday life constantly presents us with choices, for instance:

Designate your method of payment
Select your beverage from the following list
Place a check next to each book you wish to order

The objective of this chapter is to show you a variety of means by which Net Express allows you to designate choices. From this chapter, you will learn how to include the following HTML controls in a form design and the necessary CGI code to process their input.

- Check boxes—they provide the capability for accepting yes/no types of responses from a user.
- Radio buttons—they provide the capability for designating a single item from two or more items in a group.
- List selection elements that provide for selection of one or more items from a list.

A Typical Web Selection Screen

To illustrate the topics of this chapter, consider one of the services of a print shop: printing form letters for its customers. The print shop owner wants an online system in which the customer fills out a query screen such as that shown in Figure 5-1. Inspect this screen carefully and you see two types of controls for accepting user entries: squares and circles. You are probably familiar with both of these from GUI applications you've used (such as Windows and even Net Express). The two squares (entitled *Check here...*) indicate Yes/No entries. For instance, the check in the second box means that this is a reorder; the first box is not checked. Notice that these two controls are completely independent of one another. You can check one, or both, or none at all. They are called **check boxes**.

The selections in the lower portion of Figure 5-1's screen are different. For instance, in placing an order, you select *one* of four in the group entitled *Paper Color*. You do not make multiple choices. Also, the nature of most applications is almost always such that you *must* make an entry. These controls, called **radio buttons**, are arranged in groups, each group having its separate identity. So, in Figure 5-1 you see three radio button groups.

The input form definition of Figure 5-1 is part of the project Ltr01 stored in the Proj0501 folder. The output screen, which completes this project, merely confirms the user's selections as you see in Figure 5-2. You will study both of these form definitions and the CGI code modification needed to go from input to output.

Proj0501
Ltr01

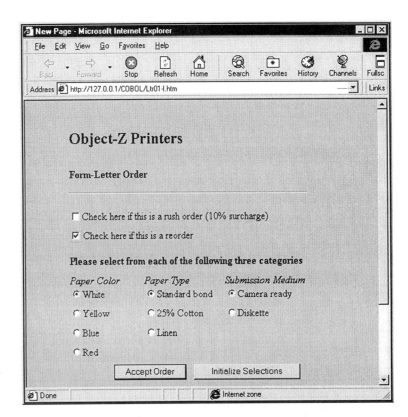

Figure 5-1.
A typical customer
order screen.

Figure 5-2.
A typical customer order verification screen.

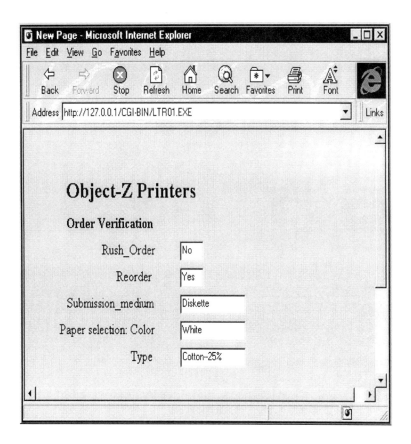

    In the descriptions that follow, you need not recreate this entire project but you will find it helpful to at least create a similar project of your own using a check box and a radio button group to ensure that you understand the details.

Check Boxes

Creating Checkboxes

Each Check Box you use in an input form produces a data item and, as does an Text Input control, results in a name/value pair being sent to the server. When you insert a check box, your screen displays two elements: a small box into which the user places the check mark, and a description. In Figure 5-3 you see two check boxes with their default entries. These two Check Box controls were inserted the same way you've inserted other controls on the screen. That is, you select the Check Box icon on the Form Designer tool bar, then click at the screen point you want the box positioned. To change the caption, you select the default text CheckBox and overtype it. However, that can be a little tricky and sometimes your attempts can produce strange results. In that respect, it helps to know exactly what you are dealing with. Look at the tree structure (top of the next page) for the first check box (taken from the tree window of Figure 5-3).

```
⊟--⊟- checkboxspan1 (Span)
   ⊟--🗐 (Paragraph)
       ☒  checkbox1 (Checkbox)
```

Here you see three HTML tags nested one within the other: a span, a paragraph, and a check box. The corresponding HTML script is as follows.

```
<SPAN id=checkboxspan1...>
  <P>
    <INPUT id=checkbox1 name=checkbox1 type=checkbox>
    CheckBox
  </P>
</SPAN>
```

Although generally you need not be concerned about generated HTML code, looking at this will eliminate some possible confusion when you begin working with check boxes (and also radio buttons). Notice the following about this code.

- The SPAN tag (terminated by /SPAN) is assigned the HTML identifier checkboxspan1 (the ellipses represent other code not shown).
- The paragraph tag (P and /P) encloses the two items of interest:
     The check box itself (identified by the INPUT tag)
     The caption CheckBox adjacent to the check box.
- The attributes of the INPUT tag identify it as a type checkbox. By default this input item is assigned the word checkbox1 as both the ID (for HTML use) and the Name (of the name/value pair returned to the server).

To give you a general idea of how to stay out of trouble with check boxes and radio buttons (and other controls, as well), let's experiment. If you have not created the form of Figure 5-3, create a new project then an HTML form. Insert a check box into the form and do the following.

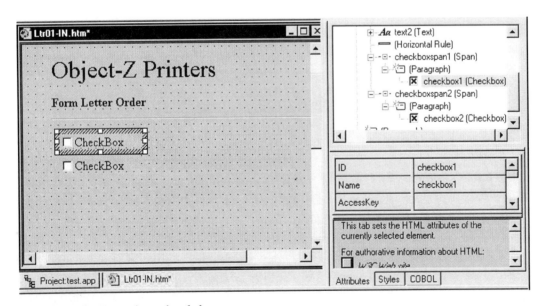

Figure 5-3. Inserting check boxes.

1. Expand the tree entry for this checkbox to show the three components (upper-right pane).
2. Click anywhere in your form to deselect the check box.
3. Click anywhere in the caption CheckBox. Notice that you have a text cursor (vertical bar) and that the Paragraph entry is selected in the component tree.
4. You can either press the Delete key to delete characters from this caption one at a time or you can select the entire caption and delete or overtype it (standard Windows practice).
5. Replace the caption CheckBox with Sample Box.
6. Using the left arrow key, move the cursor all the way to the left; make certain it is to the left of the check box itself. Notice that the control-tree highlight has shifted to the check box itself.
7. Press the Delete key and you will see that the check box is removed. Confirm this by looking at the control tree. If you were to look at the HTML code (listed on the preceding page), you would see that the INPUT tag has been deleted. For all practical purposes, you now have a simple Text control.
8. Click the Undo button in the toolbar to reinsert the check box.

What's the bottom line of all this? The answer is: "Be careful. Also don't be confused if you see something strange occur. Just click Undo and check the control tree to see what you have actually selected."

Setting Properties

The only component of the check box span structure you must change is the check box itself. To get started, click checkbox1 in the control tree and you will see the check box span highlighted. You will also see the COBOL tab in addition to the Attributes and Styles tabs beneath the lower-right window. From these, you can set the properties of the checkbox. Let's first look at the attributes.

Name. As with the Text Input control, the Name attribute designates the name of the data item the browser sends to the CGI program. The default is checkbox1 for the first check box you insert, checkbox2 for the second, and so on. Names used for the two check boxes of this example (Figure 5-1) are RushOrder and Reorder.

Checked. This property allows you to designate the default condition of the check box. If you click on False of this attribute, a drop down menu appears that displays True and False. Setting this property to True causes the browser to display this item with a check in the box (as the default).

Value. This property designates the value returned by the browser to the CGI program when the box is checked. To illustrate its use, consider the following scenario. The CGI generated for this application calls a subprogram containing the data item reorder. If this data item contains the value "R" then the current order is a reorder. Any other entry indicates a new order. Since the installation's programmers are familiar with this code, it makes sense to set up the CGI by that standard. To that end, the entry R for COBOLValue will cause the browser to return an R if the box is checked (if it is not checked, a space is returned) as summarized on the next page.

Box checked?	Name/Value
Yes	Reorder/R
No	Reorder/*space*

If you click the COBOL tab, you will see the COBOLPicture. This property designates the data type and size of the data item created in the CGI program into which the browser transmitted data value will be stored. Although not necessary, you would probably want to change from its default value X(32) to X(1).

Corresponding values for the rush order check box are as follows.

Name	RushOrder
Checked	False
Value	rush
CobolPicture	x(4)

For these two controls, you would insert into the process-business-logic section of the CGI program code something like the following.

```
If Reorder = "R"
    (Box checked action)
Else
    (Box not-checked action)
End-if
If RushOrder = "rush"
    (Box checked action)
Else
    (Box not-checked action)
End-if
```

For the sake of control-tree documentation, you might find it useful to replace the default ID with something more meaningful. Although you could change that entry for the check box itself, try changing that entry for the span, as done in the "finished product" of Figure 5-4.

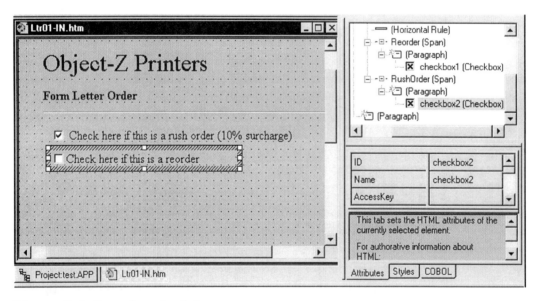

Figure 5-4. Inserting check boxes.

Radio Buttons

What are Radio Buttons?

Radio buttons enable an end-user to select a single option from a group of choices. For instance, you've made radio button selections in creating forms when you designate the HTML output type. You indicate your selection by clicking the circle corresponding to your choice. Your selection is marked by a dot within the circle.

In Figure 5-1 you see three groups of radios buttons: Paper Color, Paper Type, and Submission Medium. Each group is independent of each of the other groups. That is, from each group, you may select only one. For instance in Figure 5-1, if you clicked on the Yellow button, the White button would be deselected.

Creating a Screen With Radio Buttons

To illustrate using radio buttons, let's consider the four-button color group of Figure 5-1. Adding them to the design screen of Figure 5-4 results in the screen of Figure 5-5. Look at the control tree and you can see that radio buttons have the same structure as check boxes.

- The ID attributes are given numbered default values (radiobuttonspan1 and radiobutton1)
- Each is assigned the caption RadioButton (which you will change).
- All radio buttons are assigned the default Name entry radio (in contrast to check boxes where each is assigned a unique name).
- Although not visible in this screen, the default Checked attribute is False.
- The default entry for Value is on.
- The default COBOLPicture is x(32).

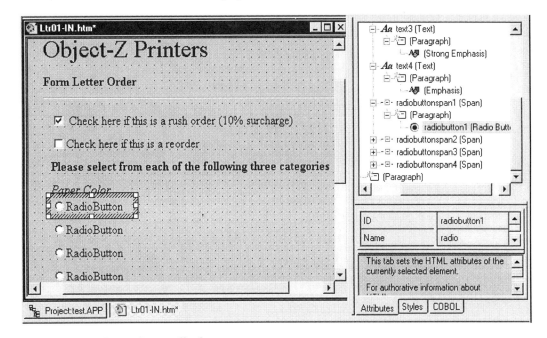

Figure 5-5. Inserting radio buttons.

Like check boxes, the Name entry serves as the data name of the name/value pair returned to the server. Unlike check boxes, the Name entry also serves the purpose of grouping two or more radio buttons. So all of the radio buttons in a group (for instance, paper color) must have the same Name entry. However, for each radio button you will assign a unique entry for its Value attribute (the value returned to the server). The assignments to be made for this group of radio buttons are as follows.

Name	All four buttons	PaperColor
Value	First button	white
	Second button	yellow
	Third button	blue
	Fourth button	red

In Figure 5-6 you see the appropriate captions assigned to each radio button and a unique ID for each radio button span—see the control tree. (The purpose of the latter is solely for control-tree documentation.) Not evident is the assignment of the above Value entries to buttons and the COBOLPicture entries of x(6), sufficient to handle the largest value (yellow).

When the form is submitted to the server, the browser returns a single name/value pair for this group as follows.

Button selected	Name/Value
White	PaperColor/white
Yellow	PaperColor/yellow
Blue	PaperColor/blue
Red	PaperColor/red

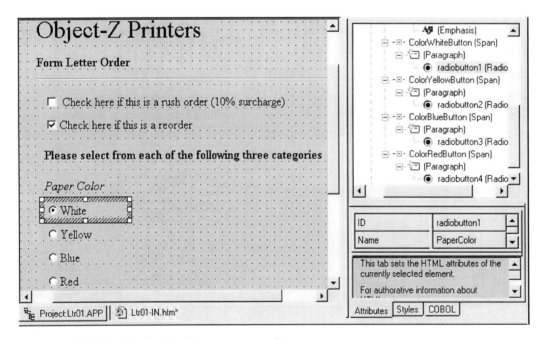

Figure 5-6. Desired radio button properties.

With Net Express 3.0 you must be careful to be consistent with case as Form Designer is case sensitive (in contrast to Cobol, which is not). For instance, if you designated one button with the group name PaperColor and another with the name Papercolor, they would be identified as belonging to two different groups. (Note: This may change with later releases of Net Express.)

In the screen definition of Figure 5-6, you see that the Checked property is set to True for the White button which makes it the default selection when you run the application. In general, it is a good idea to designate one button in each group as the default to ensure that the end user does not inadvertently forget to click an entry.

Be Consistent With Existing Cobol Applications

The Value entries white, yellow, blue, and red are reasonable choices for this group of radio buttons. However, don't create forms in a vacuum—keep in mind existing Cobol programs with which your application may be interfacing. For example, assume that existing programs for order processing include the following for paper-color processing.

```
10  paper-color        pic X(01).
    88  white-paper        value "1".
    88  yellow-paper       value "2".
    88  blue-paper         value "3".
    88  red-paper          value "4".
```

In this case, you might find it more convenient to designate the Value entries as 1, 2, 3, and 4 for these buttons. Then the following returned values returned would be consistent with the existing code.

Button selected	Name/Value
White	PaperColor/1
Yellow	PaperColor/2
Blue	PaperColor/3
Red	PaperColor/4

You probably would want to change the COBOLPicture entry to X(1) as well. Be aware that the picture entry for the group designation is taken from the first radio button listed in the control tree.

Resulting CGI Code

Let's take a look at the following portions of CGI copy-file code that will be generated for the radio buttons from this screen.

```
01 HTMLForm is external-form.
   03 f-PaperColor         pic x(6)
       identified by "PaperColor".

01 FormFields.
   03 PaperColor           pic x(6).

   Move f-PaperColor to PaperColor
```

In the 03 entry of the external-form entry you see the HTML name PaperColor associated with the Cobol name f-PaperColor. Remember that PaperColor is the Name for the group of four radio buttons—refer to Figure 5-6. The Move makes the data value available to you in a Cobol data item with the same name as the HTML name, a technique you've already encountered.

In the process-business-logic section of your CGI program, you would include code to test the value in PaperColor, for instance, look at the following code.

```
Evaluate PaperColor
   when "white"
      (White action)
   when "yellow"
      (Yellow action)
   when "blue"
      (Blue action)
   when "red"
      (Red action)
   when Other
      (Action for no selection)
End-Evaluate
```

Although Cobol names are case insensitive, don't assume the value you are testing is also case insensitive. It is a data value and as such is indeed case sensitive. For instance, if you used

```
when "White"
```

instead of   `when "white"`

your program would not detect the white button selection.

Suppose you had used Value entries of 1, 2, 3, and 4 for the respective color buttons, and had inserted the condition names of the earlier example (perhaps from one of your own copy files) into the Working-Storage section of the CGI. Then your CGI Evaluate statement would look something like the following.

```
Move PaperColor to paper-color
Evaluate TRUE
   when white-paper
      (White action
   when yellow-paper
      (Yellow action)
   when blue-paper
      (Blue action)
   when red-paper
      (Red action)
   when Other
      (Action for no selection)
End-Evaluate
```

Using Multiple Radio Button Groups

The Three Groups of Figure 5-1

Referring once again to Figure 5-1, you see that this input screen contains three radio button groups: paper color, paper type, and submission medium. You generate the paper type and submission medium groups in exactly the same way you generated the paper color group.

This application is programmed and stored in the Proj0501 folder as the project Ltr01. Following is a summary of this project's radio group properties .

Proj0501
Ltr01

Paper Color

Name: PaperColor   This is the data item name of the name/value pair transmitted to the CGI program. Net Express will define an equivalent data item of the same name to contain the transmitted data value.

Individual buttons

Button	Value	
White	white	Checked: True
Yellow	yellow	
Blue	blue	
Red	red	

COBOLPicture: x(6)

Paper Type

Name: PaperType

Individual buttons

Button	Value	
Standard bond	1	Checked: True
25% Cotton	2	
Linen	3	

COBOLPicture: x(1)

Submission Medium

Name: Medium

Individual buttons

Button	Value	
Camera ready	camera	Checked: True
Diskette	diskette	

COBOLPicture: x(8)

An Output Page

For this example, the output screen is kept relatively basic; it merely confirms the user's selections as you see in the browser screen display of Figure 5-2. The design screen for this page is shown in Figure 5-7 where you see properties of the Rush-Order Server-Side Text control VerifyRushOrder. Note that this will be the CGI program's data item name generated by Net Express. Since it will receive the value Yes or No, its COBOLPicture value is set to 3. You can see the other four data names in the tree of the upper-right window.

Reorder verification	VerifyReorder
Submission medium	VerifyMedium
Paper selection, color	VerifyColor
Paper selection, type	VerifyType

For each of these, the Style property Background-Color is set to white so that these items are more prominent when displayed by the browser.

Grouping Screen Controls

Notice that the column of descriptions (Rush order and so on) are perfectly aligned on the right; also, the Server-Side Text controls are aligned on the left. Achieving these alignments can be painstaking if you try to do it manually. Two features of Form Designer simplify the task for you. One of them involves grouping two or more controls then performing an appropriate alignment action on controls of the group. You group two or more screen controls by stretching a rectangular "rubber band" around the group. For instance, assume you want to group the Text controls (except for the heading) of Figure 5-7.

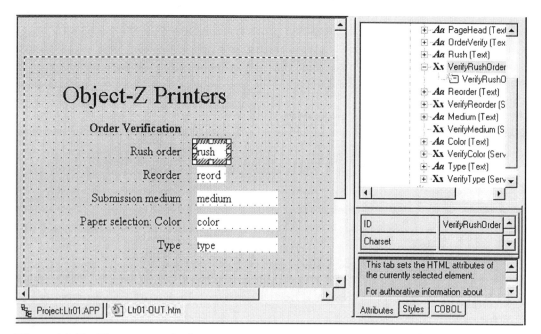

Figure 5-7. The output design screen.

1. Move the cursor to the upper left of the top-left control of the desired group.
2. Press and hold the left mouse button.
3. Drag to the lower right of the screen to encompass all the desired text objects inside a grouping rectangle; your screen will look like Figure 5-8(a).
4. Release the mouse button and the encompassed controls will be grouped as indicated by the ghost selection handles in Figure 5-8(b).

Hash marks around the **Order Verification** control indicate that it is the **dominant control**, the control against which the others are aligned when using positioning tools. You can change the dominant control by holding down the Ctrl key and clicking another control of the group. Although the grouping example of Figure 5-8 shows grouping only Text controls, a group can consist of any combination of controls.

Aligning Screen Controls

Net Express makes alignment of controls in a group easy for you by providing four alignment tools; each of these aligns based on the dominant control.

The Align Left tool aligns each control of the group against the left edge of the dominant control

The Align Right tool aligns each control of the group against the right edge of the dominant control

The Align Top tool aligns each control of the group against the top edge of the dominant control

The Align Bottom tool aligns each control of the group against the bottom edge of the dominant control

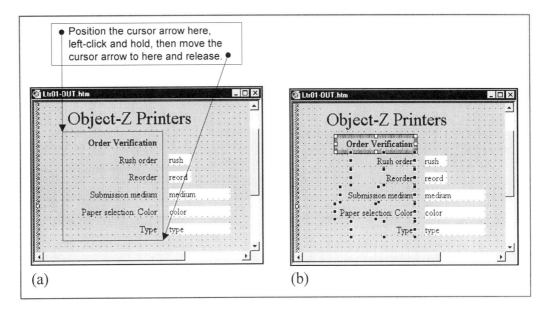

Figure 5-8. Selecting a group of objects.

To align controls of Figure 5-8(b), you would use either the Align Left or Align Right tool. You will see examples of using Align Top and Align Bottom tools in a later chapter.

Justifying Text

Positioning a group of Text controls so that they line up on the right as in Figure 5-8(b) can be a painstaking task. However, Net Express includes alignment features that make the task simple for you. For instance, assume you have created the following Text control.

Notice that it is positioned to the left within the span (justified left). If you position a text cursor anywhere within this text, you will see in the formatting toolbar that the left-justification icon is highlighted as in the following.

Because you want to align this group on the right, you should right justify each text entry within its span. (Remember, control alignment occurs on the end of the span, not the last character of text.) For instance, you select the Order Verification Text control, then click the right-justify icon ▤. You will see the text moved to the right within the span as follows.

So in creating the screen of Figure 5-7, the procedure you might follow is illustrated in Figure 5-9. The final step is to click the Align right tool.

The CGI Program

The CGI program and its associated copy files are stored in this example's folder under the name Ltr01 (the standard extensions are CBL, CPF, CPY, and CPV). In Figure 5-10 you see pertinent portions of the CGI (including appropriate parts of the three

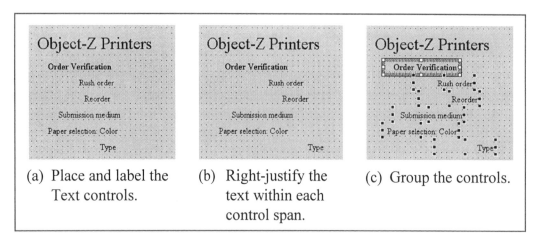

(a) Place and label the Text controls.

(b) Right-justify the text within each control span.

(c) Group the controls.

Figure 5-9. Right aligning a group of Text controls.

```
  1  IDENTIFICATION DIVISION.
  2      program-id. "Ltr01".

 10  DATA DIVISION.
 11
 12  working-storage section.
 13
 14      *> WARNING: Do not remove this copy statement
 15      *> or modify the contents of the copy file.
 16      copy "Ltr01.cpf".
 17      01 HTMLForm is external-form.
 18          03 f-Medium            pic x(8)
 19              identified by "Medium".
 20          03 f-PaperType         pic x(1)
 21              identified by "PaperType".
 22          03 f-Reorder           pic x(1)
 23              identified by "Reorder".
 24          03 f-PaperColor        pic x(6)
 25              identified by "PaperColor".
 26          03 f-VerifyReorder     pic x(3)
 27              identified by "VerifyReorder".
 28          03 f-VerifyMedium      pic x(15)
 29              identified by "VerifyMedium".
 30          03 f-VerifyRushOrder   pic x(3)
 31              identified by "VerifyRushOrder".
 32          03 f-RushOrder         pic x(4)
 33              identified by "RushOrder".
 34          03 f-ssubmit           pic x(60)
 35              identified by "ssubmit".
 36          03 f-VerifyColor       pic x(15)
 37              identified by "VerifyColor".
 38          03 f-VerifyType        pic x(15)
 39              identified by "VerifyType".
 40          03 filler              pic x.

 96      *> WARNING: Do not remove this copy statement
 97      *> or modify the contents of the copy file.
 98      copy "Ltr01.cpy".
 99      01 FormFields.
100          03 Medium            pic x(8).
101          03 PaperType         pic x(1).
102          03 Reorder           pic x(1).
103          03 PaperColor        pic x(6).
104          03 VerifyReorder     pic x(3).
105          03 VerifyMedium      pic x(15).
106          03 VerifyRushOrder   pic x(3).
107          03 RushOrder         pic x(4).
108          03 ssubmit           pic x(64).
109          03 VerifyColor       pic x(15).
110          03 VerifyType        pic x(15).
111
112  *> Enter additional working-storage items here
113
114  PROCEDURE DIVISION.
115
116  main section.
117      perform process-form-input-data
118      perform convert-input
119      perform process-business-logic
120      perform ltr01-out-cvt
121          *> ltr01-out
122      perform ltr01-out-out
123          *> ltr01-out
124      exit program
125      stop run.
126
127  process-form-input-data section.
128      *> Accept the input from the Browser
129      *> and check for errors
130      perform browser-initialize
131      accept htmlform
132      exit.
133
134  convert-input section.
135      *> Convert numeric input values
```

```
136      perform input-conversion
137      if v-all-ok = 0
138          perform output-form-error-and-stop
139      end-if
140      exit.
141
142  process-business-logic section.
143      *> Add application business logic here.
144      If RushOrder = "rush"
145          Move "Yes" to VerifyRushOrder
146      Else
147          Move "No" to VerifyRushOrder
148      End-If *>RushOrder = "rush"
149      If Reorder = "R"
150          Move "Yes" to VerifyReorder
151      Else
152          Move "No" to VerifyReorder
153      End-If *>Reorder = "R"
154      Evaluate medium
155          When "camera"
156              Move "Camera-ready" to VerifyMedium
157          When "diskette"
158              Move "Diskette" to VerifyMedium
159          When other
160              Move "No selection" to VerifyMedium
161      End-Evaluate *>medium
162      Evaluate PaperColor
163          When "white"
164              Move "White" to VerifyColor
165          When "yellow"
166              Move "Yellow" to VerifyColor
167          When "blue"
168              Move "Blue" to VerifyColor
169          When "red"
170              Move "Red" to VerifyColor
171          When other
172              Move "No selection" to VerifyColor
173      End-Evaluate *>PaperColor
174      Evaluate PaperType
175          When "1"
176              Move "Standard bond" to VerifyType
177          When "2"
178              Move "Cotton-25%" to VerifyType
179          When "3"
180              Move "Whole linen" to VerifyType
181          When other
182              Move "No selection" to VerifyType
183      End-Evaluate *> PaperType
184      exit.

219  Input-Conversion Section.

230      move 1 to v-Medium
231      move f-Medium to Medium
232      move 1 to v-PaperType
233      move f-PaperType to Paper1Type
234      move 1 to v-Reorder
235      move f-Reorder to Reorder
236      move 1 to v-PaperColor
237      move f-PaperColor to PaperColor
238      move 1 to v-RushOrder
239      move f-RushOrder to RushOrder
240      move 1 to v-ssubmit
241      move f-ssubmit to ssubmit
242      exit.

262  ltr01-out-cvt Section.
263      *> ltr01-out
264      move VerifyReorder to f-VerifyReorder
265      move VerifyMedium to f-VerifyMedium
266      move VerifyRushOrder to f-VerifyRushOrder
267      move VerifyColor to f-VerifyColor
268      move VerifyType to f-VerifyType
269      exit.
```

Figure 5-10. The CGI program Ltr01.

copy files). In inspecting this listing, keep in mind that the following was done to the original LRT01.CBL program generated by Net Express.

- Source code from the CPF, and CPY copy files is displayed following their Copy statements.
- Source lines are numbered for easy reference in ensuing descriptions.
- Code not directly pertinent to topics of discussion in this chapter is not shown (including code beyond line 269). You can spot the areas of missing code by gaps in the line numbers.

Notice the following about this program.

- The two check box data items are defined at lines 22/23 and 32/33.
- The three input radio button group names are defined at lines 18/19, 20/21, and 24/25.
- Input form field names corresponding to the HTML names are defined at lines 100-103 and 107. Input values are moved to these fields by Net Express-generated code at lines 231, 233, 235, 237, and 239.
- The output form Server-Side Text names are defined at lines 26/27, 28/29, 30/31, 36/37, and 38/39.
- Output form field names corresponding to the HTML names are defined at lines 104-106, 109, and 110.
- The If statement of lines 144-148 tests the rush-order check box to determine if it was checked. If checked, its value is rush. If not checked it contains spaces.
- Similarly, the If statement of lines 149-153 compares the data name Reorder to R, the designated Value entry for this check box.
- The three radio button groups are tested by Evaluate statements at lines 154-161, 162-173, and 174-183.
- Values of the receiving fields of the user code (VerifyRushOrder and so on) are move by the Net Express-generated code at lines 264-268 to the HTML-associated data items at lines 26-31 and 36-39 prior to the output action.

To repeat a point made earlier, Cobol data names are not case sensitive but Cobol data item values are, so you must be careful. For instance, consider the If of line 144.

```
If RushOrder = "rush"
```

RushOrder on the left of the above equal sign is a Cobol data name so it makes no difference if you use rushorder instead of RushOrder. However, rush on the right is a literal (enclosed in quotes) and it is case sensitive. If you used Rush here, your program would never detect a check in that check box. You must be careful in being consistent with names and values between the input form, the CGI program, and the output form.

The Reset Button

Look at Figure 5-1 again and you will see a button entitled Initialize Selections. When you click this button, all screen entries are set back to their default values. It is especially convenient if a user is working with a large form and has changed his or her mind about entries just made and wants them replaced with the default values. It is called a **Reset** button is is available by clicking the Reset icon [Reset] from the Form Designer screen.

The Table Control

Project Proj0502—Using a Table

There are several ways you can improve the appearance of Figure 5-1; one way is to enclose the radio buttons within a table thereby producing a screen like Figure 5-11. You can inspect this form design screen by opening the project Table and bringing up Table01.htm stored in the Proj0502 folder. (Be aware that this project contains only sample forms; it is not an application you can run.) To gain a feel for using tables, you should step through the example that follows. (Create a temporary folder for this.) Your end result will be an HTML form that generates the screen of Figure 5-11.

> Proj0502
> Table01

Table Characteristics

To step through this exercise, open a new project, create a new positional form, then proceed as follows.

1. Click on the Table icon ⊞ of the Page Elements toolbar then place a Table control on the left side of the Form Design screen. The resulting Table control will look like the element to the right.
2. Grab the right selection handle and stretch the control until it looks something like Figure 5-12. Notice the following about this control

Figure 5-11.
Enhancing appearance using a table.

Paper Color	Paper Type	Submission Medium
⊙ White	⊙ Standard Bond	⊙ Camera ready
○ Yellow	○ 25% Cotton	○ Diskette
○ Blue	○ Linen	
○ Red		

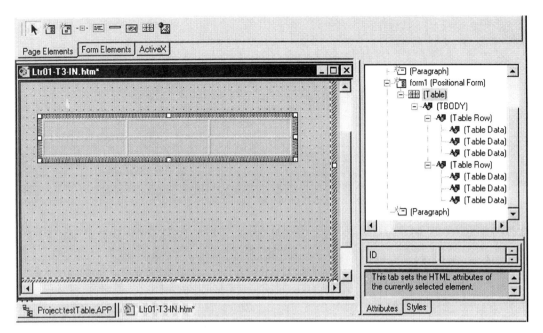

Figure 5-12. The Table control.

- The default size is two rows and three columns of individual cells.
- In the control tree there are two Table Row entries, one corresponding to each of the two rows you see in the control itself. (You will probably need to expand the elements under the Table entry.
- Subordinate to each Table Row in the tree you see three Table Data entries, one corresponding to each of the cells of Figure 5-12's table.
- In Figure 5-12, the entire Table is selected, as you see by the border around the control and the highlight on the Table entry of the control tree. You can select an entire row or an individual cell by clicking on the corresponding Table Row or on the Table Data control-tree entry.

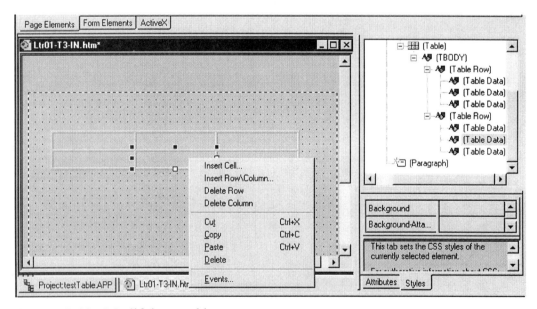

Figure 5-13. Modifying a table.

Figure 5-14. Popup menu for
modifying a table.

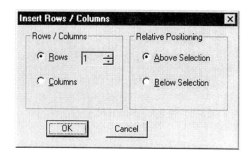

You need three more rows (total of five) for the display of Figure 5-11. So let's make that the first task.

1. Select any one of the cells by clicking within that cell or by clicking the entry in the control tree.
2. With a cell selected, right-click (anywhere on you screen) and you will see the popup menu of Figure 5-13.
3. For this exercise, you must add three rows (to obtain the five-row display of Figure 5-11). Click Insert Row/Column and you will see the popup menu of Figure 5-14.
4. With Rows selected (as in Figure 5-14) click the Up button to increase the number from 1 to 3. Since you are working with a blank form, it does not matter whether you insert them above or below the selection.
5. When you click OK, three rows will be inserted giving your desired five rows. Form Designer might compress the cell height to stay within the original table dimensions. If so, select the entire table, click on the lower-middle selection handle, and drag downward until you've restored the cell heights.
6. Referring to Figure 5-11, you see the three lower-right cells blanked out— they are not used. Select the lower-right cell then right-click to obtain the popup menu of Figure 5-13.
7. Click Delete to that cell and your table will look like Figure 5-15.
8. Delete the cell to the left and the cell above this corner cell. Your form should begin to resemble that in Figure 5-11.

Entering Column Headings

Let's next enter the column headings into the cells of the first row (refer to Figure 5-11).

9. Click anywhere within the upper-left cell. You should see a vertical-bar text cursor. Proceed as follows for the needed entry.

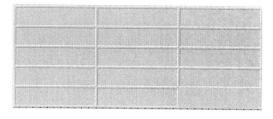

Figure 5-15. Deleting a cell.

- Type the words: Paper Color. If entry of these words has caused the width of that column to expand (narrowing the others), grab its right selection handle and restore the original dimesions.
- Highlight the text you just typed.
- On the Format toolbar, click the Bold button and the Text-center button. The words **Paper Color** will be in boldface and centered within the cell.

In Figure 5-11 you see that each of the three columns is a different shade of gray. If you inspected this form under Form Designer you saw that they are actually different colors. Change the color of this heading cell as follows.

- Select the cell.
- Click the Styles tab beneath the properties window.
- Click Background-Color then the Down button to display the pull-down list of colors (not the color palette).
- Select a color that appeals to you—don't get carried away. Remember, you want screens that are comfortable to read, not ones that "attack" the user. The first column in Figure 5-11 uses the color beige.

10. Repeat the preceding process for the next two cells by entering **Paper Type** and **Submission Medium**. Unless you have very wide cells, **Submission Medium** will wrap to the next line as you see in Figure 5-11.

Entering Radio Buttons

The next step is to place a Radio Button control in each of the remaining cells. Be aware that you do *not* insert a control into a cell the same way you place one on a form. That is, you must (1) select the cell and (2) click the control's button in the control toolbar. Furthermore, you *cannot* move a control into a cell from elsewhere in a form. For an idea of what happens, deselect the table, click the Radio Button icon on the toolbar to highlight it, move the mouse pointer to one of your cells and click. Look at you control tree and you will see that this control is not subordinate to any entry of the table. It is an independent control overlapping the table. Click the Undo button to remove this Radio Button.

Let's proceed to enter radio buttons for the paper color (first column); remember, the properties as follows.

Paper Color

Name: PaperColor

Individual buttons

Button	Value	
White	white	Checked: True
Yellow	yellow	
Blue	blue	
Red	red	

COBOLPicture: x(6)

1. Select the cell of row 2, column 1.
2. Click the Radio Button icon in the control toolbar and you table will look like Figure 5-16. Your screen may not have the group of tightly clustered selection handles around it. If not, don't worry so long as the radiobutton1 entry is selected in the control tree and the ID attribute radiobutton1 is displayed.

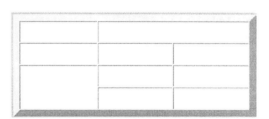

Figure 5-16.
Inserting a Radio Button in a cell.

3. Change this button's attributes to the following.

ID	White (for control-table documentation only)
Name	PaperColor (the radio button group name)
Checked	True
Value	white

4. Click the COBOL tab and change the COBOLPicture to x(6).
5. Click to the immediate right of the button control. The selection will change from the button to the cell and you will see a text cursor. Enter a space then type the description White.
6. Click the properties Style tab, click Background-Color, click the expand-down button and change the color to beige (or whatever color you selected for the cell above this one).
7. Repeat Steps 1-6 for each of the other three colors using the appropriate color entries. If the default button is not White when you are finished, click on the White button and it will register as the default.

You may proceed to add radio buttons for the paper type and submission medium columns. Use properties listed earlier in this chapter for these entries.

For the final piece of "dressing up" you can change the Background-Color of the entire table to obtain the appearance of Figure 5-11. Do this by selecting the Table in the control tree, clicking on the Style tab, and selecting a color that appeals to you (Figure 5-11 uses olive).

Other Table Features

There are numerous attributes and styles you can work with in changing the configuration and appearance of a table. For instance, the table of Figure 5-17 was generated as follows. (You can inspect this example stored as Table02 in the folder Proj0502.)

Figure 5-17.
Changing a table's appearance.

1. Insert a Table control and increase the number of rows to 4.
2. With the table selected, scroll to the attribute Cell Spacing; it determines the width of the lines separating cells. Although there may not be an entry displayed for this attribute in the properties window, the default is 2. Enter a value 0 to obtain the narrow lines you see in Figure 5-17.
3. The attribute Border determines the width of the table border (added to the spacing value); the default is 1. If you specify a wider border, you see a three-dimensional effect. If you enter 0, all table lines disappear. The value used in Figure 5-17 is 7.
4. Change the BGColor to a light color (OldLace is used in this example).
5. To achieve the double-width (second cell in first row), first select the row one, column three cell and delete it.
6. Select the row one, column two cell and change its Colspan (column span) to 2.
7. To achieve the double-height cell on the left, select the cell in row four, column one and delete it. Do not be concerned that the deleted cell is positioned in row four, column 3.
8. Select the cell in row 3, column 1 and change its Rowspan attribute to 2. The completed form should look like Figure 5-17.

The Select Control

About the Select

Look at Figure 5-18 and you see four input forms that you probably have encountered in you travels through the Internet or when using other GUI software. Although their appearances are different, each of these is an HTML **Select** control. Each of them provides a list of nine colors for selection. The example on the left displaying the single entry White, produces the drop-down list beneath it when the down button is clicked. The example in the center displays three of the nine; it uses the familiar scroll bar to view other selections. The example on the right displays all nine of the selections. Furthermore, the example in the upper-left displays the color White in its window; the example in the center displays White highlighted; the example to the right displays the color Blue highlighted. In each case, these are the default values. You will learn how to designate defaults in the example that follows.

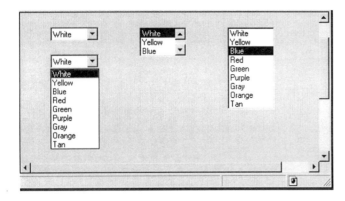

Figure 5-18. Select controls.

You can use the Select control as a substitute for radio buttons in which a user can select a single item from a list. You can also use it to display a list from which a user can make multiple selections, in essence substituting for a group of check boxes. Following are attributes of this control that will be of primary interest to you.

Name. This is the data-item name of the name/value pair transmitted to the CGI program. The default is select1 (select2, and so on for subsequently inserted Select controls). Net Express will define an equivalent data item of the same name to contain the transmitted data value.

Multiple. A value False (the default) restricts the selection to a single item of the list (like a group of radio buttons). For instance, if the end user clicked on Blue in the browser window of Figure 5-18, White would be deselected and Blue selected (highlighted).

Options. This attribute contains the list of selection items displayed in the select box. You will learn how to insert your list in the example that follows.

Selected. This attribute determines which item in the select box is highlighted as the default selection.

Visible. This property sets the number of rows displayed in the browser screen. When the value is set to 0 or1, the Select works as a drop-down list.

In creating Select controls, you will also be working with two properties listed under the COBOL tab: COBOLOccurs and COBOLPicture.

COBOLOccurs. With Multiple set to False (radio button feature) you should leave this property at 1, the default value. The selection result will be available in the CGI program as a simple Cobol data item with a data name the same as the control's Name property entry.

COBOLPicture. This property is identical to that of both radio buttons and check boxes. That is, it designates the size of the Cobol data item defined in the CGI program. It must be large enough to contain the value returned to the CGI.

Creating a Select Control

As an exercise, let's create the form that generated the controls shown in the browser screen of Figure 5-18 by proceeding as follows. (If you wish to inspect this example, it is stored in the Proj0503 folder as Select01.app).

Proj0503
Select01

1. Create a new project (click File/New/Project).
2. From the New Project window,
    a. select Project,
    b. type Select01 (or whatever name you desire) for the project name,
    c. designate the folder (use My-Examples\Proj0503 if you want to be in step with the examples of the book).
3. Click Create to generate the project. You will see the HTML Page Wizard window.
4. Select Positional Form and click Next.
5. In the ensuing window, type Select01-IN for the HTML Filename, ensure that Cross-Platform is selected, and click Next.
6. Double-check your entries in the confirmation screen and click Finish.
7. When you reach the Form Designer screen, highlight the Select icon 📵 on the

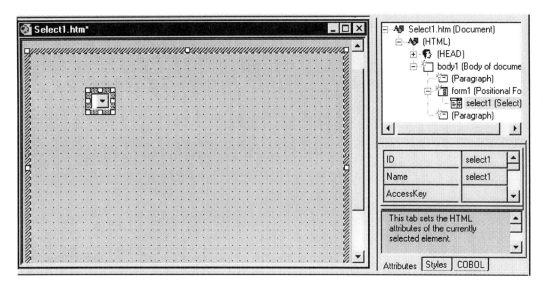

Figure 5-19. Inserting a select control.

Form Designer toolbar, then place a Select control on your design screen. At this point, your screen should look like Figure 5-19.

8. Now you must add the list of colors (see Figure 5-18) to this control's options. Do this by right-clicking on the control itself (it must be selected) or on the control's entry in the control-tree pane. From the popup menu, click Select Options. This produces the Edit Select Options window of Figure 5-20.

You see that this window is divided into three basic areas for entry/display of your selections. Let's look at how you use these by entering the color "White" as the first select option.

9. Position the cursor in the New Option box, type White, and click the Add option button (or press Enter). Your screen will look like Figure 5-21.

10. To designate White as the default, click the Selected check box. Do not enter anything for the Value attribute (let's postpone that topic).

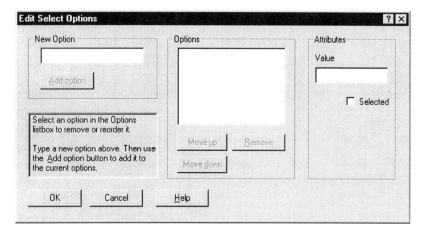

Figure 5-20. Window to add entries to the selection list.

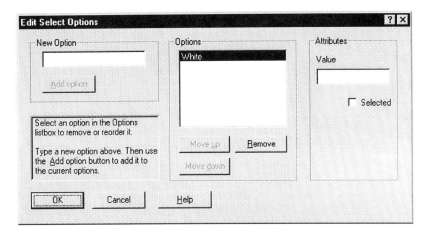

Figure 5-21. Adding an entry to the selection list.

11. Type Yellow in the New Option box and click Add option. Do not click the Selected box as you only designate one option as the default. (If you did click it, the Selected option of the White selection would be removed.)

12. Repeat this process for the remaining seven colors in the list of Figure 5-18. When you are finished, your selection list will look like Figure 5-22.

Notice the three buttons entitled Move up, Move down, and Remove. Their actions are exactly as their labels imply. The first two allow you to move the highlighted option up or down within the list; the Remove allows you to delete the highlighted option from the list.

13. Click the OK button to return to the Form Designer screen.

14. Click File/Save to save the form.

15. To view this control in your browser, click Page/Preview.

16. When the browser comes up, click on the expand button on the right side of this control and you will see the drop-down list of the lower-left example in Figure 5-18.

17. Notice that the first entry is highlighted; it is the default selection. Click on any of the other colors and you will see White deselected.

18. Close the browser.

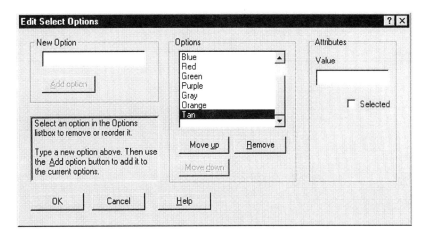

Figure 5-22. The completed selection list.

Let's review the attributes you have assigned.

- You left the Multiple entry False, making this selection control equivalent to a radio button group.
- Through the Options attribute, you have entered nine color options from which the user can select.
- You left the Size entry at its default value 0 thereby establishing the control size sufficient to display one entry, the one selected.

Other Properties

From Figure 5-19 you see that Form Designer defaults to Select1 for both the ID and Name attributes. Consistent with the choice for the corresponding radio button group, you might use PaperColor as the Name attribute for this Select control. You could also use PaperColor for the ID entry if you so desired.

Recall that when you designated this control's options, you did not make entries into the Value attribute—see Figure 5-22. This attribute is the value of the name/value pair returned to the server. In the absence of an entry, the value returned is the selected option entry itself. Thus if the user selected Green, then the value returned to the server would be the word Green. If your application is such that it is more convenient to return (and test for) values other than those of the option list, you would make an appropriate Value entry for each option (Figure 5-22).

Whether your input form returns the option entry or the value entry, you must be certain the generated Cobol data item is large enough. Click on the COBOL properties tab and you will see that the default entry for COBOLPicture is x(16). In this example, no option consists of more than six characters (Yellow and Orange) so you might want to change this entry to x(6). The default COBOLOccurs value of 1 reflects the choice of allowing only a single value to be returned to the server.

Next, let's create the middle and right Select controls as of Figure 5-18. Rather than enter them from scratch, you can simply copy and paste.

1. From the Form Design screen, highlight the current Select control's entry on the control tree.
2. Do a copy operation (click Edit/Copy or press Ctrl-C) then deselect the Select control.
3. Do a paste operation (click Edit/Paste or press Ctrl-V).
4. Your copy is positioned in the upper-left of the form. Reposition it as appropriate.
5. Do a second paste; you now have three select controls. Click File/Save to save this form.
6. For the second and third Select controls, change the Size attribute to 3 and 9, respectively.
7. For the third control, make Blue the default selection. Do this by highlighting Blue and clicking the Selected checkbox—see Figure 5-22. When you are finished, your screen will look like Figure 5-23.
8. Click Page/Preview and try various selections to gain a feel for how these work.

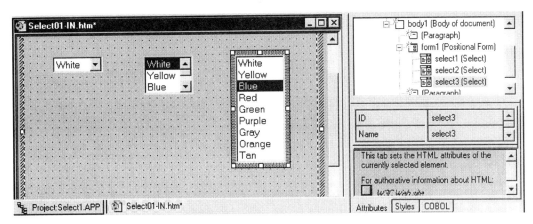

Figure 5-23. Three different forms of Select controls.

On The CGI Side

If you are curious, go ahead and generate a CGI program for this project. (You might want to include a Submit button and create a simple output screen, although neither is necessary to look at the generated CGI code.) In the resulting Cobol code you will see the three data items Select1, Select2, and Select3 corresponding to the HTML data names from the form of Figure 5-22. (Of course, in an actual application you would use only one of the versions of this selection form, not all three.) If you used the third one of Figure 5-23, then you might insert code like the following into your CGI.

```
Evaluate Select3
  When "White"
  (White action)
  When "Blue"
  (Blue action)
      .
      .
  When "Tan"
    (Tan action)
End-evaluate
```

Multiple Selection

For the next exercise you will create a project that presents the user with the input and output forms of Figure 5-24. Note that this exercise provides for multiple selection. For this, you can either step through the following procedure to create a new project (named Select02) or you can simply study the components of the Select02.app project included in the Proj0504 folder. If you create your own project, you can save yourself some work by copying one of the Select controls from Figure 5-23 to the clipboard then pasting it to your new input page.

Proj0504
Select02

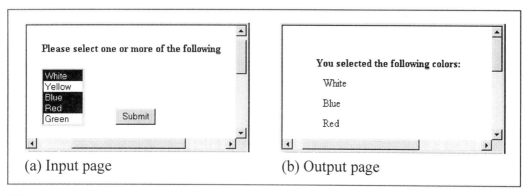

(a) Input page   (b) Output page

Figure 5-24. Using a selection control.

Creating the Input Page

First you must create a new project, then generate the input page.

1. Create a new project. Remember, the sequence is:
    Click File/New.
    Select Project.
    Select HTML Project, type Select02 for the project name and
        My-Examples\Proj0504 for the folder, then click Create.
    Select Positional Form then click Next.
    Type Select02-IN for the input form name and click Next.
    Verify your selections then click Finish.

    Now proceed to create the input form of Figure 5-25 by adding the user instruction, the Submit button, and the Select control as follows.

2. Insert a Text control and change its description to the user instruction of Figure 5-25. For emphasis, change this text to bold.
3. Insert a Submit button; change its caption if you are so inclined.

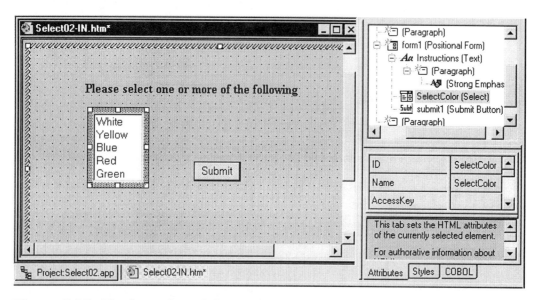

Figure 5-25. The input form Select02-IN.

4. Insert a Select control and set its properties as follows.
   - Right click on the control for the Select Options menu. Enter the five color options shown in Figure 5-25. You may set a default entry if you like.
   - Change the Name and ID to SelectColor.
   - Change the Multiple attribute to True.
   - Change the Size attribute to 5 (sufficient to display all five options).
   - Click the COBOL tab. Then change COBOLPicture to x(6).
   - Change the COBOLOccurs to 5 thereby providing for return to the server of up to five colors.
5. Save the form.

Creating the Output Page

Next you must create the output page of Figure 5-26; it consists of the description line and five Server-Side Text controls.

1. Create a new page (click File/New and proceed from there). Name the page Select02-OUT.
2. Insert the Text (*Aa*) control; change the text description as shown in Figure 5-25. You may want to change the text entry to bold.
3. Insert five Server-Side Text **Xx** controls as shown.
   - Change the ID attribute of each as indicated in the tree-view (Confirm1, Confirm2, and so on).
   - Change the COBOLPicture property to x(6) for each (this corresponds to the greatest number of letters in the output display, for instance, the color Yellow).
   - Optionally, change the screen description of each to provide better documentation of those form elements. They are included here only because their presence makes it easier to see the individual controls on the Design Screen.
4. Save the form and close the design screen.

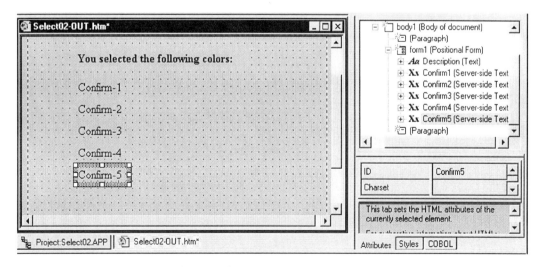

Figure 5-26. The output form Select02-OUT.

The CGI Program

Now create the CGI as follows.

1. Click File/New.
2. Select Internet Application and click OK.
3. Select Server Program and click Next.
4. Make the following entries in the ensuing Server Program Generation window.
   - Filename: Select02.
   - Generation Template: If you've been using the minimal skeleton from examples CD, select CGI-min.skl.
   - Designate Select02-IN.htm as input and Select02-OUT.htm as output.
5. Click Next.
6. Confirm your entries in the next screen. When all are correct, click the Finish button.
7. After the CGI is created, rebuild the project.
8. From the project's component tree, double-click SELECT02.CBL so that you can look at the CGI program.

Scroll down to the SELECT02.CPY expansion and you will see the following data items. (Note: Your fields may be listed in a different order—that has no consquence.)

```
01 FormFields.
   03 Confirm2              pic x(6).
   03 Confirm4              pic x(6).
   03 Confirm3              pic x(6).
   03 SelectColor           pic x(6) occurs 5.
   03 ssubmit               pic x(64).
   03 Confirm1              pic x(6).
   03 Confirm5              pic x(6).
```

Notice that the Select control of Figure 5-25 produces a table data item (SelectColor in this example) with a table size corresponding to your COBOLOccurs entry when building the input form. When run, this table will contain the names of the colors selected by the user. For example, assume that a user selects two colors: Yellow and Red. Then the contents of this table will be:

```
SelectColor(1)     Yellow
SelectColor(2)     Red
SelectColor(3)     spaces
SelectColor(4)     spaces
SelectColor(5)     spaces
```

In the above Working-Storage code, you also see the Server-Side Text items, Confirm1 through Confirm5 created from the output form. Thus, you need to copy the input items from the table elements to these output data items. For this, you need to insert the following code into the process-business-logic section of the CGI.

```
Move SelectColor(1) to Confirm1
Move SelectColor(2) to Confirm2
Move SelectColor(3) to Confirm3
Move SelectColor(4) to Confirm4
Move SelectColor(5) to Confirm5
```

After making these insertions, compile the program to ensure that you have no errors. When finished, close this program display window and rebuild the project.

Trial Runs

Make a trial run to be certain it works properly. For instance, select the colors White, Blue, and Red. (As with such Windows lists, to make more than one selection hold down the Control key as you click each entry you want.) Your browser input and output screens should look like Figure 5-24. Once in your browser, you may repeat simply by clicking the browser "Back" button.

If you find that your results are not correct, you can always use the Animator step function as described in Chapter 1. The only tricky part is in viewing the contents of the table. Try the following

1. Stop animating if you are proceeding from the previous test.
2. Click the Step ✎ icon on the Net Express toolbar.
3. Click the Run Through ⏭ three times to perform the following three sections.

```
process-form-input-data
convert-input
process-business-logic
```

4. Scroll up to the FormFields record. If you double-click on the data item SelectColor, you will see a window displaying the value for SelectColor(1).
5. To see all six entries, close the Examine window then double-click on FormFields and you will see the window of Figure 5-27(a).
6. Click the + button to the right of FormFields (to expand the list) and your screen will look like Figure 5-27(b).

Using Color in the Display Form

A Simple Example

Based on what you've seen in surfing the Web, you probably feel that the display of Figure 5-24(b) is pretty mundane. The next example shows you how to "jazz up"

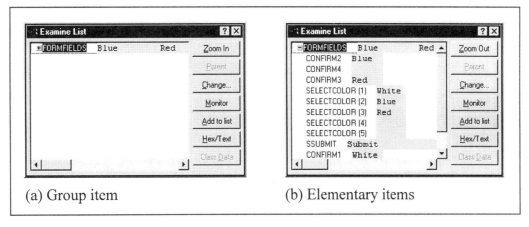

(a) Group item   (b) Elementary items

Figure 5-27. Displaying data item values.

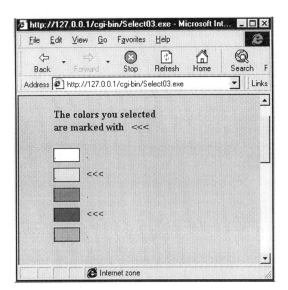

Figure 5-28.
Using color in an output screen.

your display a while using the basic tools to which you've already been introduced. It also illustrates Cobol techniques that you will find useful in process
ing input from multiple-select browser controls.

In this example, you will modify the output page of the preceding exercise to produce a screen such as that shown in Figure 5-28 in which the two colors yellow and red have been selected. (Note: The varying shades of gray in this figure are actually the colors yellow, blue, red, and green. If you run the application Select03 stored in the Proj0505 folder, you will see the correct color renderings.)

Creating the Output Form

For this exercise, the simplest path is to replace the output page Select02-OUT of the preceding project. However, if you want to save the Select02 project, create a new project (Select03) and generate Select03-IN using Select02-IN as the template. In either case, then proceed to create the output page corresponding to the display of Figure 5-28 as follows.

1. Create a new page as follows.
   - Click File/New.
   - From the popup menu select HTML Page and click Next.
   - For HTML Filename, enter Select03-OUT (or Select02-OUT) and click Next.
   - Check you entries in the Summary window then click Finish.
2. Insert a Text (*Aa*) control and change the caption to that shown in Figure 5-28 ("**The colors you…with <<<**").
3. Insert a second Text control beneath the first one. You must change its properties so that it looks like Figure 5-29.
   - Select this control and click the Styles tab.
   - In the properties window, scroll down to the Border Style option. Click on it, then click on the resulting down arrow, and select Solid.
   - Scroll to Border Width and enter 1px (for 1 pixel).

Figure 5-29. A Text control.

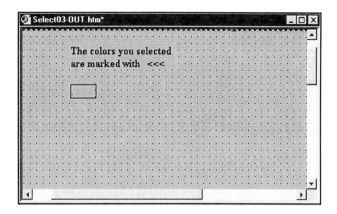

4. Delete the text New Text. If the height of the box doubles when you delete the text, insert a period—anything that will not be conspicuous.
5. Grab the right selection handle and reduce the width so that it is approximately the same as the box in Figure 5-29.
6. You need five of these, one for each of the five colors you see in Figure 5-28. You could enter four more but it is easier to copy this one and paste it four times. Select this control by clicking on its *Aa* entry in the control tree. Copy this control to the clipboard (Edit/Copy or Ctrl-C).
7. First, make certain that no control is selected. Then perform a paste (Edit/Paste or Ctrl-V). If the duplicate appears in the upper-left corner of your form move it down so that it is immediately beneath the other box.
8. Repeat Step 7 three more times. When you are finished, your screen should look like Figure 5-30. If you have difficulty aligning these five controls, group them, then click the Align Left ⊟ button.
9. Next, you must change the color of each box.
   - Select the first box.
   - Click the Style tab.
   - Click Background Color.
   - Click the expand button ▶.
   - From the resulting color palette, select the white chip then click OK.

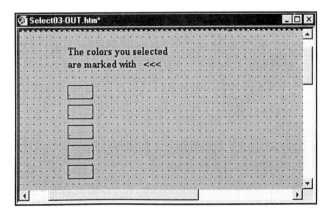

Figure 5-30.
Five Text controls with borders.

10. Repeat the preceding for each of the following four boxes using the colors:
>   yellow
>   blue
>   red
>   green

To complete this form you must insert appropriate controls to display the three less-than symbols **<<<** indicating that the color has been selected. For this you use Server-Side Text (**Xx**) controls. Your end result will look like Figure 5-31.

11. Insert a Server-Side Text control to the right of the color box.
12. Replace the caption Server-side Text with three less than symbols **<<<**. Note that this is solely for Form Designer screen documentation. Actual values will be entered by the CGI.
13. Reduce the width of this control by grabbing a selection handle and dragging.
14. Change the COBOLPicture entry to x(3).
15. Duplicate this control by copying it then pasting four times. Be certain the Xx entry of the control tree is highlighted (not the subordinate Paragraph) for the copy operation.
16. Align these controls as in Figure 5-31.
17. The ID attribute of the Server-Side Text control yields the Cobol data name you will work with in the CGI. Change this attribute for each as follows (refer also to the control tree of Figure 5-31).
>   CheckedWhite
>   CheckedYellow
>   CheckedBlue
>   CheckedRed
>   CheckedGreen
18. Referring to the control tree of Figure 5-31 you see that the Text controls are identified as ColorWhite, ColorYellow, and so on. Although not necessary, you should make these changes for their screen documentation value.

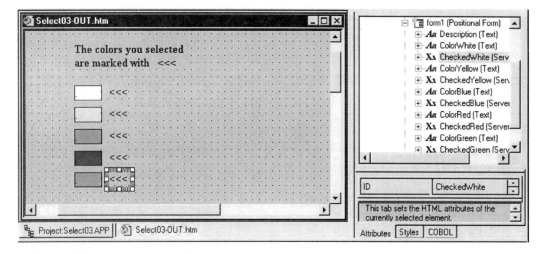

Figure 5-31. The completed output form.

19. You are finished, so save the form.

20. From the Form Designer screen, rebuild the project.

If you created a new application for this example, you must generate a CGI. Do so and name it Select03.cbl. If you working with the Select02 application and modified Select02-OUT, then you must modify Select02.cbl.

The CGI

Searching a String

From the preceding example, you know that the selected colors from the input browser screen are available in the CGI program from the table elements `SelectColor(1)` through `SelectColor(5)`. In order to place marks adjacent to the appropriate color boxes, the CGI code must search this array five times, once for each of the colors. An alternate to using a table search is to use the Inspect statement as it allows you to search an alphanumeric data item (a string) for any desired substring occurrence. For instance, consider the following statements.

```
Move zero to the-count
Inspect this-field tallying the-count for all "Red"
```

Upon completion of this statement, the value in `the-count` will be equal to the number of times the literal `Red` is found in `this-field`. For instance, if `this-field` contains

```
The color is Red or Reddish
```

The value in `the-count` will be 2. If the substring does not exist in the data item being inspected, the count will be 0. Let's apply this technique to this application.

Inserting Your Code into the CGI

If you look at your CGI program (double-click on the program name listed in the component tree), you will see the code of lines 1-8, Figure 5-32. These are inserted from the .CPY copy file. (Note: Line numbers are shown here only for convenient reference; they are not part of the code.) In order to use the Inspect statement, you need the color table defined under a separate 01. For this, you will need the addi-

Figure 5-32.
Data Division entries.

```
 1     01 FormFields.
 2        03 CheckedYellow      pic x(3).
 3        03 CheckedWhite       pic x(3).
 4        03 CheckedGreen       pic x(3).
 5        03 SelectColor        pic x(6) occurs 5.
 6        03 CheckedRed         pic x(3).
 7        03 ssubmit            pic x(64).
 8        03 CheckedBlue        pic x(3).
 9
10 *> Enter additional working-storage items here
11     01 select-fields.
12        03 select-1           PIC X(6) occurs 5.
13     01 select-pointer        pic 9.
14     01 tally-field           pic 9.
```

tional Working-Storage components shown in lines 11 through 14 (add these to your CGI). Code you must add to the process-business-logic section is shown in Figure 5-33. (If you are modifying Select02, be certain to remove the code from that application.)

- The input subscripted data items are moved to a work array by lines 102-106.
- The Server-Side Text items are initialized at lines 108 and 109. (Notice that a period is used rather than a space. When this application was tested, the absence of a non-space character in these fields caused the color box to be repositioned. Consider use of a period here as a "work-around." This may not be necessary with later versions of Net Express.)
- A search is done for each color; for instance, lines 111-116 looks for White. If found, the characters <<< are moved into the form field CheckedWhite.

Insert this code into your CGI and run a compile—correct any errors you encounter. Then rebuild the project and run trying some test cases. If the results are not similar to Figure 5-28, you've made an error somewhere, so find it and perform the necessary repairs.

```
101    *>    Move array to the group item select-fields
102          Perform varying select-pointer from 1 by 1
103                      until select-pointer > 5
104            Move SelectColor(select-pointer) to
105                      select-1(select-pointer)
106          End-perform
107    *>    Set each color to not checked
108          Move "." to CheckedWhite,CheckedYellow,
109              CheckedBlue, CheckedRed, CheckedGreen
110    *>    Look for White
111          Move 0 to tally-field
112          Inspect select-fields
113                      tallying tally-field for all "White"
114          If tally-field = 1
115            Move "<<<" to CheckedWhite
116          End-if
117    *>    Look for Yellow
118          Move 0 to tally-field
119          Inspect select-fields
120                      tallying tally-field for all "Yellow"
121          If tally-field = 1
122            Move "<<<" to CheckedYellow
123          End-if
124    *>    Look for Blue
125          Move 0 to tally-field
126          Inspect select-fields
127                      tallying tally-field for all "Blue"
128          If tally-field = 1
129            Move "<<<" to CheckedBlue
130          End-if
131    *>    Look for Red
132          Move 0 to tally-field
133          Inspect select-fields
134                      tallying tally-field for all "Red"
135          If tally-field = 1
136            Move "<<<" to CheckedRed
137          End-if
138    *>    Look for Green
139          Move 0 to tally-field
140          Inspect select-fields
141                      tallying tally-field for all "Green"
142          If tally-field = 1
143            Move "<<<" to CheckedGreen
144          End-if
```

Figure 5-33.
Required code
for the CGI.

Comments About Different Browsers

You are at the point now where you will be creating more complex screens. You must be aware that different browsers render the appearance of HTML pages differently. Consequently, Form Designer cannot match exactly what the user will see on the screen. In particular, Form Designer renders pages the same way as Internet Explorer 4.0, not Internet Explorer 3.0. The only way to see the exact appearance of the form inside a Web browser is to display it using that Web browser. If your default Web browser is either Internet Explorer or Netscape Navigator, the default view is set accordingly. If neither of these is your default, the default view is Internet Explorer.

Summing Up

Project Summary

Proj0501 (Ltr01) illustrates using check boxes and radio buttons and how you handle them in a CGI.

Proj0502 (Table01) consists only of two HTML pages (it is not a complete application). The purpose is to illustrate variations you can make on a Table control to vary data presentation.

Proj0503 (Select01) illustrates using the Select control with the capability of allowing a user to select one or more entries from a list.

Proj0504 (Select02) focuses on the CGI code necessary to process input data from a Select control

Proj0505 (Select03) is a variation on the output of Select02 illustrating use color to illustrate output.

General Summary

You can use a check box when a yes/no type of response is required to a query. The Name property designates the name of the name/value pair transmitted to the browser. The COBOLValue property designates the value of the name/value pair; if there is no entry for this property, the Caption property serves as the default.

You can use a set of radio buttons to offer the user a choice from a predetermined list of options. Unlike the check box, the name of the name/value pair is designated by the GroupName property. Like the check box, either the COBOLValue property or the Name property of the selected radio button designates the value of the name/value pair.

You can use the Select control in much the same way you use check boxes and radio buttons. If the property MultipleSelection is set to False, this control functions much like a radio button, allowing the user to select only one of the listed entries. If this property is set to True, the user can select more than one of the listed entries. In this mode, the user's selections are available in the CGI program as a Cobol table.

Coming Up

The next chapter further explores considerations when building applications using existing legacy code (subprograms). It also describes a special feature of Net Express that automatically generates both the input and output forms and the CGI from fields selected from a subprogram's Linkage Section.

Assignment

5-1

This assignment revolves around the order file (order.di); its record description is listed in Figure 5-34. Note: Only use this list of data items for the list of options to be inserted in your html form.

Input screen: The input screen must accept entries for a new order as follows.

order-ID	Text Input
customer-ID	Text Input
saddle-type	Radio Button
stirrup-covers	Check Box
padded-seat	Check Box
leather-tooling	Select (single selection with drop down menu)
silver-ornaments	Select (single selection with drop down menu)

Ignore the date determination fields.

For screen descriptions, use the 88 condition names of Figure 5-34, for instance:

    Leather tooling
        None
        Basic
        and so on

Output screen: The output screen must verify the user's selections.

Note that this assignment does not involve reading from or writing to the order file. You will use this input screen for file updating in Chapter 11.

Figure 5-34.
Record description
for **order.di**.

```
01  order-record.
    10  or-order-id              pic x(03).
    10  or-customer-id           pic x(04).
    10  or-saddle-type           pic X(01).
        88  type-western         value "W".
        88  type-english         value "E".
        88  type-spanish         value "S".
    10  or-order-options.
        20  or-stirrup-covers-sw   pic X(1).
            88  stirrup-covers      value "Y".
            88  no-stirrup-covers   value "N".
        20  or-padded-seat-sw      pic X(1).
            88  padded-seat         value "Y".
            88  no-padded-seat      value "N".
        20  or-leather-tooling     pic X(2).
            88  tooling-none        value "NO".
            88  tooling-basic       value "BA".
            88  tooling-buffalo-bill value "BB".
            88  tooling-coogan      value "CO".
            88  tooling-aurilio     value "AU".
            88  tooling-brush       value "BR".
            88  tooling-horse-tail  value "HT".
            88  tooling-custom      value "CU".
        20  or-silver-ornaments    pic X(2).
            88  silver-none         value "NO".
            88  silver-beads        value "BE".
            88  silver-horseshoes   value "BO".
            88  silver-rings        value "BA".
            88  silver-stars        value "ST".
            88  silver-binary-digit value "BD".
    10  or-date-determination-fields.
        20  or-order-date-count    pic 9(03).
        20  or-start-date-count    pic 9(03).
        20  or-promised-date-count pic 9(03).
        20  or-scheduled-date-count pic 9(03).
    10                             pic X(20).
```

Building Applications from Legacy Code

Chapter Contents

A File-Accessing Program 140
   The Patron File 140
   The Subprogram Lib-sub2.cbl 140
   The Stateless Nature of the Web 141
A Basic Subprogram Application—Proj0601 142
   Incorporating the Subprogram into the Application 142
   The Output Form Lib06-OUT. 144
   CGI Code—Lib06.cbl 145
Manipulating Subprogram Input for Display—Proj0602 146
   The Output Page Lib07-OUT 146
   CGI Code—Lib07.cbl 146
Creating Applications With Form Express 147
   About the Application Wizard 147
   Create the Application Project 148
   Create the Application 149
Modifying the HTML Pages 152
   The Input Page 152
   The Output Page 153
   The CGI 155
   Using Disabled Edit to Display Data 156
   Placing Form Express in its Proper Context 156
Data Validation 157
   Built-In JavaScript Data Validation Functions 157
   Designating Data Validation 158
Summing Up 161
   Project Summary 161
   General Summary 161
Coming Up 162
Assignment 163

Chapter

6

Chapter Introduction

The last example of Chapter 4 (Lib05 in the Proj0504 folder) uses the subprogram Lib-sub1 to access data from the patron file and display the patron name. This example is contrived in that the input and output form data items corresponded exactly to linkage section data items of the subprogram. Consequently, the CGI (Lib05.cbl) only needs a few basic moves to set up data for the output form. In practice, your task usually is not that simple. This chapter examines a more typical subprogram you are likely to encounter in practice. From the chapter you will learn about the following.

- Create an application from a subprogram using all or part of the subprogram's input data.
- Insert code into your CGI to convert subprogram input data to a more desirable form for browser display
- A feature of the Net Express Application Wizard that automatically generates input and output forms and CGI code for processing data you select from a subprogram's Linkage Section.

A File-Accessing Program

The Patron File

The indexed patron file (patron.di) contains one record for each library patron; record contents include the following.

Field	Length
Patron identification number (key field)	3
Patron last name	10
Patron first name	12
Street address	20
City	14
State	2
Zip	10
Privilege status	1
Employee status	1
Book right	1
Periodical right	1
Video right	1
Books checked out	2
Other data (not used)	18

If you want to inspect the file contents, refer to the listing in the appendix. You also can use a word processor to access its text equivalent stored as patron.dat.

The Subprogram Lib-sub2.cbl

The subprogram of Figure 6-1 contains typical file accessing code that you might find in any basic file processing program. Let's look at some of its features.

- Lines 21-25 contain the file information.
- Lines 30-46 contain the record description.
- The parameter list of lines 49-57 includes the following:

> Input
> > Patron number (ls-patron-number)
>
> Output
> > Patron name and address data (ls-patron-info)

Each data name in the Linkage Section includes the prefix ls- signifying (for documentation's sake) that the item is a Linkage Section data item.
- Notice that Linkage Section data items do not correspond exactly to the record description: not all the record fields are returned to the calling program.
- If the file does not contain the requested patron record, ls-patron-info is set to low-values.

```
         $set sourceformat "free"                      47
1  *>***********************************             48  Linkage Section.
2  *> Library Application                             49     01  ls-patron-number          pic x(03).
3  *> W. Price  1/2/99              LIB-SUB2.CBL       50     01  ls-patron-info.
4  *> This subprogram provides read access to the     51         10  ls-first-name         pic X(10).
5  *> following indexed file                          52         10  ls-last-name          pic X(12).
6  *>    PATRON.DI: Indexed by Patron Number; contains 53         10  ls-street-address     pic X(20).
7  *>    patron name, address data and other data.    54         10  ls-city               pic X(14).
8  *> Subprogram parameter is ls-patron-record        55         10  ls-state              pic X(02).
9  *>    Input: ls-patron-number (record key)         56         10  ls-zip                pic X(10).
10 *>    Output: ls-patron info.                       57         10  ls-employee-status    pic X(1).
11 *>         Set to low-values if record not found   58
12 *>***********************************             59  Procedure Division Using ls-patron-number
13                                                    60                        Ls-patron-info.
14 Identification Division.                           61
15    Program-id. LIB-SUB2.                           62     000-Main-module.
16                                                    63        Open Input Patron-File
17 Environment Division.                              64        Perform 200-process-user-request
18                                                    65        Close Patron-File
19    Input-Output Section.                           66        Exit program
20    File-Control.                                   67          .
21       Select Patron-File assign to disk            68     200-process-user-request.
22          "c:\Elements-CWP\NE-data\patron.di"       69        Move ls-patron-number to pr-patron-number
23          organization is indexed                   70        Read Patron-File
24          access is random                          71           Invalid key
25          record key is pr-patron-number.           72              Move low-values to ls-patron-info
26                                                    73           Not invalid key
27 Data Division.                                     74              Move pr-first-name     to ls-first-name
28    File Section.                                   75              Move pr-last-name      to ls-last-name
29    FD Patron-File.                                 76              Move pr-street-address to ls-street-address
30       01  patron-record.                           77              Move pr-city           to ls-city
31          10  pr-patron-number    pic x(03).        78              Move pr-state          to ls-state
32          10  pr-first-name       pic X(10).        79              Move pr-zip            to ls-zip
33          10  pr-last-key redefines                 80              Move pr-employee-status to ls-employee-status
34              pr-first-name       pic 9(03).        81        End-read
35          10  pr-last-name        pic X(12).        82          .
36          10  pr-street-address   pic X(20).
37          10  pr-city             pic X(14).
38          10  pr-state            pic X(02).
39          10  pr-zip              pic X(10).
40          10  pr-privilege-status pic X(01).
41          10  pr-employee-status  pic X(01).
42          10  pr-book-right       pic X(01).
43          10  pr-periodical-right pic X(01).
44          10  pr-video-right      pic X(01).
45          10  pr-books-out        pic 9(02).
46          10                      pic X(18).
```

Figure 6-1. The Lib-sub2 subprogram.

The Stateless Nature of the Web

Although relatively simple, Lib-sub2 contains reasonably conventional features that you will find in many existing Cobol programs. One non-conventional feature of this program is that it contains no provision for repetition: that is, there is no main loop. In the 000 module you see:

> The file is opened
> A user request is processed
> The file is closed
> The program is terminated.

This is characteristic of Web applications. Remember from Chapter 2 the nature of the Web. If a screen you are viewing includes a Submit button, the HTML script that generated the screen includes a Post method that designates a CGI program on some server. When you click the Submit, that server program is run and returns another HTML page to your browser. When this sequence is finished, the server has completed its job. It has no way of knowing whether or not you are coming back, so it closes the CGI program. Consequently, we do not have a continuously running program as we know it in conventional Cobol; hence the Web is referred to as being **stateless**. You will learn about problems and solutions associated with the stateless-ness of the Web in Chapter 10.

A Basic Subprogram Application—Proj0601

Incorporating the Subprogram into the Application

Proj0601
Lib06

The first example of this chapter (stored as Lib06.app in Proj0601) accepts an input patron number using the input screen of your first project in Chapter 3 (see Figure 3-14) and displays the output screen of Figure 6-2. Note that this application is built around the legacy subprogram Lib-sub2. When creating the application, you can first generate the input and output pages and the CGI, then add the subprogram as you did in Chapter 4. However, a more convenient approach, especially when your subprogram uses copy files, is to designate the project as being created from an existing application. You do this as follows. (Although several data items are displayed by the output form of Figure 6-2, construction of the form involves no new principles over those of preceding chapters.)

1. Create the folder into which you will build this application.
2. Copy the subprogram into this folder. This application uses Lib-sub2.cbl.
3. To create the new project, click File/New/Project. The resulting window will look like Figure 6-3.
4. In the type-of-project pane, select Project from an existing application as in Figure 6-3.

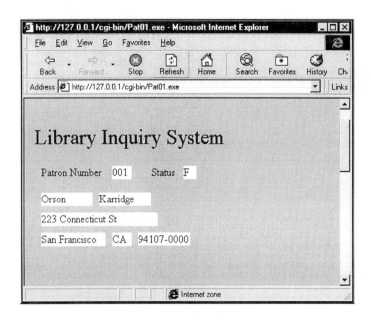

Figure 6-2.
Output screen for project Lib06.

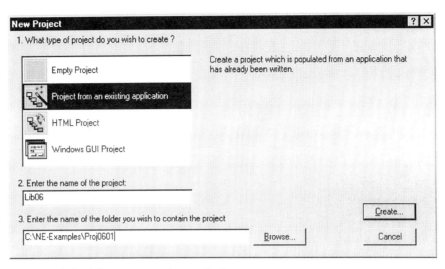

Figure 6-3. The new-project window.

5. Enter the project name and folder then click Create. The files-to-add window of Figure 6-4 will pop up.
6. To designate the program file (the subprogram you want to include in the project), click Add File(s).
7. The Add files window of Figure 6-5 lists all .cbl files in the folder—in this case, the only available file is lib-sub2.cbl.
8. Double-click on lib-sub2.cbl and it will be inserted into the display of Figure 6-4.
9. From the screen of Figure 6-4, click Next.
10. The next screen directs you to indicate the main program. As you only have one listed, no action is required. Click Next.
11. From the ensuing confirmation screen, click Finish.

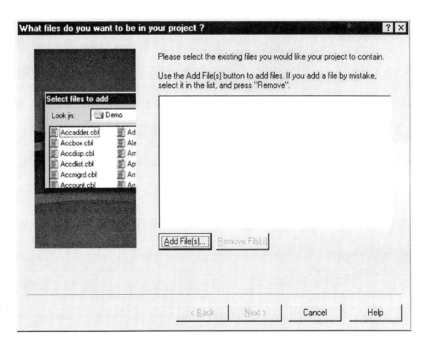

Figure 6-4.
The files-to-add window.

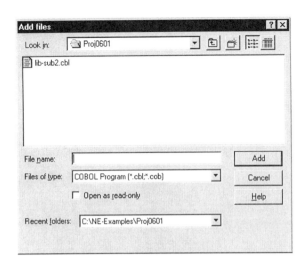

Figure 6-4.
The files-to-add window.

At this point, you will see the Net Express project screen identifying lib-sub2 as a component of this project. Had your program included one or more copy files, they would be listed in project pane. Net Express inspects each program for copy statements to identify needed copy files.

The Output Form Lib06-OUT.

By inspecting the Form Designer screen of Figure 6-6 you can see that this page consists of three Text controls and eight Server-Side Text controls to display data. The latter have been designated with a BackgroundColor property of white to make them stand out. Although you could step through the creation of this application, that would bc of limited value because no new Form Design techniques are introduced. For this example, we will focus our attention on the CGI.

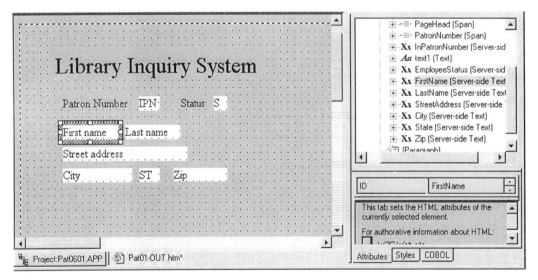

Figure 6-6. Form Designer screen for project Lib06.

CGI Code—Lib06.cbl

You see appropriate portions of the CGI's code in Figure 6-7. Lines 70-78 contain the Net Express generated form fields—compare this sequence of data names to the Form Designer control tree of Figure 6-6. At lines 81-88 you see the record patron-info that corresponds in format exactly to the Linkage section output parameter of Lib-sub2 (refer to lines 50-57 of Figure 6-1). The procedure I used in inserting these into the CGI was as follows.

1. Open both the subprogram and the CGI program in a word processor.
2. Select and copy to the clipboard the Linkage Section output record (lines 51-58) of Lib-sub2.
3. Insert the clipboard contents into the appropriate portion of the CGI's Working-Storage Section (following line 80 of Figure 6-7).
4. Perform a global replace on the entries of this record to change the prefix ls- to pi- (pi for patron-info). Although this step is not necessary, I prefer to use the prefix ls- only to identify data items defined in the Linkage Section—simply a matter of documentation.

```
 1  IDENTIFICATION DIVISION.              79
 2      program-id. "Lib06".              80  *> Enter additional working-storage items here
                                          81  01  patron-info.
 9  DATA DIVISION.                        82      10  pi-first-name       pic X(10).
10  working-storage section.             83      10  pi-last-name        pic X(12).
11                                        84      10  pi-street-address   pic X(20).
12      *> WARNING: Do not remove this copy statement    85      10  pi-city         pic X(14).
13      *> or modify the contents of the copy file.      86      10  pi-state        pic X(02).
14      copy "Lib06.cpf".                 87      10  pi-zip              pic X(10).
15      01 HTMLForm is external-form.     88      10  pi-employee-status  pic X(1).
16          03 f-City            pic x(14)   89
17              identified by "City".     90  PROCEDURE DIVISION.
18          03 f-FirstName       pic x(10)   91
19              identified by "FirstName".  92  main section.
20          03 f-InPatronNumber  pic x(3)   93      perform process-form-input-data
21              identified by "InPatronNumber".  94      perform convert-input
22          03 f-State           pic x(2)   95      perform process-business-logic
23              identified by "State".     96      perform lib06-out-cvt
24          03 f-ssubmit         pic x(60)   97          *> lib06-out
25              identified by "ssubmit".   98      perform lib06-out-out
26          03 f-EmployeeStatus  pic x(1)   99          *> lib06-out
27              identified by "EmployeeStatus".  100      exit program
28          03 f-Zip             pic x(10)  101      stop run.
29              identified by "Zip".
30          03 f-LastName        pic x(12)  118  process-business-logic section.
31              identified by "LastName".  119      *> Add application business logic here.
32          03 f-StreetAddress   pic x(20)  120      Call "lib-sub2" Using InPatronNumber
33              identified by "StreetAddress".  121                            patron-info
34          03 filler            pic x.    122      If patron-info = low-values
                                          123          Move "Record not found" to StreetAddress
66      *> WARNING: Do not remove this copy statement    124      Else
67      *> or modify the contents of the copy file.      125          Move pi-first-name      to FirstName
68      copy "Lib06.cpy".                126          Move pi-last-name       to LastName
69      01 FormFields.                   127          Move pi-street-address to StreetAddress
70          03 City              pic x(14).  128          Move pi-city           to City
71          03 FirstName         pic x(10).  129          Move pi-state          to State
72          03 InPatronNumber    pic x(3).   130          Move pi-zip            to Zip
73          03 State             pic x(2).   131          Move pi-employee-status to EmployeeStatus
74          03 ssubmit           pic x(64).  132      End-If *>patron-record = low-values
75          03 EmployeeStatus    pic x(1).   133
76          03 Zip               pic x(10).  134      exit.
77          03 LastName          pic x(12).  135
78          03 StreetAddress     pic x(20).  136
```

Figure 6-7. The CGI Lib06.cbl.

The subprogram is called by the programmer-inserted code at line 120. The If statement of the (lines 122-132) involves the same basic logic as that of Lib05.cbl (Figure 4-12). If the subprogram returns low-values, the requested patron is not contained in the file, so an error message is moved to the appropriate output form field. Otherwise, the required output data is moved.

Manipulating Subprogram Input for Display—Proj0602

The Output Page Lib07-OUT

The next example application, stored as Lib07 in the Proj0602 folder, is a minor variation of the preceding Lib06. In the sample output screen of Figure 6-8 you see that the first and last names and the city, state, and zip have been concatenated to form a single field. Furthermore, the employee status is displayed in a descriptive form (**Full-time**) rather than the one-letter code obtained from the subprogram.

You see the structure of the output page producing this display in Figure 6-9. As in the previous project, all output data is displayed with Server-Side Text controls with a designated BackgroundColor of white.

CGI Code—Lib07.cbl

Examples you've seen thus far involve relatively little code addition to the CGI. In many applications, the amount of work required in the CGI will be substantial. You will find that you can handle code insertion in the following ways.

- Type the code directly into the process-business-logic section as you have seen in preceding examples.
- If you have a large amount of code, then write it as a subprogram.
- If you have a library subprogram that performs the required functions, include an appropriate call to the subprogram in your CGI.

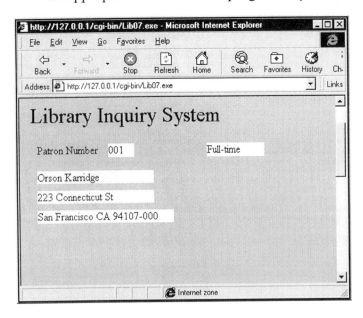

Figure 6-8.
Browser output for project Lib07.

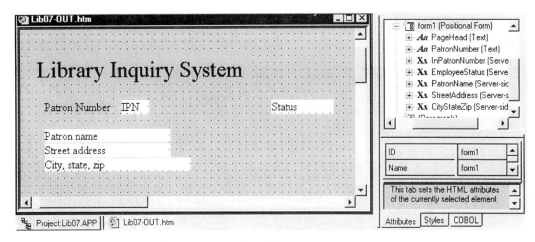

Figure 6-9. Form Designer screen for Lib07-OUT.

If you incorporate your code in the form of a subprogram, don't forget to designate the subprogram in the project components list. You can do this either when creating the project (refer to Figure 6-3 through 6-5 and the accompanying description earlier in this chapter) or you can add it later as described in Chapter 4.

In the listing of Figure 6-10 you see that necessary code for manipulating input data for output is carried out at lines 114-132. As you see, these are standard Cobol operations that we commonly use in problem solving.

Creating Applications With Form Express

About the Application Wizard

Net Express is designed to simplify your task of bringing legacy Cobol applications to the Web. This task is illustrated by the preceding examples of this chapter in which an existing subprogram is called by the Net Express generated CGI. To this end, Net Express includes a special feature of the Internet Application Wizard that automatically creates the following.

- Input page.
- Output page.
- Basic data item definitions and procedural code in the CGI.

You need only designate input and output data items from a displayed list of your subprogram's Linkage Section data items.

In earlier versions of Net Express this feature was identified as **Form Express**. However Version 3.0 integrates it into the application wizard thereby dropping the term Form Express. On the other hand, I continue to use that terminology as it is a convenient way of referring to the particular tool. Be aware that Form Express is evolving rapidly and probably will be updated on the Micro Focus Web Sync, so be

```
 1   IDENTIFICATION DIVISION.              77
 2       program-id. "Lib07".              78
                                           79  PROCEDURE DIVISION.
 9   DATA DIVISION.                        80
10   working-storage section.             81  main section.
11                                         82      perform process-form-input-data
12       *> WARNING: Do not remove this copy statement  83      perform convert-input
13       *> or modify the contents of the copy file.    84      perform process-business-logic
14       copy "Lib07.cpf".                85      perform Lib07-out-cvt
15       01 HTMLForm is external-form.    86          *> Lib07-out
16           03 f-InPatronNumber    pic x(3)    87      perform Lib07-out-out
17               identified by "InPatronNumber".  88          *> Lib07-out
18           03 f-ssubmit           pic x(60)   89      exit program
19               identified by "ssubmit".      90      stop run.
20           03 f-EmployeeStatus    pic x(12)
21               identified by "EmployeeStatus".  107  process-business-logic section.
22           03 f-StreetAddress     pic x(20)   108      *> Add application business logic here.
23               identified by "StreetAddress".  109      Call "lib-sub2" Using InPatronNumber
24           03 f-CityStateZip      pic x(28)   110                             patron-info
25               identified by "CityStateZip".   111      If patron-info = low-values
26           03 f-PatronName        pic x(23)   112          Move "Record not found" to PatronName
27               identified by "PatronName".     113      Else
28           03 filler              pic x.      114          String pi-first-name delimited by " "
                                                115              " "
57       *> WARNING: Do not remove this copy statement  116              pi-last-name
58       *> or modify the contents of the copy file.    117              into PatronName
59       copy "Lib07.cpy".                118          Move pi-street-address to StreetAddress
60       01 FormFields.                   119          String  pi-city delimited by " "
61           03 InPatronNumber     pic X(360).  120              " "
62           03 ssubmit            pic x(64).   121              pi-state
63           03 EmployeeStatus     pic x(12).   122              " "
64           03 StreetAddress      pic x(20).   123              pi-zip
65           03 CityStateZip       pic x(29).   124              into CityStateZip
66           03 PatronName         pic x(23).   125          Evaluate pi-employee-status
67                                              126              When "F"
68   *> Enter additional working-storage items here  127                  Move "Full-time" to EmployeeStatus
69   01  patron-info.                     128              When "P"
70       10  pi-first-name       pic X(10).   129                  Move "Part-time" to EmployeeStatus
71       10  pi-last-name        pic X(12).   130              When "N"
72       10  pi-street-address   pic X(20).   131                  Move "Non-employee" to EmployeeStatus
73       10  pi-city             pic X(14).   132          End-Evaluate *>pi-employee-status
74       10  pi-state            pic X(02).   133      End-If *>patron-info = low-values
75       10  pi-zip              pic X(10).   134      exit.
76       10  pi-employee-status  pic X(1).
```

Figure 6-10. The CGI program Lib07.

certain to check and make certain you have the latest upgrades. The following example was generated using the original release of Net Express 3.0 (upgrades might give you a slightly different result in some cases).

The first example using the Form Express is stored as Lib08 in the folder Proj0603. To step through the following sequence to generate this application, you must first do the following.

1. Create a working folder for the project.
2. Copy the file
       Lib-sub2.cbl
   into that folder.

Create the Application Project

For this first Form Express example, you will create an application that is roughly equivalent to Lib06 (the first example of this chapter).

1. From the Net Express screen, click File/New/Project.

Figure 6-11.
Internet Application
main screen.

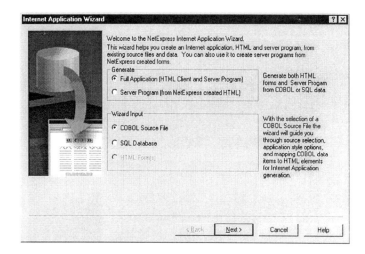

2. From the resulting New Project window, select Empty Project (Form Express will ask you for the name of the subprogram later). Make appropriate entries for the project name and the folder.

Create the Application

Now you must create the application based on the subprogram that you've included in this folder (lib-sub2.cbl).

1. Click File/New/Internet Application.
2. From the Wizard screen of Figure 6-11, you want:
   Full Application
   COBOL Source File
   Click Next.
3. In the ensuing Source Selection screen either type lib-sub2.cbl or click Browse and select lib-sub2.cbl (Figure 6-12).
4. From the next screen, select the Separate Input/Output Forms button and click Next.
5. Click Create and you will see the screen of Figure 6-13.

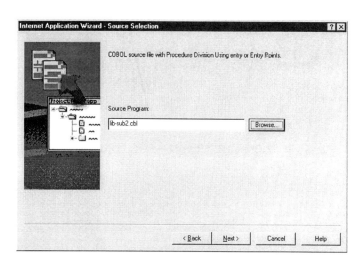

Figure 6-12.
Source program
selection screen.

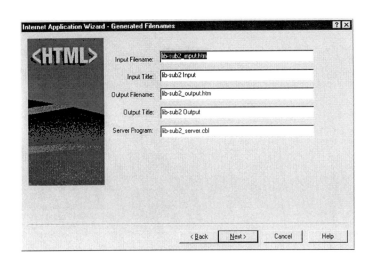

Figure 6-13.
Default filenames.

This screen contains default names for the input and output HTML files and for the CGI program (Server Program) that use the subprogram name as the base. You also see title entries for the two screens (Input Title and Output Title). You should always give each form a descriptive title.

6. In Figure 6-14 you see entries that are consistent with the naming standards use in this book. Change your entries accordingly.

Input Filename:	Lib08-IN.htm
Input Title:	Patron Inquiry Input
Output Filename:	Lib08-OUT.htm
Output Title:	Patron Information Display
Server Program:	Lib08.cbl

Figure 6-14. Default filenames.

7. Click Next and you will see the screen of Figure 6-15 (you will probably need to click the + button to expand ls-patron-info). Lets' examine each of the Parameter Assignment columns beginning with the rightmost, I/O.

8. Click on one of the entries, for instance, Both on the first line and you will see the following drop-down list.

Selection	**Creates a control for**
In	the input page
Out	the output page
Both	both input and output pages
N/A	data item not used in this application

9. Next click on any one of the Edit entries under the Control Type column and expand the list. If you scroll down, you will see the following options.

Selection	**Control Generated**
Edit	Text Input (**ab|**)
CheckBox	Check box
RadioButton	Radio button
Label	Server-Side Text (**Xx**)
Select	Select
Hidden	Hidden field (described in Chapter 10)
Password	Password (described in Chapter 10)
Disabled Edit	Input Text with change capability disabled

Figure 6-15.
Parameter list from
the subprogram.

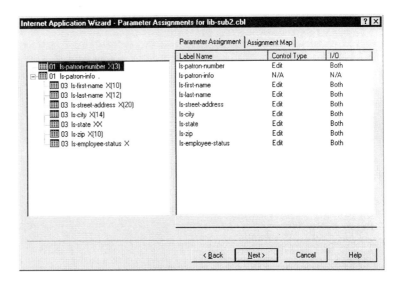

When Form Express generates your pages, for each data item you've designated, it generates the appropriate control and places a descriptive label to the left of the control. You will see this label, generated from the Label Name entry in Figure 6-15, as a Text (*Aa*) control. You can see in Figure 6-15 that Form Express uses the Linkage Section data names as the default values for Label Name entries.

10. Modify your Parameter Assignment screen to look like Figure 6-16. To speed up the process of changing the Control Type and I/O entries, click on the desired entry and type the first letter. For instance, highlight Edit for First name and press the letter L.

11. When your screen looks like Figure 6-16, click Next.

12. From the verification screen, click Finish. Next Express builds your project and returns you to the project screen.

You now have a complete application, so rebuild it and run. Your screens will be relatively crude, in need of some "dressing up." But that's the next step.

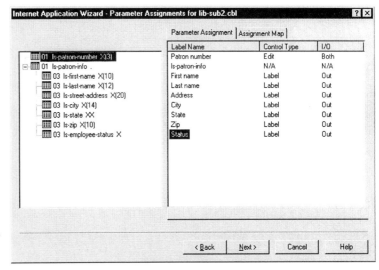

Figure 6-16.
Completed parameter
assignments.

Modifying the HTML Pages

The Input Page

Open your input page and your screen will look something like Figure 6-17. Characteristic of the way in which the original release of Version 3.0 generates forms, this one includes three primary spans. Referring to the control tree you see:

- The FORMHEADER span
- Unlabelled span containing the Input Text control. This is the body of the form; it contains all the controls that you select from your wizard screen (Figure 6-16).
- Unlabelled span containing the Submit button.

You will find it relatively easy to modify this form so that it corresponds to your original patron inquiry screen (refer to Figure 3-14 in Chapter 3).

1. Select the body span as shown in Figure 6-18.
2. Grab the lower left selection handle and pull the bottom span border down to provide room for your heading.
3. Select the I_Patron span (it is a Text control) and change the caption from Patron number to Enter your patron number. Note that you could have included this as the Label Name entry in the parameter assignments of Figure 6-16. However, as this parameter is designated for both the input and output forms, you would need to make this modification in one form or the other.
4. Lasso the two controls, this text span and the Input Text control, and move them downward in the form to allow space for the heading line.
5. Place a Text control for the heading. Type the heading line **Library Inquiry System** and increase the font size.
6. Save the form and close the form's window.

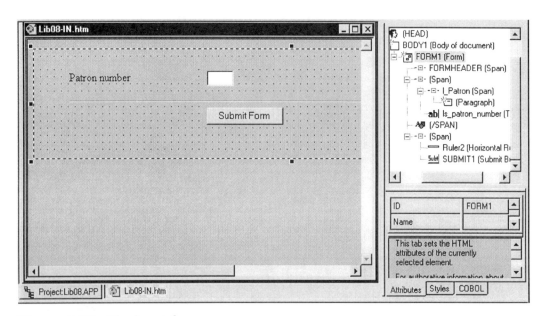

Figure 6-17. The input form.

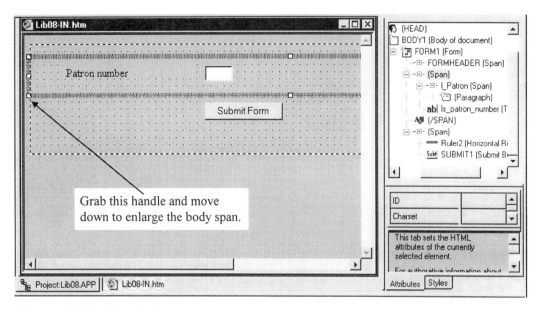

Figure 6-18. The body span.

The Output Form

The output page of Figure 6-19 provides you the basic controls from which you can work to produce a reasonable appearing browser display. For instance, look at the modified version in Figure 6-20(a); it results in the browser display of Figure 6-20(b). You can look at this final version of the page stored as Lib08-OUT in Proj0603. (Note that in Figure 6-19 you don't see the employee status control because it is off the screen to the right.) Following is the sequence of steps to produce the form of Figure 6-20(a) from Figure 6-19.

1. You may need to change the grid size from 10 pixels to 5 pixels to simplify positioning of the controls. Make this change by clicking the grid ▦ icon from the Form Designer tool bar and entering new values.

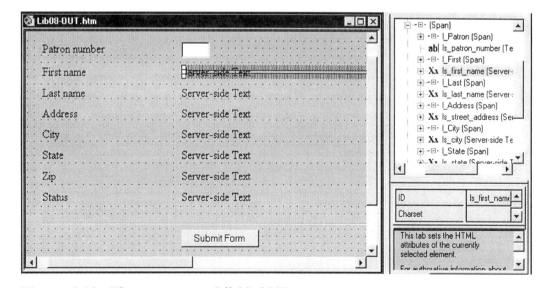

Figure 6-19. The output page Lib08-OUT.

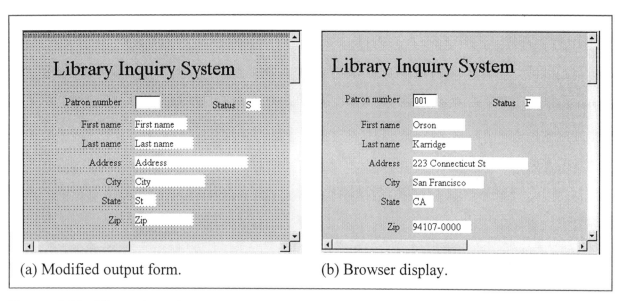

(a) Modified output form.   (b) Browser display.

Figure 6-20. The end result.

2. Expand the size of the body span to accommodate the heading.
3. Insert the heading.
4. For each of the Text controls (containing the descriptions), do the following.
    *   Shorten the span—the automatically generated span probably is longer than needed.
    *   Select the text and click on the right-justify icon of the format toolbar. The alignment of these controls should be as shown in Figure 6-20(a).
5. Set the ReadOnly attribute of the Input Text control (the patron number) to True as this control is intended for display only.
6. Delete the Submit button.
7. For each of the Server-Side Text controls do the following—in each case refer to the example in Figure 6-20(a).
    *   Change the inserted descriptive field (Server-side Text) to something that better describes the field. Note that this is solely for screen documentation.
    *   Shorten each to a size that corresponds roughly to the data that will be displayed.
    *   Set the Background-Color style property to white (or any distinctive color that appeals to you).
8. Save this form then close the form window.

You can now proceed to rebuild and run the project. When I completed these modifications and then ran the application, I experienced wrapping of descriptive lines containing two words. For instance, the words **First name** were positioned on two lines. The only way I was able to avoid this was to move each of the offending Text controls, save the form, move them back, and save the form again. Presumably, this will be corrected by updates available from Web Sync.

The CGI

You should observe the following pertaining to this applications relevant CGI's code shown in Figure 6-21.

- External form data items are defined in the same way as in preceding examples—see lines 37-56.
- The FormFields record contains only the Submit button (lines 96 and 97).
- All other data items created from this form are imported directly from the subprogram via a Net Express created copy file (Lib08.cpl in this example)—see lines 106-115.
- Actions of the Input Conversion Section and the lib08-out-cvt Section are identical to their counterparts of previous applications you've studied: move work-item values to and from corresponding external-form items.
- Net Express has generated an appropriate call statement to access the subprogram (lines 150-155).

```
  1 *>**********************************************
  2 identification division.
  3 *>**********************************************
  4     program-id. "Lib08".

 24 *>**********************************************
 25 data division.
 26 *>**********************************************
 27 file section.
 28 working-storage section.

 36     copy "Lib08.cpf".
 37     01 HTMLForm is external-form.
 38         03 f-ls-employee-status   pic x(1)
 39             identified by "ls_employee_status".
 40         03 f-ls-patron-number     pic x(3)
 41             identified by "ls_patron_number".
 42         03 f-ls-city              pic x(14)
 43             identified by "ls_city".
 44         03 f-ls-last-name         pic x(12)
 45             identified by "ls_last_name".
 46         03 f-ssubmit              pic x(60)
 47             identified by "ssubmit".
 48         03 f-ls-street-address    pic x(20)
 49             identified by "ls_street_address".
 50         03 f-ls-zip               pic x(10)
 51             identified by "ls_zip".
 52         03 f-ls-first-name        pic x(10)
 53             identified by "ls_first_name".
 54         03 f-ls-state             pic x(2)
 55             identified by "ls_state".
 56         03 filler                 pic x.

 95     copy "Lib08.cpy".
 96     01 FormFields.
 97        03 ssubmit                 pic X(60).

106     copy "Lib08.cpl".
107     01 ls-patron-number     PIC X(3).
108     01 ls-patron-info.
109        03  ls-first-name     PIC X(10).
110        03  ls-last-name      PIC X(12).
111        03  ls-street-address PIC X(20).
112        03  ls-city           PIC X(14).
113        03  ls-state          PIC XX.
114        03  ls-zip            PIC X(10).
```

```
115        03  ls-employee-status  PIC X.
124 *>**********************************************
125 Procedure Division.
126 *>**********************************************

146 process-business-logic section.
147
148 *> Add pre-call application business logic here
149
150     CALL "lib-sub2" USING
151         ls-patron-number
152         ls-patron-info
153     ON EXCEPTION
154         PERFORM handle-call-exception
155     END-CALL
156
157 *> Add post-call application business logic here
158
159     perform lib08-out-cvt
160         *> lib08-out
161     perform lib08-out-out
162         *> lib08-out
163     exit.

223 Input-Conversion Section.

236     move f-ls-patron-number to ls-patron-number

264 lib08-out-cvt Section.
265     *> lib08-out
266     move ls-employee-status
268                 to f-ls-employee-status
270     move ls-patron-number to f-ls-patron-number
272     move ls-city to f-ls-city
274     move ls-last-name to f-ls-last-name
276     move ls-street-address to f-ls-street-address
278     move ls-zip to f-ls-zip
280     move ls-first-name to f-ls-first-name
282     move ls-state to f-ls-state
283 exit.
```

Figure 6-21. Form Express-generated CGI.

Using Disabled Edit to Display Data

As you learned in an earlier chapter, you can use the Input Text control to display output. However, unless a subsequent CGI includes capabilities for acting upon any change a user makes, you should set the ReadOnly attribute to True. Form Express provides you a similar capability. For instance, Figure 6-22 is the browser display generated by an unmodified Form Express created output form. (You can inspect this application: Lib09 stored in Proj0604.) Notice that they displayed data is gray-out, the conventional Windows indication that you cannot change the values. In fact, you cannot even position the cursor within these control areas.

For an idea of how to do this, look at the Control Type entries of Figures 6-15 and 6-16. From the corresponding narrative, recall that the Control Type entry Disabled Edit produces an Input Text control in which editing of the data is disabled. Referring to this application's output form shown in Figure 6-23 you see that Form Express accomplishes this by setting the Disabled attribute to True, an action you can do yourself with any Input Text control.

Placing Form Express in its Proper Context

The basic objective of Form Express is to simplify your task of bringing legacy Cobol applications to the Web. However, don't get carried away and view it as a panacea that will provide immediate Web-ready capabilities to legacy applications. You've seen that that the generated Web forms are rudimentary; they will usually require some effort to make them truly application ready. However, in some situa-

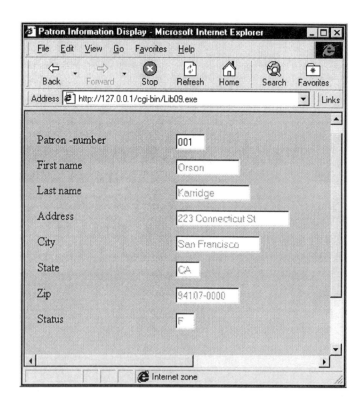

Figure 6-22.
A browser display using Input Text controls.

tions, Form Express can save you considerable effort; you will see this in examples of later chapters. Furthermore, as this component of Net Express matures, you will likely see it becoming increasingly useful. Remember, use it as you would any other tool: where it is appropriate.

Data Validation

Built-In JavaScript Data Validation Functions

As Cobol programmers, we are all familiar with the need for validation of input data—remember the well worn term GIGO: garbage-in garbage-out. In fact, data validation is such a fundamental task, that the new Cobol standard includes a Validate statement with powerful features for automatic validation of data. Data coming into a system from the Web is no different from data from any other source when it comes to the need for validation. With Web applications, there are two possibilities for validation. On one hand, all data from an input form can be validated by conventional validation code you insert into the CGI. The down side of this approach is that input is sent to the CGI, data is checked for validity, and a page is returned to the user identifying the error and requesting reentry. This is a poor scenario as Internet traffic is involved in both directions. A better approach is to include data-checking capabilities within the page itself so that all checking can be done on the local machine by appropriate components of the HTML input page without resorting to Internet traffic. The key to this approach is **JavaScript**. Net Express 3.0 includes built-in JavaScript functions to perform the input validation actions listed in Figure

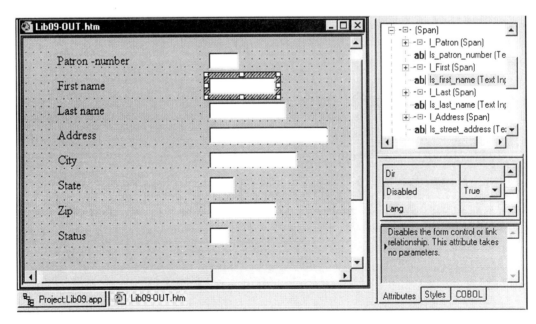

Figure 6-23. The Form Express generated output form.

6-24. (Note that WebSync updates may include other functions.) These functions are available for the following HTML controls.

- Input Text
- TextArea (described in Chapter 7)
- Hidden Input (described in Chapter 10)

Designating Data Validation

Proj0605
Verify

The folder Proj0605 contains the data verification example Verify.app. In its project window of Figure 6-25 you see the usual HTML and Cobol components. You also see several JavaScript functions (the file name extension is js). Each of these performs a validation function designated for controls of the input page for this application. You can click on any such entry and Net Express will display the JavaScript code.

Figure 6-26 is the input form Verify-IN of this application; its controls include the following validation functions.

First name	Required
Last name	Required
State	Valid state abbreviation

Type of Data	Validation Performed
American Express card number	Conforms to the format for an American Express card number
Credit card number	Conforms to all the credit card number formats (American Express, Mastercard and Visa)
e-mail address	Conforms to the format for an e-mail address
Mastercard card number	Conforms to the format for a Mastercard card number
Number	Is a whole number with no sign
Number (decimal)	Is a number containing a decimal point; may be signed
Number (signed positive)	Is a positive whole number
Number (signed)	Is a whole number with an optional sign
Phone number - international	Conforms to the format for an international phone number
US phone number	Conforms to the format for a US phone number, that is, 10 digits. There may be a space after the third digit and after the sixth digit
US social security number	Conforms to the format for a US social security number, that is, 9 digits. There may be a space after the third digit and after the fifth digit
US state code	Is one of the valid two-letter abbreviations for a US state
US zip code	Conforms to the format for a US zip code, that is, 5 or 9 digits
Visa card number	Conforms to the format for a Visa card number

Figure 6-24. Validation functions.

Figure 6-25.
JavaScript functions listed
in the project screen.

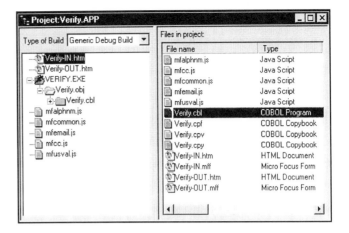

Zip	Valid zip code
Social security number	Required and valid SSN
Number of dependents	Positive integer
Additional withholding	Decimal number
Credit card number	Valid card number
Email adderss	Valid email address

You should run this application to get a feel for the form's response to an invalid entry. For instance, immediately click the submit button without making any en-

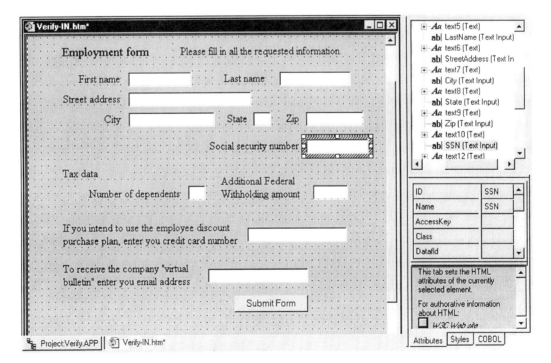

Figure 6-26. The input form Verify-IN.

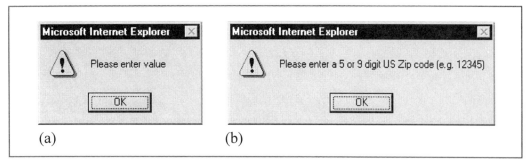

Figure 6-27. Validation messages.

tries. As the name fields are required, you will see a popup warning such as Figure 6-27(a). Notice the prompt entry of the status line (bottom of your screen). It indicates that the error relates to a required field. Click OK and the cursor will be positioned within the first-name field awaiting data entry. Next, enter anything into the two name fields. Move to the zip code field and type 123. Click the submit button and you will see the message of Figure 6-27(b). You may wish to experiment with other validated fields on this form.

To see how you assign validation to a control, open the input file Verify-IN.htm then proceed as follows.

1. Select the social security number field as shown in Figure 6-26.
2. Right-click on that control and you will see the popup menu shown here to the right.
3. Click Validation and you will see the window of Figure 6-28 describing the validation assignments for this field.
4. Click the expand button on the Validation box and you will see a list of validation functions corresponding to Figure 6-24. You can experiment with these if you so desire. Notice that the Yes radio button for the Required field is active for this control.
5. The prompt field is the message displayed when you make an invalid entry. You can leave the default or change it to any message you like. A check in the Status line prompt box causes the error prompt to be displayed on the browser's status line as well as within the warning boxes.

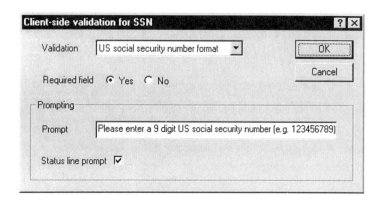

Figure 6-28. Validation assignment window.

6. Look at validation for either of the two name fields and you will see that they are designated Any value. This designation is necessary in order to set them as required fields.

7. Look at the *Additional withholding* amount field and you will see it designated as Numeric (decimal). This field will accept any entry with or without a decimal point. If you check the COBOLPicture property of this control, you will see that it is 999V99. Following are typical entries you might make and the way in which the CGI interprets the input.

12345	123.45
1.2	001.20
1.234	001.23
1234.5	Not detected by the form's JavaScript functions in the first release of Net Express. The CGI detects this as a data error and returns an error message to the browser. You can insert code to handle this—see the output-form-error-and-stop section of the CGI.

When you are finished experimenting with this application, close it. This example is not used in applications of the next chapter.

Summing Up

Project Summary

Proj0601 (Lib06) illustrates accessing data from the indexed file Patron by calling an existing file-accessing subprogram.

Proj0602 (Lib07) is a minor variation of Lib06—its CGI includes programmer-added code to manipulate data for better display.

Proj0603 (Lib08) uses Form Express which allows you to create an application by selecting fields from the linkage section of the application subprogram.

Proj0604 (Lib09) is a minor variation of Lib08—it shows you how to set Input Text controls so that the displayed data cannot be changed.

Proj0605 (Verify) includes as its main focus an input page containing a variety of JavaScript data verification examples.

General Summary

If you intend to include a subprogram in an application, create the project by designating Project from an existing application in the New Project screen. Net Express will automatically include the subprogram in the project-build screen.

You can create an application using input from a subprogram in either of two ways. One approach is to build the forms with Form Designer and insert code into the CGI as you have done with examples of preceding chapters.

The second approach is to use Form Express, a tool for automatically generating input and output forms and a limited amount of CGI code. In general, you will find that these forms require a certain amount of "dressing up."

Form Express allows you to designate each Linkage Section data item as either input, output, or input/output form elements. Available control types are Edit (Input Text), Check Box, Radio Button, Label (Server-Side Text), Select, Hidden, Password, and Disabled Edit (Input Text with the Disable attribute set to True).

Net Express includes versatile JavaScript functions for validating input from three HTML controls: Text Input, TextArea, and Hidden Input. Figure 6-24 is a summary list of validation controls furnished with the first release of 3.0. The validation facility also provides you the capability to designate the an entry is required for a given field.

Coming Up

Chapter 7 expands on the topics you've learned in this chapter. The primary focus is on displaying repeating data derived from a subprogram that returns a Cobol table.

Assignments

6-1

Create an application "from scratch" using the subprogram Cus-sub2.cbl. This subprogram accesses data from the indexed file Customer.di. The input specifications and data listing are shown on page 341. The Cus-sub2.cbl program listing is on page 344. Use pages 139-146 and 157-161 as a guide.

Input	Customer ID	Validate as an integer
	Social Security Number	Validate as SSN
	Credit Card Number	Validate as credit card number. You may use your own number or the number 5410654131211614 for a test.
Output	Customer ID	
	Customer name (first and last name as a single string)	
	Social Security Number	
	Credit Card Number	
	Street address	
	City, State and Zip as a single string	
	Customer rating as **Excellent** (if an 'A'), **Limited** (if a 'B'), or **Advance Pay** (if a 'C')	
	Credit Limit	
	Credit Balance	

6-2

Generate an application using Form Express from the subprogram Cus-sub2.cbl (it accesses data from the indexed file Cus.di). You will find listings of the subprogram and the data file in the Appendix.

Your input and output pages should include the following.

Input	Customer ID
Output	Customer ID
	Customer first name
	Customer last name
	Street address
	City
	State
	Zip
	Customer credit rating

Make the following modifications to the form generated by Form Express.

- Rearrange the controls to give a balanced display such as that of Figure 6-6.
- For the file's credit rating values A, B, and C substitute the following.

A	Excellent
B	Limited
C	Advance pay

To do this, you will need to delete the existing spanned credit rating controls and create new label and server side controls.

Processing Cobol Tables

Chapter Contents

Multiple-File Data Access 166
   A Conventional Cobol Screen Display 166
   The Data Files 166
   The Subprogram Lib-sub3 167
Textarea Control Display 167
   Displaying a List of Books 167
   The Output Page—Lib11-OUT 170
   The CGI Program 171
Using the Table Control 172
   About the Lib11 Project 172
   Creating the HTML Table—Lib10-OUT 173
   CGI Code 177
Managing Repeating Data—Lib12 178
   Handling Subscripted Cobol Data Items 178
   Features of the Lib12 CGI 178
   The Output Page Lib12-OUT 182
Using Form Express to Generate Table Output 184
   Creating the Application 184
   The End Result 184
Summing Up 187
   Project Summary 187
   General Summary 187
Coming Up 188
Assignment 188

Chapter

7

Chapter Introduction

Your Chapter 1 introduction to the Micro Focus IDE featured a library inquiry system example program designed around access to data in two indexed files. You typed a patron number and the program responded with a screen displaying the patron data and a list of books checked out by the patron. The subprogram used in that example forms the basis for multi-line display examples of this chapter. From the chapter you will learn about the following.

- Using the multi-line Textarea control with a scroll bar feature.
- Displaying Cobol table data in HTML Table controls
- A COBOLTableType property that allows you to designate an HTML table row as a variable-row unit thereby providing the programmer complete control over the number of table rows displayed by the browser.
- Automatic generation of variable-row forms with Form Express.

Multiple-File Data Access

A Conventional Cobol Screen Display

The examples of Chapter 6 use the subprogram Lib-sub2 to access data from the patron file and display the patron name and address data. The conventional Cobol example of Chapter 1 (used to illustrate the IDE) is more extensive in that it displays both the name/address information for a patron and the library books checked out by that patron. When you ran the application in Chapter 1, you entered a library patron number and received a screen display similar to that of Figure 7-1. This displayed data is derived from two files: a patron file and a book file. As these files are basic to some of the techniques of this chapter, let's examine each.

The Data Files

The indexed patron file contains one record for each library patron; record contents include the following.

- Patron identification number—the key field.
- Patron name.
- Address.
- Other data not used in this chapter's examples.

The indexed book file contains one record for each book in the library; record contents include the following.

- Book identification code—the key field.
- Title.
- Author.
- Data to determine due date.
- Patron identification number of person to whom book is checked out—an alternate key field.
- Other data not used in this chapter's examples.

```
Sandy Beech
1247 Main Street
Woodside  CA  94062-0000

   Book-ID Title                   Author
     0005    General Economics       Wheels, Helen
     0019    C                       Leets, Ethyl
     0024    Unix Hater's Reference   O'Shea, Rick
```

Figure 7-1.
Library patron
screen display.

The Subprogram Lib-sub3

The subprogram of Figure 7-2 (on the next page) contains typical file accessing code that you might find in any basic file-processing program. Let's look at some of its features.

- It contains two file/record definitions, one for the patron file (lines 26-30 and lines 43-59) and the other for the book file (lines 32-38 and 62-72).
- The parameter list (lines 107-110) includes the following:

    Input
        Patron number (ls-in-patron-number)
    Output
        Patron name and address (ls-patron-info)
        Number of books checked out by patron (ls-book-counter)
        List of books checked out by patron (the table ls-book-info-array)

- A date computation is performed to obtain the book due date—refer to the inline comments (lines 145-149)
- The first and last name fields are concatenated into a single data item (lines 195-198) for return to the calling program. The same is done for the city-state-zip fields (lines 201-206).
- If the patron number is not found in the file, ls-patron-info is set to low-values at line 164 (as in previous versions of this subprogram series).
- The data item ls-book-counter is set to 0 at line 169. If the patron has no books checked out, further processing within the Read statement is aborted by the Continue at line 173. The value 0 is then returned to the calling program for this parameter.

Notice that in subprogram, you are dealing with a Cobol table (ls-book-info-array) in which each entry contains information for one book checked out by the patron. As patrons are allowed to check out up to 10 books, the table is dimensioned to 10 (line 101).

Textarea Control Display

Displaying a List of Books

One way to display a list of data items is with a box that includes a scroll bar as shown in Figure 7-3. In this example you see five books displayed. You can inspect others by moving the scroll bar down, a standard Windows technique.

This screen was generated from the project Lib10 stored in the folder Proj0701. The input and output pages, Lib10-IN and Lib10-OUT, were created from the existing corresponding pages of Lib07. Let's look at the additions made to the output page for this example. (Note that the input page is unchanged from Lib07.)

Proj0701
Lib10

```
 1  $set sourceformat "free"
    *>*****************************************
 2  *> Library Application
 3  *> W. Price  9/13/97                    LIB-SUB3.CBL
 4  *> The subprogram accesses data from the following
 5  *> two data files.
 6  *>   PATRON.DI: Indexed by Patron Number; contains
 7  *>     patron name and address data.
 8  *>   BOOK.DI: Indexed by Book ID; contains book
 9  *>     title and other book information. If book is
10  *>     checked out, also includes Patron Number and
11  *>     due date. Patron number is secondary key.
12  *> The input parameter is the patron number
13  *> Output parameters are:
14  *>   Patron name and address data
15  *>   Count of number of books checked out
16  *>   Array containing book information
17  *>*****************************************
18
19  Identification Division.
20    Program-id. Library-Subprogram.
21
22    Environment Division.
23
24    Input-Output Section.
25    File-Control.
26      Select Patron-File assign to disk
27          "c:\Elements-CWP\NE-data\patron.di"
28          organization is indexed
29          access is random
30          record key is pr-patron-number.
31
32      Select Book-File assign to disk
33          "c:\Elements-CWP\NE-data\book.di"
34          organization is indexed
35          access is dynamic
36          record key is br-book-id
37          alternate key is br-patron-number
38            with duplicates.
39
40  Data Division.
41    File Section.
42    FD  Patron-File.
43      01  patron-record.
44          10  pr-patron-number     pic x(03).
45          10  pr-first-name        pic X(10).
46          10  pr-last-key redefines
47              pr-first-name        pic 9(03).
48          10  pr-last-name         pic X(12).
49          10  pr-street-address    pic X(20).
50          10  pr-city              pic X(14).
51          10  pr-state             pic X(02).
52          10  pr-zip               pic X(10).
53          10  pr-privilege-status  pic X(01).
54          10  pr-employee-status   pic X(01).
55          10  pr-book-right        pic X(01).
56          10  pr-periodical-right  pic X(01).
57          10  pr-video-right       pic X(01).
58          10  pr-books-out         pic 9(02).
59          10                       pic X(18).
60
61    FD  Book-File.
62      01  book-record.
63          10  br-book-id           pic x(04).
64          10  br-book-title        pic X(25).
65          10  br-last-key redefines
66              br-book-title        pic 9(04).
67          10  br-book-author       pic X(13).
68          10  br-book-publisher    pic X(11).
69          10  br-publication-year  pic X(04).
70          10  br-patron-number     pic X(03).
71          10  br-remaining-days    pic 9(02).
72          10                       pic X(20).
73
74    Working-Storage Section.
75      01  program-switches.
76          10  end-of-file-sw   pic X(01).
77              88  end-of-file      value "Y".
78              88  not-end-of-file  value "N".
79      01  book-pointer             pic 9(02).
80
81      01  todays-date-info.
82          05  todays-date          pic 9(08).
83          05                       pic X(13).
84      01  due-date                 pic 9(08).
85      01  due-day-count            pic 9(08).
86      01  ws-due-date.
87          05  ws-month             pic Z9.
88          05                       pic X(01) value "/".
89          05  ws-day               pic X(02).
90          05                       pic X(01) value "/".
91          05  ws-year              pic X(04).
92
93  Linkage Section.
94      01  ls-in-patron-number      pic X(03).
95      01  ls-patron-info.
96          05  ls-patron-name       pic X(23).
97          05  ls-street-address    pic X(20).
98          05  ls-city-state-zip    pic X(30).
99      01  ls-book-counter          pic 9(02).
100     01  ls-book-info-array.
101         05  ls-book-info         occurs 10 times.
102             10  ls-book-id     pic X(04).
103             10  ls-book-title  pic X(25).
104             10  ls-book-author pic X(13).
105             10  ls-due-date    pic X(10).
106
107 Procedure Division Using ls-in-patron-number
108                          ls-patron-info
109                          ls-book-counter
110                          ls-book-info-array.
111
112 000-Main-module.
113     Perform 100-Open-Files
114     Perform 200-process-user-request
115     Perform 300-close-files
116     Exit program
117     .
118 100-Open-Files.
119     Open Input Patron-File
120               Book-File
121     .
122
123 200-process-user-request.
124     Move spaces to ls-book-info-array
125     Move spaces to ls-patron-info
126     Move 0 to ls-book-counter
127     Move ls-in-patron-number to pr-patron-number
128     Perform 800-read-patron-record
129     If ls-patron-info NOT = low-value
130         Perform 850-string-patron-data
131         Perform 820-read-book-records
132     End-if
133     .
134
135 300-Close-files.
136     Close Patron-File
137           Book-File
138     .
139 400-set-up-book-info-line.
140     Move br-book-id to ls-book-id(ls-book-counter)
141     Move br-book-title
142             to ls-book-title(ls-book-counter)
143     Move br-book-author
144             to ls-book-author(ls-book-counter)
145     *> The input record includes due date as the
146     *> number of days from the date the program is
147     *> run. I do the following so that displayed
148     *> output looks current. Otherwise, the data
149     *> file would soon appear outdated.
150     Move Function current-date to todays-date-info
151     Compute due-day-count =
152         function integer-of-date (todays-date)
153                 + br-remaining-days
154     Compute due-date =
155         function date-of-integer (due-day-count)
```

Figure 7-2. The Lib-sub3 subprogram (continued next page).

```
156        Move due-date(1:4) to ws-year           193    850-string-patron-data.
157        Move due-date(5:2) to ws-month          194        Move spaces to ls-patron-name
158        Move due-date(7:2)   to ws-day          195        String pr-first-name delimited by "  "
159        Move ws-due-date to ls-due-date (ls-book-counter)  196                "  "
160     .                                          197            pr-last-name
161    800-read-patron-record.                     198            into ls-patron-name
162        Read Patron-File                        199        Move pr-street-address to ls-street-address
163        Invalid key                             200        Move spaces to ls-city-state-zip
164            Move low-values to ls-patron-info   201        String  pr-city delimited by "   "
165        End-read                                202                "  "
166     .                                          203            pr-state
167                                                204                "  "
168    820-read-book-records.                      205            pr-zip
169        Move 0 to ls-book-counter               206            into ls-city-state-zip
170        Move ls-in-patron-number to br-patron-number  207     .
171        Read Book-File key is br-patron-number
172         invalid key
173            Continue
174         not invalid key
175            Add 1 to ls-book-counter
176            Perform 400-set-up-book-info-line
177            Set not-end-of-file to true
178            Perform until end-of-file
179               Read Book-File next
180                 at end
181                    Set end-of-file to true
182                 not at end
183                    If ls-in-patron-number = br-patron-number
184                       Add 1 to ls-book-counter
185                       Perform 400-set-up-book-info-line
186                    Else
187                       Set end-of-file to true
188                    End-If *>ls-in-patron-number ...
189               End-Read *>Book-File next
190            End-Perform *>until end-of-file
191        End-Read *>Book-File
192     .
```

Figure 7-2. The Lib-sub3 subprogram (continued).

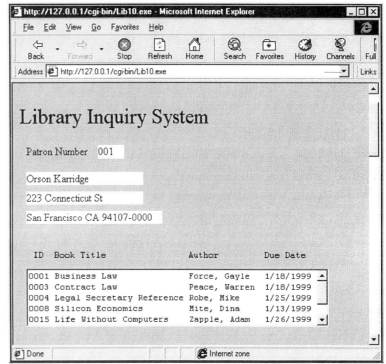

Figure 7-3.
Displaying data in a
scrolling text area.

The Output Page—Lib10-OUT

In Figure 7-4 you see the familiar patron information output page to which a Textarea control has been added. (Refer to Lib10-OUT of the project.) You insert this control in the usual way: highlight the Textarea icon 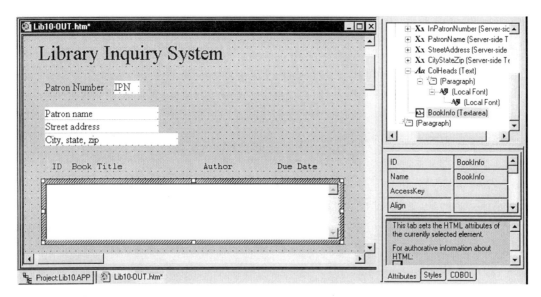 of the Net Express control tool bar then click at the appropriate position in the Form Designer screen. Notice that the entire area is identified by a single Name entry, BookInfo in this example. There is nothing to distinguish one line of the area from another. Following are critical properties of this control.

- COBOLPicture. The value X(560) is selected to hold the entire list of books checked out to a patron. (The need for 560 is described in the next section's CGI discussion.)
- Columns. This property, found under the Attributes tab, is set to the value 56, corresponding to the width of the line to be displayed, that is, the number of columns occupied by one book. You must count carefully in selecting this number or your output might wrap at the wrong place.
- Rows. This property, also found under the Attributes tab, is set to the value 5; it determines the number of rows you want displayed in the text area.

The column heading line above the text box was created by inserting a Text control then changing the font type and size. That is, the default font is proportional spacing (Times); the display from the Textarea is fixed pitch (Courier). The sequence is:

1. Insert the Text control.
2. Change the font style from Times to Courier. You can do this from the format toolbar or by changing the Font-Family entry under the Styles tab.
3. The default font size is 12 point; the output display from the Textarea is 10 point. Change the font size of this text display either by clicking the reduce-size icon on the font toolbar or by changing the Font-Size entry under the Styles tab.

Figure 7-4. The output form with a Textarea Control.

4. Expand the control's width to correspond to the Textarea's width.

The CGI Program

The creativity of this project lies in the CGI code shown in Figure 7-5. In the Data Division code, notice the following.

- BookInfo (line 63) is name of the Textarea control of the output form; remember, its length was designated 560.
- The subprogram call parameters are defined in lines 71-82; these are essentially duplicates of the subprogram's Linkage Section (see lines 94-105 of Figure 7-2).
- book-pointer (line 84) is required in the Procedure Division as a subscript in processing the input book information array book-info.

Notice the following in the process-business-logic section of the Procedure Division.

- No record for the requested patron returns low-values for patron-info. This case is handled by the Move at line 121. Otherwise name and address data items are moved to the form fields. (This sequence is the same as that used in preceding examples.)

```
  1 IDENTIFICATION DIVISION.
  2     program-id. "Lib10".

 10 DATA DIVISION.
 11
 12 working-storage section.

 16     copy "Lib10.cpf".
 17     01 HTMLForm is external-form.
 18        03 f-BookInfo          pic x(560)
 19           identified by "BookInfo".

 61     copy "Lib10.cpy".
 62     01 FormFields.
 63        03 BookInfo            pic x(560).
 64        03 InPatronNumber      pic X(60).
 65        03 ssubmit             pic x(64).
 66        03 StreetAddress       pic x(20).
 67        03 CityStateZip        pic x(29).
 68        03 PatronName          pic x(23).
 69
 70 *> Enter additional working-storage items here
 71 01   in-patron-number         pic X(03).
 72 01   patron-info.
 73      05   patron-name         pic X(23).
 74      05   street-address      pic X(20).
 75      05   city-state-zip      pic X(30).
 76 01   book-counter             pic 9(02).
 77 01   book-info-array.
 78      05   book-info      occurs 10 times.
 79         10  bi-book-id        pic X(04).
 80         10  bi-book-title     pic X(25).
 81         10  bi-book-author    pic X(13).
 82         10  bi-due-date       pic X(10).
 83
 84 01   book-pointer             pic 9(02).
 85

 86 PROCEDURE DIVISION.

114 process-business-logic section.
115    *> Add application business logic here.
116    Call "lib-sub3" Using InPatronNumber
117                         patron-info
118                         book-counter
119                         book-info-array
120    If patron-info = low-values
121       Move "No record for patron" to PatronName
122    Else
123       Move patron-name to PatronName
124       Move street-address to StreetAddress
125       Move city-state-zip to CityStateZip
126       If book-counter = 0
127          Move "This patron has no books checked out"
128              to BookInfo
129       Else
130          *> Build each of the 10 output lines
131          Move X"FF" to BookInfo
132          Perform with test after
133              varying book-pointer from 1 by 1
134              Until book-pointer = book-counter
135          String BookInfo delimited by X"FF"
136              bi-book-id (book-pointer) " "
137              bi-book-title (book-pointer) " "
138              bi-book-author (book-pointer) " "
139              bi-due-date (book-pointer) " " X"FF"
140              delimited by size
141              into BookInfo
142          End-Perform *>varying book-counter
143          Inspect BookInfo replacing all X"FF" by " "
144       End-If *>book-counter = 0
145    End-If *>patron-info = low-values
146    exit.
```

Figure 7-5. Pertinent code from Lib10.cbl.

- If the returned book-counter value is 0, the patron has no books checked out so an appropriate message is moved to BookInfo (lines 127 and 128). Otherwise, book data is processed for output.

Although the loop of lines 132-142 might at first look foreboding, it is not nearly as complicated as it appears. The String statement builds each output line for the Text Area display as if the line were defined as in Figure 7-6. Be aware that the space in the last position of this string, inserted by line 139 (Figure 7-5), is necessary for browser separation of book groups. That is, without the space, the browser can treat the date of one book group and the book number of the next book group as a single field thereby causing a line break and forcing the two items to the next line in the Textarea.

The purpose of the character X"FF" is to serve as a delimiter in the repetitive action of concatenating to BookInfo. When the loop is completed, the last book line is followed by this character, so it is replaced with a space at line 143.

You can now see the length requirements rationale of the Text Area properties. Sum the pic values in Figure 7-6 (the equivalent of the string actions in Figure 7-5) and you'll see that they total 56, the Columns entry used in this Textarea. As there can be up to 10 books, 56 time 10 yields 560, the value used for theTextarea's COBOLPicture.

Note that you can use the Multi-line Text Area for input, but your CGI program will need to include code that separates individual lines because the field is returned as a single string.

Using the Table Control

About the Lib11 Project

Like the preceding example, the next example (stored as Lib11.app in Proj0702) accepts a patron number and displays patron and book information. Instead of the Textarea tool for the Cobol table output, this example uses Server-Side Text controls in conjunction with an HTML table, as you can see by inspecting the sample output screen of Figure 7-7.

The objective of this example is twofold. First, it will introduce a rudimentary technique for handling Cobol tables—a method that you will find useful for some types of applications. Second, it will give you some more experience in using HTML

```
01  book-line.
    10  bi-book-id        pic X(04).
    10                    pic X(01) value space.
    10  bi-book-title      pic X(25).
    10                    pic X(01) value space.
    10  bi-book-author     pic X(13).
    10                    pic X(01) value space.
    10  bi-due-date        pic X(10).
    10                    pic X(01) value space.
```

Figure 7-6.
Equivalent line definition.

Figure 7-7.
Sample output screen
from Lib11-OUT.

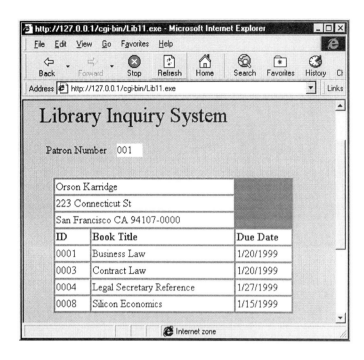

tables. In the interest of reducing the amount of repetitive work you must do in creating this output form, the display is limited to four books (even though a patron can check out up to ten).

Creating the HTML Table—Lib11-OUT

If you wish to recreate this entire project (Lib11) you can do so by generating the input page directly from Lib10-IN. Lib10-OUT is a good starting point for the output page although most of the display fields will require replacement. If you take this approach, delete all but the heading line and the line containing the patron number. Your objective is to create a form that looks like Figure 7-8.

1. From the Page Elements tab, insert a Table into the form by highlighting the table icon ▦ then clicking in the appropriate position of the form.
2. Grab one of the end selection handles and stretch the table to a reasonable width.
3. Select any one of the table cells, right click, and from the ensuing popup menu, insert 6 rows (giving a total of eight).
4. From each of the first three rows, delete two cells. (For this, you will need to delete selected cells one at a time.)
5. Set the Colspan attribute (the column span) to 2 for each of the remaining cells in the first three rows. When you are finished, your table should look like Figure 7-9.

Be aware that with the first release of Net Express 3.0 maintaining desired column widths and inserting controls into tables can be tricky (and frustrating). So if you are stepping through this exercise, be careful to perform the steps exactly as described here. If a given action results in something undesirable, click the undo. Presumably, WebSync updates will simplify working with tables.

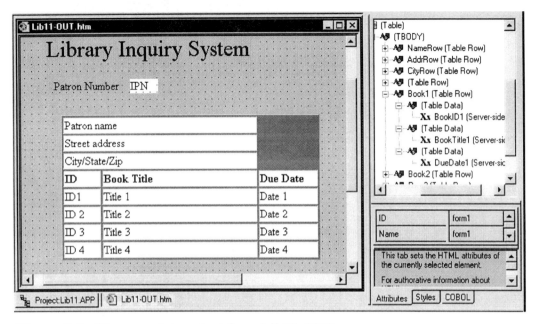

Figure 7-8. The complete output form Lib11-OUT.

6. Select the cell at row 4, column 1. Click the Style tab, scroll down to the Width property and set it to 50px (50 pixels). For an idea of this width, remember that the Form Designer grid points are 10 pixels apart. Repeat this for the first cell in the next four rows.
7. Repeat Step 6 for the five cells in the second column—use a width of 220px.
8. Select the entire table, grab the right selection handle, and resize to obtain a table that has the proportions of Figure 7-8's form.

You may optionally change colors for better contrast table elements. To this end, you will change the background color of each cell and the background color of the table itself.

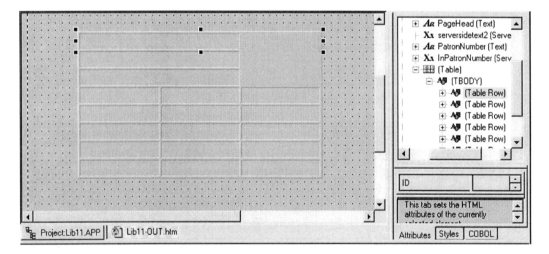

Figure 7-9. The reconfigured table.

9. Select a row by clicking the Table Row entry in the control tree. In Figure 7-9, the first row is selected.

10. Click the Styles tab, click the Background-Color property and obtain the color palette. Change the color to something that appeals to you. Lib11-OUT uses white for the cell color.

11. Repeat Step 10 for each of the other table rows.

12. Select the table (click on Table in the control tree).

13. Assign a background color; Lib11-OUT uses a dark gray. When finished, your table should look like Figure 7-10. Next you must insert Sever-Side Text controls into appropriate cells.

14. At this point, you've put a lot of work into the form. Save it so that if you really mess up as you proceed, you have something to fall back on.

15. Select the row 1 cell. Click the Server-Side Text icon (**Xx**) in the control bar. This inserts the control into the selected cell. Remember, this is the only way you can insert controls into cells of a table.

16. Change the control's ID attribute to PatronName.

17. Click the COBOL tab and change the COBOLPicture value to x(23).

18. Highlight the description **Server-side Text** (within the cell itself) and overtype it with **Patron name**. This is for documentation only. Do not delete the description before typing or the control itself is removed (possibly changed with WebSync updates). As you are working with Server-Side Text controls within table cells, always keep an eye on the control tree to be certain you (1) have the proper element selected as you make changes, and (2) don't accidentally delete the control.

19. In the control tree window, right-click the Table Row entry for the cell you're working on. From the resulting popup menu, click Set ID. Then type the word **NameRow**—see Figure 7-11. This is for control-tree documentation only.

20. Repeat Steps 15-19 for row 2 using the following:

   ID   StreetAddress
   COBOLPicture   x(20)
   Type **Street address** for the cell descriptive entry
   Change the TableRow name to AddrRow.

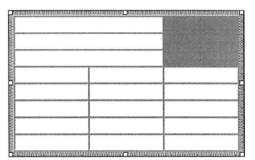

Figure 7-10. Using color for emphasis.

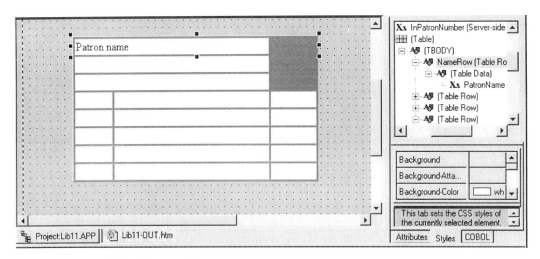

Figure 7-11. Selecting a table row.

21. Repeat Steps 15-19 for row 3 using the following:
    ID   CityStateZip
    COBOLPicture   x(30)
    Type **City/State/Zip** for the cell descriptive entry
    Change the TableRow name to CityRow.

22. Type the column headings in the cells of row 4—see Figure 7-8. Do this by selecting each cell and typing the desired heading. (Note that you need not place a Text control in the cell to do this.) These headings will stand out if you change them to boldface.

23. To be safe, save the form again.

24. In the control tree window, right-click the Table Row entry for row 5 (the first book-information row). Change the its ID to Book1.

25. Select the cell at row 5, column 1 and do the following.
    • Insert a Server-Side Text control
    • Change the description within the cell to ID1 (documentation).
    • Change the control's ID to BookID1.
    • Change the COBOLPicture to x(4).

26. Repeat Step 25 for the remaining three cells in column 1. Use BookID2, BookID3, and BookID4 for the ID entries; see Figure 7-8 for the cell descriptive entries.

27. Save the form.

28. Repeat Steps 24-26 for the four cells of column 2 using:
    COBOLPicture   x(25)
    ID entries   BookTitle1, BookTitle2, BookTitle3, and BookTitle4.
    See Figure 7-8 for the documentation cell descriptions.

29. Save the form.

30. Repeat Steps 24-26 for the four cells of column 3 using:
    COBOLPicture   x(10)
    ID entries   DueDate1, DueDate2, DueDate3, and DueDate4.
    See Figure 7-8 for the documentation cell descriptions.

31. Save the form.

```
  1   IDENTIFICATION DIVISION.              107        03 StreetAddress         pic x(20).
  2      program-id. "Lib11".               108        03 CityStateZip          pic x(30).
                                            109        03 DueDate2              pic x(10).
 10   DATA DIVISION.                        110        03 BookID4               pic x(4).
 11   working-storage section.             111        03 PatronName            pic x(20).
 12                                         112
 13      *> WARNING: Do not remove this copy statement   113   *> Enter additional working-storage items here
 14      *> or modify the contents of the copy file.     114   01  in-patron-number         pic X(03).
 15      copy "Lib11.cpf".                  115   01  patron-info.
 16      01 HTMLForm is external-form.      116        05  patron-name           pic X(23).
 17         03 f-BookTitle2         pic x(25)   117        05  street-address        pic X(20).
 18            identified by "BookTitle2".      118        05  city-state-zip        pic X(30).
 19         03 f-DueDate3           pic x(10)   119   01  book-counter             pic 9(02).
 20            identified by "DueDate3".        120   01  book-info-array.
 21         03 f-BookTitle3         pic x(25)   121        05  book-info               occurs 10 times.
 22            identified by "BookTitle3".      122             10  bi-book-id         pic X(04).
 23         03 f-BookID1            pic x(4)    123             10  bi-book-title      pic X(25).
 24            identified by "BookID1".         124             10  bi-book-author     pic X(13).
 25         03 f-BookID2            pic x(4)    125             10  bi-due-date        pic X(10).
 26            identified by "BookID2".         126
 27         03 f-BookTitle4         pic x(25)   127   PROCEDURE DIVISION.
 28            identified by "BookTitle4".
 29         03 f-DueDate4           pic x(10)   155   process-business-logic section.
 30            identified by "DueDate4".        156        *> Add application business logic here.
 31         03 f-DueDate1           pic x(10)   157        Call "lib-sub3" Using InPatronNumber
 32            identified by "DueDate1".        158                             patron-info
 33         03 f-InPatronNumber     pic x(60)   159                             book-counter
 34            identified by "InPatronNumber".  160                             book-info-array
 35         03 f-ssubmit            pic x(60)   161        If patron-info = low-values
 36            identified by "ssubmit".         162          Move "No record for patron" to PatronName
 37         03 f-BookID3            pic x(4)    163        Else
 38            identified by "BookID3".         164          Move patron-name to PatronName
 39         03 f-BookTitle1         pic x(25)   165          Move street-address to StreetAddress
 40            identified by "BookTitle1".      166          Move city-state-zip to CityStateZip
 41         03 f-StreetAddress      pic x(20)   167          If book-counter = 0
 42            identified by "StreetAddress".   168            Move "Patron has no books" to BookTitle1
 43         03 f-CityStateZip       pic x(30)   169          Else
 44            identified by "CityStateZip".    170            If book-counter >= 1
 45         03 f-DueDate2           pic x(10)   171              Move bi-book-id(1) to BookID1
 46            identified by "DueDate2".        172              Move bi-book-title(1) to BookTitle1
 47         03 f-BookID4            pic x(4)    173              Move bi-due-date(1) to DueDate1
 48            identified by "BookID4".         174            End-if
 49         03 f-PatronName         pic x(20)   175            If book-counter >=  2
 50            identified by "PatronName".      176              Move bi-book-id(2) to BookID2
 51         03 filler               pic x.      177              Move bi-book-title(2) to BookTitle2
                                             178              Move bi-due-date(2) to DueDate2
 93      copy "Lib11.cpy".                  179            End-if
 94      01 FormFields.                     180            If book-counter >= 3
 95         03 BookTitle2           pic x(25).   181              Move bi-book-id(3) to BookID3
 96         03 DueDate3             pic x(10).   182              Move bi-book-title(3) to BookTitle3
 97         03 BookTitle3           pic x(25).   183              Move bi-due-date(3) to DueDate3
 98         03 BookID1              pic x(4).    184            End-if
 99         03 BookID2              pic x(4).    185            If book-counter >= 4
100         03 BookTitle4           pic x(25).   186              Move bi-book-id(4) to BookID4
101         03 DueDate4             pic x(10).   187              Move bi-book-title(4) to BookTitle4
102         03 DueDate1             pic x(10).   188              Move bi-due-date(4) to DueDate4
103         03 InPatronNumber       pic X(60).   189            End-if  *> book-counter >= 4
104         03 ssubmit              pic x(64).   190          End-if *>  book-counter = 0
105         03 BookID3              pic x(4).    191        End-if *> patron-info = low-values
106         03 BookTitle1           pic x(25).   192        exit.
```

Figure 7-12. Pertinent code from Lib11.

CGI Code

The CGI's code in which we are interested is shown in Figure 7-12—look at the following Data Division entries.

- Lines 95-111 contain the Net Express generated form fields—those the programmer specified when creating the form.
- Lines 114-125 contain additional Working Storage items entered by the programmer. These correspond in number and size to the subprogram's Linkage Section parameters.

The If statement of the programmer-inserted code (lines 161-190) involves the same basic logic as that of Lib10.cbl (see line 120 of Figure 7-5). If the subprogram returns low-values, the requested patron is not contained in the file so an error message is moved to the appropriate output form field (line 162). Otherwise, the required output data is moved (lines 164-189).

- The patron name and address are moved at lines 164-166.
- As the data item book-counter contains the number of books checked out by the patron (the number of table entries from the subprogram containing data), it controls book data output. If a value 0 is returned, the patron has no books so an appropriate message is moved to one of the output fields (line 168). A non-zero value, for instance 2, results in data from table elements 1 and 2 being moved to the corresponding form fields (lines 170-174 and 175-179).

Although handling of the output book data might appear to be a brute-force approach, it is characteristic of the way we set up an output line in generating a printed report with Cobol. Fortunately, as you will see in the next example, Net Express does provide a more convenient method for handling table displays. However, there will likely be instances in which you will need to use the technique of this example.

Managing Repeating Data—Lib12

Handling Subscripted Cobol Data Items

The four browser displays of Figure 7-13 illustrate some of the versatility you can achieve with Net Express's table capabilities. All of them were created from the single Net Express generated output page of Figure 7-14 (stored as Lib12.app in the folder Proj0703). In the control tree you see the second table row (BookData) highlighted and its COBOL properties displayed. That is, this row can occur up to 10 times, reminiscent of a Cobol table. If you look at the first row, you will see that its COBOLOccurs value is 2. For this example, let's first look at the CGI; it will illustrate the significance of these properties.

Proj0703
Lib12

Features of the Lib12 CGI

The first code to look at in the CGI segments of Figure 7-15 are the FormFields of lines 93-102. Based on their descriptive names, you can easily relate most of them to their corresponding controls in Figure 7-14. The difference you see is inclusion of the occurs clause at lines 93, 94, 96, and 98, the data items pertaining to books, of which there can be up to 10. (Ignore line 95 for the moment.) Notice that the corresponding external-form entries (lines 19, 22, 28, and 33) also include the same occurs. Net Express generates these for the second row of the table because that table's row is assigned a COBOLOccurs value of 10—see Figure 7-14. Next, look at the HTML-Counters in lines 80-87. These are provided for you, the programmer, to use in controlling input from a table or output to a table. In particular, you use the

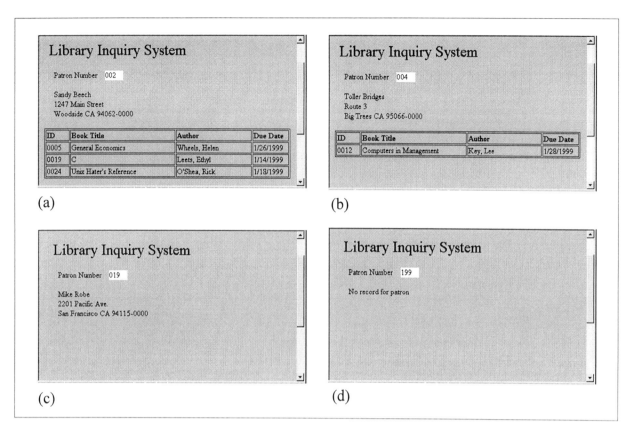

Figure 7-13. Four output displays.

item c-BookData, the name assigned to the second table row (see Figure 7-14) to control the number of table rows sent for output. If the value is zero, then no rows are displayed. Similarly, c-ColumnHeads is the name assigned to the first table row (the column headings) in Figure 7-14.

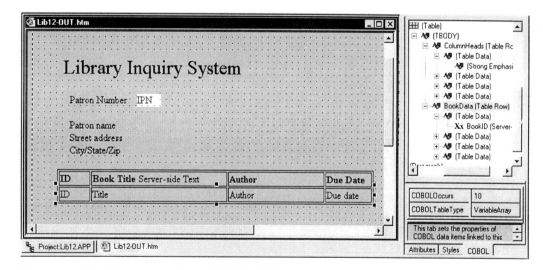

Figure 7-14. The output form Lib12-OUT.

```
  1  IDENTIFICATION DIVISION.              111  01  book-info-array.
  2      program-id. "Lib12".              112      05  book-info            occurs 10 times.
                                           113          10  bi-book-id          pic X(04).
 11  DATA DIVISION.                        114          10  bi-book-title       pic X(25).
 12                                        115          10  bi-book-author      pic X(13).
 13  working-storage section.             116          10  bi-due-date         pic X(10).
 14                                        117
 15      *> Do not remove this copy statement   118  01  book-pntr             pic 9(02).
 16      *> or modify the contents of the copy file.  119
 17      copy "Lib12.cpf".                120  PROCEDURE DIVISION.
 18      01 HTMLForm is external-form.    121
 19         03 f-BookAuthor       pic x(13)  occurs 10   122  main section.
 20            identified by "BookAuthor"   123      perform process-form-input-data
 21               count in c-BookAuthor.    124      perform convert-input
 22         03 f-BookTitle        pic x(25)  occurs 10   125      perform process-business-logic
 23            identified by "BookTitle"    126      perform lib12-out-cvt
 24               count in c-BookTitle.     127          *> lib12-out
 25         03 f-serversidetext1  pic x(1)  occurs 2   128      perform lib12-out-out
 26            identified by "serversidetext1"   129          *> lib12-out
 27               count in c-serversidetext1.   130      exit program
 28         03 f-BookID           pic x(4)  occurs 10   131      stop run.
 29            identified by "BookID"
 30               count in c-BookID.        148  process-business-logic section.
 31         03 f-InPatronNumber   pic x(3)   149      *> Add application business logic here.
 32            identified by "InPatronNumber".   150      Call "lib-sub3" Using InPatronNumber
 33         03 f-DueDate          pic x(10)  occurs 10   151                          patron-info
 34            identified by "DueDate"       152                          book-counter
 35               count in c-DueDate.        153                          book-info-array
 36         03 f-ssubmit          pic x(60)   154      Move 0 to c-ColumnHeads, c-BookData
 37            identified by "ssubmit".      155      If patron-info = low-values
 38         03 f-StreetAddress    pic x(20)   156        Move "No record for patron" to PatronName
 39            identified by "StreetAddress".   157      Else
 40         03 f-CityStateZip     pic x(30)   158        Move patron-name to PatronName
 41            identified by "CityStateZip".   159        Move street-address to StreetAddress
 42         03 f-PatronName       pic x(23)   160        Move city-state-zip to CityStateZip
 43            identified by "PatronName".    161        If book-counter > 0
 44         03 filler             pic x.      162          Move book-counter to c-BookData
                                              163          Move 1 to c-ColumnHeads
 76  *> The following fields are used to count the   164        End-If *>book-counter > 0
 77  *> number of values input for fields that occur   165        Perform varying book-pntr from 1 by 1
 78  *> more than once or can return multiple values   166                until book-pntr > book-counter
 79      01 HTML-Counters.                    167          Move bi-book-id(book-pntr)
 80         03 c-BookData     PIC 9(4) comp-5 value 0.   168                       to BookID(book-pntr)
 81         03 c-ColumnHeads  PIC 9(4) comp-5 value 0.   169          Move bi-book-title(book-pntr)
 82         03 c-BookAuthor   PIC 9(4) comp-5 value 0.   170                       to BookTitle(book-pntr)
 83         03 c-BookTitle    PIC 9(4) comp-5 value 0.   171          Move bi-book-author(book-pntr)
 84         03 c-serversidetext1                         172                       to BookAuthor(book-pntr)
 85                           PIC 9(4) comp-5 value 0.   173          Move bi-due-date(book-pntr)
 86         03 c-BookID       PIC 9(4) comp-5 value 0.   174                       to DueDate(book-pntr)
 87         03 c-DueDate      PIC 9(4) comp-5 value 0.   175        End-Perform
 88                                          176      End-If *>patron-info = low-values
 89      *> Do not remove this copy statement   177      exit.
 90      *> or modify the contents of the copy file.
 91      copy "Lib12.cpy".                   263  lib12-out-cvt Section.
 92      01 FormFields.                      264      *> lib12-out
 93         03 BookAuthor      pic x(13) occurs 10.   265      perform varying MF-SEL-INDEX from 1 by 1
 94         03 BookTitle       pic x(25) occurs 10.   266              until MF-SEL-INDEX > c-BookData
 95         03 serversidetext1 pic x(1) occurs 2.   267          move BookAuthor(MF-SEL-INDEX) to
 96         03 BookID          pic x(4) occurs 10.   268                     f-BookAuthor(MF-SEL-INDEX)
 97         03 InPatronNumber  pic X(3).        269      end-perform
 98         03 DueDate         pic x(10) occurs 10.
 99         03 ssubmit         pic x(64).        305      exec html
100         03 StreetAddress   pic x(20).        306          copy "Lib12-OUT.htm".
101         03 CityStateZip    pic x(30).
102         03 PatronName      pic x(23).           (Embedded HTML code)
103
104  *> Enter additional working-storage items here   392      <!--/*MF NE embedded COBOL begin*/ end-exec
105  01  in-patron-number        pic X(03).   393      perform varying MF-SEL-INDEX from 1 by 1
106  01  patron-info.                          394          until MF-SEL-INDEX > c-BookData
107      05  patron-name         pic X(23).   395      exec html /*MF NE embedded COBOL end*/-->
108      05  street-address      pic X(20).
109      05  city-state-zip      pic X(30).        (More embedded HTML code)
110  01  book-counter            pic 9(02).
```

Figure 7-15. CGI code—Lib12.

Before looking at the procedural code, let's consider the different scenarios that can occur for a given patron number request.

- The requested patron has from 1 to 10 books checked out. The first two examples in Figure 7-13 illustrate this. Notice that the displayed table consists only of the number of rows required for the books checked out by the patron.
- The requested patron has no books checked out—Figure 7-13(c) is such an example. Notice that there is no table display as it is not needed.
- There is no patron in the file for the input patron number, in which case only the message is displayed—see Figure 7-13(d).

Now let's take a look at the procedural code to see how you implement this feature of Net Express. For the first sequence, assume the user has entered patron number 002, thereby producing the screen of Figure 7-13(a) in which the patron has three books.

1. After calling the subprogram to access patron/book data (line 150), the program initializes the counters c-ColumnHeads and c-BookData to zero at line 154.
2. Name and address data is moved from the subprogram parameter area to the form output data items at lines 158-161. This is identical to previous examples of this chapter.
3. As book-counter contains a value greater than 0 (3 for this example), the moves of lines 163 and 164 are executed thereby setting c-BookData to 3 and c-ColumnHead to 1.
4. Book output data is moved from the subprogram parameter arrays (lines 113-116) to the FormFields arrays within the Perform loop beginning line 166.
5. With completion of the process-business-logic section code, processing progresses to the lib12-out-cvt section (line 263) via the perform of line 126.
6. At lines 265-269 you see a loop to move the FormFields-defined author data (line 93) to corresponding elements of the external-form fields (beginning line 19). At line 266 you see that repetition is controlled by the HTML-Counters data item c-BookData. (This program includes similar code for the other table items following line 269.) Be aware that this portion of the CGI is contained in the copy file Lib12.cpv. Every application you have created to this point contains similar Move statements, although they move simple data items rather than tables.
7. Embedded within the HTML script (lines 392-395 and beyond) you see similar Cobol looping code to cause output of a table containing the number of rows corresponding to the data to be displayed.

Now, handling the cases of no books and no patron should be evident. That is, the counters c-ColumnHeads and c-BookData are initialized to zero at line 154. If the value in c-BookData is not changed to a non-zero value (through the If statement at lines 162-165) the loops beginning 166, 265, and 393 are never executed. Therefore, no HTML output is generated for this table row (the second row in Figure 7-14) and nothing appears on the screen.

If you inspect the CGI for this project, you will find similar code for the heading row (the first table row in Figure 7-14). Its counter, c-ColumnHeads, contains a value of either 0 (from line 154) which suppresses its display by the browser, or 1 (from line 164) which forces its display by the browser.

The Output Page Lib12-OUT

It is hardly necessary to recreate the entire project Lib12 to familiarize yourself with these table-processing principles. I suggest you build your own table in the existing Lib12-OUT page as follows.

1. Open the project Lib12 stored in the Proj0703 folder.
2. Double-click Lib12-OUT.htm to open it in Form Designer. Your screen should display the page of Figure 7-14.
3. Make certain no existing controls are selected then place a table control on the form just beneath the existing table.
4. Insert a fourth column, position and stretch it out so that it looks like Figure 7-16.
5. With this alignment completed, delete the original table as you will recreate it in your newly inserted table.
6. Let's first work with the second row. Look at the structure of this row in the control tree of Figure 7-14 where the entire row is selected. You modify the second row of your form to give this.
7. Select the entire row by clicking on the second Table Row element in your control tree. The selection should be depicted as shown in Figure 7-14.
8. Right-click to obtain a drop-down menu from which you click Set ID.
9. Type BookData for the ID entry of this table row. Net Express generates the HTML counter c-BookData from this.

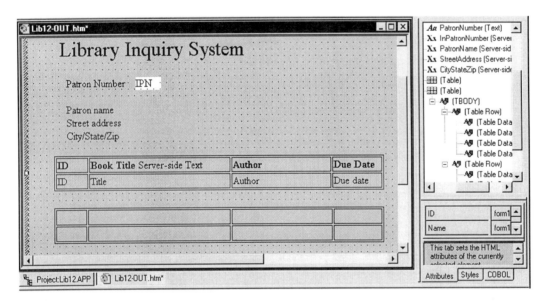

Figure 7-16. Inserting another table into Lib12-OUT.

10. Click the COBOL tab and set the entries to:

    COBOLOccurs   10 (the maximum number of elements in the array)
    CobolTableType VariableArray

    The latter causes Net Express to generate the code for processing a variable number of table rows—see lines 265-269 and 393-395 of Figure 7-15.

11. To insert Server-Side Text controls, begin by selecting the first cell of the second row.

12. With that cell selected, click the Server-Side Text icon (**Xx**) from the Form Elements toolbar to insert the control. The cell's width is increased to hold the text description—don't worry about that yet.

13. Highlight the text Server-side Text and overtype it with ID (as your descriptive entry). Resize the cell to its original width if necessary.

14. Ensure that the Server-Side Text control is selected by checking the control tree and make the following entries (under the appropriate tag, Attributes or COBOL).

    ID   BookID
    COBOLPicture x(4)

15. Insert Server-Side Text controls into the remaining three cells of this row and make corresponding entries as follows.

Description	**Book Title**	**Author**	**Due Date**
ID	BookTitle	BookAuthor	DueDate
COBOLPicture	x(25)	x(13)	x(10)

16. Select the first table row and change its ID to ColumnHead. Set its COBOL properties as follows.

    COBOLOccurs   2
    CobolTableType VariableArray

    Even though you will never want the browser to display more than one row of column headings on output, you must designate 2 for the COBOLOccurs or you will be unable to use this technique (variable array). Recall from the CGI description that the value for its counter c-ColumnHead is set either to 0 (no output) or 1 (producing the heading row).

17. Type the descriptive text (**ID, Book Title, Author**, and **Due Date**); make them boldface.

18. Position the cursor following the descriptive entry **Book Title** in the second cell and click the Server-Side Text icon to insert that that control. Change its COBOLPicture entry to x(1).

Insertion of the Server-Side Text control in the last step is necessary as Net Express will not generate needed subscripted code (which provides the capability to display or not display) unless the row contains at least one data-type control. Since no data is place in the result data item (serversidetext1 at line 95 of Figure 7-15), nothing is displayed for it when the application is run.

Using Form Express to Generate Table Output

Creating an Application

Proj0704
Lib13

The next example, Lib13 stored in the Proj0704 folder, was created using Form Express, described in Chapter 6. For this application, Form Express proved to be a real time-saver. If you wish to try it, create a new folder and copy the file Lib-sub3.cbl into it. Then create the application following the detailed steps of Chapter 6. When you get to the Generated Filenames window of the application wizard, make the entries of Figure 7-17.

When you reach the Parameter Assignment screen, make the entries of Figure 7-18. Notice the following about these values.

- Control Type assignments are Edit for the patron number (it serves as the input field in the input form) and Label (Server-Side Text) for the other elementary items.
- The I/O assignments are Both for patron number (it is displayed on the output form) and Out for the other elementary items. The exception is the book counter which is designated N/A as it is not displayed on either form.
- Default values for Label Name are replaced with the entries entered shown in Figure 7-18. Be aware that when I made these name changes using the first release of Net Express, it crashed. Presumably WebSync updates correct this problem.

The End Result

Upon completing the build process, you can run the application. You should get an output screen that looks something like Figure 7-19. This is a reasonable appearing output obtained with a minimum amount of effort. If you look at the output page, see Figure 7-20, and the CGI you will see that Form Express uses a fixed table in

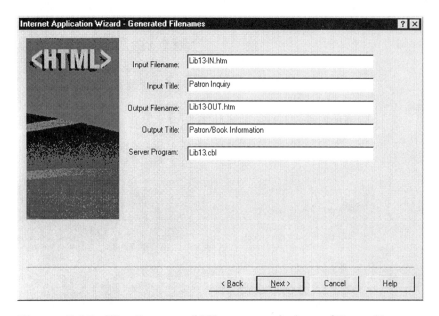

Figure 7-17. The Generated Filenames window of Form Express.

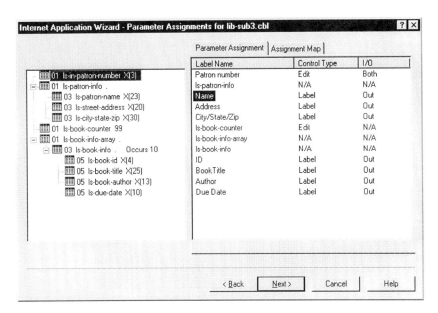

Figure 7-18. Parameter assignments.

which the subscripted data items are moved one at a time as in Lib11. Following are two other features to notice.

- Form Express creates form fields from linkage section names and places them in the separate **.cpl** file which is copied into your CGI. For instance, where you saw InPatronNumber in Lib12, you will see ls-in-patron-number in this application.

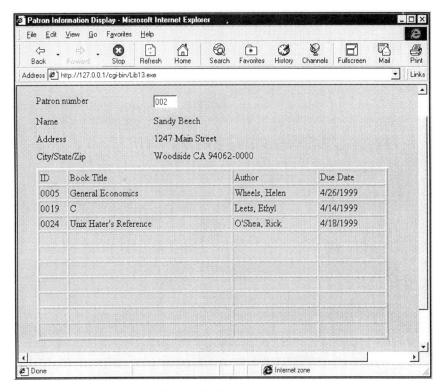

Figure 7-19. Browser displayLib13.

- Correspondence is maintained between the linkage section names and the external form names as illustrated by the following fragment of code from Lib13.cbl.

```
01 HTMLForm is external-form.
   03 f-ls-in-patron-number  pic x(3)
            identified by "ls_in_patron_number".
```

Suppose your objective was to create an output page to produce the browser displays of Figure 7-13 (that is, duplicate the Lib12 application). In addition to adding the heading line to both the input and output pages, you would need to make the following changes to Lib13-OUT.

1. Remove the Text controls containing the line descriptions Patron name, Street address, and City/State/Zip.
2. Change each entry in the first row of the table (the heading row) to display as bold.
3. Insert a Server-Side Text control into the Book Title cell of the first row. To avoid Form Designer inserting the control on a second line (thereby destroying the alignment of the column headings, fully expand the control tree entry for this cell and select the Strong Emphasis element. Then click the Server-Side Text icon on the control bar. The Server-Side Text control should be inserted immediately to the right of the caption.
4. Change this Server-Side Text control's COBOLPicture to 1.

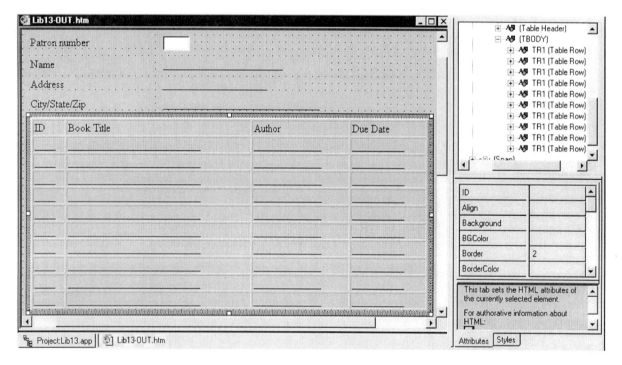

Figure 7-20. The Form Designer generated output page Lib13-OUT.

5. Select the first Table Row and change its properties as follows.
   ID to ColumnHeads
   COBOLOccurs to 2
   COBOLDataType to VariableArray

6. You must now delete rows from the bottom of the table until only the first two remain. When you are finished, your table should resemble Figure 7-1.

7. Select the second Table Row and change its properties as follows.
   ID to BookData
   COBOLOccurs to 10
   COBOLDataType to VariableArray

6. Insert the following code after the CALL statement in the process-business-logic section; it must follow the comment line shown here.

```
*> Add post-call application business logic here
    Move 0 to c-ColumnHeads, c-BookData
    If ls-patron-info = low-values
      Move "No record for patron" to ls-patron-name
    Else
      If ls-book-counter > 0
        Move ls-book-counter to c-BookData
        Move 1 to c-ColumnHeads
      End-If *>book-counter > 0
    End-If *>patron-info = low-values
```

Compare this code to the corresponding to programmer-inserted code of Figure 7-15 (lines 154-177). Notice that they are the same except the series of Move statements is omitted in this example. Form Express generates data items so that Form Designer-generated Move statements in the **.cpv** file handle the task for you.

When finished with these relatively simple steps, you have an application identical to the one created for Lib12. As indicated in Chapter 6, Form Express is a powerful tool to quickly provide you basic elements of an HTML page from which you can build an application.

Summing Up

Project Summary

Proj0701 (Lib10) shows you how to display table data with a multi-line Textarea control. This example, as do all in this chapter, displays patron name/address data and a list of books checked out by the patron.

Proj0702 (Lib11) uses a Table control to display Cobol table data.

Proj0703 (Lib12) uses the Table control designated as a VariableArray Cobol type to display Cobol table data.

Proj0704 (Lib13) illustrates using Form Express to generate an application that includes the output of Cobol table data.

General Summary

The Multi-Line Text Area control gives you the capability to display multiple lines of text within a box that includes a scroll bar.

The table-row properties provide for the convenient handling of subscripted Cobol data items. It allows you to output repeating controls on a form under control of the CGI program. Specifically, for any row you want to display Cobol table data you designate the following properties:

ID	Any valid HTML data name.
COBOLOccurs	The maximum number of rows you want displayed for the form row.
COBOLTableType	VariableArray

Each VariableArray designated table row produces an HTML counter data item (numeric) in the CGI. You assign that item a value designating the number of rows you want displayed. A value of zero suppresses the row display entirely.

Form Express provides for the automatic generation of table output for Cobol table items. The resulting COBOLTableType is FixedArray in which the displayed table always shows the number of rows assigned the COBOLOccurs property (obtained by Form Express from the Occurs clause of the corresponding Linkage Section data items). You can easily change the type to VariableArray.

Coming Up

This chapter has provided you many of Form Designer's working tools. Chapter 8 shows some of the tools you can use to make your applications more functional. You will learn how to insert graphics into your forms, provide for repetition, create applications that use multiple output forms, create applications using multiple Submit buttons, and display help information at the click of a button.

Assignment

7-1

The Harmon's Saddle application includes two files, Customer.di and Order.di and the subprogram Cus-sub3.cbl that provides access to the data of the files. The subprogram contains the Linkage Section shown in Figure 7-21—refer to the Appendix for a more detailed description of these files and the subprogram. In Figure 7-21, the field ls-in-customer-id is the input parameter; all others are output parameters. For this assignment, you are to display customer and order information for a user-requested customer.

- The input page is identical to the input form of previous customer record access assignments—it must accept a customer number
- The output page must display at least the following items:

> Customer information
> > Name
> > Street address
> > City/State/Zip
>
> Order information (one line for each order)
> > Order number
> > Saddle type
> > Order date (see the Linkage Section listing in Figure 7-21)
> > Scheduled date (see the Linkage Section listing in Figure 7-21)

If you want to display the customer's credit limit and/or current balance (not required), use X(6) and X(9), respectively, for the COBOLPicture entries of the output controls.

```
01  ls-in-customer-id              pic X(04).
01  ls-customer-info.
    10  ls-customer-name           pic X(23).
    10  ls-street-address          pic X(20).
    10  ls-city-state-zip          pic X(28).
    10  ls-phone-number            pic X(12).
    10  ls-credit-rating           pic X(01).
        88  credit-excellent       value "A".
        88  credit-limited         value "B".
        88  advance-pay-only       value "C".
    10  ls-credit-limit            pic $$,$$9.
    10  ls-current-balance         pic $$,$$9.99.

01  ls-order-counter               pic 9(02).
01  ls-order-info-array.
    05  ls-order-info occurs 5 times.
        10  ls-order-id            pic x(03).
        10  ls-customer-id         pic x(04).
        10  ls-saddle-type         pic X(07).
        10  ls-order-options.
            20  ls-stirrup-covers  pic X(3).
            20  ls-padded-seat     pic X(3).
            20  ls-leather-tooling pic X(12).
            20  ls-silver-ornaments pic X(12).
        10  ls-date-determination-fields.
            20  ls-order-date      pic X(10).
            20  ls-start-date      pic X(10).
            20  ls-promised-date   pic X(10).
            20  ls-scheduled-date  pic X(10).
```

Figure 7-21. Linkage section from Cus-sub3.cbl.

Hyperlinks and Other Good Stuff

Chapter Contents

Web Administration for Solo 192
    Web Shares 192
    Creating a New Web Share 193
Adding Images to HTML Pages 195
    About Graphics in the Web 195
    Inserting an Image Into Lib12 195
The Input Image Control 197
    Project Border 197
    Including an Input Image Control in a Form 199
    CGI Code for Handling Input Image 200
Providing for Repetition 201
    Using a Text Control as a Hyperlink 201
    A Graphic as a Hyperlink 203
Defining Events 204
    What is an Event? 204
    The Script Assistant 204
    Displaying Help 205
    Event Handler Code—JavaScript 208
Modifying Properties with Event Handlers 208
    Duplicating Data 208
    JavaScript Code for Duplicating Data Items 209
    Creating the Event Handler 210
    More on Setting the Value 211
    Setting Check Boxes and Radio Button 212
Using an Input Button to Transfer Control 213
A Word of Caution 213
Summing Up 214
    Project Summary 214
    General Summary 214
Coming Up 214
Assignment 215

Chapter

8

Chapter Introduction

Chapter 6 introduced you to a variety of tools for creating output screens. This chapter focuses on additional tools and techniques for meeting the variety of needs in form design. From this chapter you will learn about the following

- Inserting graphics into your pages.
- Providing for repetition.
- Hyperlinks.
- Events and event handlers.
- Creating an event handler with a simple JavaScript program.

Web Administration for Solo

Web Shares

File processing subprograms in this book include a Select clause telling the system the location of the file to be accessed, for instance:

```
Select Patron-File assign to disk
        "c:\Elements-CWP\NE-data\patron.di"
```

Similarly, when you run a Web application, you must tell the browser where to find the HTML file containing the opening page script. For instance, the starting point for project Lib12 is

```
Subdirectory   C:\Elements-CWP\NE-examples\Proj0703
File name      Lib12-IN.htm
```

However, when you run a Web application from Net Express you see a screen such as that in Figure 8-1. (This example is from the Lib12 application, stored in the Proj0703 folder. You may want to bring it up to give you a better feel for the descriptions that follow.) Notice that execution is to begin with:

```
HTTP://127.0.0.1/COBOL/Lib12-IN.htm
```

From Chapter 2 you know that the IP (Internet Protocol) address 127.0.0.1 maps to Net Express's Solo, the server simulator that provides you a complete client/server environment on you own computer. Perhaps you have wondered about the significance of the COBOL component of this designation. The answer is that Solo sets up three special **web shares**, identifying names that designate the local paths to the folders of your computer containing components required by Solo. With the Lib12 application open, if you double click on the Solo icon 🌐 (or click Windows Start then Programs/Micro Focus Net Express/Solo) you will see a display like Figure 8-2. Here you see the special shares COBOL and cgi-bin set up by Solo to make working with Net Express simple for you. Thus the Internet starting instruction you see in Figure 8-1 is equivalent to

```
C:\Elements-CWP\NE-Examples\Proj0703\Lib12-IN.htm
```

If you check the contents of the DEBUG folder, you the will see that it contains the executable CGI Cobol program required of this project (Lib12.exe).

Although you've had no need to consider these concepts in learning basic principles of Net Express so far, you will need an insight to these principles for some examples of this chapter.

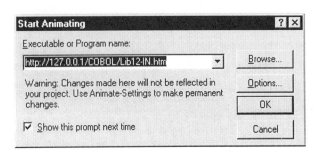

Figure 8-1.
The Net Express run window.

Creating a New Web Share

In Chapter 3 you specified an image file to use as form background by listing the image filename, EggShell.gif, for the Background-Image style property. You did not need to designate the location (folder) of this file because the project folder Proj0301 contains a copy of the file. In general, requiring that any displayed image be stored in the project folder in which it is used is a clumsy process. Generally, it is better to store all images in a separate image folder then identify each by its name and location (in the image file). If you loaded this book's Examples CD into default folders, you will find a complete set of images in the folder Elements-CWP\NE-images. Thus, in Chapter 3's example, you could have designated the Background-Image style property as:

url(C:\Elements-CWP\NE-images\EggShell.gif)

Better yet, if you set up a Web share in which this folder is designated as the share Images, you would enter your Background-Image style property as:

url(/Images/EggShell.gif)

At first glance you may feel there is no advantage to setting up a Web share and using it in this way. However, remember that ultimately your application will be deployed from your development environment (using Solo) to a server in which you have no control over names of folders. For instance, one NT server to which you deploy may store all image files in a folder named Graphics and another in a folder named Image-Files. If you've designated folders in you image references, you will need to change every reference in each component of the application. However, by

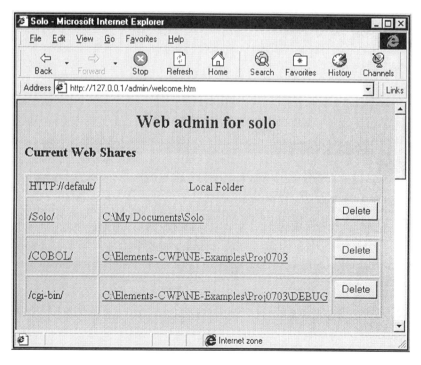

Figure 8-2. Web shares displayed by Internet Explorer.

using Web share references, you need only define a Web share for the image folder. Let's create a Web share for the folder C:\Elements-CWP\NE-images that you can use for image reference in examples that follow.

1. Start Windows Explorer
2. Locate the folder NE-Images; right-click it.
3. From the resulting menu, click the Properties option.
4. From the Properties window, click the Web Share tab and you will see a window that looks like Figure 8-3.
5. Click the Share name radio button.
6. The folder name appears as the default share name. Change it to Images, the name you will use in all future image references.
7. Click OK and the share name is assigned.
8. With Lib12 open, double-click on the solo icon and you will see a display like Figure 8-4 listing your newly added share.

Figure 8-3. Defining a Web share.

If you want to know more about Web shares, double-click the Solo. Scroll down the resulting screen and click **Questions and Answers**.

Figure 8-4. Web shares.

Adding Images to HTML Pages

About Graphics in the Web

Up to this point your pages have all consisted of only text. Adding graphics to your pages with Form Designer is a relatively easy process. (Creating the graphics may not be as easy.) In general, graphics should have a clear purpose on any Web page; Don't include graphics merely for the sake of having pictures. Most Web surfers are looking for information and/or services and have little time for an "art gallery" display. However, a company logo and the like can be valuable in creating a comfortable and functional Web page. (For instance, the library application of this book might show a graphic of an open textbook to set the tone of the site.) Furthermore, icons can be used to get a particular point across much more effectively than words (the basis for Windows).

In general, multimedia files (including graphics) are files that store information outside the capabilities of HTML. By designating any desired multimedia file in your HTML script, the browser can access it and bring it into your presentation. Four common formats for graphics files are:

File Format	Filename Extension
Graphics Image Format	GIF
JPEG (compressed)	JPG
Tag Image File Format	TIF
Windows Bitmap	BMP

Inserting an Image Into Lib12

The folder NE-images contains two book image files Book.gif, a rendering of a book lying open, and BookShelf.gif, several books on a shelf. Let's insert Book.gif into the input page Lib12-IN.

1. If you have not already done so, bring up the project Lib12 (in the Proj0703 folder).
2. Double-click Lib12-IN.htm to open it in Form Designer.
3. From the Page Elements tab, select the Image icon.
4. Click an Image control anywhere on your screen, for instance, refer to Figure 8-5.

You will change two attributes: ID (merely for the sake of documentation in the component tree) and SRC. The latter property, tells the browser the name and location of the image file. On one hand, you could use the standard DOS path format. However, as this is a Web application, using Web identification capabilities is superior in that it provides good portability.

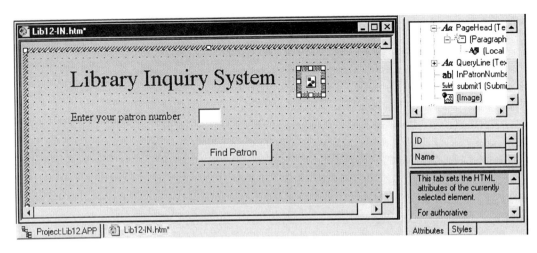

Figure 8-5. The Image control.

5. As the image files are available to HTML through the Web share name Images, type the following for the SRC entry.

    /Images/Book.gif

    Also, change the ID attribute to BookPicure. Your screen should look like Figure 8-6 when you are finished.

6. You can resize the image in the usual Windows fashion by grabbing and dragging one of the selection handles. Resize and reposition as you see appropriate.

7. While you're at it, you may as well assign a form background image (as you did in Chapter 3). To do this, highlight the Body of document entry (probably named body1) in the control tree.

8. Click the Style tab.

9. Enter the following for the Background-Image property.

    url(/Images/BG01.jpg)

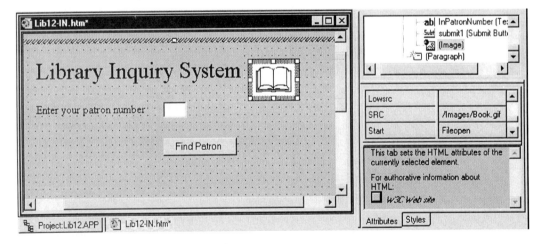

Figure 8-6. Designating the image.

Notice the form of this entry; to designate a background image, you must include the abbreviation URL and enclose the Webshare and file name in parentheses. The file BG01.jpg is one of the image files in the NE-Images folder.

10. Save this form file and close the Form Designer screen.
11. Run the project and your browser screen will look something like Figure 8-7.
12. When you are finished, close the project.

The Input Image Control

Project Border

Project Border.app stored in the folder Proj0801 illustrates using an area-sensitive image to serve both a selection function and as a submit. For an insight to this example, load and run that application. In the resulting browser screen of Figure 8-8 you see that the image is divided into six areas. Click anywhere within, for instance, the second row, first column (the area identified as **Wave**). This action causes the form to be submitted and the CGI to return a page with a description of the Wave border. Click the browser Back button and try another border. As you see, the browser is sensitive to the position of the mouse pointer when you click.

Proj0801
Borders

First let's look at the image (stored in the NE-images folder as Patterns.gif) shown in Figure 8-9. The dimensions you see (when imported into the input form) are in pixels. That is, the image is 137 pixels in height and 269 pixels in width. Also shown are "coordinates" of boundary points between the different areas of the image. For instance, 135,0 means an x-position of 135 and a y-position of 0; similarly, 269,137 means an x-position of 269 and a y-position of 137 (the lower-right corner of the image). Using these coordinate values, you can identify a specific border pattern. For example, the coordinate 125,48 lies within the wave pattern area.

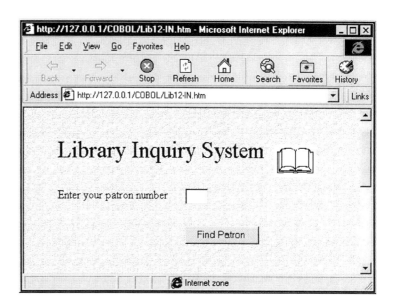

Figure 8-7.
The book image displayed by the browser.

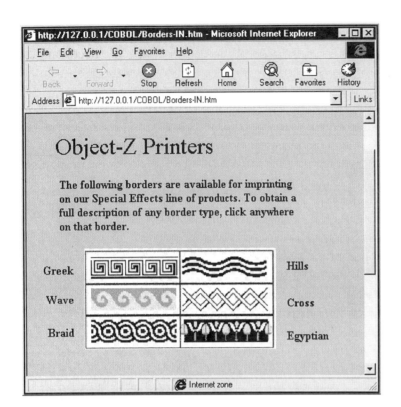

Figure 8-8.
Browser input
screen from the
Border project.

When you ran the application and clicked within the wave pattern, the browser returned to the CGI, the exact coordinate (for instance, x-coordinate 125 and y-coordinate 48) at which you clicked. As you will see, the user-inserted code in the CGI evaluates the coordinates and acts accordingly.

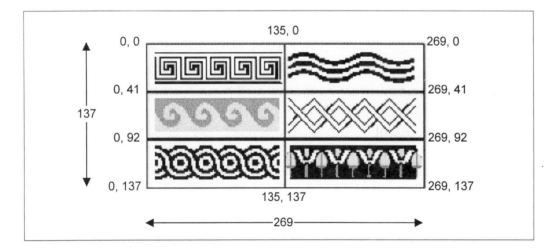

Figure 8-9. Image dimensions.

Including an Input Image Control in a Form

Although you could recreate the entire Borders application, that's not necessary as you are already familiar with most of the techniques. However, you might find it useful to bring up the application (in Proj0801) and correlate its features to the descriptions that follow.

When incorporating an Input Image into a form, your first action should be to determine its dimensions. Unfortunately, with the initial release of 3.0 you cannot obtain that information from the Input Image control when you place it on your form. [Check after you load any WebSync updates to see if this has changed.] To obtain those dimensions, proceed as follows.

1. Open Borders-IN.htm.
2. Scroll down to the empty area at the bottom of the form.
3. Click the Page Elements tab.
4. Select the Image icon .
5. Insert the image control beneath the current image.
6. Scroll to the SRC attribute and enter /images/Patterns.gif, the location and image filename.
7. Click the Styles tab and scroll down to the Height style property; you should see a value 137. Record this value as you will use it when creating your CGI code. [Note: When I was experimenting with this, sometimes Form Designer did not automatically display the value. If you encounter this problem, grab the bottom selection handle, move the bottom edge slightly down then move it back again. The needed dimensions should appear.] Scroll to the Width property and record its value (should be 269).
8. Delete this Image control—you don't need it anymore.

If you wish to step through the following for setting up the Input Image, you may do so by positioning it beneath the existing image. However, don't save the form when you are finished—simply close the Form Designer display without saving.

9. Select the Input Image icon of the Form Elements toolbar and insert the control beneath the existing Input Image control.
10. From the Attributes tab, change the ID and Name to Borders2 (the existing image uses Borders).
11. In the original release of Version 3.0, the browser displayed the text descriptions (on each side of the image) in different positions than set up on the Form Designer screen. To force correct positions, click to the Style tab and enter the height and width values that you determined earlier: 137px and 269px. You may not need to do this after you update from Web Sync.

That's all there is to create in Input Image control. Let's take a look at the code required in the CGI.

CGI Code for Handling Input Image

First, look at the CGIs FormFields shown in Figure 8-10 where you see Borders-x and Borders-y (lines 55 and 56). Net Express generates these items from the name of the Input Image as the input elements from that control. (The item BorderDescription pertains to the output form.) Clicking within the image on the browser screen returns the x-coordinate in Borders-x and the y-coordinate in Borders-y.

The Evaluate statement beginning line 114 tests these value and performs the appropriate Move. For instance, coordinates of 95, 30 (within the Greek area—see Figures 8-8 and 8-9) match the condition of line 116. Similarly, coordinates of 250,50 (within the Cross area) match the condition of line 124.

```
  1          IDENTIFICATION DIVISION.
  2             program-id. "Borders".

 10          DATA DIVISION.
 11
 12          working-storage section.
 13
 14             *> WARNING: Do not remove this copy statement
 15             *> or modify the contents of the copy file.
 16             copy "Borders.cpf".
 17             01 HTMLForm is external-form.
 18                03 f-BorderDescription    pic x(160)
 19                   identified by "BorderDescription".
 20                03 f-Borders-x            pic x(9)
 21                   identified by "Borders.x".
 22                03 f-Borders-y            pic x(9)
 23                   identified by "Borders.y".
 24                03 filler                 pic x.

 53             01 FormFields.
 54                03 BorderDescription      pic x(160).
 55                03 Borders-x              PIC 9(9).
 56                03 Borders-y              PIC 9(9).
 57
 58          *> Enter additional working-storage items here
 59          01  border-descriptions.
 60              02  greek
 61                  value   "The Greek border is one of two that we consider
 62          -               "classics. It provides a fine, two-dimensional look
 63          -               "that is ideal for dark colored background.".
 64              02  wave
 65                  value   "The Wave trim is designed to provide a light,
 66          -               "outdoor feel. Use it in an informal environment.
 67          -               "We recommend pastel colors for this border.".

 84          PROCEDURE DIVISION.

112          process-business-logic section.
113             *> Add application business logic here.
114             Evaluate
115                 Borders-x < 136 also Borders-y < 47 also Borders-y < 93
116             When    TRUE     also    TRUE     also        ANY
117                Move greek to BorderDescription
118             When    TRUE     also    FALSE    also        TRUE
119                Move wave to BorderDescription
120             When    TRUE     also    FALSE    also        FALSE
121                Move braide to BorderDescription
122             When    FALSE    also    TRUE     also        ANY
123                Move hills to BorderDescription
124             When    FALSE    also    FALSE    also        TRUE
125                Move cross to BorderDescription
126             When    FALSE    also    FALSE    also        FALSE
127                Move egyptian to BorderDescription
128             End-Evaluate
129
130             exit.
```

Figure 8-10. The CGI Borders.cbl.

Providing for Repetition

Using a Text Control as a Hyperlink

Thus far, your projects have involved the simple sequence of a browser screen to a CGI program, to a second browser screen. You have been able to repeat (return from the output browser screen to the input browser screen) by clicking the Back button of the browser. This is a rather mundane way of repeating; generally, it is clearer to a user to have a screen control specifically for repetition. Furthermore, you will frequently encounter the need to go from one HTML page to another, an action you cannot accomplish with the browser Back button. As a simple illustration of accessing one page from another, let's consider the project Lib14.app in the folder Proj0802. (This project was created by duplicating Lib12.) If you run it, you will see the output screen of Figure 8-11. The text <u>Click here to view another patron</u> is called a **hyperlink** (or a **hotspot**), an area on your browser screen that causes a transfer to another Web element. The procedure for inserting a hyperlink is relatively simple. The easiest way to try it out is to open Lib12.app in the folder Proj0703 and modify the output page Lib12-OUT.

Proj0802
Lib14

1. Insert a Text control immediately above the right edge of the table.
2. Replace the caption
      New Text
    with
      Click here to view another patron.
3. Enter any appropriate description for the ID (documentation only).

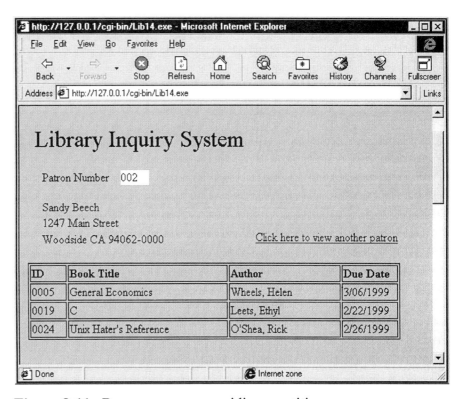

Figure 8-11. Browser screen providing repetition.

4. With the entire text highlighted, click the Edit Hyperlink icon 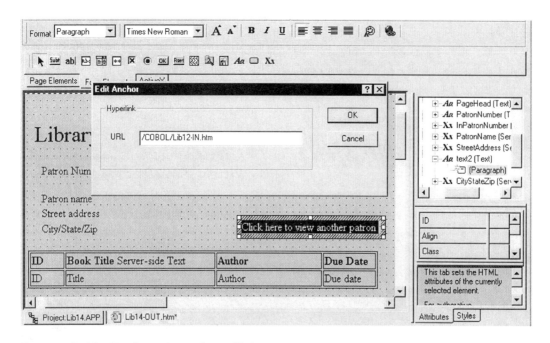 on the Format toolbar. You will see the popup window of Figure 8-12 (without the URL entry).
5. Type in the URL shown in Figure 8-12.

Net Express lets you designate any Text control, whole or part, as a hyperlink thereby providing a Web surfer the ability to bring up another Web page. (As a conventional programmer, you might think of this as equivalent to some type of branching instruction.) To accomplish this, your hyperlink must identify the desired Web location and document. In this example, you want the to call up (link to) the input page of this application, Lib12-IN.htm (Note: The example application in the Proj0802 folder links to Lib14-IN.htm.) Although you could designate the particular folder (c:Elements-CWP\NE-Examples\Proj0703), you would have an application that is clumsy to move to another site. This is precisely the reason for Web shares described at the beginning of this chapter.

The required entry is the Web share, COBOL, and the document to be accessed is Lib12-I.htm, the input page for this application.

6. Type /COBOL/Lib12-IN.htm for the URL—see Figure 8-12. (HTML is not case sensitive, so upper/lower case is not an issue.) Be certain to use forward slashes (used by Unix) not backslashes (used by DOS). Also, do not forget the extension .htm or else the browser will be unable to find the Web page.
7. Click OK on the Edit Anchor window. Notice that the Text is underscored and is displayed in a different color (blue is the default); this identifies it as a hyperlink.
8. Save the form, rebuild the project, and run some trials. Click on the hyperlink to repeat.

Figure 8-12. Designating a hyperlink.

A Graphic as a Hyperlink

In many instances you will want to use a Text control as a hyperlink. However, Web pages that consist of nothing but text are not very appealing. From your own experience with the Internet, you are familiar with graphics serving as hyperlinks. Let's modify the example you've been working on to produce the browser screen of Figure 8-13.

1. From the Lib12 project, open the output .
2. Delete the Text hyperlink from Lib12-OUT that you inserted in the preceding example.
3. From the Page Elements control toolbar, click the Image icon 📇 .
4. Place an image control at approximately the same position you had the hypertext link.
5. Type some descriptive entry for the ID attribute (for screen documentation).

All browsers allow the user to turn off graphics in order to speed up downloading of forms. Under this condition, the graphic is displayed as a generic symbol thereby losing all meaning to the user. Fortunately, HTML includes the capability for you to define alternate text that is displayed under this circumstance. Another feature is that this text serves as a "help" to the graphic. That is, if a user does not understand the meaning of the graphic, he/she can hold the mouse pointer on the graphic for a moment and this description appears on the screen.

6. For the Alt attribute enter any descriptive text, such as the following.
   Access another patron
7. To identify the image file and source, enter the following for the SRC attribute.
   /Images/another.gif
8. Resize the image as appropriate.

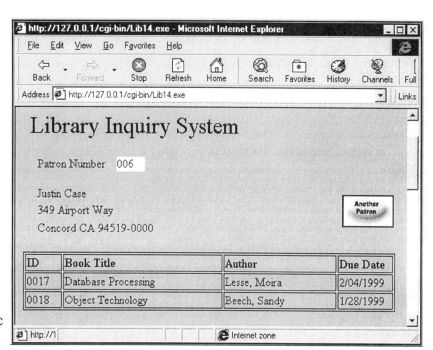

Figure 8-13.
Using a graphic as a hyperlink.

9. Click the Edit Hyperlink icon ⬛ on the Format toolbar. Make the following
    URL entry (same as Figure 8-12).
    /COBOL/Lib12-IN.htm
10. You are finished, so save the form, rebuild the project, and run some test
    cases.

Defining Events

What is an Event?

The focus in this book is on creating HTML forms and corresponding CGI code to
perform server-side actions necessary to the application. The forms you have been
creating are static and, in a sense "dumb" in that once sent to the browser they are
not capable of performing any processing functions. However, you have seen an
exception in the built-in validation features of Net Express. By embedding JavaScript
functions within the HTML script, your page can interactively check data entries
without returning to the server-side program.

Underlying the Web pages you have been creating is the notion of events and
event handlers. An **event** is any action the user takes such as clicking on a button or
moving a window on the screen. An **event handler** is code describing actions to be
taken when an event occurs. So making a change to a value in, for instance, a Text
Input field is an event; the event handler is the Net Express JavaScript function
(program) for validating the entry.

In addition to the prewritten validation functions, Net Express includes provisions for you to designate events and create event handlers in JavaScript. Without
knowing JavaScript, you can use the Net Express **Script Assistant** to generate code
to do simple tasks such as:

*   Link to another HTML page or server-side program
*   Display help screens
*   Change data values in input controls
*   Change a control's properties

The Script Assistant

Considering that most Cobol programmers don't know JavaScript (or even have an
interest in learning it), Micro Focus includes in Net Express a special **Script Assistant** to simplify the creation of event handlers. In the sample assistant screen of
Figure 8-14 you see the following five tabs.

*   Scripts
*   Events
*   Methods
*   Properties
*   Styles

Your primary focus in the book will be on the Events tab (shown in Figure 8-14) and the Methods tab. All tabs except the Style tab produce a screen similar to the Events tab.

- Objects pane. This pane lists, in tree form, all the objects (controls and other elements) comprising your HTML page. This is the same tree you see under Form Designer.
- Events pane. From this pane you designate the event for which you want to create an event handler. In Figure 8-14 the onclick event is checked. For Methods, Properties, and Styles tabs, this pane is similar in appearance but provides options appropriate to the tab selected.
- Help pane. This pane (middle-right) provides information about the selected event. In Figure 8-14, this pane describes the onclick event.
- Event Handler Code pane. The bottom pane contains the event handler JavaScript code assigned to the event. The Script Assistant includes point-and-click features to assist you in creating this code.

Displaying Help

In designing a Web page, it is a good idea to avoid too much information that the user will normally ignore. For instance, consider a data entry screen with which most users are familiar. The average person won't want detailed instructions when he or she is already familiar with the procedures. However, the new user will want instructions for unfamiliar procedures. A simple way of accomplishing this is through JavaScript-created help displays.

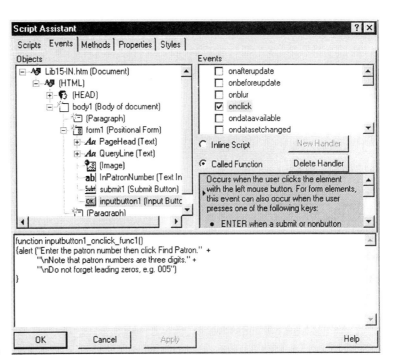

Figure 8-14.
The Script Assistant.

The next example, Events01 stored in the Proj0803 folder, includes two different (but similar) event definitions to produce the Help pane of Figure 8-15. Load and run this application to get a feel for how it works. You will find that the help screen is displayed by either of the two actions: (1) clicking the Help button, and (2) passing the mouse pointer over the international information symbol. When you are finished, close this application and open Lib12 (in Proj0703); then step through the following example to add these components to the input form.

1. Bring up Lib12-IN.htm in Form Designer.
2. If you are interested in some variety, specify a background image as follows.
    - In the control tree, select the entry body1 (Body of document).
    - Under the Styles tab, enter the following for Background-Image
        url(/Images/eggshell.gif)   (or use any other image that appeals to you)
3. Select the Input Button icon ⛶ from the Form Elements control bar and position it to the right of the current Find Patron button. You may want to move controls around to obtain the balance of Figure 8-15.
4. Make certain the cursor is positioned within the control and type the label Help. Also, change its ID attribute to Help.
5. The international information ⓘ graphic is stored in the NE-Images folder as Information.jpg. To insert it into this form, select the Image icon from the Page Elements tab and place an image control in the Form Designer page—for positioning, use Figure 8-15 as a guide.
6. Type the following for its SRC attribute.
        /Images/Information.jpg
7. Next, let's add the event handlers. Right-click anywhere in the form screen and select Events from the resulting popup menu to produce the Script Assis-

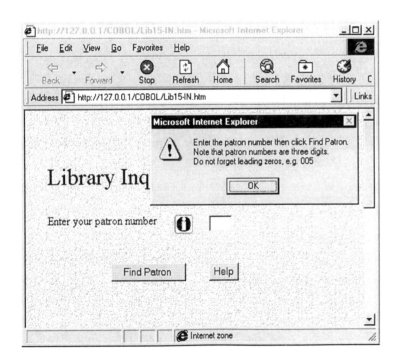

Figure 8-15.
Including help capabilities in a Web screen.

tance. Click to expand the body1 and form1 elements and your screen will look like Figure 8-16.

6. You can designate an event for any control-tree element in the body (or the body itself) by highlighting that element. Click Help (Input Button) to begin with that control.

7. You want the help message displayed when the user clicks on the Help button (refer to Figure 8-15) so double-click on the onclick check box in the Events pane. Alternately, select that option and click the New Handler button. You will see the following JavaScript function inserted into the event-handler pane.

```
function inputbutton1_onclick_func()
{
}
```

8. Position the cursor immediately following the open brace { and press the Enter key to insert a new line (for easy reading). Then type the following

```
alert ("Enter the patron number then click Find Patron." +
    "\nNote that patron numbers are three digits." +
    "\nDo not forget leading zeros e.g. 005")
```

Use lower-case exactly as shown here. When you are finished, this pane should contain the following. Check your entry to make certain you've not made any typing errors.

```
function inputbutton1_onclick_func()
{
alert ("Enter the patron number then click Find Patron." +
    "\nNote that patron numbers are three digits." +
    "\nDo not forget leading zeros e.g. 005")
}
```

9. Click OK to close the Script Assistant.

10. Save the form and make a test run. Click on the Help button to make certain it works properly. If you have an error in the event handling code, your browser will display an error message.

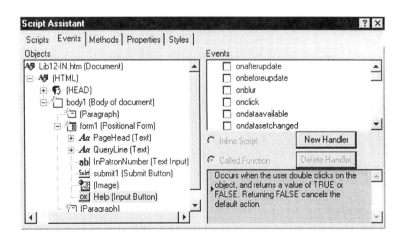

Figure 8-16.
The Events window.

11. Repeat Steps 7-11 for the Image control. Instead of an onclick event, click the onmouseover checkbox.
12. Save the form and make another test run. Move the mouse over the screen image—the help screen should appear.

Event Handler Code—JavaScript

The event handler code of this example is written in JavaScript; it has the following features.

- The keyword alert is a "verb" describing the action that is to occur. Be certain to type this in all lower case.
- Script for display within the popup must be quoted (as we do in Cobol with a literal). The output text must be enclosed within the parentheses.
- The code \n causes the following text to be positioned on a new line (forces a line break). Be aware that JavaScript, like HTML, ignores spaces and carriage returns.
- The entire message could have been placed on a single line such as the following. However, entering it on three lines makes it easier to see what you've typed.

      alert ("Enter the patron number then click Accept\nPatron...005")

Modifying Properties with Event Handlers

Duplicating Data

Assume you are entering data into the screen of Figure 8-17 and for you, as with most of us, your mailing address is the same as your home address. This particular form requires full entries—the word "Same" is not sufficient. What a nuisance: retype the address data. But that's not necessary here as you can click the Repeat key and the home address data is duplicated to the mailing address fields. You should try this application, stored as Events02.app in Proj0804, to see how it works. Then you will delete and recreate the event handler as an exercise. Be aware that this is not a complete application—the project consists only of the input page Events02-IN, which produces the screen of Figure 8-17. To test it, proceed as follows.

Proj0804
Events02

1. Open the application.
2. Bring up Events02-IN.htm in Form Designer.
3. Click the Preview icon ![icon] on the Form Designer toolbar (or click Page/ Preview on the Form Designer toolbar). The browser will be activated displaying the input screen.
4. Fill in the name and home address fields—as in Figure 8-17.
5. Click the Repeat button and you will see the home address data duplicated to the mailing address fields.
6. Close the browser thus returning to Form Designer.

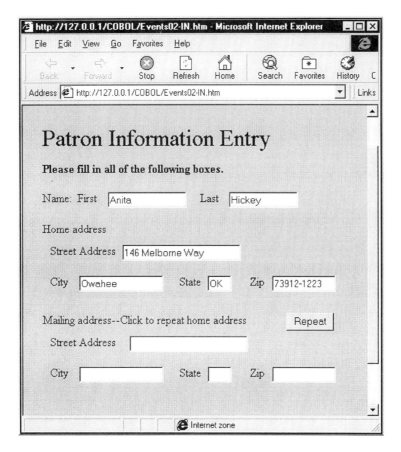

Figure 8-17. Duplicate data on an input screen.

Before proceeding, look at entries of the control tree and you will see that the home address Input Text controls are named StreetAddress, City, State, and Zip. Similarly, the mailing address controls are named MStreetAddress, MCity, MState, and MZip.

JavaScript Code for Duplicating Data Items

This example accesses the value from each of the home address fields and places it into the corresponding mailing address fields. Let's consider, for instance, the following JavaScript code to access the value (one of its properties) of the home street address input control.

```
document.form1.StreetAddress.value
```

Inspecting these components from left to right, this syntax denotes that you are interested in the value stored in the object StreetAddress (the name of the street address Input Text control) contained in the form named form1, which is itself contained in this document.

JavaScript includes an assignment statement, which is similar to Cobol's Compute statement. For instance, the following JavaScript code will place the value stored in StreetAddress into the object (Input Text control) MstreetAddress.

```
Document.form1.MStreetAddress.value = Document.form1.StreetAddress.value
```

Creating the Event Handler

There is no need to recreate the entire form for this application—you can simply delete the existing event handler then rebuild it by stepping through this exercise. If you do not have this page on your Form Designer screen, then open the project (Events02.app in Proj0804) and bring up Events02-IN.htm.

1. Right-click anywhere in the page then click Events from the popup menu.
2. In the Objects pane of the resulting Script Assistant, highlight the OK button inputbutton1. Click the onclick event and you will see the Script Assistant display of Figure 8-18. Notice that the event handler contains one JavaScript assignment statement for each of the four fields to be duplicated.
3. Click the Delete Handler button then click Yes on the resulting popup menu. You want to remove this event, then recreate it.
4. Check to ensure that the inputbutton1 control-tree entry is still selected.
5. Double-click the onclick checkbox.
6. Click the Properties tab and scroll down the control tree to the MstreetAddress Input Text entry and click on it. This is the item that goes on the left of the = sign in the JavaScript assignment statement.
7. In the Events pane, scroll down and click the Value checkbox. The upper part of your screen should look like Figure 8-19.
8. You want code that will "set" a value for this control (MstreetAddress). To this end, click the Insert Set Code button.
9. If you wanted to insert a literal into this control you would enter it into the resulting popup screen (Figure 8-20). You do not want a literal, so click OK without making an entry. The following will be inserted into your event handler (in the bottom part of the screen).

    document.form1.MStreetAddress.value = ""

10. You don't want the quote marks so delete them.

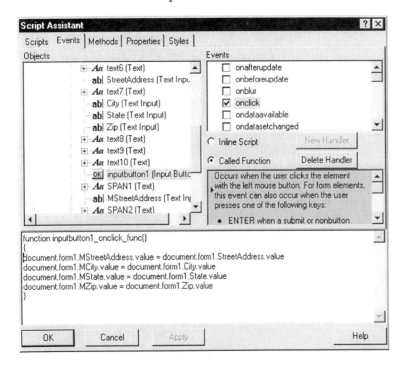

Figure 8-18.
Script Assistant with the event handler.

Figure 8-19.
Inserting JavaScript
code into an event
handler.

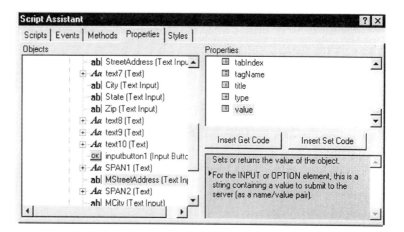

11. With the cursor positioned after the equal sign, select the StreetAddress Input Text control in the tree.

12. Scroll down the Properties list and click the value checkbox. Your screen will again look like Figure 8-19 except StreetAddress will be selected.

13. Now you want code to "get" the value from this control (StreetAddress), so click the Insert Get Code button. If you've carefully followed these steps, this line of your event handler should be as follows.

    document.form1.MStreetAddress.value = document.form1.StreetAddress.value

14. Repeat this process for each of the other three controls: city, state, and zip. Alternately copy this line of code and paste it three times. Then change successive occurrences of StreetAddress appropriately: City, State, and Zip.

15. Save the page and do a trial run. If the fields to not duplicate correctly, go back to the Script Assistant and correct any errors you have in the JavaScript code—refer to Figure 8-18.

More on Setting the Value

Sometimes you will want JavaScript code that sets a value to spaces. For instance, if you wanted FormCity set to spaces you would insert the following code.

    document.HTMLForm.FormCity.value = ""

On the other hand, had you typed an entry into the Object Property window (Figure 8-20), for instance Winnemuccu, the JavaScript statement would have taken the following form.

    document.HTMLForm.FormCity.value = "Winnemuccu"

When the user clicked the button the browser would enter Winnemuccu into the control.

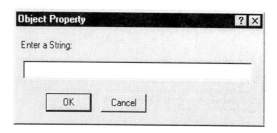

Figure 8-20. Specifying the set value.

Setting Check Boxes and Radio Button

Sometimes you will want to set check boxes or radio buttons in an event handler. The process is nearly identical to that you have just seen. Let's try it by inserting a check box in Events02-IN and inserting JavaScript code to set it to checked.

1. Get back to the Form Designer screen for Events02-IN.htm.
2. Insert a checkbox anywhere on this page.
3. Bring up the Script Assistant as in Figure 8-18; the button event must be displayed (as in Figure 8-18).
4. Click the Properties tab.
5. In the object tree, find the newly added checkboxspan1, expand it, and select the Check Box itself as shown in the left pane of Figure 8-21.
6. In the Properties pane, click Checked.
7. Click the Insert Set Code button.
8. From the resulting popup Object Property window, you see that you can designate a value True or False. True is the default so click OK. The required JavaScript statement will be inserted at the cursor position as shown in the lower pane of Figure 8-21.

You can change a selected radio button with the same procedure. If you try this, don't be confused with the number enclosed within brackets; this is simply the way JavaScript handles radio buttons.

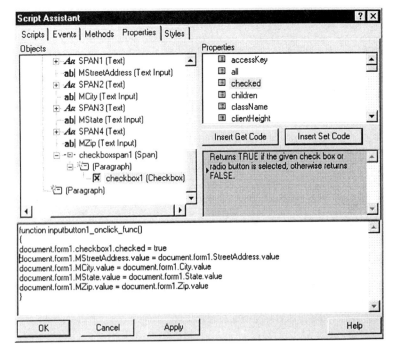

Figure 8-21.
Inserting JavaScript code to set a check box value.

Using an Input Button to Transfer Control

From preceding examples of this chapter you've learned how to create hyperlinks both from a Text control and from an image. This allows you to transfer control from one screen to another thereby achieving repetition. You can also do this with an Input Button—try it with Lib12.app in Proj0703.

1. Open Lib12.app and bring up Lib12-OUT in Form Designer.
2. If you have one of the hyperlinks from the earlier exercises, delete it.
3. Insert an Input Button control to the right of the address fields and change its caption to Next Patron.
4. Bring up the Script Assistant.
5. Highlight the button control in the control-tree pane.
6. Double-click the onclick checkbox.
7. Following the open brace, type the command:

```
location.href="Lib12-IN.htm"
```

Your completed event handler should be as follows.

```
function inputbutton1_onclick_func1()
{
location.href="Lib12-IN.htm"
}
```

8. Click OK to save and close the Script Assistant.
9. Save the form and close Form Designer.
10. Run the application and click the Next Patron button to ensure that your modification works properly.

The location statement tells the browser to load the HTML page Lib12-I.htm from the same location as the current page was loaded. The latter results from location.href, which returns the complete URL of the current document.

A Word of Caution

Errors that you make in defining events sometimes are very difficult to find, especially if you do not know JavaScript. To that end, don't get carried away and attempt creating sophisticated scripts. One specific piece of advice is to be certain you have the correct element highlighted on the control tree of the object list window before stipulating your event. For instance, if you've inadvertently selected the form to designate an onclick event, then the handler will be triggered whenever you click anywhere on the form.

If you have a burning desire to get fancy with event handlers, then purchase a good book on JavaScript.

Summing Up

Project Summary

Proj0801 (Borders) features the input page—it includes an Input Image (sensitive image area on the screen) as the form's input control. CGI code evaluates the position of the image on which the user clicked.

Proj0802 (Lib14) uses a Text control as a hyperlink text transfer from one form to another.

Proj0803 (Events01) is the first example illustrating creating an event handler. This one displays a help screen when a button is clicked.

Proj0804 (Events02) consists only of an example data-entry input page, a typical form in which a user enters successive data records. An event handler is included to offer data from the preceding record entry as defaults for the current record.

General Summary

Solo, the simulated Web server, sets up two Web shares. COBOL identifies the subdirectory containing the HTML forms and cgi-bin designates the location of the executable code of the CGI program.

You insert graphics into your forms with the Image tool. For each graphic, you must designate its location and its file name, for instance, /Images/book-picture.gif.

Hyperlinks (hot spots) give you the ability to pass control from one Web document to another. You create a hyperlink from a Text control or an image by designating a hypertext reference.

An **event** is any action the user takes such as clicking on a button or moving a window on the screen. An **event handler** is code describing actions to be taken when an event occurs. Net Express includes the Script Assist which allows you to create simple JavaScript event handlers without the need for a knowledge of JavaScript.

To use the Button control in a form, you write a JavaScript event handler (program) describing the required action when the button is clicked.

Coming Up

Thus far you have studied applications consisting of an input form, a CGI, and an output form. In the next chapter you will begin to see variations on this theme. The three example applications illustrate: a CGI in which the same form serves for both input and output, using multiple output forms, and providing a user access to either patron or book data.

Assignment

8-1.

This assignment involves modifying Assignment 5-1 as follows.

Input page

1. In the original form definitions, set the following default values (refer to the record description in Figure 5-34):

    Stirrup coves: No
    Padded seat: No
    Leather tooling: Basic
    Silver ornaments: None

2. Insert a Reset Button to reset entries to their default values.

3. Insert an Input Button (give it the caption Std Deluxe) with an event handler that sets values as follows:

    Stirrup coves: Yes
    Padded seat: Yes
    Leather tooling: Brush
    Silver ornaments: Beads

4. Place an international information symbol (see Figure 8-15) adjacent to each of the Select controls (leather tooling and silver ornaments) with an onclick event that displays a brief description for the user via a help window.

Output page

1. Provide for repetition.

More Complex Applications

Chapter Contents

One Form for Input and Output 218
   Asymmetric and Symmetric Programs 218
   Features of Proj0901 218
   Creating the Application 219
   Creating the CGI 221
   CGI Code 221
   Finish-Up Tasks 224
Multiple Output Pages 226
   The Nature of the Project 226
   The CGI Program 228
Multiple Actions—Two Submit Buttons 229
   Project Input and Output 229
   About the Subprogram Book-sub.cbl 230
   The Input Form and Multiple Submit Buttons 232
   Selecting Names For Form Items 232
   The Generated CGI Program 233
Summing Up 235
   Project Summary 235
   General Summary 235
Coming Up 236
Assignment 236

Chapter

9

Chapter Introduction

From the preceding chapters you've learned how to use basic tools to create input and output pages and how to modify CGI programs to carry out needed server-side actions. To this end, you have created applications consisting of an input form, a CGI, and an output form. As you are well aware from you experiences with the Web, in real applications life is much more than this simple trio of components. From this chapter you will learn about the following variation on that basic theme.

- Creating a CGI that uses the same form for input and output.
- CGI code necessary to return either of two HTML pages to the browser.
- Using multiple Submit buttons on an input form.

One Form for Input and Output

Asymmetric and Symmetric Programs

Each server-side program you've created to this point includes one input form and one output form as illustrated in Figure 9-1(a). Micro Focus designates this as an **asymmetric program:** different forms for input and output. A **symmetric program**, illustrated in Figure 9-1(b), uses the same form for input and output. An application based on a symmetric server-side program typically works like this.

1. The user clicks a link on a Web page hyperlink that starts the server-side program running [Lib15 in Figure 9-1(b)].
2. The server-side program runs (usually without the normal processing procedures) and returns an HTML page.
3. The user makes appropriate entries (the form's input) into the form and clicks to submit.
4. The server-side program processes input from the user, accesses data, and returns it via the form to the user's browser.

This has some interesting ramifications, as you will see in the next project.

Features of Proj0901

The next project, Lib15.app stored in the folder Proj0901, consists of the components illustrated in Figure 9-2. Note that Lib15-INI does *not* provide input to the server-side program Lib15, it only sends a message to the server to run this program. The single page Lib15-IO provides serves as both input to and output from Lib15. Therefore, Lib15 is a symmetrical program.

Open this application and make some trial runs for a feel of how it works. For instance, consider the screen sequence of Figure 9-3.

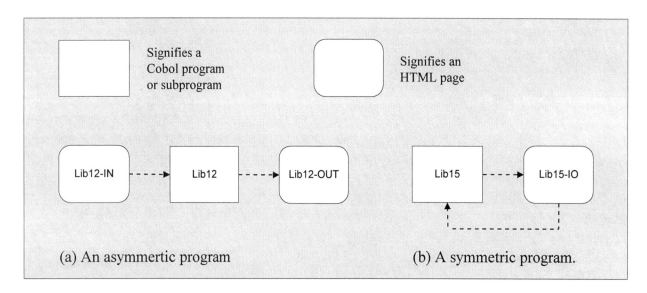

Figure 9-1. Graphical representations of Web applications.

(a) The opening screen (from Lib15-INI).

(b) Clicking the Continue button in the screen of (a) activates the CGI Lib15 which returns this screen.

(c) Entering the patron number 005 in the screen of (b) and clicking the Submit button sends the input 005 to the CGI program which returns the data of this screen.

(d) Entering the patron number 020 in the screen of (c) and clicking the Submit button sends the input 020 to the CGI program which returns the data of this screen.

Creating the Application

It would be a good idea to step through creating this application as it will give you an insight to some subtleties that are best appreciated by doing.

1. Create a new folder for your version of this project and copy the file Lib-sub3.cbl into it.

2. Create the project Lib15; designate Project from an existing application. In the creation sequence, add the file lib-sub3.cbl to the project.

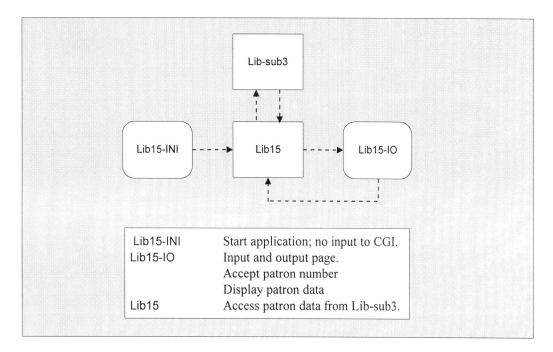

Figure 9-2. The Lib15 application.

As your applications become more complex, you might find it difficult to visualize the interrelationships between components. To that end, each of the remaining examples in this book includes a **component diagram** like those of Figures 9-1 and 9-2. Server-side programs are represented by rectangles; HTML pages are represented by rectangles with rounded corners.

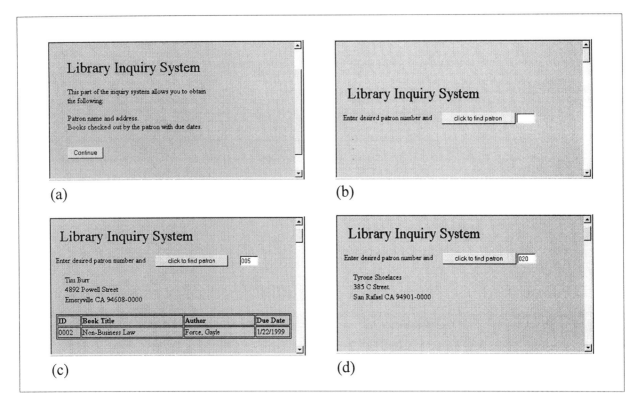

Figure 9-3. Sequence of browser displays for Lib15.

3. Create a new HTML page (click File/New/HTML page). Designate a Positional Form and use the name Lib15-INI. This will be the page to produce the startup screen of Figure 9-3(a).

4. Create an HTML page to produce the screen of Figure 9-3(a). All of the items on this screen are Text except the Input Button (OK) labeled Continue. When you are finished, save and close.

5. Create another page but for this one click the From Existing tab then select Lib12-OUT from the folder Proj0703.

6. Name this page Lib15-IO then complete the form generation.

7. Modify this form so it looks like Figure 9-4 as follows.
   - Change the caption.
   - Delete the patron number Server-Side Text control.
   - Insert a Submit button to the right of the user instruction "Enter desired..." and change its caption as shown.
   - Insert an Text Input control. Change its properties as follows.

Name	InPatronNumber
ID	InPatronNumber
MaxLength	3
Size	3
COBOLPicture	x(3)

8. Save the form.

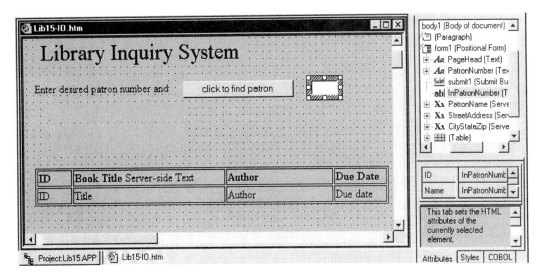

Figure 9-4. The HTML page Lib15-IO.htm.

Creating the CGI

From the descriptions in Figure 9-2 you see that Lib15-INI, which begins execution of this application, provides no input (no patron number) to the CGI. Therefore, you need code in Lib15.cbl to prevent executing the subprogram to read a record. Fortunately, Net Express automatically generates the needed code for you. Recall that the Server Program Generation screen lists as a default the generation template CGI.skl. You have used in its place CGI-min.skl, a version provided with this book in which a large number of comments and some code (all confusing to the beginner) have been removed. For this application, you need some of that code. So, let's create the CGI then look at the differences over preceding CGIs.

1. Click File/New/Internet Application/Server Program/Next and you will see a screen like Figure 9-5.
2. Enter Lib15.cbl for Filename.
3. For Generation Template, scroll down and select CGI-nibi.skl (nibi for no initial browser input).
4. For both input and output, select Lib15-IO.htm. Ignore Lib15-INI.htm at this point.
5. Complete the action of building this CGI.

The programmer-inserted code for this program is identical to that of preceding examples that display the patron and his/her books. To that end, proceed as follows.

6. Copy and paste code from, for instance, Lib12.cbl (in the Proj0703 folder). Referring to Figure 9-6, this consists of lines 100-113 and 153-180.
7. Insert the Move of line 125—you will see why in the next section.

CGI Code

The main section of all CGI programs you've created in previous exercises contains five Perform statements, for instance:

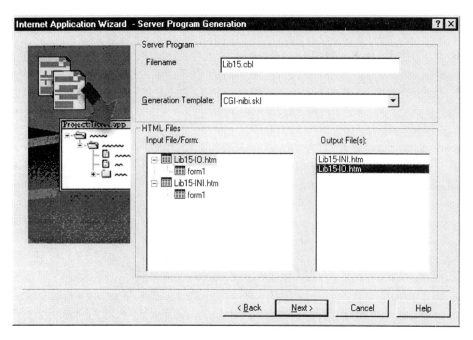

Figure 9-5. Creating a symmetric CGI—Lib15.

```
perform process-form-input-data
perform convert-input
perform process-business-logic
perform lib12-out-cvt
perform lib12-out-out
```

Obviously, for a symmetric application, you do not want the process-business-logic section performed the first time this CGI is executed. Likewise, you do not want output conversion (in this example, the lib12-io-cvt section) carried out as there is no output data to convert. The standard Net Express template (CGI.skl) contains code to accommodate this need; the template CGI-nibi.skl, included with this book, contains that code.

The data item MF-SERVER-EXEC at line 47 of Figure 9-6 serves as a flag to indicate whether or not input was received from the browser (see the comment lines 41-46). Next, look at how that data item is used in the procedural code of lines 122-130. Lets' follow the sequence of actions for the first execution of this program.

1. From line 118 the process-form-input-data section (line 136) is performed This causes execution of the accept statement at line 140 to be executed. As there is no input from Lib15-INI the entire HTML input record HTMLForm (line 17) contains spaces.
2. From line 119 the convert-input-section (line 143) is performed thereby performing (line 145) the input-conversion-section (line 204).
3. The test at line 206 is true therefore causing the data item MF-SERVER-EXEC to be set to no.
4. Control is returned to main section where the test at line 122 is true therefore causing the Lib15-io-ini to be performed (from line 123). This sets all data items of the HTML page to their designated initial values.

```
  1    IDENTIFICATION DIVISION.                    120    *> If there is no input from the Browser,
  2        program-id. "Lib15".                    121    *> then initial field values are output
                                                   122    if MF-SERVER-EXEC = z"no"
 10    DATA DIVISION.                              123        perform lib15-io-ini
 11                                                124            *> lib15-io
 12    working-storage section.                    125        Move 0 to c-BookData, c-ColumnHeads
                                                   126    else
 16        copy "Lib15.cpf".                        127        perform process-business-logic
 17        01 HTMLForm is external-form.            128        perform lib15-io-cvt
 18           03 f-BookAuthor    pic x(13)  occurs 10    129            *> lib15-io
 19               identified by "BookAuthor"        130    end-if *>MF-SERVER-EXEC = z"no"
 20               count in c-BookAuthor.            131    perform lib15-io-out
                                                   132        *> lib15-io
 41    *>    The following field indicates if input was    133    exit program
 42    *>    received from the Browser              134    stop run.
 43    *>    z"yes" indicates that business logic   135
 44    *>        should be executed                 136    process-form-input-data section.
 45    *>    z"no" indicates an "initial load" condition    137    *> Accept the input from the Browser
 46    *>    (the null terminator is required by JScript)    138    *> and check for errors
 47    01 MF-SERVER-EXEC          pic x(4).        139        perform browser-initialize
                                                   140        accept htmlform
 72    *> The following fields are used to count the    141        exit.
 73    *> number of values input for fields that occur    142
 74    *> more than once or which can return multiple values    143    convert-input section.
 75    01 HTML-Counters.                           144        *> Convert numeric input values
 76       03 c-BookData       PIC 9(4) comp-5 value 0.    145        perform input-conversion
 77       03 c-ColumnHeads    PIC 9(4) comp-5 value 0.    146        if v-all-ok = 0
                                                   147            perform output-form-error-and-stop
 84    *> WARNING: Do not remove this copy statement    148        end-if
 85    *> or modify the contents of the copy file.    149        exit.
 86    copy "Lib15.cpy".                           150
 87    01 FormFields.                              151    process-business-logic section.
 88       03 BookAuthor        pic x(13) occurs 10.    152        *> Add application business logic here.
 89       03 BookTitle         pic x(25) occurs 10.    153        Call "lib-sub3" Using InPatronNumber
 90       03 serversidetext1   pic x(1) occurs 2.    154                              patron-info
 91       03 BookID            pic x(4) occurs 10.    155                              book-counter
 92       03 InPatronNumber    pic x(3).            156                              book-info-array
 93       03 DueDate           pic x(10) occurs 10.    157        Move 0 to c-ColumnHeads, c-BookData
 94       03 ssubmit           pic x(64).           158        If patron-info = low-values
 95       03 StreetAddress     pic x(20).           159            Move "No record for patron" to PatronName
 96       03 CityStateZip      pic x(30).           160        Else
 97       03 PatronName        pic x(23).           161            Move patron-name to PatronName
 98                                                162            Move street-address to StreetAddress
 99    *> Enter additional working-storage items here    163            Move city-state-zip to CityStateZip
100    01  in-patron-number         pic X(03).     164            Move book-counter to c-BookData
101    01  patron-info.                            165            If book-counter > 0
102        05  patron-name          pic X(23).     166                Move book-counter to c-BookData
103        05  street-address       pic X(20).     167                Move 1 to c-ColumnHeads
104        05  city-state-zip       pic X(30).     168            End-If *>book-counter > 0
105    01  book-counter             pic 9(02).     169            Perform varying book-pntr from 1 by 1
106    01  book-info-array.                        170                        until book-pntr > book-counter
107        05  book-info        occurs 10 times.   171                Move bi-book-id(book-pntr)
108            10  bi-book-id       pic X(04).     172                        to BookID(book-pntr)
109            10  bi-book-title    pic X(25).     173                Move bi-book-title(book-pntr)
110            10  bi-book-author   pic X(13).     174                        to BookTitle(book-pntr)
111            10  bi-due-date      pic X(10).     175                Move bi-book-author(book-pntr)
112                                                176                        to BookAuthor(book-pntr)
113    01  book-pntr                pic 9(02).     177                Move bi-due-date(book-pntr)
114                                                178                        to DueDate(book-pntr)
115    PROCEDURE DIVISION.                         179            End-Perform
116                                                180        End-If *>patron-info = low-values
117    main section.                               181
118        perform process-form-input-data        182        exit.
119        perform convert-input                  
                                                   204    Input-Conversion Section.
                                                   205
                                                   206        if HTMLForm = spaces
                                                   207            move z"no" to MF-SERVER-EXEC
                                                   208        else
                                                   209            move z"yes" to MF-SERVER-EXEC
                                                   210        end-if
```

Figure 9-6. Selected codes segments of Lib15.cbl.

5. One action of the initialization section (not shown in this listing) is to set HTML counters (variable array items) to their maximum values. In this application, as you do not want repeating rows of the table displayed, you must insert the Move of line 125 to set the row counters to 0.

6. Note that business-logic-section is not performed as the statements of lines 127 and 128 are not executed this first pass.

7. The initialized HTML page is returned to the client by action of the lib15-io-out section performed from line 131.

During subsequent executions of this CGI, the value of HTMLForm will be other than spaces. Therefore, you will see execution of the customary five-statement sequence in the main section (lines 118, 119, 127, 128, and 131).

Finish-Up Tasks

If you clicked on Run for your version of this application, you would see the Start Animating window of Figure 9-7 in which execution is to begin with the CGI. Net Express always designates the CGI as the starting point when you create a symmetric CGI. It had no idea that you want to begin execution with the initial HTML page as you made no reference to it when you created the CGI (see Figure 9-5). You have two remaining tasks to complete this project.

- Tell Net Express to begin execution with Lib15-INI.htm.
- Define an event in the initial screen that transfers control to the CGI.

As described in the window of Figure 9-7, you can change the starting point for an application by simply typing an entry, but it does not become a permanent change. For a permanent change, proceed as follows.

1. Click Animate/Settings to produce a settings window that looks like Figure 9-8.
2. Change the Start Animating at: entry from

    http://127.0.0.1/CGI-bin/Lib15.exe

to

    http://127.0.0.1/COBOL/Lib15-INI.htm

3. Click OK.

The final step is to define an onclick event and create an event handler for the Input Button of Lib15-INI.htm. This event handler must instruct the server to run this application's CGI.

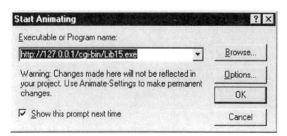

Figure 9-7. Application starting point.

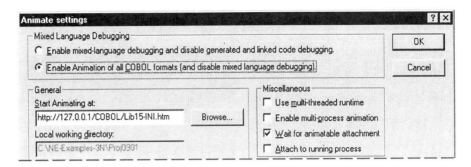

Figure 9-8. Animate settings window.

1. Bring up Lib15-INI.htm.
2. Right-click in the form and select Events.
3. Highlight the Input Button on the control tree of the Objects pane—see Figure 9-9.
4. Double-click the onclick event.
5. For the event handler, type the entry shown in Figure 9-9, that is:

    location.href="/cgi-bin/Lib15.exe"

6. Click OK.

Your project is now complete. You can rebuild then run. Enter both valid and invalid patron numbers to make certain everything works as it should.

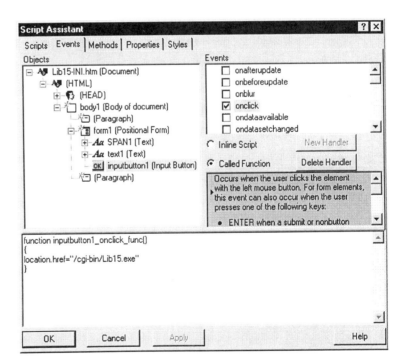

Figure 9-9.
Entering an event handler for the Input Button.

Multiple Output Pages

The Nature of the Project

Each of the previous examples you've studied includes one output page. However, often your application will require different output screens as determined by your CGI's processing logic. Features of HTML that allow for multiple output pages from a CGI are available to you through Net Express. As a simple illustration of an application with two output pages, consider the project Lib16.app (in the folder Proj0902). It is much like preceding projects in that it accepts a patron number and displays the patron and book data. However, it is expanded to produce the error output screen of Figure 9-10. You see the relationship between components of this project in the diagram of Figure 9-11. This application was created from components of Lib12 in the folder Proj0703.

- Lib16-IN.htm and Lib16-OUT1.htm were created from corresponding pages of the Lib12 project.
- Basic CGI code was duplicated from the Lib12 CGI.

1. Create a new folder for this project. Place a copy of the files Lib-sub3.cbl in the folder.
2. Create the new project Lib16 using the Project from existing application option. Designate Lib-sub3.cbl.
3. Generate the HTML page Lib16-IN.htm using Lib12-IN.htm (from Proj0703) as the template. No changes are required to the resulting page.

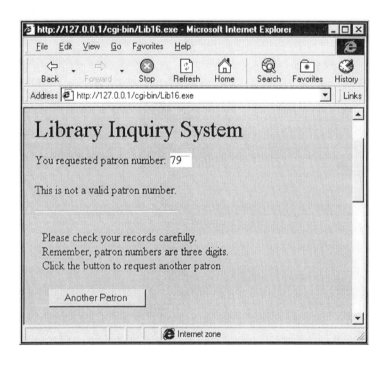

Figure 9-10.
The Invalid-patron-number output screen.

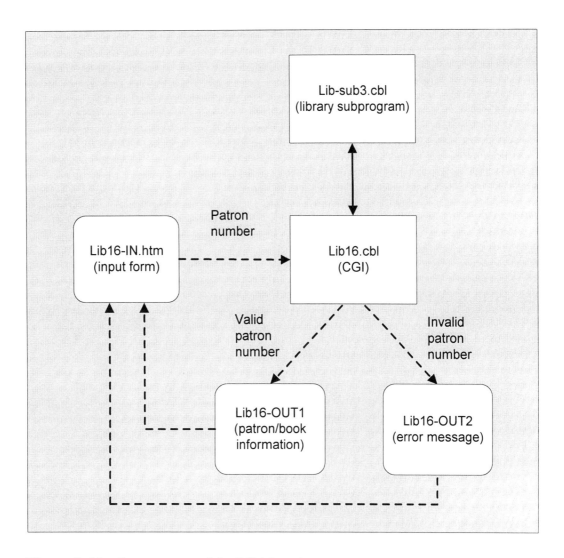

Figure 9-11. Components of the Lib16 project.

4. Generate the HTML page Lib16-OUT1.htm using Lib12-OUT.htm as the template. Insert an Input Button with an event handler to return control to Lib16-IN.htm.

5. Create the page for Lib16-OUT2.htm—refer to Figure 9-10.
   - The patron number is displayed by a Server-Side Text control with the ID entry InPatronNumber.
   - The button is an Input Button with an event handler to return control to Lib16-IN.htm.
   - All other displays are produced by Text controls.

6. Create the CGI by selecting both Lib16-OUT1.htm and Lib16-OUT2.htm as output—see Figure 9-12.

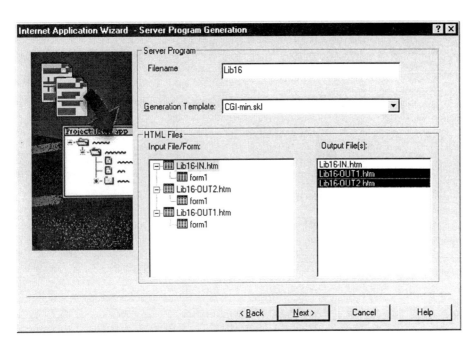

Figure 9-12. Selecting input and output forms for the CGI.

The CGI Program

The first thing to do is to insert process-business-logic section entries into this CGI by copying and pasting from Lib12.cbl. When finished, look at the main section and you will see the following familiar code.

```
perform process-form-input-data
perform convert-input
perform process-business-logic
perform lib16-out1-cvt
perform lib16-out1-out
```

The last two performs handle processing for the HTML page Lib16-OUT1.htm. Scroll down and you will find the designated sections. (You must be viewing the CGI through Net Express as these sections are in the copy file Lib16.cpv.) Look further (beyond the HTML code) and you will find corresponding sections lib16-out2-cvt and lib16-out2-out containing the code to be executed for an invalid patron number.

Look at Figure 9-13 for modifications necessary to control which HTML page is returned to the browser.

- The section process-business-logic (beginning line 147) is identical to that of the previous project except no action is taken when the file-accessing program returns low-values—see the Continue statement at line 155. In previous versions of this application, a Move statement placed an appropriate error message in an output field.
- The key to this program's logic is the If statement of the main section where patron-info is tested thereby causing the appropriate pair of conversion/output sections to be performed—see lines 122-128.

```
  1  IDENTIFICATION DIVISION.              147  process-business-logic section.
  2      program-id. "Lib16".              148    *> Add application business logic here.
                                           149    Call "lib-sub3" Using InPatronNumber
116  PROCEDURE DIVISION.                   150                       patron-info
117                                        151                       book-counter
118  main section.                         152                       book-info-array
119      perform process-form-input-data   153    Move 0 to c-ColumnHeads, c-BookData
120      perform convert-input             154    If patron-info = low-values
121      perform process-business-logic    155      Continue
122      If patron-info = low-values       156    Else
123          perform lib16-out2-cvt        157      Move patron-name to PatronName
124          perform lib16-out2-out        158      Move street-address to StreetAddress
125      Else                              159      Move city-state-zip to CityStateZip
126          perform lib16-out1-cvt        160      Move book-counter to c-BookData
127          perform lib16-out1-out        161      If book-counter > 0
128      End-If *>patron-info = low-values 162        Move book-counter to c-BookData
129      exit program                      163        Move 1 to c-ColumnHeads
130      stop run.                         164      End-If *>book-counter > 0
                                           165      Perform varying book-pntr from 1 by 1
                                           166              until book-pntr > book-counter
                                           167        Move bi-book-id(book-pntr)
                                           168               to BookID(book-pntr)
                                           169        Move bi-book-title(book-pntr)
                                           170               to BookTitle(book-pntr)
                                           171        Move bi-book-author(book-pntr)
                                           172               to BookAuthor(book-pntr)
                                           173        Move bi-due-date(book-pntr)
                                           174               to DueDate(book-pntr)
                                           175      End-Perform
                                           176    End-If *>patron-info = low-values
                                           177
                                           178    exit.
```

Figure 9-13. Selected segments of `Lib16.cbl`.

Multiple Actions—Two Submit Buttons

Project Input and Output

The next project, Lib17 stored in the Proj0903 folder, provides the user the option of obtaining information about either patrons or books. To this end, the input screen looks like Figure 9-14. Entering a patron number and clicking the Find Patron button produces the same result as earlier projects—for instance, see Figure 8-11. On the other hand, entering a book number and clicking the Find Book button produces one of the three screens shown in Figure 9-15.

> Proj0903
> Lib17

The project's components and their relationships are shown in Figure 9-16; its significant features are as follows.

- The CGI must access either of two subprograms: `Lib-sub3.cbl` or `Book-sub.cbl`, depending upon the request from the input form (patron number or book number).
- The CGI sends either of two output pages to the browser. You know how to do this from the preceding example (Lib16).
- With required access to either of two subprograms, the CGI will require additional logic beyond that of, for instance, Lib16.

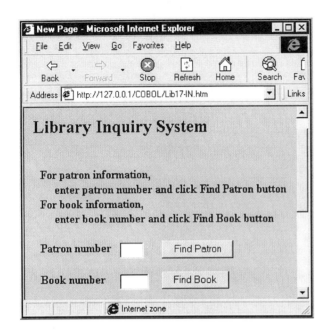

Figure 9-14.
Input screen for the
Lib17 project.

About the Subprogram Book-sub.cbl

The subprogram to access book information is stored in the project's folder Proj0903 as Book-sub.cbl. You can inspect it if you wish (refer to the listing in the Appendix), but that is not necessary. You only need to know the subprogram parameters in order to understand its use in this project. To that end, consider the portion of its code listed on the opposite page.

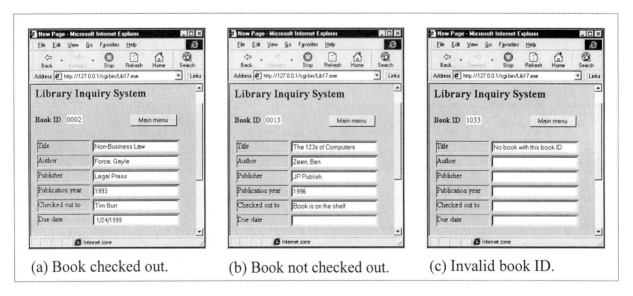

(a) Book checked out.   (b) Book not checked out.   (c) Invalid book ID.

Figure 9-15. Output screens for the Lib17 project.

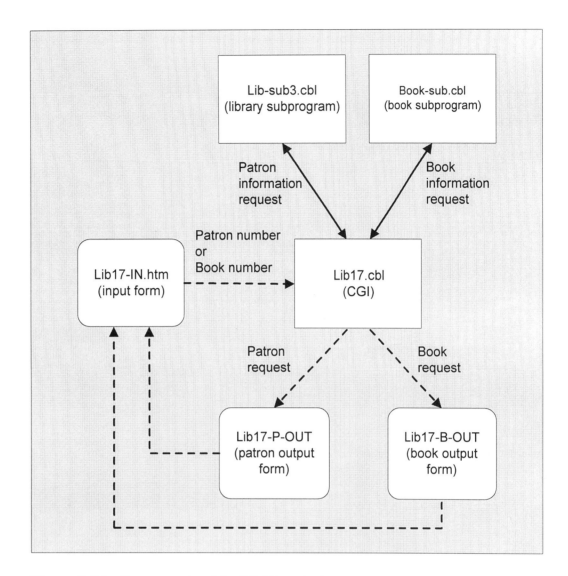

Figure 9-16. Components of the Lib17 project.

```
Linkage Section.
    01  in-book-id              pic X(04).    Input parameter
    01  book-info.                            Output parameter
        10  ls-book-title        pic X(25).
        10  ls-book-author       pic X(13).
        10  ls-due-date          pic X(10).
        10  ls-book-publisher    pic X(11).
        10  ls-publication-year  pic X(04).
        10  ls-patron-name       pic X(23).

Procedure Division Using in-book-id
                        book-info.
```

Compare the elementary items of the output parameter to the display of Figure 9-15(a) and you see that they are the six required display items.

If there is no record in the file for the submitted book ID, the data item book-info is set to low-values. If the book is on the shelf (not checked out) the data item ls-patron-name is set to low-values.

The Input Form and Multiple Submit Buttons

Until now you've had no need to focus on properties of the Submit button; the only change you've made is the caption on the button itself. In this application, your input page Lib17-IN.htm contains two Submit buttons and the CGI must determine which one was clicked. In a sense, two or more Submit buttons are handled like Radio buttons. That is, they belong to a group and the group name designates the name (of the name/value pair) sent to the CGI. Furthermore, you program for multiple Submit controls in exactly the same way you program for a group of radio buttons. If you bring up this input page you will see the following properties.

ID. You can leave the ID attribute at its default value or change it to something meaningful for its control-tree documentation value.

Name. Net Express assigns the default Name attribute ssubmit for all Submit buttons, there is no need to change this default. It is the name of the name/value pair sent to the CGI program.

Value. This attribute is displayed on the button and it is the value of the name/value pair sent to the CGI program.

COBOLPicture. This property designates the size of the Cobol data item to contain the value from the input form. The default value is x(64). The value returned to the CGI will be either Find Patron or Find Book; x(11) is adequate to handle these values.

Selecting Names For Form Items

This application includes two different output pages displaying much of the same data, as you can see by comparing Figures 9-17(a) and 9-17(b). From the patron output page (Lib17-P-OUT.htm), book data is displayed from subscripted data items. For example, Net Express wants to define the book title in Working-Storage as:

```
03 BookTitle        pic x(25) occurs 10.
```

However, from the book output page (Lib17-B-OUT.htm), Net Express wants to define the book title in Working-Storage as:

```
03 BookTitle        pic x(25).
```

Although the first release of Net Express does not generate both of these Working-Storage entries, it does produce a compiler error in code generated in the .CPV copy file code. This is resolved here by adding a prefix of B to all book fields in the output page Lib17-B-OUT.htm; for instance the book page uses BBookTitle and the patron page uses BookTitle. You will see this in the CGI.

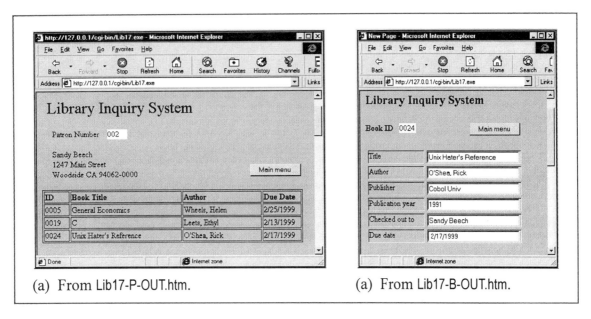

Figure 9-17. Two output screens—Lib17.

The Generated CGI Program

With the preceding preliminaries, the CGI code segments of Figure 9-18 are reasonably straightforward.

- The form fields of lines 109-111 were generated from the input page Lib17-IN.htm. (Note: For convenient reference here, I have altered the sequence of these form fields over the sequence produced by Net Express.)
- The form fields of lines 112-116 were generated from the output page Lib17-B-OUT.htm, the book page.
- The form fields of lines 117-124 were generated from the output page Lib17-P-OUT, the patron page.
- Determination of data to be accessed (patron or book) is made by the If statement of line 182. Note that the test involves the Value attribute assigned the Submit button. It is also the label on the button.
- Processing for a patron request uses the same code (lines 183-210) as earlier projects.
- Processing for a book request is handled by the code of lines 212-230—this is new code that calls the book subprogram. Its logic is similar to that for handling patron data.
- Determination of the output page to be sent to the browser is made by the If statement of line 154. This code has exactly the same form as the corresponding code of Lib16.

```
  1   IDENTIFICATION DIVISION.                    161       exit program
  2       program-id. "Lib17".                    162       stop run.

 10   DATA DIVISION.                              180   process-business-logic section.
 11                                               181       *> Add application business logic here.
 12   working-storage section.                    182       If ssubmit = "Find Patron"
                                                  183           Call "lib-sub3" Using InPatronNumber
105       *> WARNING: Do not remove this copy statement  184                             patron-info
106       *> or modify the contents of the copy file.    185                             book-counter
107       copy "Lib17.cpy".                       186                             book-info-array
108       01 FormFields.                          187           Move 0 to c-ColumnHeads, c-BookData
109           03 InBookID          pic X(4).      188           If patron-info = low-values
110           03 InPatronNumber    pic X(3).      189               Move "No record for patron" to PatronName
111           03 ssubmit           pic x(12).     190           Else
112           03 BBookAuthor       pic X(13).     191               Move patron-name to PatronName
113           03 BBookTitle        pic X(25).     192               Move street-address to StreetAddress
114           03 BPublicationYear  pic X(4).      193               Move city-state-zip to CityStateZip
115           03 BBookPublisher    pic X(11).     194               Move book-counter to c-BookData
116           03 BDueDate          pic X(10).     195               If book-counter > 0
117           03 BookID            pic x(4) occurs 10.  196                   Move book-counter to c-BookData
118           03 BookAuthor        pic x(13) occurs 10. 197                   Move 1 to c-ColumnHeads
119           03 BookTitle         pic x(25) occurs 10. 198               End-If *>book-counter > 0
120           03 DueDate           pic x(10) occurs 10. 199               Perform varying book-pntr from 1 by 1
121           03 serversidetext1   pic x(1) occurs 2.   200                       until book-pntr > book-counter
122           03 StreetAddress     pic x(20).     201                   Move bi-book-id(book-pntr)
123           03 CityStateZip      pic x(30).     202                             to BookID(book-pntr)
124           03 PatronName        pic x(23).     203                   Move bi-book-title(book-pntr)
                                                  204                             to BookTitle(book-pntr)
125                                               205                   Move bi-book-author(book-pntr)
126   *> Enter additional working-storage items here  206                             to BookAuthor(book-pntr)
127   01    patron-info.                          207                   Move bi-due-date(book-pntr)
128       05    patron-name        pic X(23).     208                             to DueDate(book-pntr)
129       05    street-address     pic X(20).     209               End-Perform
130       05    city-state-zip     pic X(30).     210           End-If *>patron-info = low-values
131   01  book-counter             pic 9(02).     211       Else
132   01  book-info-array.                        212           Call "book-sub" Using InBookID
133       05  book-info    occurs 10 times.       213                             b-book-info
134           10  bi-book-id       pic X(04).     214           If b-book-info = low-values
135           10  bi-book-title    pic X(25).     215               Move "No book with this book ID"
136           10  bi-book-author   pic X(13).     216                       to BBookTitle
137           10  bi-due-date      pic X(10).     217           Else
138   01  book-pntr                pic 9(02).     218               Move bbi-book-title to BBookTitle
139                                               219               Move bbi-book-author to BBookAuthor
140   01  b-book-info.                            220               Move bbi-book-publisher to BBookPublisher
141       10  bbi-book-title       pic X(25).     221               Move bbi-publication-year
142       10  bbi-book-author      pic X(13).     222                       to BPublicationYear
143       10  bbi-due-date         pic X(10).     223               If bbi-patron-name = low-values
144       10  bbi-book-publisher   pic X(11).     224                   Move "Book is on the shelf"
145       10  bbi-publication-year pic X(04).     225                       to BPatronName
146       10  bbi-patron-name      pic X(23).     226               Else
147                                               227                   Move bbi-due-date to BDueDate
148   PROCEDURE DIVISION.                         228                   Move bbi-patron-name to PatronName
149                                               229               End-If *>bbi-patron-name = low values
150   main section.                               230           End-If *>b-book-info = low values
151       perform process-form-input-data         231       End-If *>ssubmit = "Find Patron"
152       perform convert-input                   232
153       perform process-business-logic          233       exit.
154       if Ssubmit = "Find Patron"
155           perform lib17-p-out-cvt
156           perform lib17-p-out-out
157       else
158           perform lib17-b-out-cvt
159           perform lib17-b-out-out
160       end-if *>Ssubmit = "Find Patron"
```

Figure 9-18. Code segments for the Lib17 CGI.

Summing Up

Project Summary

Proj0901 (**Lib15**) contains a symmetric CGI program, one in which the same form is used for both input and output.

Proj0902 (**Lib16**) is an application in which the CGI sends either of two output forms (one displaying patron information and the other an error message).

Proj0903 (**Lib17**) includes two Submit buttons in the input form. The CGI includes code that determines required action depending on the button clicked.

General Summary

A symmetric CGI uses the same form for input and output. As execution begins with the CGI, the CGI must include code to prevent performing the business code upon first entry. Use either CGI.skl or CGI-nibi.skl as the CGI code template and Net Express will generate code such as the following.

```
main section.
    perform process-form-input-data
    perform convert-input
    *> If there is no input from the Browser,
    *> then initial field values are output
    if MF-SERVER-EXEC = z"no"
      perform lib15-io-ini *> lib15-io
    else
        perform process-business-logic
        perform lib15-io-cvt *> lib15-io
    end-if *>MF-SERVER-EXEC = z"no"
    perform lib15-io-out *> lib15-io
```

An application can include any number of output forms. However, you must insert appropriate logic within the CGI program to determine which output form is sent to the browser. Following is that code form Lib16.

```
main section.
    perform process-form-input-data
    perform convert-input
    perform process-business-logic
    If patron-info = low-values
      perform lib16-out2-cvt
      perform lib16-out2-out
    Else
      perform lib16-out1-cvt
      perform lib16-out1-out
    End-If *>patron-info = low-values
```

Multiple submit buttons on an input form are treated somewhat like a group of radio buttons. Logic you include in the CGI program must determine the action to be taken depending upon the clicked submit button, for instance:

```
If ssubmit = "Find Patron"
   Call "lib-sub3" Using InPatronNumber
                         patron-info
                         book-counter
                         book-info-array
   . . .
Else
   Call "book-sub" Using InBookID
                         b-book-info
   . . .
End-If *>ssubmit = "patron"
```

Coming Up

You've already learned about the stateless nature of the Web from Chapter 6 in which a file-accessing subprogram must open the file with each execution. File processing is not the only circumstance under which the Web's statelessness is significant. Indeed, there are many applications in which you must preserve information across multiple components of an application. HTML includes two capabilities for preserving state: the Hidden Input control and the cookie. Net Express includes a third technique: a server-side state-preservation file. You will learn about these in the next chapter.

Assignment

9-1
Create the application illustrated by the component diagram of Figure 9-19.

- The menu page must give the user the option of viewing either customer information or order information.
- The customer and order CGIs are both symmetric.
- The output pages must provide for appropriate data and error messages.

This assignment is amenable to expansion through Chapter 11's Assignment 11-2.

9-2
Create the application illustrated by the component diagram of Figure 9-20.

- The input page allows the user to select either customer or order information by clicking either of two Submit buttons.
- This application uses a single CGI so code must be included to determine the Submit button clicked by the user in the input page.
- The output pages must provide for appropriate data and error messages.

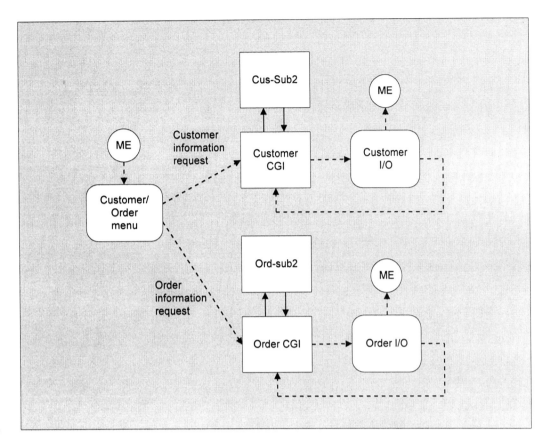

Figure 9-19.
Component diagram for Assignment 9-1.

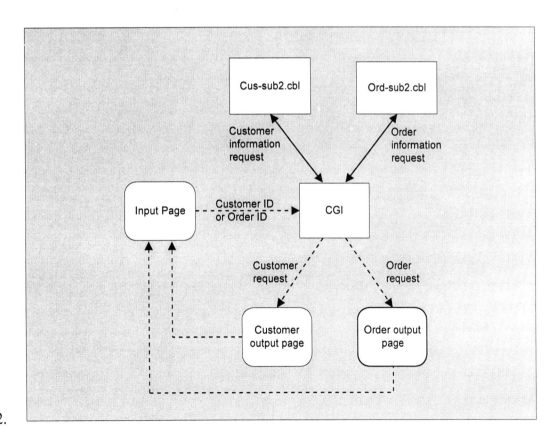

Figure 9-20.
Component diagram for Assignment 9-2.

Maintaining State

Chapter Contents

Techniques for Maintaining State 240
   Scenarios Requiring State Maintenance 240
   Three State-Maintenance Mechanisms 240
   Considerations 241
Controlling Repetition With a Hidden Input 241
   Overview of the Application 241
   Inserting a Hidden Input Control 242
   Creating the CGI programs 243
   CGI Code 244
   Some Other Observations 244
Restricting Data Access With a Hidden Input Control 245
   About this Example 245
   The Input Password Control 246
   CGI Code 247
Multiple Screen Input 247
   The Order Processing Example 247
   Project Hidden03 249
   The Application's CGI programs 250
   A Form With Hidden Input controls 250
Using a Cookie in the Form-Letter Order System 251
   About This Example 251
   Inserting a Cookie into a Form 252
   Cookie Data Preparation by the CGI 253
   Retrieving Cookie Data 255
Using a Cookie to Store an Access Code 258
   The Project Proj1005 Pages 258
   The Project's CGI Programs 259
Maintaining State Across Browser Sessions 259
   Persistent Cookies 259
   Setting a Cookie Expiration Date 262
   Accessing Cookie Data with the Accept 263
Maintaining State Using a Server-Side File 264
   The Micro Focus Sstate.cbl Subprogram 264
   Preserving Name/Address Data Within a Browser Session 265
   The CGI Programs 266
   Building the Project 268
Using a Cookie with a Server-Side File 269
   State Preservation Between Sessions 269
   Component Diagram—Proj1008 271
   CGI Code—Project 1008 272
   Removing Aged Server-Side Records 272
Summing Up 274
   Project Summary 274
   General Summary 275
   Summarizing the Sstate Subprogram Entry Points 276
Coming Up 278
Assignment 278

Chapter

10

Chapter Introduction

One of the problems with Web-based applications is maintaining application state. Each time a CGI program is run, it has no "knowledge" of what went before. This chapter focuses on techniques you can use to preserve state. From the chapter you will learn about the following.

- The Hidden Input control that allows you to transport data between pages without being displayed on the form.
- Using cookies, data stored by the Web browser on the client computer thereby being available to CGI programs the duration of a browser session.
- Assigning an expiration date to cookie thereby allowing the cookie data to exist on the client computer for a designated period of time.
- Preserving state by writing data to a server-side file.

Techniques for Maintaining State

Scenarios Requiring State Maintenance

None of the examples of preceding chapters have exhibited the need to save data from one part of the application to another, or preserve **state**. To illustrate this need, let's consider three scenarios.

Library inquiry system examples of Chapters 8 and 9 feature the ability to repeat thereby allowing the user to inquire about successive patrons. Assume that management has decided to limit the number of inquiries allowed a user during a single session to two. For this, the file-accessing CGI must include a counter to increment for each access of the patron file. Here we have a state problem. That is, with each inquiry, the CGI is run and then shut down, thereby losing any counter value required for access control.

Another scenario involves management's decision to implement security features thereby limiting each user's access to data according to "need to know." To begin a session, the user enters his/her access code which the CGI evaluates to determine access level. The access-level code must be retained throughout the duration of the session. Here we have another state problem.

The third scenario pertains to the Object-Z Printers example of Chapter 5. Because of the large amount of data a user must enter, management has decided to to spread data entry over three screens, thereby avoiding an overwhelming cluttered appearance. Data from all three screens must be passed to the processing CGI. As you will see, this involves a state consideration.

Three State-Maintenance Mechanisms

There are three mechanisms you can use to maintain the state of an application.

Hidden Input. The Hidden Input control is much like the Text Input control in that its properties include Name, Caption, and COBOLPicture. However, during a run its value is set by a CGI. Furthermore, it is not displayed on the screen by the browser—therefore the name "Hidden Input" control. By passing a Hidden Input control value from one form to another, information is retained, thus a degree of state is maintained.

Cookie. A cookie contains data stored by the browser on at the client side. By default, such data remains available for the duration of the browser run and is accessible by an Accept statement to any CGI. The CGI originating the cookie can set an expiration date thereby causing the client to retain the cookie information in a file.

Server-Side File. Net Express includes a mechanism that enables you to preserve state information by writing it to a server-side indexed file. Appropriate routines in their file-handling subprogram provide controlled access to data stored in the file.

Considerations

If a large amount of data is involved in state maintenance, speed may become an issue as sending the state data over a network in the form of hidden input can slow down the application.

Where data security is an issue, some organizations are not comfortable sending sensitive data over the Internet via hidden input or cookies. In some cases, using a server-side file can provide better security.

A significant consideration with employing a cookie is that some users set their browsers to prohibit cookies. So if your application will be functioning in an environment where you have no control over the users, you should consider hidden input. Or at the least, you will need to include provisions in your code for the absence of a cookie.

The server-side file approach of Micro Focus has much to offer including a higher degree of security and less data being transported back and forth on the Internet. However, their technique requires the ability to write a cookie to the client's browser.

Controlling Repetition With a Hidden Input

Overview of the Application

The representation of Figure 10-1 shows the components and their relationships of the project Hidden01 stored in the Proj1001 folder. This project is based on earlier projects that accept a patron number and display patron and book information (for instance, Lib12 in Proj0703). Its feature is the inclusion of a counter to limit the number of accesses allowed a user during a given session. Before proceeding, you should run this application to gain a feel for how it works. Then read the following.

Proj1001
Hidden01

- Hidden01-INI produces a greeting form that welcomes the user to the system.
- The CGI Hidden01ini sets the value of the field AccessCount to zero then sends Hidden01-IN to the client
- Hidden01-IN produces the familiar library input form into which the user enters the patron number of the record to be obtained. This form also includes the Hidden Input control AccessCount, which was initialized to zero by the CGI Hidden01ini.
- The CGI Hidden01get is a modified version of the corresponding CGI programs from earlier examples to read the patron and book files.
- Patron data, together with the hidden field is returned to the browser by Hidden01-OUT.
- The CGI Hidden01cnt increments and tests the counter AccessCount. If the count has not exceeded the limit, Hidden01cnt sends Hidden01-IN to the browser whereby the user can submit a request for another patron. If the count has reached the limit, Hidden01cnt sends Hidden01-MAX to the browser thereby terminating access to the file.

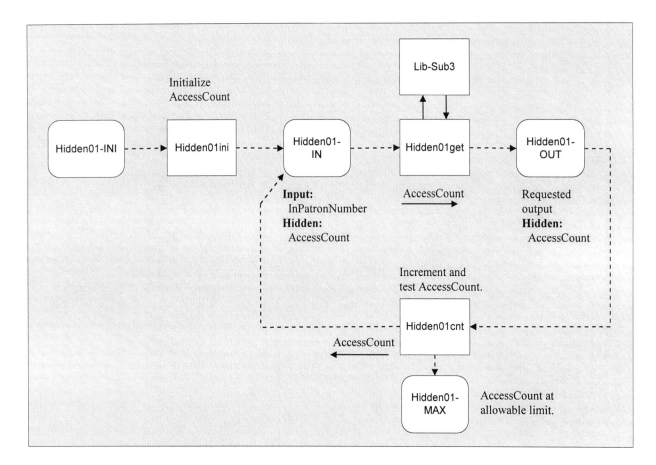

Figure 10-1. Component diagram for project Hidden01.

Inserting a Hidden Input Control

Bring up Hidden01-IN in Form Designer and highlight the control containing the caption hidden; your screen will look like Figure 10-2. Inserting a Hidden Input control into a form is no different than inserting, for instance, a Text Input control. That is, highlight the Hidden Input icon ▨ on the Form Designer screen, then place it anywhere on the form; its position is not important. For this application, the default entries were changed to:

ID	AccessCount
Name	AccessCount
Caption	hidden (For Form Designer documentation only—similar to use with the Text control)
Size	5 (This is screen size of the element—make it large enough to show the caption)
COBOLPicture	9(1) (Make this a numeric item as it will be incremented)

Bring up the output page Hidden01-OUT and you will see an identical entry. By using the same name, this field is automatically passed through from the input page to the output page by the CGI Hidden01get.

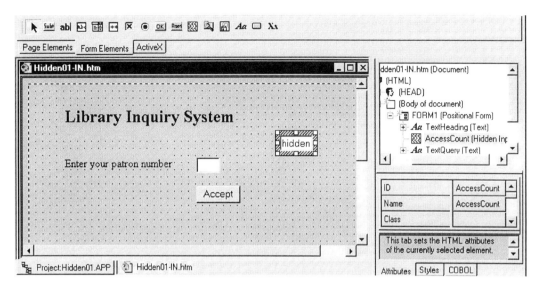

Figure 10-2. Inserting a Hidden Input into a form.

Creating the CGI programs

Refer to Figure 10-1 and you see that this project contains three CGIs. When you build such a project, you need to go through the process of CGI generation three times. For each CGI, be careful that you select the correct input and output files. For instance, the component diagram of Figure 10-1 is helpful when designating Hidden01-INI.htm as input and Hidden01-IN.htm as output for Hidden01ini in Figure 10-3.

Although you can generate the three CGIs in any order you wish, generating Hidden01ini last has an advantage. That is, Net Express uses as its start-animating

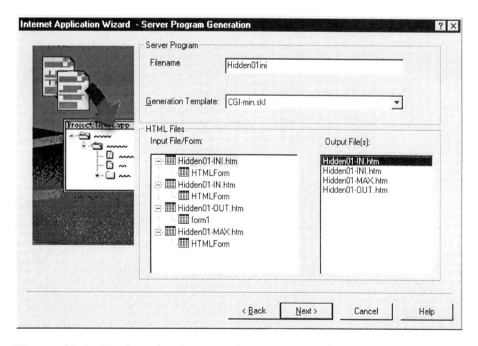

Figure 10-3. Designating input and output pages for CGI generation.

point the input form of the last CGI you generated. If you generated Hidden01cnt last, then Net Express would log Hidden01-OUT as its start-animating point. However, this is not a disaster as you can easily make an appropriate change (as illustrated in Chapter 9's Figure 9-8).

CGI Code

You will find little new in the code added to the CGI programs of this application. As a Cobol programmer, you can see Figure 10-1's component diagram as illustrating a simple "counted loop." The Cobol data item AccessCount (resulting from the Hidden Input control AccessCount shown in Figure 10-2) is:

- initialized to 0 in Hidden01ini
- incremented and tested for a maximum value in Hidden01cnt.

Specifically, programmer-required code in each of these three CGI programs is as follows.

Hidden01ini. The following statement is inserted into the section process-business-logic.

```
Move 0 to AccessCount
```

Hidden01get. This CGI is identical to those of preceding examples for accessing data from the patron and book files.

Hidden01cnt. This CGI increments the counter AccessCount and sends the appropriate page to the browser depending on the value stored in the counter.

```
main section.
    perform process-form-input-data
    perform convert-input
    Add 1 to AccessCount
    If AccessCount >= 2
      perform hidden01-max-cvt *> hidden01-max
      perform hidden01-max-out *> hidden01-max
    Else
      perform hidden01-in-cvt *> hidden01-in
      perform hidden01-in-out *> hidden01-in
    End-If *>AccessCount >= 2
    exit program
    stop run.
```

You can see that this If statement structure is identical to that in the CGI of Chapter 9's Lib16 (see Figure 9-13). If you ran this application, you found you were allowed only two accesses. Needless to say, you the programmer could set that limit to any appropriate value by changing the test value of the If statement.

Some Other Observations

There is a subtle point pertaining to Hidden01-IN (refer to Figure 10-1). That is, it is the input to CGI Hidden01get and also the output from CGI Hidden01ini. As such, Net Express automatically generates code to send a value to its input field InPatronNumber. Assume that you decide to eliminate Hidden01-INI and its corresponding CGI Hidden01ini. (Note that you could do this as Micro Focus COBOL initializes

Figure 10-4.
A confusing display.

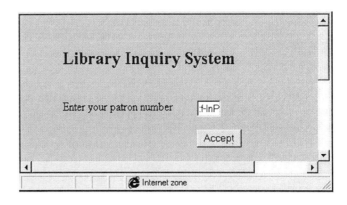

numeric values to zero at load time.) For your first run, your browser screen will look like Figure 10-4. This occurs because as an output form (from Hidden01cnt) it wants to display something for the patron number. As it has no value, the browser displays the field name. The user can delete the name and enter a valid patron number, but most users will be confused by the display. If you would like to check this yourself, click to run the application. Then in the Start Animating window, change the name Hidden01-INI.htm (in HTTP://127.0.0.1/COBOL/Hidden01-INI.htm) to Hidden01-IN.htm.

If the wrong HTML page is listed in the Start Animating window you can change the starting point by making the change in that window. However, that change will not be permanent. For a permanent change, click Animate/Settings and you will see a popup window like Figure 10-5—make the desired change here. For instance, in this example the starting point is Hidden01-OUT.htm (scroll to the right to see the full extension); it must be changed to Hidden01-INI.htm.

Restricting Data Access With a Hidden Input Control

About this Example

The second example of using a Hidden Input control involves the library management's decision to implement security features thereby limiting each user's access to the system's data. (Although the example is somewhat contrived, it illustrates an important use of a Hidden Input control.) Library employees can access

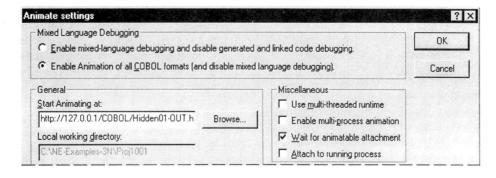

Figure 10-5. Setting the starting point.

patron/book information as before. Non-employees can also access the patron/book information but their screen displays will not show the patron address data. To this end, the system functions as follows.

1. The opening screen requests the user to enter an access code.
2. An employee enters the employee access code (given only to employees).
3. The user (employee or non-employee) enters a patron number.
4. The CGI accesses the requested patron/book data and returns the appropriate output page. If the user has employee access rights, the display includes address data; otherwise address data is excluded.
5. The user is allowed to repeat.

The relationship between system elements and its overall flow is similar to that of the preceding example as you can see by inspecting Figure 10-6. The key element of this application, stored in the Proj1002 folder as Hidden02, is the need to retain the user's access code as the user repeats.

You will find it useful to run the application to get a feel for how it works. When the screen requests your access code, type super for employee privilege—this will cause the patron address to be displayed. Then try another run and enter anything for the access code and the system will not display the patron address.

The Input Password Control

If you made a trial run, you probably noticed that the screen echoes asterisk characters as you typed the password. This is a commonly encountered security feature

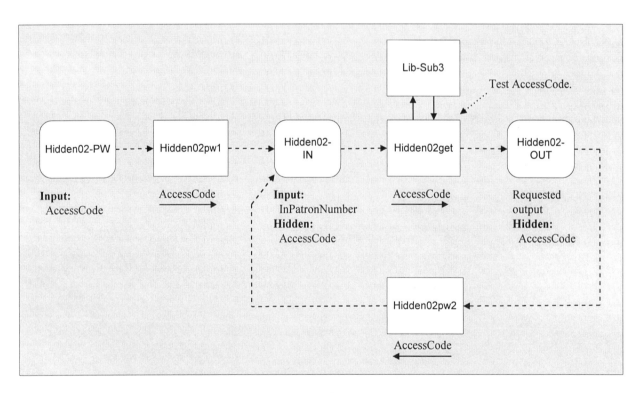

Figure 10-6. Component diagram for project Hidden02.

and one available to you through Net Express. Figure 10-7 is the page Hidden02-PW during its construction. To insert an Input Password control, highlight the Input Password icon ⟦**⟧ of the control bar and click wherever you wish to place it. Notice that its properties are identical to those of the Text Input control. For this application, the follow entries are used.

ID	AccessCode
Name	AccessCode
Size	5
COBOLPicture	X(5)

You can leave the row of asterisks within the control as a Page Designer indication to you that the control is a password.

When run, the Input Password control returns a name/value pair exactly the same as the conventional Input Text control you have been using.

CGI Code

Referring to the components illustrated in Figure 10-6, the CGI Hidden02pw1 has no additional code beyond that generated by Net Express. Its sole purpose is to pass the field AccessCode (as a Hidden Input control) on to the CGI Hidden02get via Hidden02-IN.

The CGI Hidden02get contains the file accessing code of previous examples with the addition of the following code to determine whether or not the address is to be displayed.

```
process-business-logic section.
    Call "lib-sub3" Using InPatronNumber
                          patron-info
                          book-counter
                          book-info-array
    If patron-info = low-values
      Move "No record for patron" to PatronName
    Else
      Move patron-name to PatronName
      If function upper-case (AccessCode) = "SUPER"
        Move street-address to StreetAddress
        Move city-state-zip to CityStateZip
      End-if
      Move "ID" to BookID(1)
      ...
```

Finally, the function of the CGI Hidden02pw2 is to provide a vehicle for passing the field AccessCode back, thereby maintaining state for this element.

Multiple Screen Input

The Order Processing Example

Look at the form-letter order screen of Figure 10-8 (reproduced from Figure 5-1). Assume that management has decided to change the look-and-feel of this application whereby ordering information is collected through three screens as follows.

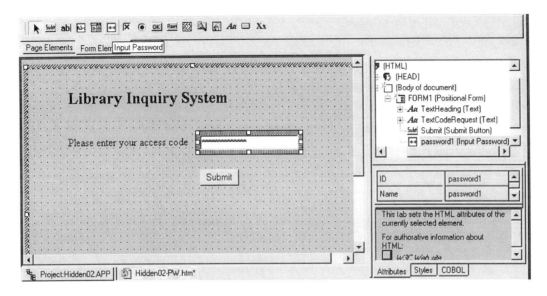

Figure 10-7. Inserting an Input Password control.

1. Through a customer information form, the customer enters customer-specific data—no such data is collected in the example application of Chapter 5.
2. The customer data is submitted to the server for checking/verification.
3. Through a second form, the customer enters general ordering information such as the check box entries of Figure 10-8.

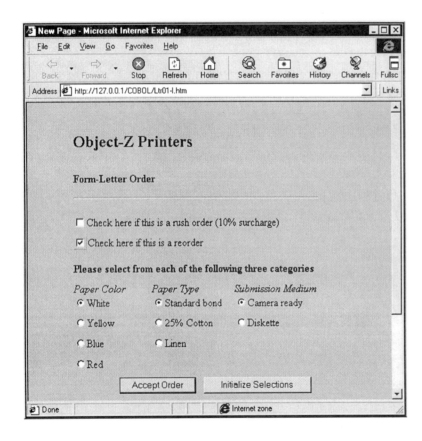

Figure 10-8. Order processing screen.

4. The general ordering information is submitted to the server for checking/verification.
5. Through a third form, the customer enters specific ordering information such as the radio buttons of Figure 10-8.
6. The specific ordering information is submitted to the server for checking/verification.
7. After the final screen of data is verified, the order data from all three forms is written to an order file.

Once again, we need state preservation abilities. That is, data from the first two forms must be retained and be available for writing to the file after verification of the third form's input.

Project Hidden03

To illustrate the technique, the project Hidden03 (in folder Proj1003) includes a bare minimum of input data.

> Proj1003
> Hidden03

First page	Customer number
Second page	Reorder and rush order
Third page	Paper color, paper type, and submission medium

In the project components diagram of Figure 10-9 you see the following technique for preserving state from one form to the next.

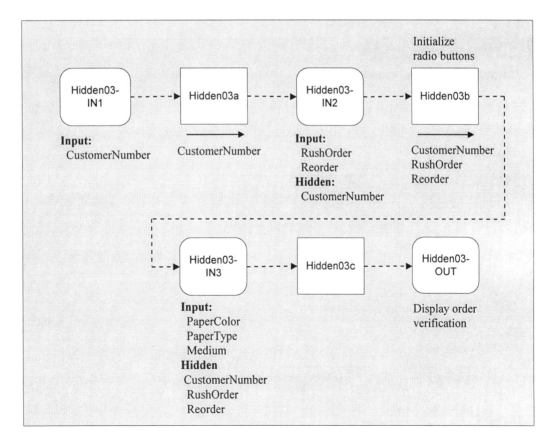

Figure 10-9. Application components diagram—Hidden03.

1. The customer number is accepted by Hidden03-IN1.
2. The customer number is passed through the CGI Hidden03a to Hidden03-IN2 as a hidden field.
3. The rush order and reorder values are accepted by Hidden03-IN2.
4. The rush order, reorder, and customer number values are passed through the CGI Hidden03b to Hidden03-IN3 as hidden fields.
5. The paper color, paper type, and medium values are accepted by Hidden03-IN3.
6. The entire data set is passed to the CGI Hidden03c for processing. In this example, the order confirmation screen is displayed.

The Application's CGI Programs

If you look at the CGI programs of this example, you will find no code beyond that generated by Net Express except for Hidden03b. In most real applications, standard Cobol verification techniques would be employed depending on the particular application's needs. Regarding Hidden03b, remember that in the Chapter 5's example, default values are assigned the input page radio buttons. Because Hidden03-IN3 (which includes the radio buttons) is an output page (from the CGI Hidden03b), the screen-defined defaults are nullified. Therefore, they are given their desired initial values by the following code included in Hidden03b.

```
Move "white" to PaperColor
Move "1" to PaperType
Move "camera" to Medium
```

A Form With Hidden Input controls

Figure 10-10 shows the Hidden Input controls of Hidden03-IN3 with the field RushOrder highlighted. If you open this project and bring up this page you will see that field names and sizes are identical to those defined for this application in Chapter 5. (Refer to that chapter's *Using Multiple Radio Button Groups* in which the characteristics of these fields are specified.)

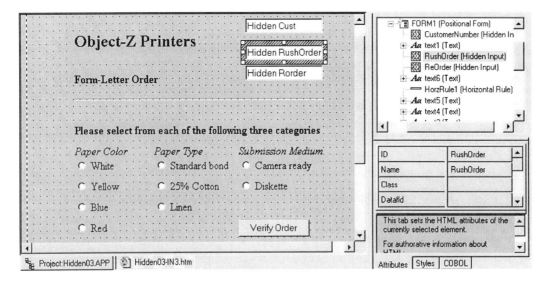

Figure 10-10. Three Hidden Input controls in the input form.

Using a Cookie in the Form-Letter Order System

About This Example

As described at the beginning of this chapter, a cookie contains data stored by the browser on at the client side. A cookie can be defined to contain up to 4K bytes of data. By default, such data remains available for the duration of the browser run and can be accessed with an Accept statement from a CGI. The CGI originating the cookie can set an expiration date thereby causing the client to retain the cookie information in a file.

The first example of using a cookie, Cookie01 in folder Proj1004, is a variation of Hidden03 in which the Hidden Input control is replaced by a cookie—compare Figure 10-11 to Figure 10-9. Notice the actions of each component.

1. The customer number is accepted from Cookie01-IN1.
2. The CGI Cookie01a sets up the customer number as an output field corresponding to the cookie defined in Cookie01-IN2.
3. When the server sends Cookie01-IN2 to the browser, the cookie defined within that page is automatically written to a work area of the browser.
4. Order data is accepted from Cookie01-IN2. The preceding process is repeated in which Cookie01-IN3 includes a second cookie (containing order data) that is saved by the browser.

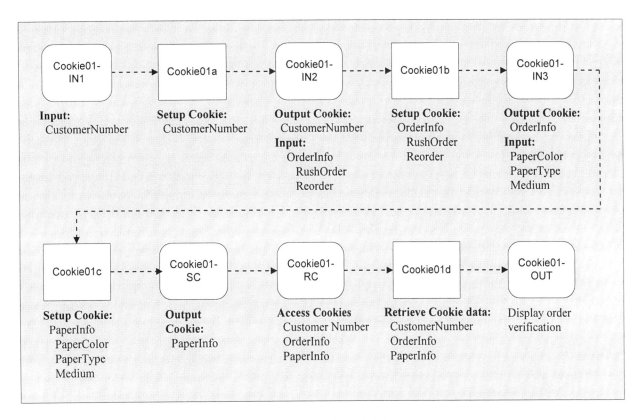

Figure 10-11. Application component diagram—Cookie01.

5. A third cookie in Cookie01-SC (containing the input from Cookie01-IN3) is saved by the browser .
6. When control is transferred from Cookie01-SC to Cookie01-RC all "memory" of previous activities is lost, except for data stored in the browser as cookies. Cookie01-RC provides access to those cookies and sends their values to the CGI Cookie01d.
7. The CGI Cookie01d processes ordering data from the three cookies and prepares output for the verification screen.

Inserting a Cookie into a Form

The procedure you use to insert a cookie into a form is different from that for controls. If you want to try it, open any of the example pages in Form Designer. (Don't worry about which one—you're not going to save the change.)

1. With some form open, click Page/Cookies and you will see the window of Figure 10-12(a).
2. Type the name you want to use for the cookie, for instance, CustomerNameCookie (this is the name used for the cookie inserted into Cookie01-IN2).
3. The Add cookie button will be activated, so click it and the cookie will be designated as in Figure 10-12(b).

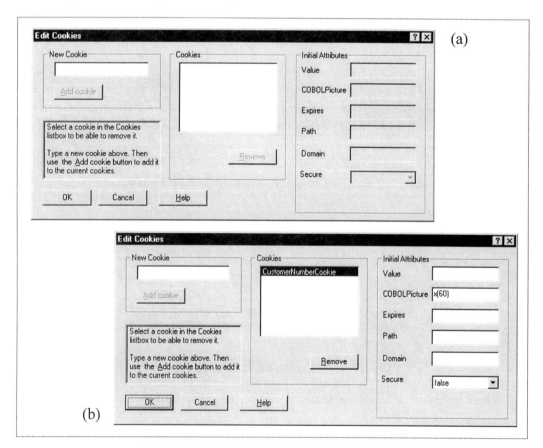

Figure 10-12. Inserting a cookie into a form.

4. Change the COBOLPicture entry to match the size of the data you intend to store [CustomerNumberCookie is x(4)].
5. Click OK to save this cookie definition.

Look at your page and you will see no visual indication that a cookie is associated with it—the only way you can tell is by clicking Page/Cookies and inspecting the cookie window (Figure 10-12(b)). If you don't want this cookie in your form, simply close the Form Designer window and click No to saving.

Cookie01-IN3 and Cookie01-SC also require cookies with the following characteristics.

Cookie01-IN3

| Name | OrderInfoCookie |
| COBOLPicture | X(10) |

Cookie01-IN3 will contain data for the check boxes fields rush-order (9 bytes) and reorder (1 byte)—hence its length of 10.

Cookie01-SC

| Name | PaperInfoCookie |
| COBOLPicture | X(19) |

Cookie01-SC will contain data for the radio button fields paper-type (1 byte), paper-color (10 bytes), and the medium (8 bytes)—hence its length of 19.

Cookie01-RC contains all three cookies. Thus with this design (refer to Figure 10-11), the CGI Cookie01d has access to all of the ordering data from the following cookies.

Customer number	from CustomerNumberCookie
Rush order	from OrderInfoCookie
Reorder	from OrderInfoCookie
Paper color	from PaperInfoCookie
Paper type	from PaperInfoCookie
Medium	from PaperInfoCookie

Cookie Data Preparation by the CGI

For in insight to how cookie's work, let's focus our attention on the CGI Cookie01a and its input Cookie-IN1 and output Cookie-IN2. In their control trees shown in Figure 10-13 and Figure 10-14, you see the following control names.

Control Name	Page of Origin
CustomerNumber	Cookie01-IN1 (Text Input)
RushOrder	Cookie01-IN2 (Check Box)
ReOrder	Cookie01-IN2 (Check Box)
CustomerNumberCookie	Cookie01-IN2 (from the Edit Cookies window)

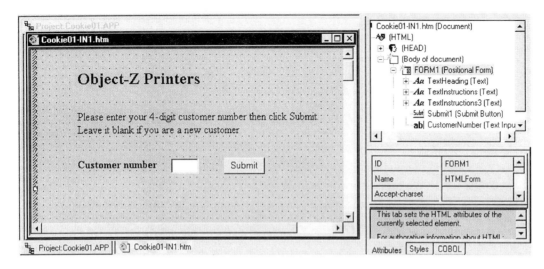

Figure 10-13. The HTML page Cookie01-IN1.

Figure 10-15 is relevant code extracted from the CGI Cookie01a. By comparing these three figures, you can correlate the external form fields (lines 18-28) and form fields (lines 68-73) to the their sources in the two HTML pages. The data items of interest here pertain to the customer number cookie. You see that Net Express generates data items for it (lines 18/19 and 68) exactly as it does with any other control. (The data item f-CustomerNumberCookie-exp pertains to the expiration date of the cookie. You will learn about this topic from the next example.)

When this application is run, a normal sequence of events occurs including writing of the cookie data to the client computer.

1. From the form displayed by Figure 10-13's page, the user enters a customer number then clicks the Submit button.
2. Net Express accepts the form's input data and moves it to the data item CustomerNumber (line 70 in Figure 10-15).

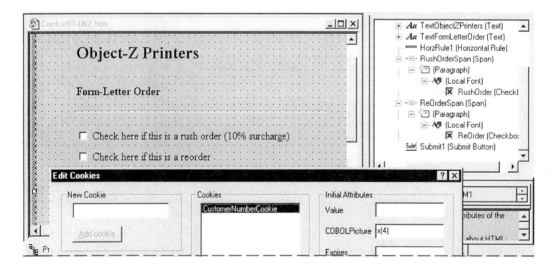

Figure 10-14. The HTML page Cookie01-IN2.

```
 1  IDENTIFICATION DIVISION.                    67     01 FormFields.
 2      program-id. "Cookie01a".                68        03 CustomerNumberCookie    pic X(4).
                                                69        03 CustomerNumberCookie-exp pic x(32).
12  working-storage section.                    70        03 CustomerNumber          pic X(4).
13                                              71        03 ReOrder                 pic X(1).
14      *> WARNING: Do not remove this copy statement  72   03 RushOrder              pic X(9).
15      *> or modify the contents of the copy file.    73   03 ssubmit               pic X(60).
16      copy "Cookie01a.cpf".                   74
17      01 HTMLForm is external-form.           75  *> Enter additional working-storage items here
18         03 f-CustomerNumberCookie pic x(4)   76
19            identified by "CustomerNumberCookie".  77  PROCEDURE DIVISION.
20         03 f-CustomerNumberCookie-exp pic x(32).   78
21         03 f-CustomerNumber        pic x(4)  79  main section.
22            identified by "CustomerNumber".   80      perform process-form-input-data
23         03 f-ReOrder               pic x(1)  81      perform convert-input
24            identified by "ReOrder".          82      perform process-business-logic
25         03 f-RushOrder             pic x(9)  83      perform cookie01-in2-cvt
26            identified by "RushOrder".        84         *> cookie01-in2
27         03 f-ssubmit               pic x(60) 85      perform cookie01-in2-out
28            identified by "ssubmit".          86         *> cookie01-in2
29         03 filler                  pic x.    87      exit program
                                                88      stop run.

                                               105  process-business-logic section.
                                               106      *> Add application business logic here.
                                               107      Move CustomerNumber to CustomerNumberCookie
```

Figure 10-15. Relevant code from CGI Cookie01a.cbl.

3. Programmer-inserted code moves the customer number to the cookie data item CustomerNumberCookie (line 107).

4. Code executed by the Perform of line 85 includes embedded HTML script defining the HTML page of Figure 10-14. That script is sent to the user's browser.

5. Execution of the script by the browser produces the script-defined screen and causes cookie data to be saved.

Data in a cookie is stored as a single string. If you must store two or more data items, then you must define them under a group item, that group item corresponding to your cookie. For instance, in Cookie01b of Figure 10-16 look at lines 99-101. Data from the input screen is moved to the data items of this group item at lines 138 and 139 . Then line 140 moves the group item to the cookie field. Note that you could avoid using the intermediate item group-info by moving Reorder and RushOrder directly into CookieOrderInfo using reference modification. I personally prefer using the group item as it seems to provide better documentation.

If you look at the CGI Hidden01c you will see that the three data items from the radio buttons are handled in much the same way as the check box data of Hidden01b. The end result is radio button cookie data for this CGI's output page from Cookie01-SC.

Retrieving Cookie Data

You can use two different techniques for retrieving cookie data:

- Define a cookie within the page that accesses the CGI requiring the data.
- Include an appropriate external-page entry in the CGI's Data Division and an Accept statement in the Procedure Division.

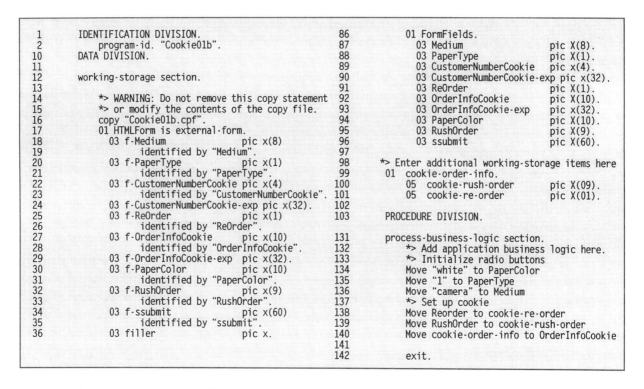

```
1       IDENTIFICATION DIVISION.                     86      01 FormFields.
2          program-id. "Cookie01b".                  87         03 Medium                    pic X(8).
10      DATA DIVISION.                                88         03 PaperType                 pic X(1).
11                                                    89         03 CustomerNumberCookie      pic x(4).
12      working-storage section.                      90         03 CustomerNumberCookie-exp pic x(32).
13                                                    91         03 ReOrder                   pic X(1).
14         *> WARNING: Do not remove this copy statement  92     03 OrderInfoCookie           pic X(10).
15         *> or modify the contents of the copy file.    93     03 OrderInfoCookie-exp       pic x(32).
16         copy "Cookie01b.cpf".                      94         03 PaperColor                pic X(10).
17      01 HTMLForm is external-form.                 95         03 RushOrder                 pic X(9).
18         03 f-Medium              pic x(8)          96         03 ssubmit                   pic X(60).
19            identified by "Medium".                 97
20         03 f-PaperType           pic x(1)          98      *> Enter additional working-storage items here
21            identified by "PaperType".              99      01  cookie-order-info.
22         03 f-CustomerNumberCookie pic x(4)         100        05  cookie-rush-order        pic X(09).
23            identified by "CustomerNumberCookie".   101        05  cookie-re-order          pic X(01).
24         03 f-CustomerNumberCookie-exp pic x(32).   102
25         03 f-ReOrder             pic x(1)          103     PROCEDURE DIVISION.
26            identified by "ReOrder".
27         03 f-OrderInfoCookie     pic x(10)         131     process-business-logic section.
28            identified by "OrderInfoCookie".        132        *> Add application business logic here.
29         03 f-OrderInfoCookie-exp pic x(32).        133        *> Initialize radio buttons
30         03 f-PaperColor          pic x(10)         134        Move "white" to PaperColor
31            identified by "PaperColor".             135        Move "1" to PaperType
32         03 f-RushOrder           pic x(9)          136        Move "camera" to Medium
33            identified by "RushOrder".              137        *> Set up cookie
34         03 f-ssubmit             pic x(60)         138        Move Reorder to cookie-re-order
35            identified by "ssubmit".                139        Move RushOrder to cookie-rush-order
36         03 filler                pic x.            140        Move cookie-order-info to OrderInfoCookie
                                                      141
                                                      142     exit.
```

Figure 10-16. Relevant code from CGI Cookie01b.cbl.

This application uses the former method, the cookies of Figure 10-17 contained in Cookie01-RC. When this form is sent to the browser, each of the three cookies is accessed.

Let's now move on to the CGI Cookie01d; notice the following features in its partial listing of Figure 10-18.

- Following are the cookie data items generated by Net Express.

Cookie	Lines
CustomerNumberCookie	18, 19, 78
OrderInfoCookie	23, 24, 81
PaperInfoCookie	30, 31, 85

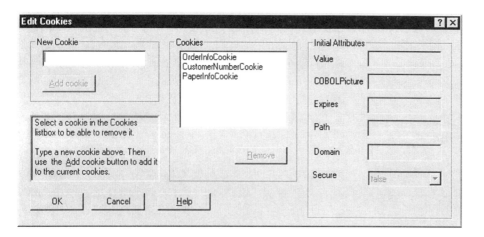

Figure 10-17. Cookie definitions in Cookie01-RC.

```
1   IDENTIFICATION DIVISION.                          97    01  cookie-paper-info.
2       program-id. "Cookie01d".                      98        10  cookie-paper-color   PIC X(10).
                                                       99        10  cookie-paper-type    PIC X(01).
10  DATA DIVISION.                                     100       10  cookie-medium        PIC X(08).
11
12  working-storage section.                          130   process-business-logic section.
13                                                     131       *> Add application business logic here.
14      *> WARNING: Do not remove this copy statement  132       Move CustomerNumberCookie to CustomerNumber
15      *> or modify the contents of the copy file.    133       Move OrderInfoCookie to cookie-order-info
16      copy "Cookie01d.cpf".                          134       Move PaperInfoCookie to cookie-paper-info
17      01 HTMLForm is external-form.                  135
18          03 f-CustomerNumberCookie pic x(4)         136       If cookie-rush-order = "RushOrder"
19              identified by "CustomerNumberCookie".  137         Move "Yes" to VerifyRushOrder
20          03 f-CustomerNumberCookie-exp pic x(32).   138       Else
21          03 f-CustomerNumber       pic x(4)         139         Move "No" to VerifyRushOrder
22              identified by "CustomerNumber".        140       End-If *>RushOrder = "RushOrder"
23          03 f-OrderInfoCookie      pic x(10)        141       If cookie-re-order = "R"
24              identified by "OrderInfoCookie".       142         Move "Yes" to VerifyReorder
25          03 f-OrderInfoCookie-exp  pic x(32).       143       Else
26          03 f-VerifyReorder        pic x(3)         144         Move "No" to VerifyReorder
27              identified by "VerifyReorder".         145       End-If *>Reorder = "R"
28          03 f-VerifyMedium         pic x(15)        146
29              identified by "VerifyMedium".          147       Evaluate cookie-medium
30          03 f-PaperInfoCookie      pic x(19)        148         When "camera"
31              identified by "PaperInfoCookie".       149             Move "Camera-ready" to VerifyMedium
32          03 f-PaperInfoCookie-exp  pic x(32).       150         When "diskette"
33          03 f-VerifyRushOrder      pic x(3)         151             Move "Diskette" to VerifyMedium
34              identified by "VerifyRushOrder".       152         When other
35          03 f-ssubmit              pic x(60)        153             Move "No selection" to VerifyMedium
36              identified by "ssubmit".               154       End-Evaluate *>medium
37          03 f-VerifyColor          pic x(15)        155       Evaluate cookie-paper-color
38              identified by "VerifyColor".           156         When "white"
39          03 f-VerifyType           pic x(15)        157             Move "White" to VerifyColor
40              identified by "VerifyType".            158         When "yellow"
41          03 filler                 pic x.           159             Move "Yellow" to VerifyColor
                                                       160         When "blue"
76      copy "Cookie01d.cpy".                          161             Move "Blue" to VerifyColor
77      01 FormFields.                                 162         When "red"
78          03 CustomerNumberCookie   pic x(4).        163             Move "Red" to VerifyColor
79          03 CustomerNumberCookie-exp pic x(32).     164         When other
80          03 CustomerNumber         pic X(4).        165             Move "No selection" to VerifyColor
81          03 OrderInfoCookie        pic x(10).       166       End-Evaluate *>PaperColor
82          03 OrderInfoCookie-exp    pic x(32).       167       Evaluate cookie-paper-type
83          03 VerifyReorder          pic X(3).        168         When "1"
84          03 VerifyMedium           pic X(15).       169             Move "Standard bond" to VerifyType
85          03 PaperInfoCookie        pic x(19).       170         When "2"
86          03 PaperInfoCookie-exp    pic x(32).       171             Move "Cotton-25%" to VerifyType
87          03 VerifyRushOrder        pic X(3).        172         When "3"
88          03 ssubmit                pic X(60).       173             Move "Whole linen" to VerifyType
89          03 VerifyColor            pic X(15).       174         When other
90          03 VerifyType             pic X(15).       175             Move "No selection" to VerifyType
91                                                     176       End-Evaluate *> PaperType
92  *> Enter additional working-storage items here     177
93                                                     178       exit.
94      01  cookie-order-info.
95          10  cookie-rush-order  pic X(09).
96          10  cookie-re-order    pic X(01).
```

Figure 10-18. Partial listing of the CGI Cookie01d.

- User inserted records to designate components of the cookies are defined at lines 94-100.
- Cookie data is moved to the additional Working-Storage data items at lines 133 and 134. Then they are readily available for setting up the output items. The remainder of the code in this section is identical to that of the corresponding example in Chapter 5.

The folder Proj1004B contains an identical project to this one except the external page and Accept are used. This technique is slightly more complicated and offers no advantages over cookies in Cookie01-RC. However, you will find it useful in when dealing with persistence across browser sessions, the third cookie example of this chapter.

Using a Cookie to Store an Access Code

The Project Proj1005 Pages

This example, Cookie02 in the folder Proj1005, is a variation of Hidden02 in which user-access persistence is maintained by a cookie rather than a Hidden Input control. You should run this application to gain a feel for how it works. The following commentary pertains to the pages of the component diagram in Figure 10-19.

The user is queried for the access code in Cookie02-PW. The code "super" provides full access as with project Hidden02. The code "patron" provides access to all data except the patron's address. Any other entry is rejected and the server returns Cookie01-RP to the browser notifying the user that he/she has entered an invalid code.

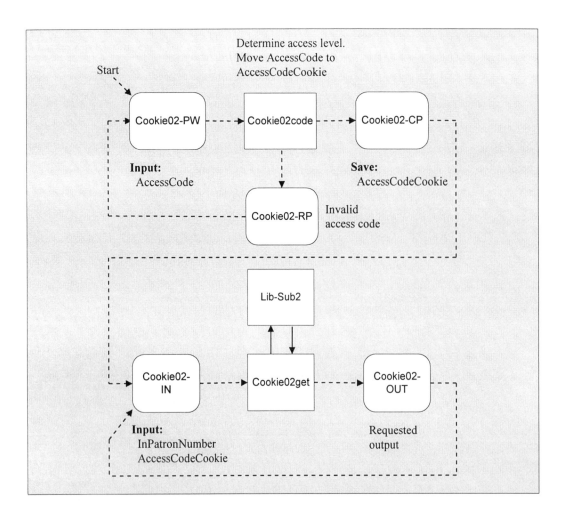

Figure 10-19. Component diagram—Proj0805.

The user is then permitted to retry. In an actual environment, you would probably want to limit the number of times the user could retry by including a counter (the technique of Hidden01).

Cookie02-CP (output from Cookie02code, refer to Figure 10-19) includes the following components.

- The Server-Side Text control ConfirmationMessage [x(45)] to confirm the user's status.
- The cookie AccessCodeCookie in which the access code is stored. When this page is sent to the client by the CGI, the browser automatically saves the cookie.

Cookie02-IN requests a patron number from the user as do previous versions of the library system. It is identical to Hidden02-IN. Cookie02-OUT displays patron/book information exactly as does Hidden02-OUT. However, where Hidden02-OUT includes a Hidden Input control to maintain persistence of the access code, Cookie02-OUT does not contain a cookie. The access code remains on the client (as cookie data) so it need not be passed to Cookie02-OUT and back again.

In Hidden02, the sole purpose of the CGI Hidden02c between the output and input pages (refer to Figure 10-9) is to pass the hidden field back to the input page. As this is not necessary when using a cookie, flow progresses directly from Cookie02-OUT to Cookie02-IN. For this, Cookie02-OUT includes a button with the event handler location.href="Cookie02-IN.htm".

The Project's CGI Programs

If you look at the code for these two CGIs and you won't find anything spectacular. Significant elements of Cookie02code are included in Figure 10-20. You see at line 101 the user-entered AccessCode is first moved to the cookie. Then it is tested to determine the confirmation message displayed by Cookie02-CP. If the code is neither SUPER or PATRON, it is changed to DENIED. In the main section the value in AccessCode determines which page is returned to the browser. You are familiar with this technique from previous examples.

Cookie02get, is identical to its counterpart in the Hidden02 project except that the access code is obtained from the cookie (made available to the CGI by its input Cookie02-IN). In Figure 10-21 you see the cookie definitions at lines 27, 28, and 96; you see the cookie tested at line 160.

Maintaining State Across Browser Sessions

Persistent Cookies

The cookie, as used in preceding examples, maintains state within a browser session. However, when you close the browser session, all state information is gone. Let's now see how easy it is to create a cookie that maintains state across browser sessions. Such a cookie is referred to as a **persistent cookie** and is created by designating an expiration date.

```
  1       IDENTIFICATION DIVISION.
  2         program-id. "Cookie02code".

 10       DATA DIVISION.
 11
 12       working-storage section.
 13
 14           *> WARNING: Do not remove this copy statement
 15           *> or modify the contents of the copy file.
 16           copy "Cookie02code.cpf".
 17           01 HTMLForm is external-form.
 18              03 f-AccessCode          pic x(10)
 19                 identified by "AccessCode".
 20              03 f-ConfirmationMessage pic x(45)
 21                 identified by "ConfirmationMessage".
 22              03 f-AccessCodeCookie     pic x(6)
 23                 identified by "AccessCodeCookie".
 24              03 f-AccessCodeCookie-exp pic x(32).
 25              03 f-ssubmit              pic x(60)
 26                 identified by "ssubmit".
 27              03 filler                 pic x.

 56           copy "Cookie02code.cpy".
 57           01 FormFields.
 58              03 AccessCode             pic X(10).
 59              03 ConfirmationMessage    pic x(45).
 60              03 AccessCodeCookie       pic x(6).
 61              03 AccessCodeCookie-exp   pic x(32).
 62              03 ssubmit                pic X(60).
 63
 64       *> Enter additional working-storage items here
 65
 66       PROCEDURE DIVISION.
 67
 68       main section.
 69           perform process-form-input-data
 70           perform convert-input
 71           perform process-business-logic
 72           Evaluate AccessCode
 73              When "DENIED"
 74                 perform Cookie02-RP-cvt *> Cookie02-RP
 75                 perform Cookie02-RP-out *> Cookie02-RP
 76              When other
 77                 perform Cookie02-CP-cvt *> Cookie02-CP
 78                 perform Cookie02-CP-out *> Cookie02-CP
 79           End-Evaluate *>AccessCode
 80           exit program
 81           stop run.

 98       process-business-logic section.
 99           *> Add application business logic here.
100           Move function upper-case (AccessCode) to AccessCode
101           Move AccessCode to AccessCodeCookie
102           Evaluate AccessCode
103              When "SUPER"
104                 Move "Supervisor access to patron system approved"
105                    to ConfirmationMessage
106              When "PATRON"
107                 Move "Access to patron system approved"
108                    to ConfirmationMessage
109              When other
110                 Move "DENIED" to AccessCode
111           End-Evaluate *>AccessCode
112
113           exit.
```

Figure 10-20. Code segments from the CGI Cookie02code.

This example consists of two projects stored in the Proj1006 folder: Cookie031 to create a persistent cookie and Cookie032 to retrieve the cookie. The structure of both is relatively simple as you can see by the component diagram of Figure 10-22. To run this application you must do the following.

1. Open the project Cookie031.
2. The input form requests name/address data. After you make your entries, your screen will look something like Figure 10-23.

```
1    IDENTIFICATION DIVISION.                     121    PROCEDURE DIVISION.
2        program-id. "Cookie02get".

10   DATA DIVISION.                                149    process-business-logic section.
11                                                 150        *> Add application business logic here.
12   working-storage section.                      151        Call "lib-sub3" Using InPatronNumber
13                                                 152                               patron-info
14       *> WARNING: Do not remove this copy statement  153                         book-counter
15       *> or modify the contents of the copy file.    154                         book-info-array
16       copy "Cookie02get.cpf".                   155        Move 0 to c-ColumnHeads, c-BookData
                                                   156        If patron-info = low-values
27       03 f-AccessCodeCookie      pic x(6)       157          Move "No record for patron" to PatronName
28           identified by "AccessCodeCookie".     158        Else
                                                   159          Move patron-name to PatronName
90       copy "Cookie02get.cpy".                   160          If AccessCodeCookie = "SUPER"
91       01 FormFields.                            161            Move street-address to StreetAddress
                                                   162            Move city-state-zip to CityStateZip
96           03 AccessCodeCookie    pic x(6).      163        End-if
```

Figure 10-21. Code segments from the CGI Cookie02get.

3. Click the Save button and you will see a confirmation screen.
4. Close your browser screen
5. Open the project Cookie032.
6. Run the application. At the introductory form (Cookie031-INI) click the Retrieve cookie button. Control passes to the CGI Cookie032 which retrieves the cookie.
7. Your name/address entries from the preceding project are displayed.

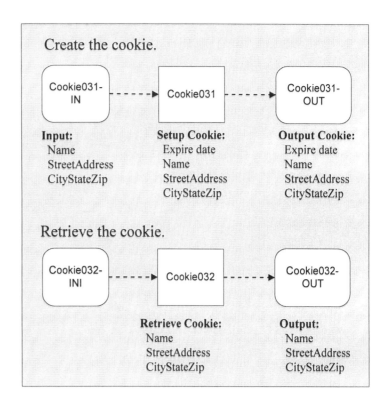

Figure 10-22.
Component diagrams for Cookie031 and Cookie032.

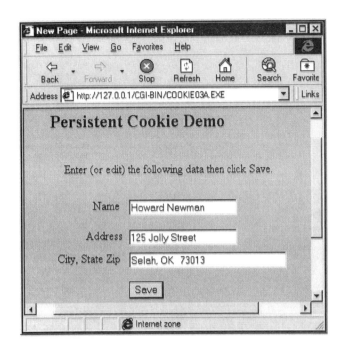

Figure 10-23.
Input screen for
project Cookie031.

Setting a Cookie Expiration Date

The cookie is set in this example by the same technique you've seen in previous examples: that is, the cookie defined in the output page Cookie031-OUT is saved by the browser when the CGI sends that page to the client. The feature of this example is designating an expiration date for the cookie. Look at the Edit Cookies window from Cookie031-OUT shown in Figure 10-24 where you see an Expires entry of +2. From this, Net Express generates appropriate code designating to the browser that this cookie must be retained for a period of 2 days. Thus, if you run Cookie031 today a cookie is created and will be accessible to Cookie032 for the next two days However, after two days it will be gone.

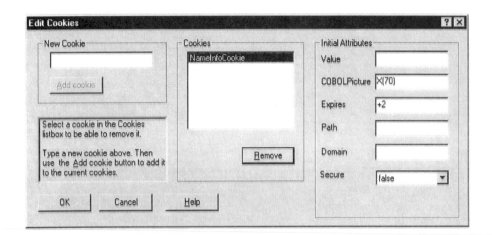

Figure 10-24. Setting a cookie expiration.

Sometimes you will need to set a specific date for the cookie to expire; you can do that using any of the following forms.

- **Short date**

Formats:	mm/dd/yyyy
	mm-dd-yyyy
Examples:	12/31/1999
	3/13/2000
	6-15-2001
Comment:	The forms mm/dd/yy and mm-dd-yy could be used for the brief period prior to 1/1/2000

- **Long date**

Formats:	Long dates can be supplied with the year month and day in any order, and the year in two- or four-digit form.
Examples:	July 10 1999
	9 Mar 2000
	Tuesday November 9 1996
Comments:	Month and day names must be at least two characters. Where there are two possible matches for a month name, the last one is always taken. For example, JU is always matched as July rather than June. The day of the week is ignored if it is incorrect based on the remainder of the date.

- **Time**   You can append a time to a long format date.

Format:	hh:mm:ss or hh:mm:ss AM|PM. Minutes and seconds are optional	
Examples:	10 10:45 10:45:30	
	10 PM 10:45PM	
	22:30	
Comments:	If you use the 24-hour clock, it is an error to specify PM for times later than 12 noon. For example, 23:15 PM is an error. You can append a time zone to the end - all standard time zones, as well as GMT and UTC are acceptable.	

Accessing Cookie Data with the Accept

Based on preceding cookie examples, you might expect to find a cookie definition in the input page Cookie032-INI. However, this example does not use that technique but rather accesses the cookie through self-contained code within the CGI Cookie032. This gives the versatility to the CGI to be used independent of any a specific input form to start its execution. For instance, control to this form could be transferred by the user clicking a button on some other form or directly from another server-side program. Also, when I ran this example with the first release of Version 3.0, I found that a cookie in Cookie032-INI to return the cookie data required an expiration entry corresponding to that of the HTML page from which the browser stored the cookie. Each access of the cookie by Cookie032-INI prolonged the life of the cookie. (This may not be the case with later versions of Net Express.)

Let's look at Figure 10-25 for Cookie032's pertinent code to retrieve the cookie data.

- An external-form is defined at line 63 and is given the internal name TheNameInfoCookie.
- This form is related to the external file NameInfoCookie at line 64. This is the name of the cookie saved by Cooki031-OUT.
- To access the cookie's individual fields within this program, name-info is defined as a group item (line 64) composed of the elementary items corresponding to the data fields stored in the cookie (lines 65-67).
- The Accept statement of line 99 accesses the cookie.
- Data items from the cookie (lines 65-67) are moved (lines 100-102) to fields generated by the output form Cooke032-OUT (lines 57, 59, and 60).

Maintaining State Using a Server-Side File

The Micro Focus Sstate.cbl Subprogram

The third means for maintaining state of an application is to write state information to a file on the server—a **server-side file**. At first thought, you might feel that a subprogram to maintain data in a server-side file would be relatively simple. However, as we programmers often discover, "simple" tasks frequently end up with a lot of painstaking details. To this end, Net Express includes the subprogram **sstate.cbl** for managing state preservation in a server-side file. (You will find source code for

```
  1   IDENTIFICATION DIVISION.
  2       program-id. "Cookie032".

 10   DATA DIVISION.
 11
 12   working-storage section.

 56       01 FormFields.
 57          03 YourName              pic X(20).
 58          03 ssubmit               pic X(60).
 59          03 StreetAddress         pic X(20).
 60          03 CityStateZip          pic X(30).
 61
 62   *> Enter additional working-storage items here
 63   01  NameInfoCookie is external-form.
 64       03 name-info    identified by "NameInfoCookie".
 65          06 C-YourName               PIC X(20).
 66          06 C-StreetAddress          PIC X(20).
 67          06 C-CityStateZip           PIC X(30).

 97   process-business-logic section.
 98       *> Add application business logic here.
 99       Accept TheNameInfoCookie
100       Move C-YourName to YourName
101       Move C-StreetAddress to StreetAddress
102       Move C-CityStateZip to CityStateZip
103
104       exit.
```

Figure 10-25. Relevant code of the CGI Cookie032.

the program in the next project's folder Proj1007. Version 3.0 of Net Express includes it in the \Net Express\base\demo\state folder.) Through its multiple entry points, you can perform all the operations necessary to preserve data and later retrieve it. Typically, in saving state data for an application, you will include code in your CGI to do the following.

- Provide **Sstate** the name of the server-side file to which your data must be saved. Your calling program designates the name of the server-side file to be used for storing your data. If the file does not exist, **Sstate** creates it.
- Request **Sstate** to create a new (empty) record in the file.
- Assemble your state data in a "state" record.
- Send this state record to **Sstate** for writing to the file. **Sstate** returns a record key identifying this record.

When execution of your CGI is terminated, your state data remains in the server-side file. At some later point in the application (usually in another CGI) you will retrieve your state record from the server-side file as follows.

- Provide **Sstate** the name of your server-side file to which your data was saved.
- Retrieve the state record by sending **Sstate** its record key.

The server-side file created by **Sstate** is indexed and is defined with variable-length records. Your save-record can be up to 63,000 bytes in length. The next two examples illustrate using **Sstate**.

Preserving Name/Address Data Within a Browser Session

The first example of using a server-side file for state preservation, Sstate01 stored in the folder Proj1007, consists of the components illustrated in Figure 10-26. The following occurs with execution of this application.

Proj1007
Sstate01

1. The user enters name and address data into the input form from Sstate01-IN.
2. The CGI Sstate01sav assembles the data into a record then calls the subprogram

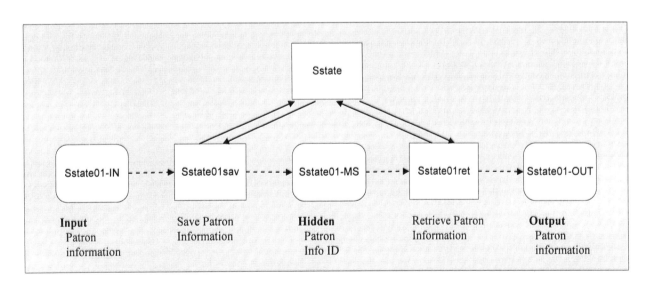

Figure 10-26. Component diagram for Sstate01.

Sstate. Sstate writes the record to a designated index file and returns the record key. Sstate01sav moves the record key into a Hidden Input control data item (derived from the page Sstate01-MS).

3. The purpose of the page Sstate01-MS is to isolate the two CGI programs Sstate01sav and Sstate01ret in order to demonstrate using a server-side file for state preservation. In an actual application, numerous other activities would probably take place.

4. The CGI Sstate01ret includes the record key (from the hidden field) as a parameter in calling Sstate. Sstate retrieves the record from the file.

5. Sstate01-OUT displays the name address data.

Notice that use of a hidden field is required with this technique as retrieval of the server-side record requires the key field value for that record. The implication is that the server-side file technique as implemented here maintains state only within the current browser session. When the browser session is completed, the hidden field, containing the record key, is lost. (The next example uses a cookie thereby providing persistence across browser sessions.)

The CGI Programs

Figure 10-27 lists relevant code from the two CGI programs of this example: Sstate01sav saves (writes) name/address data to the server-side file and Sstate01ret retrieves it. As described earlier, writing the record is a three-step process, each step implemented by calling the appropriate entry point of the subprogram Sstate.cbl. Let's look at the partial listing of Sstate01sav to see how this is done.

1. The entry point MF_CLIENT_STATE_FILE (the call is at line 114) designates the name of the server-side file. The state file name is defined at lines 67 and 68.

2. The entry point MF_CLIENT_STATE_ALLOCATE (the call is at line 127) requires the length of the record to be written as input and returns the record key value of the empty record created for this run.

3. The entry point MF_CLIENT_STATE_SAVE (the call is at line 144) writes your data to the state file.

Retrieving the record is a two-step process—refer to Sstate01ret.

1. Designate the name of the server-side file via the entry point MF_CLIENT_STATE_FILE (the call at line 120).

2. Retrieve the data from the file via the entry point MF_CLIENT_STATE_RESTORE (the call at line 126).

Together with included comment lines, the programs of Figure 10-27 are reasonably self-explanatory. For each of the subprogram's entry points (for instance, MF_CLIENT_STATE_FILE), listed parameters are identified as the subprogram's input or output. Parameters used in these examples are described on the page following the program listings.

```
  1  IDENTIFICATION DIVISION.                         1  IDENTIFICATION DIVISION.
  2     program-id. "Sstate01sav".                    2     program-id. "Sstate01ret".

 10  DATA DIVISION.                                   10  DATA DIVISION.
 11                                                   11
 12  working-storage section.                         12  working-storage section.

 58     copy "Sstate01sav.cpy".                        58     copy "Sstate01ret.cpy".
 59     01 FormFields.                                 59     01 FormFields.
 60        03 InName              pic X(25).           60        03 TheCityStateZip    pic X(25).
 61        03 ssubmit             pic X(60).           61        03 TheStreetAddress   pic X(25).
 62        03 HiddenStateRecordInfo  pic X(35).        62        03 ssubmit            pic X(60).
 63        03 StreetAddress       pic X(25).           63        03 HiddenStateRecordInfo  pic X(35).
 64        03 CityStateZip        pic X(25).           64        03 TheName            pic X(25).
 65                                                   65
 66  *> Enter additional working-storage items here    66  *> Enter additional working-storage items here
 67  01   state-filename        pic x(255)             67  01   state-filename       pic x(255)
 68                             value "nameinfo.di".   68                            value "nameinfo.di".
 69  01   state-record-info.                           69  01   state-record-info.
 70     10  state-record-ID      pic X(30).            70     10  state-record-ID     pic X(30).
 71     10  state-record-length-9 pic 9(05).           71     10  state-record-length-9 pic 9(05).
 72                                                   72
 73  01   state-record-length    pic X(04) comp-x.     73  01   state-record-length   pic X(04) comp-x.
 74                                                   74
 75  01   state-data-record.                           75  01   recovered-state-data.
 76     03  save-name           pic X(25).             76        03  recovered-name          pic X(25).
 77     03  save-street-address  pic X(25).            77        03  recovered-street-address pic X(25).
 78     03  save-city-state-zip  pic X(25).            78        03  recovered-city-state-zip pic X(25).
 79                                                   79
 80  01   state-status          pic x comp-x.          80  01   state-status         pic x comp-x.
 81                                                   81
 82  PROCEDURE DIVISION.                               82  PROCEDURE DIVISION.

110  process-business-logic section.                 110  process-business-logic section.
111     *> Add application business logic here.      111     *> Add application business logic here.
112  * Designate the name of the state file to be    112  * Move hidden field data to file variables
113  * accessed by this application                  113        Move HiddenStateRecordInfo
114     Call "MF_CLIENT_STATE_FILE"                   114                          to state-record-info
115              using state-filename *>Input         115        Move state-record-length-9
116                    state-status   *>Output        116                          to state-record-length
117                                                   117
118  * Move size of the data to be saved to          118  * Designate the name of the state file to be
119  * data-length field.                            119  * accessed by this program
120     Move function length (state-data-record)     120     Call "MF_CLIENT_STATE_FILE"
121                    to state-record-length        121              using state-filename *>Input
122     Move state-record-length                     122                    state-status   *>Output
123                    to state-record-length-9      123
124  * Allocate a record for the name/address data   124  * Recover the name/address "state" record from
125  * that is to be saved.                          125  * the server state file
126  * Receive the record key for this record.       126     Call "MF_CLIENT_STATE_RESTORE"
127     Call "MF_CLIENT_STATE_ALLOCATE"               127              using state-record-id      *>Input
128              using state-record-id    *>Output   128                    recovered-state-data *>Output
129                    state-record-length *>Input    129                    state-record-length  *>Input
130                    state-status        *>Output   130                    state-status         *>Output
131                                                   131
132  * Move record ID and length to hidden field     132  * Move data from recovered record to form fields
133     Move state-record-info                       133        Move recovered-name to TheName
134                    to HiddenStateRecordInfo       134        Move recovered-street-address
135                                                   135                          to TheStreetAddress
136  * Save the form input data to "state" record. This  136        Move recovered-city-state-zip
137  * record will be written to the server-side file.  137                          to TheCityStateZip
138     Move InName to save-name                     138
139     Move StreetAddress to save-street-Address    139  * Remove the current record from the server file
140     Move CityStateZip to save-city-state-zip     140     Call "MF_CLIENT_STATE_DELETE"
141                                                   141              using state-record-id *>Input
142  * Send the name/address "state" record to       142                    state-status   *>Output
143  * the server file.                               143
144     Call "MF_CLIENT_STATE_SAVE"                   144     exit.
145              using state-record-id   *>Input
146                    state-data-record *>Input
147                    state-record-length *>Input
148                    state-status       *>Output
149
150     exit.
```

Figure 10-27. CGI programs State01sav and State01ret.

state-filename	The name of the file you want to use to contain your state data. The filename used in this example is defined at lines 67 and 68 in both Sstate01sav Sstate01ret.
state-record-id	The key field value for the current data record to be saved. This is a pic X(30) data item—refer to line 70 in both listings.
state-data-record	The data item (line 75) containing the data to be saved by Sstate01sav. This is your record—it can be up to 63,000 bytes in length. This field is name recovered-state-record in Sstate01ret.
state-record-length	The data item (line 73) containing the length of your data record. The length is determined at lines 120 and 121 of State01sav.
state-status	A code (line 80) indicating success or failure of your operation as follows:

0	Successful completion.
1	Any error during a file operation READ, REWRITE, or OPEN.
2	Duplicate key found.
3	Key not found.
4	Record length exceeds 63000.

At lines 73 and 80 the comp-x usage for state-record-length and state-status produces numeric binary data items consisting of four bytes and one byte, respectively. Because of the way in which binary numbers are internally stored with this usage, including state-record-length in the hidden field produced a problem I could not resolve. So I took the easy way out and store the value in a Pic 9 field as done at lines 122 and 123.

As this record's key is only available during the current browser session, the record itself is deleted from the file by the call to MF_CLIENT_STATE_DELETE at line 140 of Sstate01ret.

Building the Project

In previous examples involving called subprograms, you created the project by selecting the Project from existing application option of the project creation screen. Then you selected the subprogram(s) you wanted included in the project. I was unable to gain access to entry points of the subprogram using this method. However, the following alternative approach is successful.

1. Click on either Empty Project or HTML Project in the project creation screen.
2. Create the HTML pages.
3. Create the CGIs.
4. Right click in the Files in project pane to produce the popup menu in Figure 10-28(a). Note that if you click below the list of file names you see the three-entry menu shown here; otherwise you several entries. It makes not difference for this operation.

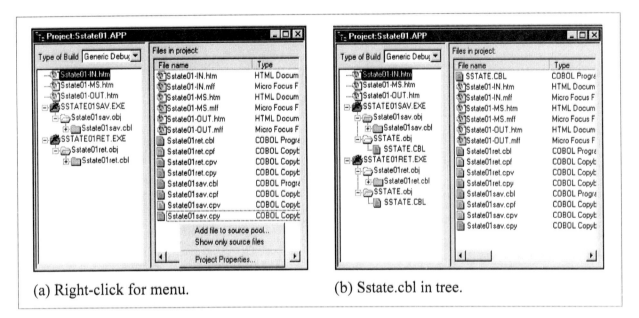

(a) Right-click for menu.   (b) Sstate.cbl in tree.

Figure 10-28. Adding Sstate to the project.

5. Click the option Add files to source pool.
6. From the resulting window, select Sstate.cbl. This file will be added to the list of files in the right pane of your window.
7. Double-click on this filename to open Sstate.cbl.
8. Compile it.
9. You want to add Sstate.cbl to the tree of the left-pane as shown in Figure 10-28(b). To do this, select SSTATE.CBL (pane on the right), drag it to the left, and deposit it on SSTATE01SAV.EXE. It should be inserted into the tree as shown in Figure 10-28(b).
10. Repeat this process placing it subordinate to SSTATE01RET.EXE.
11. Rebuild the project and it is ready to run. Note: If you have an error message pertaining to SState, open it, compile it again, then rebuild the project.

Using a Cookie with a Server-Side File

State Preservation Between Sessions

The next example is another variation of the online form-letter ordering of Chapter 5. The sales manager has found that, in placing an order, a customer often makes the same selections as her/his preceding order. So to simplify repeat orders, she wants the order screen to display as defaults the values from the preceding order. Thus a customer placing an order for the first time would see a screen like Figure 10-29(a); a repeat customer would see a screen like Figure 10-29(b). In the latter case, there are two ways to retain the preceding order's data: as a cookie or as a record written to a server-side file. This example uses the latter technique.

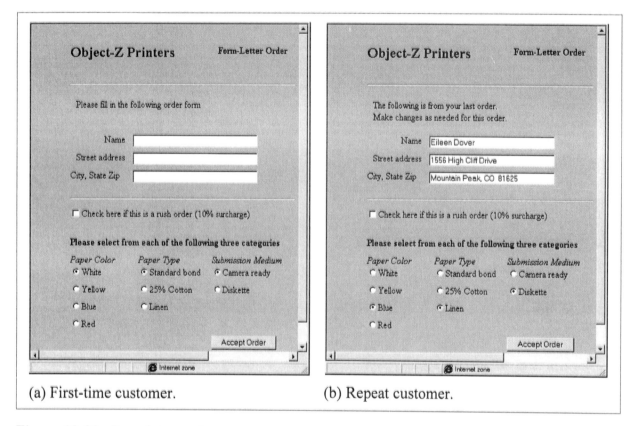

(a) First-time customer.   (b) Repeat customer.

Figure 10-29. Page-letter order entry.

To keep this type of application in the proper perspective, remember the environment: one or more users accessing a server as illustrated in Figure 10-30.

1. A user enters an order.
2. A CGI writes a record containing the order data to the server-side file.
3. The record key is written to the user's browser as a cookie.

Whenever that user logs on to place another order, the previous order data is available from the server-file through the record key saved on the user's machine. In Figure 10-30, the server-side file can contain many such records, each specifically identified by the key value stored on the individual user's computer by his/her browser. Before digging into the components of this application, you should run it to see how it works.

1. Open and run the application Sstate02 stored in the folder Proj1008.
2. From the introductory form, click the Place Order button. The data entry form will look like Figure 10-29(a).
3. Fill in the form as directed and click the Accept Order button.
4. In the resulting confirmation form, you could click the Main Menu button. However, to demonstrate persistence, close the browser screen.
5. In the Net Express screen click Animate/Stop Animating.

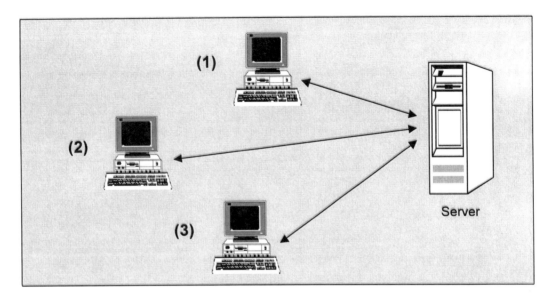

Figure 10-30. Multiple users accessing a server.

6. Run the application again; you will see your entries of the first run displayed as defaults.

Component Diagram—Proj1008

This project's component diagram is identical to that of Project 1007 as you can see by inspecting Figure 10-31. (If you look at the project you will find two additional HTML pages, but they are not relevant to the main features of this example.) In this example, Sstate02-MENU displays a set of options. The only enabled option, place an order, transfers control to the CGI Sstate02find as you observed in running the application.

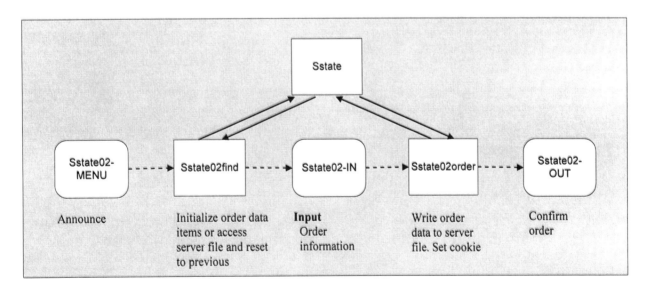

Figure 10-31. Component diagram—Proj1008.

The CGI Sstate02find queries the user's browser for a cookie. If one is found, the CGI calls the subprogram Sstate using key field value from the cookie. The returned data is provided as default values to Sstate02-IN. If no cookie is found, input items for Sstate02-IN are set to spaces. The CGI Sstate02order assembles data entered through Sstate02-IN's form and calls the subprogram Sstate thereby writing to the server-side file. The returned key value is moved to the cookie.

If you open Sstate02-OUT under Form Designer and click Page/Cookies you will see the cookie OrderRecordIDCookie defined as X(30), sufficient for the record key. The expiration entry is +2 meaning that the cookie will persist after termination of the browser session.

CGI Code—Project 1008

Both programs are relatively straightforward and correspond closely to their counterparts of Proj1007. The following commentary pertains to the order-processing CGI Sstate02order shown in Figure 10-32.

- The call at line 149 to identifies the server-side file to which this sales data will be written.
- The call at line 156 allocates the server-side record and returns the key field value.
- Data is moved from the input form to the output record at lines 161-167.
- The call at line 170 writes the record to the server-side file.
- The key-field value for this record is moved (line 176) to the cookie field (line 90, created from the cookie definition in Sstate02-OUT).

The following commentary pertains to the code segments of Figure 10-33 extracted from the CGI Sstate02find.

- Cookie defining code is at lines 109-112.
- The cookie is accessed by the Accept statement of line 142.
- If the user has not placed an order within the time span allocated for the cookie life, then no cookie will exist. The cookie field order-record-id will contain spaces.
- The If at line 143 tests the cookie contents. If spaces, all page fields are set to spaces and radio buttons are set to desired initial values and the user message is set (lines 144-151). Processing within this section is completed.
- If the cookie contents are non-zero the value is the previously stored key-id of the server-side file record containing the previous sale data.
- The file is defined by the call of line 154.
- The record is accessed by the call of line 159.
- Data fields are moved to the form fields (of Sstate02-IN) by lines 165-171 thereby providing the customer's previous-order data as the default. The user message is set by the Move of lines 172-175.

```
   1   IDENTIFICATION DIVISION.                        1   IDENTIFICATION DIVISION.
   2       program-id. "Sstate02order".                2       program-id. "Sstate02find".

  10   DATA DIVISION.                                  10   DATA DIVISION.
  11                                                   11
  12   working-storage section.                        12   working-storage section.

  17       01 HTMLForm is external-form.               82       copy "Sstate02find.cpy".
                                                       83       01 FormFields.
  22         03 f-OrderRecordIDCookie  pic x(30)        84          03 Medium                pic x(8).
  23             identified by "OrderRecordIDCookie".   85          03 PaperType             pic x(1).
                                                       86          03 UserMessage           pic x(75).
  86       copy "Sstate02order.cpy".                   87          03 PaperColor            pic x(6).
  87       01 FormFields.                               88          03 InName                pic x(30).
  88          03 Medium                pic x(8).        89          03 RushOrder             pic x(4).
  89          03 PaperType             pic x(1).        90          03 ssubmit               pic X(60).
  90          03 OrderRecordIDCookie   pic X(30).       91          03 StreetAddress         pic x(30).
  91          03 OrderRecordIDCookie-exp pic x(32).     92          03 CityStateZip          pic x(30).
  92          03 PaperColor            pic x(6).        93
  93          03 InName                pic x(30).       94   *> Enter additional working-storage items here
  94          03 RushOrder             pic x(4).        95   01 persistent-file-record.
  95          03 ssubmit               pic x(64).       96          03 Previous-InName       PIC X(30).
  96          03 StreetAddress         pic x(30).       97          03 Previous-StreetAddress PIC X(30).
  97          03 CityStateZip          pic x(30).       98          03 Previous-CityStateZip PIC X(30).
  98                                                    99          03 Previous-RushOrder    PIC X(9).
  99   *> Enter additional working-storage items here  100         03 Previous-PaperColor   PIC X(10).
 100   01 persistent-file-record.                      101         03 Previous-PaperType    PIC X(1).
 101      03 Save-InName        PIC X(30).             102          03 Previous-Medium       PIC X(8).
 102      03 Save-StreetAddress PIC X(30).             103
 103      03 Save-CityStateZip  PIC X(30).             104   01  server-file-name    pic x(255)
 104      03 Save-RushOrder     PIC X(9).              105                              value "nameinfo.di".
 105      03 Save-PaperColor    PIC X(10).             106   01  server-status       pic x comp-x.
 106      03 Save-PaperType     PIC X(1).              107   01  record-length       pic x(4) comp-x.
 107      03 Save-Medium        PIC X(8).              108
 108                                                   109   01  OrderRecordIDCookie is external-form.
 109   01  server-file-name    pic x(255)             110       05  order-record-id
 110                             value "nameinfo.di".  111           identified by "OrderRecordIDCookie"
 111                                                   112           pic x(30).
 112   01  key-id              pic x(30).             113   PROCEDURE DIVISION.
 113   01  server-status       pic x comp-x.
 114   01  record-length       pic x(4) comp-x.        141   process-business-logic section.
 115                                                   142       Accept OrderRecordIDCookie
 116   PROCEDURE DIVISION.                              143       If order-record-id = spaces
                                                       144          Move space to InName
 144   process-business-logic section.                 145                       StreetAddress
 145       *> Add application business logic here.     146                       CityStateZip
 146                                                   147                       RushOrder
 147       *>Set the file name used to store the       148          Move "white" to PaperColor
 148       *> client application data                  149          Move "1" to PaperType
 149       call "MF_CLIENT_STATE_FILE"                 150          Move "camera" to  Medium
 150                using server-file-name             151          Move "Please fill in the following form."
 151                      server-status                152             to UserMessage
 152                                                   153       Else
 153       Move length of persistent-file-record       154          Call "MF_CLIENT_STATE_FILE"
 154               to record-length                    155               using server-file-name
 155       *> Allocate a record and receive the key.   156                     server-status
 156       call "MF_CLIENT_STATE_ALLOCATE"             157          Move length of persistent-file-record
 157                using key-id                        158                       to record-length
 158                      record-length                159          Call "MF_CLIENT_STATE_RESTORE"
 159                      server-status                160               using order-record-id
 160                                                   161                     persistent-file-record
 161       Move InName        to Save-InName          162                     record-length
 162       Move StreetAddress to Save-StreetAddress    163                     server-status
 163       Move CityStateZip  to Save-CityStateZip     164
 164       Move RushOrder     to Save-RushOrder        165          Move Previous-InName       to InName
 165       Move PaperColor    to Save-PaperColor       166          Move Previous-StreetAddress
 166       Move PaperType     to Save-PaperType        167                       to StreetAddress
 167       Move Medium        to Save-Medium          168          Move Previous-CityStateZip  to CityStateZip
 168                                                   169          Move Previous-RushOrder     to RushOrder
 169       *> Send client state data to server file    170          Move Previous-PaperColor    to PaperColor
 170       call "MF_CLIENT_STATE_SAVE"                 171          Move Previous-PaperType     to PaperType
 171                using key-id                        172          Move Previous-Medium        to Medium
 172                      persistent-file-record       173          Move "Following is from your last order"
 173                      record-length                174              & X"0A0D"
 174                      server-status                175              & "Change as needed for this order"
 175       *> Save the state-data key value            176              to UserMessage
 176       Move key-id to OrderRecordIDCookie          177       End-if
 177                                                   178
 178       exit.                                       178   exit.
```

Figure 10-32. Relevant code of the   **Figure 10-33.** Relevant code of the
CGI Sstate02order.   CGI Sstate02find.

Removing Aged Server-Side Records

Assume you've written the order processing application of this example and that you've designated an expiration date 120 days from date the cookie is written. When the cookie is deleted from the user's browser, there is no need to retain the record in the file. The file processor Sstate includes a procedure for removing a record based on its age. Its use is illustrated by the following sample code. Presumably, you would include this code in a maintenance program run daily on the server.

```
Working-Storage Section.
...
01   state-filename            pic x(255) value "nameinfo.di".
01   age-in-days               pic X(04) comp-x.
01   state-status              pic x comp-x.
...
PROCEDURE DIVISION.
...
       *> Open the state file
        call "MF_CLIENT_STATE_FILE" using state-filename
                                          state-status

       *> Remove all records more than 120 days old
        Move 120 to age-in-days
        call "MF_CLIENT_STATE_PURGE" using age-in-days
                                          state-status
```

Summing Up

Project Summary

Proj1001 (Hidden01) includes an access count maintained in a Web "loop" through a hidden field to limit the number of repetitions

Proj1002 (Hidden02) limits access to patron data of this application through an access code retained throughout a browser session within a hidden field.

Proj1003 (Hidden03) includes multiple input forms to accept data from a user. Each form's input is passed to the next input form through a hidden field.

Proj1004 (Cookie01) accomplishes state preservation of Hidden03's example by using a cookie.

Proj1005 (Cookie02) accomplishes state preservation of access code data of Hidden02 through use of a cookie.

Proj1006 (Cookie03) illustrates preserving state across browser session with a cookie assigned an expiration date.

Proj1007 (Sstate01) is a simple illustration of using a server-side file to preserve name/address data for the duration of a browser session. The key-field value for later access to the file is retained in a hidden field.

Proj1008 (Sstate02) preserves customer order data (to offer as default for subsequent orders) by writing the needed data to a server-side file. The key-field value for later access to the file is retained in a cookie.

General Summary

HTML includes two facilities for maintaining state: the hidden field and the cookie. Net Express adds a third: a server-side state file.

The Hidden Input control has the same properties as the Text Input control. To maintain state, this control must be included in each HTML page of the application. Consequently, the name/value pair is passed back and forth between components of an application.

A cookie allows you to designate name/value pairs that the browser stores on the client for later retrieval.

- A cookie can contain up to 4K of data.
- Insert a cookie into an HTML page by clicking on Page/Cookies. From the resulting popup menu designate its Name and COBOLPicture properties.
- By default a cookie exists only for the duration of the browser session. Make the cookie persistent by designating an expiration date.
- Access a cookie from the browser by including a corresponding cookie definition in an HTML page or by including an external-form entry and Accept statement in a CGI.

Net Express includes the subprogram Sstate.cbl for maintaining state in a server-side indexed file. To save a record to the file you must:

1. Provide Sstate the name of the server-side file to be used.
2. Request Sstate to create an empty record.
3. Assemble desired state data in a record.
4. Send the record to Sstate. Sstate returns the record key for this record.

To retrieve a record from a server-side file you must:

1. Provide Sstate the name of the server-side file to which the record was written.
2. Retrieve the record by sending Sstate the record key.

The record key of data saved to the server-side file must be available to subsequent components of an application. Do this with either a hidden field or a cookie.

The Input Password control accepts input from an input form the same as the Input Text control. They differ only in that asterisks are echoed to the screen rather than the user's typed input.

Summarizing the Sstate Subprogram Entry Points

MF_CLIENT_STATE_ALLOCATE

Allocates a new empty record for the state information.

```
call "MF_CLIENT_STATE_ALLOCATE" using key-ID
                                       ecord-length
                                       erver-status
```

Parameters: key-ID   pic x(30).
              record-length   pic x(4) comp-x.
              server-status   pic x comp-x.

Input: record-length: The length of the server-side state record to be
         created.

Output: key-ID: The key field value of the newly created server-side record
         that will contain the state information.
         server-status: The status of the operation.

MF_CLIENT_STATE_FILE

Designates the file to be used on the server to store state information.

```
call "MF_CLIENT_STATE_FILE" using filename
                                  server-status
```

Parameters: filename   pic x(255)
              server-status   pic x comp-x

Input: filename: The name of the server-side indexed state file to which
         access is desired

Output: server-status: The status of the operation.

MF_CLIENT_STATE_RESTORE

Reads the designated record from the server-side state file.

```
call "MF_CLIENT_STATE_RESTORE " using key-ID
                                      state-data
                                      record-length
                                      server-status
```

Parameters: key-ID   pic x(30)
              state-data   Size as required for record from server.
              record-length   pic x(4) comp-x
              server-status   pic x comp-x

Input: key-ID: The key field value of the server-side record to be read.
         record-length: The length of the buffer to be used for the record
         accessed from the server-side file—make this the same size as original
         record when written.

Output: state-data: The record accessed from the server-side state file.
         server-status: The status of the operation.

MF_CLIENT_STATE_SAVE
   Writes a client record to the server-side state file.

   call "MF_CLIENT_STATE_SAVE" using key-ID
                                    state-data
                                    record-length
                                    server-status

   Parameters: key-ID   pic x(30)
               state-data   Size as required for record from server.
               record-length pic x(4) comp-x
               server-status pic x comp-x

        Input: key-ID: The key field value of the server-side record to be read.
               state-data: The record accessed from the server-side state file.
               record-length: The length of the record (state-data) to be written to
               the server-side file.
       Output: server-status: The status of the operation.

    Comments: This routine saves a previously allocated key-ID and state-data, or
              rewrites a previously saved key-ID and client state. The record-
              length can be updated.

MF_CLIENT_STATE_DELETE
   Deletes an existing record from the server-side state file.

   call "MF_CLIENT_STATE_DELETE" using key-ID
                                    server-status

   Parameters: key-ID   pic x(30)
               server-status pic x comp-x

        Input: key-ID: The key field value of the server-side record to be deleted.
       Output: server-status: The status of the operation.

MF_CLIENT_STATE_PURGE
   Deletes all client information older than the number of days specified.

   call "MF_CLIENT_STATE_PURGE" using date-criteria
                                    server-status

   Parameters: date-criteria pic x(4) comp-x
               server-status pic x comp-x

        Input: date-criteria The number of days after which client information
               should be purged.

       Output: server-status: The status of the operation.

Coming Up

The next chapter covers file and database processing. You will examine a basic file-maintenance application for editing existing records and adding new ones. You will also learn how to access data from a database using embedded SQL (structured query language).

Assignment

10-1

This assignment involves breaking the order entry application of Assignment 5-1 into separate input forms for accepting different portions of an order. Use as a guideline the component diagram of Figure 10-34—its basic functions are as follows.

Page 1   Accept the customer number of the ordering customer.

CGI 1   Verify that the customer number is valid (that there is a record for this customer in the customer file).

Page 2   Display an error message indicating that this is not a valid customer number.

Page 3   Display the customer number and name. Accept the customer request for saddle type

CGI 2   Perform actions as required by your application.

Page 4   Accept the customer request for order options (stirrup covers, padded seat, leather tooling, and silver ornaments.

Page 5   Verify the customer's order; include customer number and name.

   Select whichever state preservation technique (hidden field, cookie, or server-side file) appeals to you for this assignment.

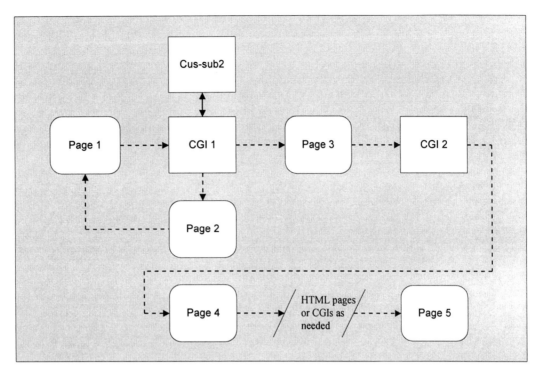

Figure 10-34. The component diagram for Assignment 10-1.

File and Database Processing

Chapter Contents

Components of the Patron File-Maintenance Projects 282
    About the Patron File 282
    Patron File-Access Subprograms 283
    Copy Files 284
Adding Records to the Patron File 284
    The Project Screens 284
    The CGI 286
One Page for Input and Output 287
    Features of Proj1102 287
    CGI Considerations 288
    The Project's Event Handlers 290
Record Maintenance—Pat03 290
    About the Pat03 Project 290
    The HTML Page Pat03U-DIS 293
    The CGI Programs 293
Accessing a Relational Database from NetExpress 294
    Relational Databases and SQL 294
    Setting Up to Use ESQL in NetExpress Programs 297
First Look at OpenESQL Assistant 299
    Starting Point 299
    Host Variables 300
    Creating a Simple Query 300
    Basic Nature of the SQL Select 302
    Establishing Search Critera 302
Inserting ESQL into the CGI 304
    The Query Code 304
    Connect and Disconnect 305
    Inserting Working-Storage Code 306
    SQL Compiler Directive 307
    The CGI Program with Embedded SQL 307
Required User-Inserted Code 309
    Input Code 309
    Output Code 309
Linking Tables and Accessing Multiple Rows. 309
Joining Two Tables 309
    The SQL Cursor 310
    The Need for Two Queries 311
Creating the Queries 311
    Generating the Query for Patron Data 311
    Generating the Query for Book Data 312
    Inserting Auxiliary Code into the CGI 314
    User-Inserted Code 315
Using the Application Wizard for an SQL Database 317
    Using the Application Sql03 317
    Creating an SQL Application 318
    Modifying and Expanding a Wizard-Built SQL Application. 320
Summing Up 322
    Project Summary 322
    General Summary 323
Assignment 324

Chapter

11

Chapter Introduction

Most examples of preceding chapters have accessed data from files—none has written output to a file. The objective of this chapter is to explore file and database processing in much more detail. From this chapter you will learn how to do the following.

- Create and write a new record to the patron file.
- Create a general file maintenance project for adding new records and editing existing one.
- Access data from an Access database using embedded SQL (ESQL).
- Use the ESQL Wizard for creating queries into a database.

Components of the Patron File-Maintenance Projects

About the Patron File

Figure 11-1 shows the patron file's record layout and its first four records. Notice that the first record is different from subsequent records—it maintains a count of the number of patron records in the file. This is accommodated in the record description where the field pr-first-name is redefined to handle the counter pr-last-key. When a new record is added, the counter's value is incremented by 1 and used as the patron number. In other words, patron numbers are assigned automatically as a new record is entered. You will see evidence of this in the first example of this chapter.

Looking again at Figure 11-1, you see five one-position fields with the following features

pr-privilege-status   Determines special privileges due the patron
                       Permissible values are: G—Gold
                                                  P—Premium
                                                  R—Regular
pr-employee-status   The patron's employment status with the company.
                       Permissible values are: F—Full time employee
                                                  P—Part time employee
                                                  N—Non-employee

```
    01  patron-record.
        10  pr-patron-number      pic x(03).
        10  pr-first-name         pic X(10).
        10  pr-last-key redefines
            pr-first-name         pic 9(03).
        10  pr-last-name          pic X(12).
        10  pr-street-address     pic X(20).
        10  pr-city               pic X(14).
        10  pr-state              pic X(02).
        10  pr-zip                pic X(10).
        10  pr-privilege-status   pic X(01).
        10  pr-employee-status    pic X(01).
        10  pr-book-right         pic X(01).
        10  pr-periodical-right   pic X(01).
        10  pr-video-right        pic X(01).
        10  pr-books-out          pic X(01).
        10                        pic X(18).


    000024
    0010rson      Karridge    223 Connecticut St  San Francisco CA94107-0000GFYYY07
    002Sandy      Beech       1247 Main Street    Woodside      CA94062-0000RFYNY03
    003Bill       Board       1532 Bancroft Road  Berkeley      CA94703-0000RFYNN02
```

Figure 11-1. Record format for the patron file.

`pr-book-right`   Book check-out privilege
`pr-periodical-right` Periodical check-out privilege
`pr-video-right`   Video check-out privilege

For each of the above checkout privileges,
permissible values are: Y—Yes
N—No

You will see code to handle these fields and their values in the CGI programs of this chapter's examples.

As with many of the other example projects of this book, you will find it especially useful to run each patron-file-processing project before reading about it. Since the file processing subprograms of these projects write to the patron file, all three write to Patron2.di rather than Patron.di (used by previous examples). This preserves the contents of Patron.di, the file you've been using until now.

Patron File-Access Subprograms

The first three projects of this chapter process the patron file and include one or more of the subprograms Pat-sub1.cbl, Pat-sub2.cbl, and Pat-sub3.cbl. Each of these requires a single parameter, the patron record.

Pat-sub1.cbl Writes a new record to the patron file.

Input: All fields of the record `patron-record` (see Figure 11-1) except the patron number `pr-patron-number`.
Output: The subprogram-assigned patron number (`pr-patron-number`.
        If the subprogram is unable to write the record, `patron-record` is returned with low-values.

If you inspect Pat-sub1, you will see that the action of adding a record involves the following sequence of steps.

- Read the counter record (key value 000).
- Add 1 to the field `pr-last-key`.
- Use that value for the patron number of the new record.
- Write the new record.
- Rewrite the updated counter record.

Pat-sub2.cbl Reads a record from the patron file.

Input: The patron number `pr-patron-number`.
Output: The patron record.
        If there is no record for the input key value, the patron record is returned with low-values.

Pat-sub3.cbl Rewrites a previously read record to the patron file.

Input: The patron record.
Output: None unless the subprogram is unable to rewrite the record, then the patron record is returned with low-values.

Copy Files

If you look at the listings in the Appendix for these subprograms you will see that each includes an FD with the record description for the patron file. Similarly, other subprograms used in these applications include that same record description; some also include a record description for the book file. Normally, you would define these record descriptions as copy files, place them in a separate folder, then include a an appropriate copy statement in the subprogram. In the original design of these examples, I had done that. However, upon reflection, I replaced all Copy statements with the correspoinding data records solely to minimize the number of elements with which you must deal.

Adding Records to the Patron File

The Project Screens

Proj1101
Pat01

This chapter's first file-processing project, Pat01 stored in Proj1101, allows you to add records to the patron file. As you can see by inspecting the diagram of Figure 11-2, this project is relatively basic. Input to the CGI consists of all data required to create a new patron record—see the Form Designer view of this page of Figure 11-3. The output page, illustrated in Figure 11-4, confirms the customer name and displays the program-generated patron number. Look at the buttons in these two forms (refer to the control trees) and you see:

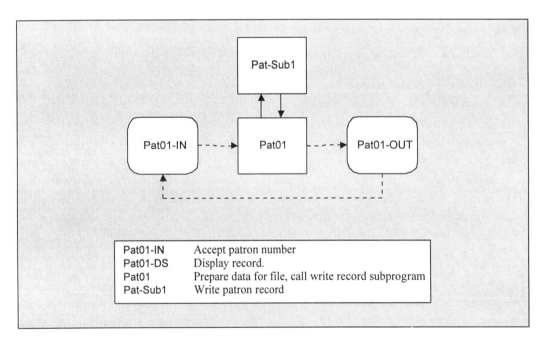

Figure 11-2. The project component diagram—Proj1101.

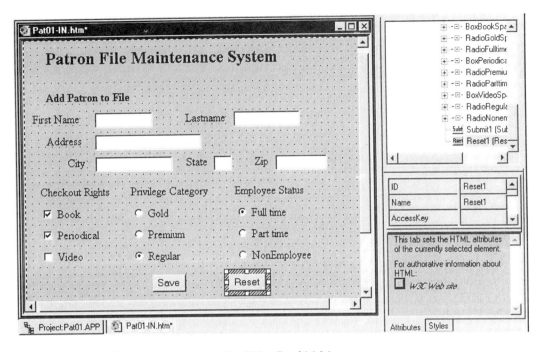

Figure 11-3. The input page Pat01-IN—Proj1101.

- Save is a Submit button.
- Reset is a Reset button; it sets all entries to their original values, spaces in the example. This is convenient if, for instance, you totally mess up an entry and decide to start over.
- Add Another (Figure 11-4) is an Input Button control assigned an onclick event that returns control to the input page.

Note that the output page uses Server-Side Text controls to display the patron name and newly assigned patron number.

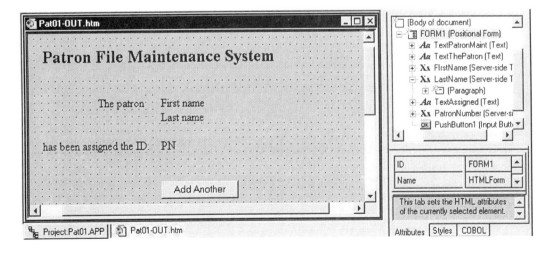

Figure 11-4. The output pagePat01-OUT—Proj1101.

The CGI

In the CGI of Figure 11-5 there is little you have not already seen in previous examples. Notice the following about this listing.

- Form fields are defined at lines 100-112.
- The Call statement of line 203 includes patron-record (line 118) as its parameter. Remember, all fields of this record except pr-patron-number serve as input to the subprogram. The field pr-patron-number contains the subprogram's output.

```
  1   IDENTIFICATION DIVISION.              134   PROCEDURE DIVISION.
  2       program-id. "Pat01".              135

 10   DATA DIVISION.                        162   process-business-logic section.
 11                                         163       *> Add application business logic here.
 12   working-storage section.             164
                                            165       Move FirstName     to pr-first-name
 98       copy "Pat01.cpy".                 166       Move LastName      to pr-last-name
 99       01 FormFields.                    167       Move StreetAddress to pr-street-address
100          03 BoxVideo        pic X(15).  168       Move FormCity      to pr-city
101          03 BoxBook         pic X(15).  169       Move FormState     to pr-state
102          03 FirstName       pic X(10).  170       Move FormZip       to pr-zip
103          03 FormState       pic X(2).   171       Evaluate EmployeeRadio
104          03 BoxPeriodical   pic X(15).  172         when "RadioFulltime"
105          03 FormZip         pic X(10).  173           Move "F" to pr-employee-status
106          03 PatronNumber    pic X(3).   174         when "RadioParttime"
107          03 PrivilegeRadio  pic X(15).  175           Move "P" to pr-employee-status
108          03 FormCity        pic X(14).  176         when "RadioNonemployee"
109          03 submit          pic X(60).  177           Move "N" to pr-employee-status
110          03 LastName        pic X(12).  178         when other
111          03 StreetAddress   pic X(20).  179           Move "X" to pr-employee-status
112          03 EmployeeRadio   pic X(15).  180       End-evaluate *>EmployeeRadio
113                                         181
114   *> Enter additional working-storage items here  182   Evaluate PrivilegeRadio
115                                         183         when "RadioGold"
116   01  patron-record.                   184           Move "G" to pr-privilege-status
117       10  pr-patron-number  pic x(03).  185         when "RadioPremium"
118       10  pr-first-name     pic X(10).  186           Move "P" to pr-privilege-status
119       10  pr-last-key redefines         187         when "RadioRegular"
120           pr-first-name     pic 9(03).  188           Move "R" to pr-privilege-status
121       10  pr-last-name      pic X(12).  189       End-evaluate *>PrivilegeRadio
122       10  pr-street-address pic X(20).  190       Move "N" to pr-book-right
123       10  pr-city           pic X(14).  191                      pr-periodical-right
124       10  pr-state          pic X(02).  192                      pr-video-right
125       10  pr-zip            pic X(10).   193       If BoxBook = "BoxBook"
126       10  pr-privilege-status pic X(01). 194         Move "Y" to pr-book-right
127       10  pr-employee-status pic X(01).  195       End-If *>BoxBook = "BoxBook"
128       10  pr-book-right     pic X(01).   196       If BoxPeriodical = "BoxPeriodical"
129       10  pr-periodical-right pic X(01). 197         Move "Y" to pr-periodical-right
130       10  pr-video-right    pic X(01).   198       End-If *>BoxPeriodical = "BoxPeriodical"
131       10  pr-books-out      pic 9(02).   199       If BoxVideo = "BoxVideo"
132       10                    pic X(18).   200         Move "Y" to pr-video-right
133                                          201       End-If *>BoxVideo = "BoxVideo"
                                             202
                                             203       Call "pat-sub1" Using patron-record
                                             204       Move pr-patron-number to PatronNumber
                                             205
                                             206       exit.
```

Figure 11-5. The Proj1101 CGI Pat01.cbl.

One Page for Input and Output

Features of Proj1102

Designers of data entry applications, are always alert to making the entry process as simple and efficient as possible. One means to that end is to give appropriate entries default values. For instance, you see this done in the input page of Figure 11-3 in which the check boxes and radio buttons are displayed with default values. These defaults were selected because they are the most commonly entered—for example, most patrons are full-time employees.

If this application were for a selected geographic area, say Portland, in which almost all patrons resided in Portland, then the city and state defaults should be set to Portland, OR. For patrons residing in Vancouver, Washington, those two entries would be replaced. Another common scenario is fields that are the same for several consecutive entries. As an example, assume that in the source documents, entry data is sorted on Zip code. So all new patrons from, for example, Modesto, California will be grouped together. In that case, carrying over the city, state, and Zip values from the preceding record as defaults (see Figure 11-6) would probably be a good idea. Notice that this screen has a button for clearing these entries in case they are not appropriate for the next patron.

The next example, Pat02 stored in Proj1102 provides for data "carry-over" by using a symmetric CGI, one in which the same HTML page is used for both input and output (you saw this in Lib15 of Proj0901). You see the component diagram for this application in Figure 11-7. Pat02-IO, the input/output HTML page component of this application, was created by using Pat01-IN as a template. Recall from Chapter 9

Proj1102
Pat02

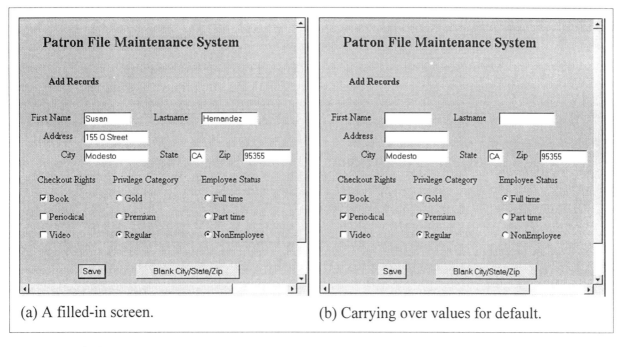

(a) A filled-in screen.   (b) Carrying over values for default.

Figure 11-6. Data entry screens.

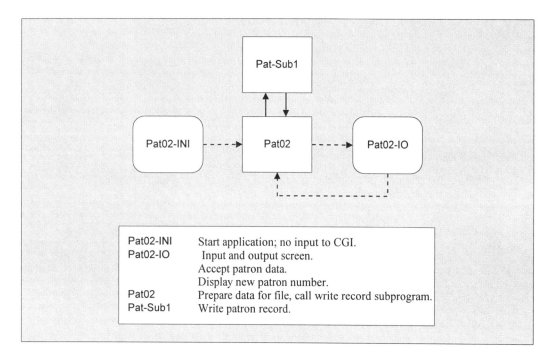

Figure 11-7. Component diagram for Pat02.

that even though the diagram shows the CGI being executed from the page Pat02-INI, this page was not designated as input when the CGI was created.

CGI Considerations

Recall from Chapter 9 that when generating the symmetric CGI, you used the generation template CGI-nibi.skl (no initial browser input). The resulting main section code (see Figure 11-8) prevents performing the business logic section the first run. Thus the following sequence prevents an empty record (no data has been entered) being written to the file.

1. As a result of the `perform` at line 136, `MF-SERVER-EXEC` contains the value no causing the section `pat02-IO-ini` (not shown in this partial listing) to be performed—see line 140.
2. Check boxes and radio buttons are set to their initial values by `pat02-IO-ini`.
3. The output page is sent to the browser by the embedded HTML code in the section Pat02-IO-out (performed from line 147).

During subsequent executions of this CGI, `MF-SERVER-EXEC` will not contain the value no. Therefore, you will see execution of the customary five-statement sequence in the main section (lines 135, 136, 143, 144, and 147.

For the other consideration of this project structure, assume you have entered the data of Figure 11-6(a) and clicked the Save button. When the CGI completes its processing, it returns to the browser the same page, now serving as the output. As such, it returns (and displays) all values stored in the page's Text Input data items. So your CGI must contain code to initialize all fields that you want returned to their default values, as done at lines 211-218 of Figure 11-8. In this case, only the city, state, and zip values carry over (refer to Figure 11-6).

```
  1  IDENTIFICATION DIVISION.              151
  2      program-id. "Pat02".              152  process-form-input-data section.
                                           153      *> Accept the input from the Browser
 10  DATA DIVISION.                        154      *> and check for errors
 11                                        155      perform browser-initialize
 12  working-storage section.              156      accept htmlform
                                           157      exit.
 44  *>    The following field indicates if input was  158
 45  *>    received from the Browser       159  convert-input section.
 46  *>    z"yes" indicates executethat business logic  160      *> Convert numeric input values
 47  *>    z"no" indicates an "initial load" condition  161      perform input-conversion
 48  *>    (null terminator is required by JScript)     162      if v-all-ok = 0
 49      01 MF-SERVER-EXEC        pic x(4).            163          perform output-form-error-and-stop
                                           164      end-if
 95      copy "Pat02.cpy".                 165      exit.
 96      01 FormFields.                    166
 97          03 BoxVideo        pic X(15). 167  process-business-logic section.
 98          03 BoxBook         pic X(15). 168      *> Add application business logic here.
 99          03 FirstName       pic X(10). 169
100          03 FormState       pic X(2).  170      Move FirstName     to pr-first-name
101          03 BoxPeriodical   pic X(15). 171      Move LastName      to pr-last-name
102          03 FormZip         pic X(10). 172      Move StreetAddress to pr-street-address
103          03 PrivilegeRadio  pic X(15). 173      Move FormCity      to pr-city
104          03 FormCity        pic X(14). 174      Move FormState     to pr-state
105          03 ssubmit         pic X(60). 175      Move FormZip       to pr-zip
106          03 LastName        pic X(12). 176      Evaluate EmployeeRadio
107          03 StreetAddress   pic X(20). 177        when "RadioFulltime"
108          03 EmployeeRadio   pic X(16). 178          Move "F" to pr-employee-status
109                                        179        when "RadioParttime"
110  *> Enter additional working-storage items here  180          Move "P" to pr-employee-status
111      copy "Pat-record.cpy".            181        when "RadioNonemployee"
112  *> PAT-RECORD.CPY                     182          Move "N" to pr-employee-status
113                                        183        when other
114  01  patron-record.                    184          Move "X" to pr-employee-status
115      10  pr-patron-number   pic x(03). 185      End-evaluate *>EmployeeRadio
116      10  pr-first-name      pic X(10). 186
117      10  pr-last-key redefines         187      Evaluate PrivilegeRadio
118          pr-first-name      pic 9(03). 188        when "RadioGold"
119      10  pr-last-name       pic X(12). 189          Move "G" to pr-privilege-status
120      10  pr-street-address  pic X(20). 190        when "RadioPremium"
121      10  pr-city            pic X(14). 191          Move "P" to pr-privilege-status
122      10  pr-state           pic X(02). 192        when "RadioRegular"
123      10  pr-zip             pic X(10). 193          Move "R" to pr-privilege-status
124      10  pr-privilege-status pic X(01). 194      End-evaluate *>PrivilegeRadio
125      10  pr-employee-status pic X(01). 195      Move "N" to pr-book-right
126      10  pr-book-right      pic X(01). 196                    pr-periodical-right
127      10  pr-periodical-right pic X(01). 197                    pr-video-right
128      10  pr-video-right     pic X(01). 198      If BoxBook = "BoxBook"
129      10  pr-books-out       pic 9(02). 199        Move "Y" to pr-book-right
130      10                     pic X(20). 200      End-If *>BoxBook = "BoxBook"
131                                        201      If BoxPeriodical = "BoxPeriodical"
132  PROCEDURE DIVISION.                   202        Move "Y" to pr-periodical-right
133                                        203      End-If *>BoxPeriodical = "BoxPeriodical"
134  main section.                         204      If BoxVideo = "BoxVideo"
135      perform process-form-input-data   205        Move "Y" to pr-video-right
136      perform convert-input             206      End-If *>BoxVideo = "BoxVideo"
137      *> If there is no input from the Browser,  207
138      *> then initial field values are output   208      Call "pat-sub1" Using patron-record
139      if MF-SERVER-EXEC = z"no"         209
140          perform pat02-IO-ini          210      *> Initialize for next loop
141          *> pat02-io                   211      Move spaces to firstname
142      else                              212                   lastname
143          perform process-business-logic 213                   streetaddress
144          perform pat02-IO-cvt          214      Move "BoxBook" to BoxBook
145          *> pat02-io                   215      Move "BoxPeriodical" to BoxPeriodical
146      end-if *>MF-SERVER-EXEC = z"no"    216      Move spaces to BoxVideo
147      perform pat02-IO-out              217      Move "RadioRegular" to PrivilegeRadio
148      *> pat02-io                       218      Move "RadioFulltime" to EmployeeRadio
149      exit program                      219
150      stop run.                         220      exit.
```

Figure 11-8. Selected parts of the CGI Pat02.

The Project's Event Handlers

If you've run this application, you know that the first screen is introductory and includes the single button Proceed. Clicking that button puts you into an input screen like Figure 11-6. If you look at the event handler for this button, you will see that it instructs the server to run the CGI via the following JavaScript instruction.

```
location.href="/cgi-bin/pat02.exe"
```

This is similar to code inserted in the initial page of Chapter 9's symmetric example.

From running this application you also know that clicking on the Blank City/State/Zip button does exactly that: blanks the three fields. Open Pat02-IO.htm and look at the onclick event handler for this button; you will see the following.

```
function PushButton1_onclick_func()
{
document.HTMLForm.FormCity.value = ""
document.HTMLForm.FormState.value = ""
document.HTMLForm.FormZip.value = ""
}
```

From the event handler examples in Chapter 8, you know that these JavaScript lines set the designated control values to spaces.

Record Maintenance—Pat03

About the Pat03 Project

The third file-processing example of this chapter, Pat03 stored in Proj1103, allows you to edit existing records of the patron file as well as add new records. You see its overall structure in the component diagram of Figure 11-9. In addition to the brief descriptions included below the diagram, following are some of its features.

- Pat03-ME is the "front-end" menu (Figure 11-10) that provides the user access to the record update features (beginning at Pat03U-INI) and the record addition component (beginning at Pat03A-IN) The record-addition component is a minor variation of Pat01.
- To avoid an excessive number of flow lines, connector symbols are used, corresponding to conventional program flowchart standards.
- Within the system, there are a number of "paths" the user can take. For instance, from Pat03U-DIS, she/he can elect to save the updated record (progress to Pat03Uwrite), abort this record and select another (progress to Pat03U-INI), or abort this record and go back to the main menu (progress to Pat03-ME).
- This application uses three different subprograms (described later) to access the patron file.

You will find it especially useful to run this application before proceeding. Try all of the options to gain a good feel for its overall functionality. When you do,

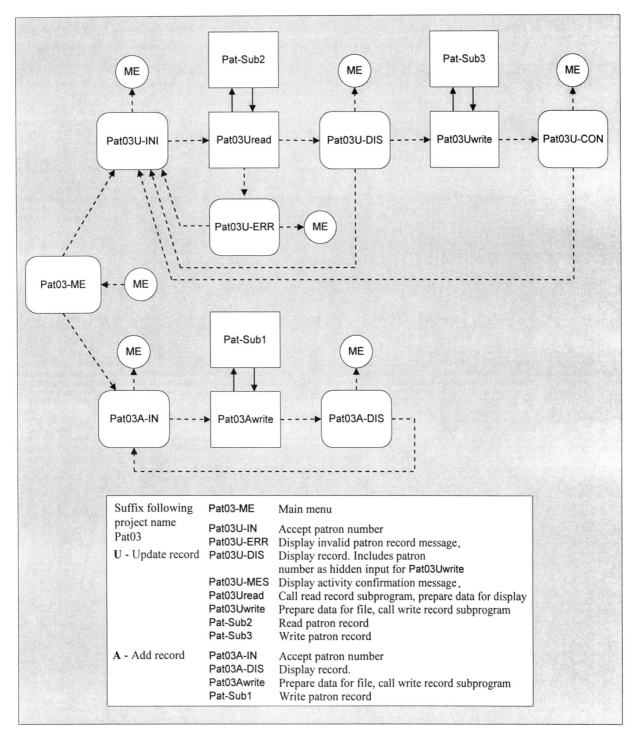

Figure 11-9. Component diagram—Project Pat03.

notice that you cannot modify the patron number. It is the record key field and is assigned automatically by the system when the record is entered. You observed this if you ran Pat01.

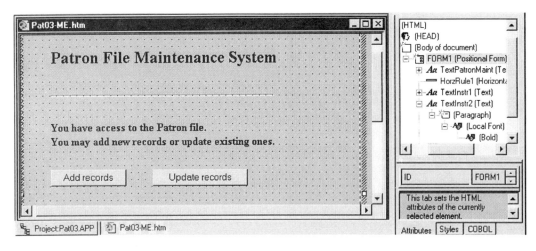

Figure 11-10. The front-end menu page Pat03-ME.

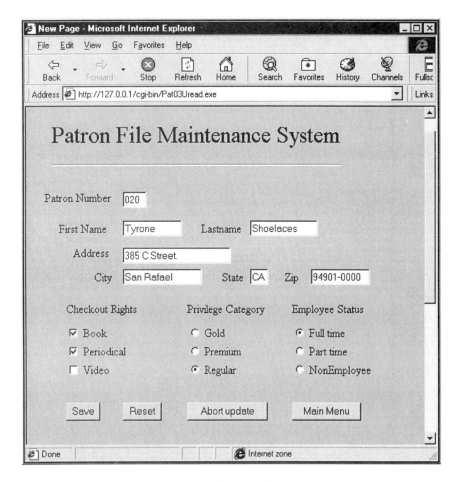

Figure 11-11. The patron data display from Pat03U-DIS.

The HTML Page Pat03U-DIS

Although the diagram of Figure 11-9 may appear complex, this application introduces no new principles. Let's focus on the portion of this application to edit a patron record, the "upper" portion in Figure 11-9 in which the following sequence of events takes place.

1. A user enters the desired patron number into Pat03-INI's form.
2. The PatUread CGI calls the subprogram Pat-Sub2 to read the selected record.
3. Pat03U-DIS displays patron data read from the file, for instance, as in Figure 11-11.
4. The user modifies the displayed data as appropriate. Upon clicking the Save button, the data is sent to the CGI Pat03Uwrite.
5. Pat03Uwrite calls the subprogram Pat-Sub3 to rewrite the record.
6. Pat03U-CON displays a message confirming the rewrite action.

All fields on the page of Figure 11-11 can be modified except the patron number: it is the record's key field value. If you look at the attributes of this control (InPatronNumber) you will see that Readonly is set to True thereby disabling the user's ability to change it. Note that you must not protect it by changing the Disabled attribute to True as this will sever its link to the CGI Pat03Uwrite where it is required in order to rewrite the record.

You should also look at the four buttons at the bottom of this form; they are as follows.

- Save   A Submit button—activates the CGI Pat03Uwrite..
- Reset   A Reset button—resets all controls to default values.
- Abort update   An Input Button with an event handler to load Pat03U-INI.
- Main Menu   An Input Button with an event handler to load Pat03-ME.

Notice that the record read and rewrite actions are contained in separate subprograms. This means that Pat-Sub2 will open, read, and close the patron file; then Pat-Sub3 will open, rewrite, and close the file. In a conventional Cobol application, all of this activity would likely be within a single run unit in which the file would be opened, the record read, its data updated, and the record rewritten. Then processing would progress to the next record. Again the absence of state comes into play. (In this example it would be possible to combine these subprogram actions into one subprogram with multiple entry points. Because of the of absence state, that offers no significant advantage here.)

The CGI Programs

The CGI Pat03Awrite and its corresponding subprogram Pat-sub1 are identical to those of the Pat01 project for writing a new record. The CGI Pat03Uread and its corresponding subprogram Pat-sub2 are similar to earlier Lib projects to read a patron record. Pat03Uwrite, although similar to the other CGI's, includes some features worthy of note—refer to Figure 11-12.

- Look at the Call statement of line 214 and you see that the subprogram parameter is the data record defined at lines 127-142 (the entire patron record).
- Name and address data is moved to this record at lines 175-180.
- Codes corresponding to the check boxes and radio buttons of Figure 11-11 are defined in the patron record at lines 137-142. These values are set according to input from the HTML page by conditional code at lines 181-211.
- The key-field value is moved to the key field at line 213.
- If a rewrite error occurs in Pat-sub3, the call parameter is returned with low-values. The occurrence of an error on the rewrite, is a serious problem. Remember that the record to be rewritten is the previously read record. Therefore, an invalid key error upon writing should never occur. If it does, a serious file error has occurred. The code of Figure 11-12's lines 216-219 advises the user to discontinue processing.

There's not much to the subprogram Pat-Sub3 as you can see by inspecting the following code taken from its Procedure Division.

```
Open I-O Patron-File
Rewrite patron-record from ls-patron-record
  Invalid key
    Move low-values to ls-patron-number
End-rewrite
Close Patron-File
Exit program
```

Accessing a Relational Database from NetExpress

Relational Databases and SQL

Every Cobol programmer is familiar with conventional files (sequential, indexed, and direct) and file management systems provided to simplify access to data of the files. In this "traditional" programming environment, overall management of the data is achieved through a combination of user-written Cobol application programs and file-handling support software. On the other hand, **relational database management systems** include the capabilities to define data and attributes of that data, establish relationships among data items, and manipulate/manage the data.

Preceding examples of this chapter access data from the two indexed files Patron.di and Book.di (and their corresponding index files, Patron.idx and Book.idx). The relationship between the files is established in the Cobol code of Lib-sub2. The remainder of this chapter deals with the **Microsoft Access relational database** Library.mdb; it contains two tables, Patron and Book, corresponding to the index files. If you have Microsoft Access on your computer, you can look at them as follows.

1. Bring up Access.
2. From the initial screen, with More files highlighted, click OK.
3. For the Look in box select C:\Elements-CWP\NE-data.
4. The file in which you are interested is Library.mdb. Open it.

```
  1  IDENTIFICATION DIVISION.              178  Move FormCity     to pr-city
  2     program-id. "Pat03Uwrite".         179  Move FormState    to pr-state
                                           180  Move FormZip      to pr-zip
 10  DATA DIVISION.                        181  Evaluate EmployeeRadio
 11                                        182    when "RadioFulltime"
 12  working-storage section.             183      Move "F" to pr-employee-status
                                           184    when "RadioParttime"
106     copy "Pat03Uwrite.cpy".           185      Move "P" to pr-employee-status
107     01 FormFields.                    186    when "RadioNonemployee"
108        03 BoxVideo        pic X(15).   187      Move "N" to pr-employee-status
109        03 BoxBook         pic X(15).   188    when other
110        03 FirstName       pic X(10).   189      Move "X" to pr-employee-status
111        03 FormState       pic X(2).    190  End-evaluate *>EmployeeRadio
112        03 BoxPeriodical   pic X(15).   191
113        03 FormZip         pic X(10).   192  Evaluate PrivilegeRadio
114        03 ExitMessage2    pic X(40).   193    when "RadioGold"
115        03 PrivilegeRadio  pic X(15).   194      Move "G" to pr-privilege-status
116        03 FormCity        pic X(14).   195    when "RadioPremium"
117        03 ExitMessage1    pic X(40).   196      Move "P" to pr-privilege-status
118        03 InPatronNumber  pic x(3).    197    when "RadioRegular"
119        03 submit          pic X(60).   198      Move "R" to pr-privilege-status
120        03 ExitMessage3    pic X(30).   199  End-evaluate *>PrivilegeRadio
121        03 LastName        pic X(12).   200  Move "N" to pr-book-right
122        03 StreetAddress   pic X(20).   201               pr-periodical-right
123        03 EmployeeRadio   pic X(15).   202               pr-video-right
124                                        203  If BoxBook = "BoxBook"
125  *> Enter additional working-storage items here  204    Move "Y" to pr-book-right
126                                        205  End-If *>BoxBook = "BoxBook"
127  01  patron-record.                   206  If BoxPeriodical = "BoxPeriodical"
128     10  pr-patron-number  pic x(03).   207    Move "Y" to pr-periodical-right
129     10  pr-first-name     pic X(10).   208  End-If *>BoxPeriodical = "BoxPeriodical"
130     10  pr-last-key redefines         209  If BoxVideo = "BoxVideo"
131         pr-first-name     pic 9(03).   210    Move "Y" to pr-video-right
132     10  pr-last-name      pic X(12).   211  End-If *>BoxVideo = "BoxVideo"
133     10  pr-street-address pic X(20).   212
134     10  pr-city           pic X(14).   213  Move InPatronNumber to pr-patron-number
135     10  pr-state          pic X(02).   214  Call "pat-sub3" using patron-record
136     10  pr-zip            pic X(10).    215  If pr-patron-number = low-values
137     10  pr-privilege-status pic X(01). 216    Move "Record not saved—file problem."
138     10  pr-employee-status  pic X(01). 217         to ExitMessage1
139     10  pr-book-right      pic X(01).  218    Move "Do not continue" to ExitMessage2
140     10  pr-periodical-right pic X(01). 219    Move spaces to ExitMessage3
141     10  pr-video-right     pic X(01).  220  Else
142     10                     pic X(20).  221    Move "Record successfully updated."
143                                        222         to ExitMessage1
144  PROCEDURE DIVISION.                   223    Move "You may edit another patron record."
                                           224         to ExitMessage2
172  process-business-logic section.      225    Move "or return to the main menu."
173     *> Add application business logic here.  226         to ExitMessage3
174                                        227  End-If *>pr-patron-number = low-values
175     Move FirstName     to pr-first-name    228
176     Move LastName      to pr-last-name     229  exit.
177     Move StreetAddress to pr-street-address
```

Figure 11-12. The CGI Pat03Uwrite.cbl.

You will see the screen of Figure 11-13 displaying the names of the two tables comprising this database. These tables correspond to the indexed files Book.di and Patron.di of preceding examples.

Figure 11-13.
Opening the Access
database Library.mdb.

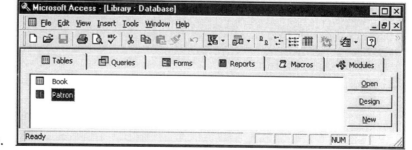

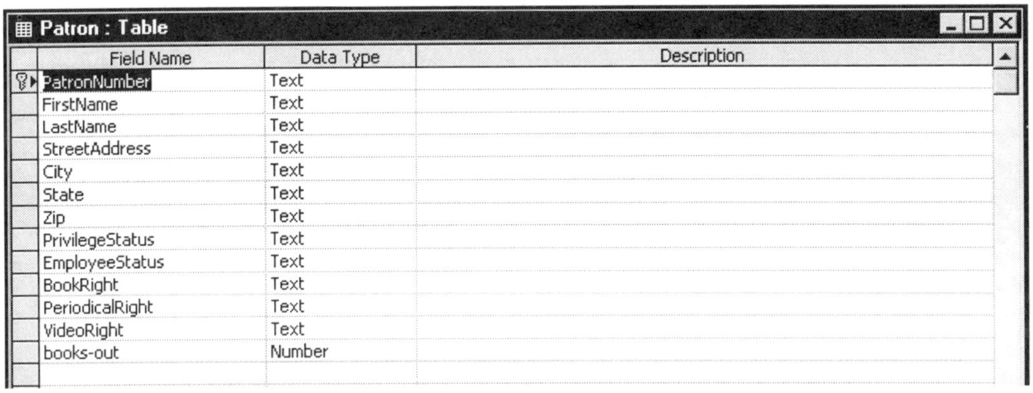

Patron : Table

Field Name	Data Type	Description
PatronNumber	Text	
FirstName	Text	
LastName	Text	
StreetAddress	Text	
City	Text	
State	Text	
Zip	Text	
PrivilegeStatus	Text	
EmployeeStatus	Text	
BookRight	Text	
PeriodicalRight	Text	
VideoRight	Text	
books-out	Number	

Figure 11-14. Field names of the patron table.

Highlight the Patron entry then click the Design button. Your resulting screen will contain the list of field names (data items) of Figure 11-14. You should recognize these from past examples using the patron file.

Close this window then click the Open button and you will see a window something like that of Figure 11-15. Again, you should recognize these data values from the runs you have made of the example projects. Notice that data appears in the form of columns and rows—this is the nature of the relational database model. The columns correspond to data items (fields) that we define in a Cobol program's FD (file description). The rows correspond to records of the file.

A widely used tool for accessing data from a database is the **Structured Query Language** (**SQL**). SQL can be used interactively or it can be embedded into application programs, in which case it is often referred to as **Embedded SQL** (**ESQL**). In this chapter, you will learn how to embed SQL into your Cobol CGI programs using the SQL wizard of NetExpress. Although you would find it helpful to know SQL, that knowledge is not necessary to create meaningful applications.

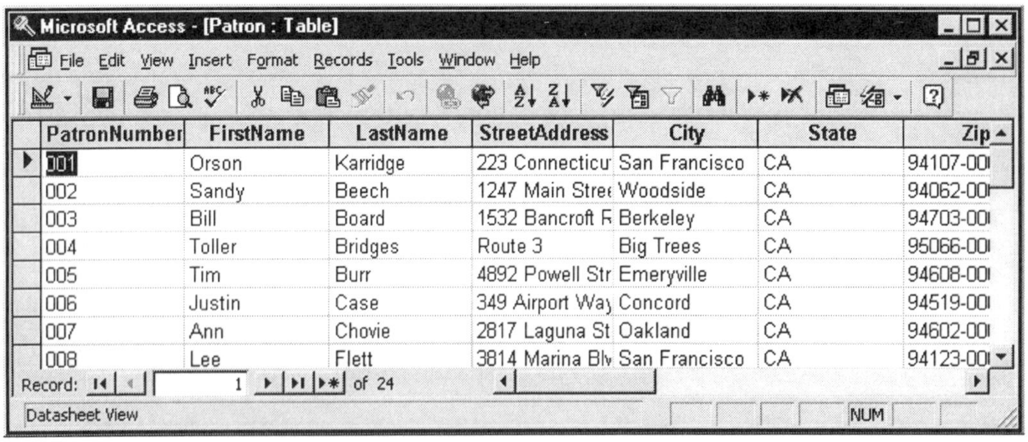

Microsoft Access - [Patron : Table]

PatronNumber	FirstName	LastName	StreetAddress	City	State	Zip
001	Orson	Karridge	223 Connecticu	San Francisco	CA	94107-00
002	Sandy	Beech	1247 Main Stre	Woodside	CA	94062-00
003	Bill	Board	1532 Bancroft R	Berkeley	CA	94703-00
004	Toller	Bridges	Route 3	Big Trees	CA	95066-00
005	Tim	Burr	4892 Powell Str	Emeryville	CA	94608-00
006	Justin	Case	349 Airport Wa	Concord	CA	94519-00
007	Ann	Chovie	2817 Laguna St	Oakland	CA	94602-00
008	Lee	Flett	3814 Marina Blv	San Francisco	CA	94123-00

Record: 1 of 24

Datasheet View

Figure 11-15. Part of the patron table.

Setting Up to Use ESQL in NetExpress Programs

To provide language-independent access to database-stored data, industry has defined a non-proprietary interface to database management systems called **Open Database Connectivity** (**ODBC**). Most relational database vendors supply an ODBC driver that can be used to access their database management system. The ODBC driver is accessed by code of the application program thereby providing the necessary bridge between a given language and a database management system.

NetExpress includes two special preprocessors that translate embedded SQL code into calls that access the OBDC driver of the particular database management system being used. In this chapter, you will be using the preprocessor OpenESQL to access data in a Microsoft Access database.

Before you can use ESQL in a Cobol program, you must provide the Windows operating system certain information regarding your data source (in this case, the Access database name) and the OBDC driver to be used for accessing it. If you currently have NetExpress open, close it then proceed with the following. (If you leave NetExpress open, you will not be able to see the results of the following without closing then reopening.)

1. From the Windows Start menu, click Settings/Control Panel.
2. From the popup window, click the 32Bit OBDC icon (it will look something like the one to the right).
3. The resulting screen will look like Figure 11-16; the tab User DSN identifies User Data Source Names. You must add a data source to this list identifying the Library database. Click the Add button.
4. Your screen will look like Figure 11-17 (it may include other entries). You want the NetExpress Microsoft Access driver so scroll down to that entry (as in Figure 11-17) then click Finish.

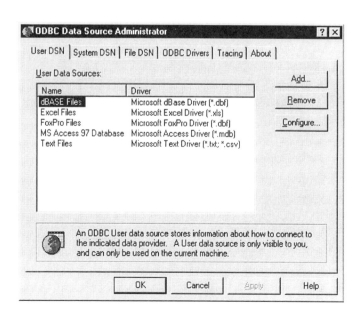

Figure 11-16.
List of data sources.

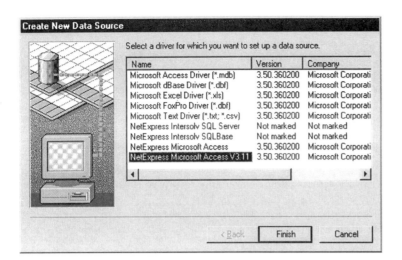

Figure 11-17.
Selecting the data
source driver.

5. You will see an OBDC setup screen similar to Figure 11-18. Type the data source name and description entries shown in this figure.

6. Click the Select button and you will see a screen like Figure 11-19. The data source you want is the Library database stored in the folder Elements-CWP\NE-data (the database use by this chapter's examples). Using standard Windows techniques, locate the NE-data folder and you should see Library.mdb listed in the left pane as in Figure 11-19. Note that if you loaded your files from the Examples CD into another folder, you will need to access that folder

7. When you have Library.mdb selected, click OK and you will be returned to the screen of Figure 11-18.

8. Click OK and your ODBC Administrator screen should include your newly added data source name as shown in Figure 11-20.

9. Click OK again, then close the Control Panel window.

The data source Library Application is now available system-wide; you will use it in the next tutorial.

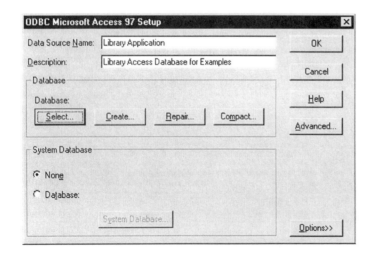

Figure 11-18.
Data source setup.

Figure 11-19.
Selecting the data source.

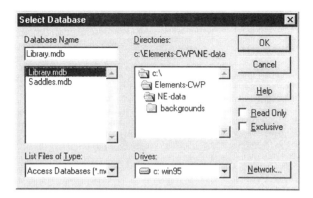

First Look at OpenESQL Assistant

Starting Point

The project Sql01 stored in the folder Proj1104 obtains data from an Access database using SQL embedded in the Cobol CGI. The application is relatively simple: you enter a patron number into the input page, the CGI accesses the patron's data, and the output page displays the name and address.

To simplify your first excursion with database access through ESQL, the folder Proj1104-2 contains a complete copy of Sql01 except the CGI has no user inserted code—creating that is the activity of this exercise. The project's components are as follows.

- Sql01-IN.htm: Input page to accept the input patron number.
- Sql01-OUT.htm: Output page to display patron name and address information.
- Sql01.cbl: The CGI program generated by NetExpress; it contains no code beyond that of NetExpress. You will add the needed code in this exercise for accessing data from the database.

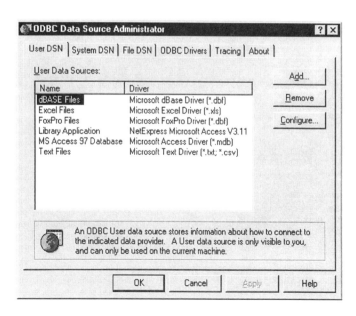

Figure 11-20.
Data source list with
Library Application.

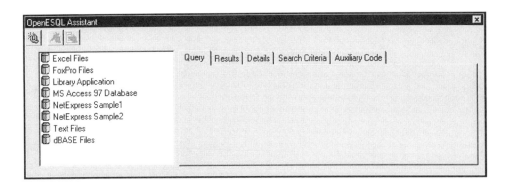

Figure 11-21.
The OpenSQL
Assistant screen.

Host Variables

Within your Cobol CGI programs, you know you must deal with both form data items (from name/value pairs brought into your program by the Accept statement) and conventional Cobol data items. NetExpress code and Cobol code created by NetExpress simplify our programming lives by parsing out name value pairs and presenting us the data in conventional Cobol form. Similarly, embedded SQL statements create Cobol data items corresponding to database table field names and make the data available in corresponding Cobol data items. The latter are commonly called **host variables**. Code that you will need to include in your CGI programs involves moving HTML input form-field values to host variables (for input to the database table) and host variable data (from the database) to HTML form-fields for display on the output page.

Creating a Simple Query

For your first look at the OpenSQL Assistant, let's create a few simple SQL queries. Although you could work from any project (even an empty one), you may as well open Sql01 (Proj1104-2) as that is the one you will be using later in this exercise. Then proceed as follows.

1. Click Tools/OpenSQLAssistant. Your screen should look like Figure 11-21. Notice that the data source Library Application you created under Windows is included in your list.

2. Double-click on Library Application to expand it thereby showing the tables subordinate to this source. This expansion will include Book and Patron, the two tables of the library database.

3. Double-click on the Patron icon and you will see the popup window of Figure 11-22. Highlight the SELECT (Singleton) option and click OK.

4. This expands Patron thereby listing its fields as in Figure 11-23. Notice that the Patron icon now includes a check mark indicating this table is selected for the query.

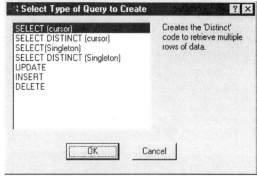

Figure 11-22.
Tables of the Library database.

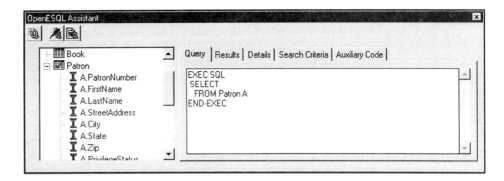

Figure 11-23. Creating a query.

In left pane of Figure 11-23 you see that each field name is preceded by the letter A and a period, for instance, A.PatronNumber. The letter A is called an **alias** and is used to distinguish data items of one table from those of another. You will see this in the next example which accesses data from both tables of this database. The icon to the left of the table name is a graphic for a column, indicating a column of the table. (In relational database terminology, a column name corresponds to the Cobol field name of a record definition.)

Now you must select the database fields you want in your Cobol CGI. For this, remember your application: you enter a patron number and the application displays the patron's name and address data. To that end proceed as follows.

5. Double-click on A.PatronNumber. That column (field) will be selected and inserted into the query screen. Also, a check is placed over the column icon of that field.

6. Proceed to select the next six columns. When you are finished, your screen should look like Figure 11-24.

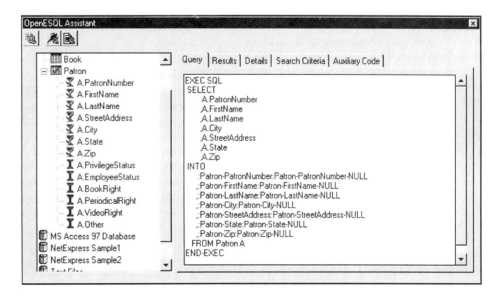

Figure 11-24. Selected columns for the query.

Although you are not finished with this query, you can actually run it at this point to satisfy yourself that it actually works. For this, click the Results tab then the run icon 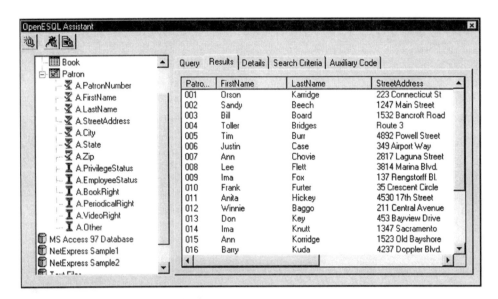 and the right-side pane will display the selected fields from the patron table—see Figure 11-25. (You can scroll across the pane to see all the fields.) Look at the top of this pane and you will see that you have the Results tab; click the Query tab and the SQL code will reappear.

Basic Nature of the SQL Select

Look at the SQL Select statement in Figure 11-24 and you see it is almost self-documenting. For instance, consider the following fragments of this code.

```
SELECT
    A.PatronNumber
    ...
INTO
    :Patron-PatronNumber:Patron-PatronNumber-NULL
    ...
    FROM Patron A
```

Read this as: "Obtain (SELECT) the value from the A-table field PatronNumber and copy it INTO the host variable named Patron-PatronNumber. The data field is FROM the table Patron identified by the alias A. (Ignore the second host data field Patron-PatronNumber-NUL; NetExpress uses it for internal checking.) If you look closely, you will see that each host data name is preceded by a colon—this is SQL's method of identifying a name as a host data name.

Establishing Search Critera

If you ran the query, your screen displayed all the rows (records) of the table. For this application, you want only a single row returned to your CGI: the one corre-

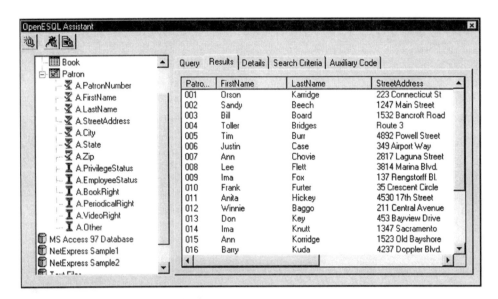

Figure 11-25. A query display.

sponding to the patron number you entered. To accomplish this, you must designate a **table-search criterion** based on finding the row whose patron number field is equal to the input patron number. For this, click the Search Criteria tab and your screen will look like Figure 11-26. Here you see the Assistant's default entries: exactly what you need for this application. Think of this as roughly equivalent to the following Cobol If statement.

```
If A.PatronNumber = :Patron-PatronNumber then ...
```

- The table field (column) on which the search is to be performed is PatronNumber.
- The comparison is to be based on a Host Variable Target Type—that is, a Cobol data item.
- The item against which the comparison must be made (the Target Value) is the host variable Patron-PatronNumber.
- The condition to be satisfied is equal (=).

If your comparison were on another field, you would simply expand the Column list and select the appropriate field. Target entries would change automatically. Although this criterion is exactly the one you want, let's experiment by designating a specific patron number and running the query. Do this as follows.

1. Expand the Target Type and select Literal.
2. Either type '001' into the Target Value box, or click the Edit button and type 001.
3. To create this search criterion, click the ▷ button. The following entry should be displayed in the right-side pane.

    A.PatronNumber = '001'

4. Click the Run icon and you will see the single row for patron 001 displayed (you may need to click the Results tab).
5. Click the Search Criteria tab to redisplay your search criteria.

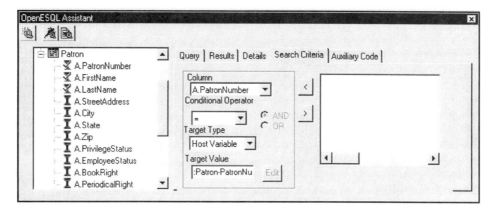

Figure 11-26. Designating a search criteria.

6. Although the preceding is a nice demonstration, you want the default criteria of Figure 11-26. To remove the current criteria highlight the search criteria (right-side pane), and click the ⟨ button.

7. Change the Target Type entry back to Host Variable. This will also change the Target Value entry back to :Patron-PatronNumber.

8. Click the ⟩ button to insert the search criteria in the right-side pane.

9. Click the Query tab and your completed query will be as shown in Figure 11-27. Notice the entry WHERE; it establishes the criterion for obtaining the single patron record (row) you want when the application is run. (Caution: Do not run the query at this point—some users have reported a Net Express crash here.)

Inserting ESQL into the CGI

The Query Code

Figure 11-27's SQL code to access data for a selected patron is equivalent to the subprogram call of earlier examples for reading a record from the indexed file. Consequently, you must insert it into the process-business-logic section of the CGI.

1. Open the CGI Sql01.cbl by double-clicking on its name in the Files window of the NetExpress window; you may need to move the OpenESQL Assistant window to do this. Your screen should look like Figure 11-28.

2. Position the cursor preceding the exit statement of process-business-logic section—refer to Figure 11-28

3. Click the Insert 📖 icon.

NetExpress will insert your code into the CGI. Check to be certain that it is positioned in the right place. If not, you did not position the cursor correctly before clicking the Insert button. So delete the inserted code, position the cursor correctly in the CGI, and click the Insert button again.

```
EXEC SQL
 SELECT
     A.PatronNumber
     A.FirstName
     A.LastName
     A.StreetAddress
     A.City
     A.State
     A.Zip
 INTO
     :Patron-PatronNumber:Patron-PatronNumber-NULL
     ,:Patron-FirstName:Patron-FirstName-NULL
     ,:Patron-LastName:Patron-LastName-NULL
     ,:Patron-StreetAddress:Patron-StreetAddress-NULL
     ,:Patron-City:Patron-City-NULL
     ,:Patron-State:Patron-State-NULL
     ,:Patron-Zip:Patron-Zip-NULL
 FROM Patron A
 WHERE ( A.PatronNumber = :Patron-PatronNumber )
END-EXEC
```

Figure 11-27.
The completed SQL query.

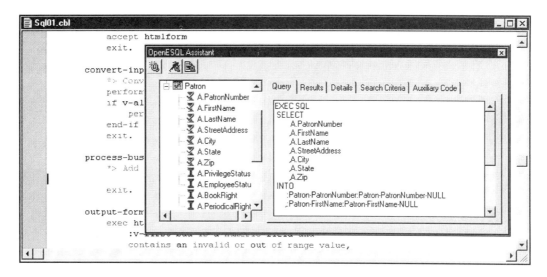

Figure 11-28. Inserting SQL code into the CGI.

Connect and Disconnect

File processing includes opening a file, accessing records of the file, and closing the file. Similarly, database processing involves connecting to a database, accessing the database, and disconnecting from the database. You can insert the needed SQL code into your CGI much as you did the query code. Your CGI source listing should still be on the screen. Similarly, the OpenESQL Assistant window should still be open.

1. From the OpenESQL Assistant click the Auxiliary Code tab. Your Assistant window will look like Figure 11-29.
2. Click the CONNECT Statement radio button and NetExpress will display the needed SQL code in the right pane as in Figure 11-30.

This SQL code is equivalent to a Cobol Open statement. It must be executed prior to executing the SQL code for accessing the file. Therefore, you must insert it into the CGI so that it precedes the query code. A good place to insert this code is in the main section just preceding the statement:

```
perform process-business-logic
```

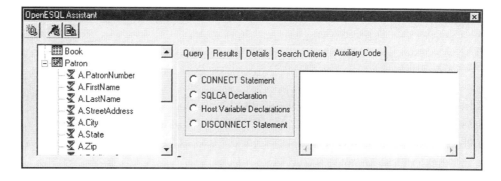

Figure 11-29. The Auxiliary Code pane.

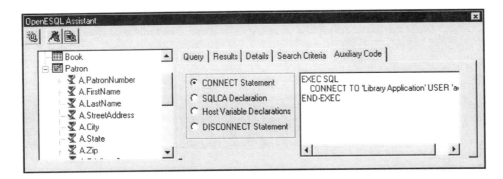

Figure 11-30. SQL CONNECT TO code.

3. Position the cursor to the extreme left on the same line as the perform. Click the Insert button 🖺.

You will see these three lines inserted into your CGI. Make certain that they precede the subject perform statement. If they are incorrectly positioned, either move them or delete them and reinsert. You must now insert the database equivalent of Cobol's Close statement: the DISCONNECT.

4. Position the CGI's cursor on the line following the subject perform statement.
5. In the OpenSQL Assistant window, click the DISCONNECT Statement radio button. The SQL statement in the right pane should be DISCONNECT CURRENT.
6. Click the Insert button to insert this code into the CGI.

At this point you main section should look like the following. Move the SQL statements if they are not positioned correctly.

```
main section.
    perform process-form-input-data
    perform convert-input
    EXEC SQL
        CONNECT TO 'Library Application' USER 'admin'
    END-EXEC
    perform process-business-logic
    EXEC SQL
        DISCONNECT CURRENT
    END-EXEC
    perform sql01-out-cvt *> sql01-out
    perform sql01-out-out *> sql01-out
```

Inserting Working-Storage Code

From earlier descriptions, you know that data from embedded SQL field names is made available to your program through host variables. For instance, referring to Figure 11-24, Patron-PatronNumber identifies the Cobol data item into which the database value for patron number will be stored. Therefore, each of these host variables (data items) must be defined in the program's Data Division. Fortunately, OpenESQL Assistant provides these elements as well as the previously inserted executable code.

1. Within the CGI, position the cursor on the line immediately following the comment line:

   ```
   *> Enter additional working-storage items here
   ```

2. In the OpenESQL Assistant click the Host Variable Declarations radio button. The right pane should display:

   ```
   EXEC SQL INCLUDE Patron END-EXEC
   ```

3. Click the Insert button to insert this code into your Working-Storage Section. Confirm that it is correctly positioned.

   After each embedded SQL statement is executed, error and status information is returned in the SQL Communications Area (SGLCA). To accommodate this, you need one more SQL entry in your Working-Storage Section. You can leave the CGI's cursor where it is (one the previously inserted EXEC SQL line), or you can move it down to the next line.

4. In the OpenESQL Assistant click the SQLCA Declarations radio button. The right pane should display:

   ```
   EXEC SQL INCLUDE SQLCA END-EXEC
   ```

5. Click the Insert button to insert this code into your Working-Storage Section. Confirm that it is correctly positioned.
6. This completes insertion of necessary embedded SQL entries. You can close the OpenSQL Assistant window.

SQL Compiler Directive

Each program in which you include embedded SQL must contain the following SQL compiler directive.

```
$SET SQL(dbman=ODBC)
```

You should type it into you CGI immediately *following* the NetExpress inserted directive:

```
$set preprocess(htmlpp) endp
```

The CGI Program with Embedded SQL

To see the SQL code in Working-Storage of your cgi, click the compile button; after the compile, your program should contain the code of Figure 11-31. As usual, code not pertinent to our current focus is not shown in this listing as is evident by the line number gaps.

Lines 69-81 contain the list of field names used by SQL—you will not reference them. On the other hand, lines 87-99 define the host variables—Cobol data items that ESQL uses for making data available to your program.

```
      $set preprocess(htmlpp) endp          142  PROCEDURE DIVISION.
      $set SQL(dbman=ODBC)                   143
   1  IDENTIFICATION DIVISION.               144  main section.
   2      program-id. "Sql01".               145      perform process-form-input-data
                                             146      perform convert-input
  11                                         147      EXEC SQL
  12  working-storage section.               148          CONNECT TO 'Library Application'
                                             149                                 USER 'admin'
  58      copy "Sql01.cpy".                  150      END-EXEC
  59      01 FormFields.                     151      perform process-business-logic
  60         03 InPatronNumber    pic X(3).  152      EXEC SQL
  61         03 ssubmit           pic X(60). 153          DISCONNECT CURRENT
  62         03 StreetAddress     pic X(20). 154      END-EXEC
  63         03 CityStateZip      pic X(30). 155      perform Sql01-OUT-cvt
  64         03 PatronName        pic X(23). 156          *> sql01-out
  65                                         157      perform Sql01-OUT-out
  66  *> Enter additional working-storage items here 158          *> sql01-out
  67  EXEC SQL INCLUDE Patron END-EXEC       159      exit program
  68      EXEC SQL DECLARE Patron TABLE      160      stop run.
  69      ( PatronNumber          TEXT(3)
  70       ,FirstName             TEXT(10)   176  process-business-logic section.
  71       ,LastName              TEXT(12)   177      *> Add application business logic here.
  72       ,StreetAddress         TEXT(20)   178      Move InPatronNumber to Patron-PatronNumber
  73       ,City                  TEXT(14)   179      EXEC SQL
  74       ,State                 TEXT(2)    180        SELECT
  75       ,Zip                   TEXT(10)   181              A.PatronNumber
  76       ,PrivilegeStatus       TEXT(1)    182             ,A.FirstName
  77       ,EmployeeStatus        TEXT(1)    183             ,A.LastName
  78       ,BookRight             TEXT(1)    184             ,A.StreetAddress
  79       ,PeriodicalRight       TEXT(1)    185             ,A.City
  80       ,VideoRight            TEXT(1)    186             ,A.State
  81       ,Other                 TEXT(20)   187             ,A.Zip
  82      ) END-EXEC.                        188        INTO
  83  *********************************************  189          :Patron-PatronNumber
  84  * COBOL DECLARATION FOR TABLE Patron  *  190                     :Patron-PatronNumber-NULL
  85  *********************************************  191         .:Patron-FirstName
  86  01  DCLPatron.                         192                     :Patron-FirstName-NULL
  87      03 Patron-PatronNumber     PIC X(3).   193         .:Patron-LastName:Patron-LastName-NULL
  88      03 Patron-FirstName        PIC X(10).  194         .:Patron-StreetAddress
  89      03 Patron-LastName         PIC X(12).  195                     :Patron-StreetAddress-NULL
  90      03 Patron-StreetAddress    PIC X(20).  196         .:Patron-City:Patron-City-NULL
  91      03 Patron-City             PIC X(14).  197         .:Patron-State:Patron-State-NULL
  92      03 Patron-State            PIC X(2).   198         .:Patron-Zip:Patron-Zip-NULL
  93      03 Patron-Zip              PIC X(10).  199        FROM Patron A
  94      03 Patron-PrivilegeStatus  PIC X(1).   200        WHERE ( A.PatronNumber =
  95      03 Patron-EmployeeStatus   PIC X(1).   201                     :Patron-PatronNumber )
  96      03 Patron-BookRight        PIC X(1).   202      END-EXEC
  97      03 Patron-PeriodicalRight  PIC X(1).   203
  98      03 Patron-VideoRight       PIC X(1).   204      If SQLCODE NOT = 0
  99      03 Patron-Other            PIC X(20).  205        Move "Invalid patron number" to PatronName
                                             206      Else
 117  EXEC SQL INCLUDE SQLCA END-EXEC        207        String Patron-FirstName delimited by " "
 118  01 SQLCA.                              208                " "
 119      05  SQLCAID  PIC X(8)    VALUE "SQLCA   ".  209             Patron-LastName
 120      05  SQLCABC  PIC S9(9) COMP-5 VALUE 136.    210             into PatronName
 121      05  SQLCODE  PIC S9(9) COMP-5 VALUE 0.      211      Move Patron-StreetAddress to StreetAddress
                                             212      Move spaces to CityStateZip
 140      05  SQLSTATE PIC X(5).             213        String Patron-City delimited by " "
 141                                         214                " "
                                             215             Patron-State
                                             216                " "
                                             217             Patron-Zip
                                             218             into CityStateZip
                                             219      End-If *>SQLCODE NOT = 0
                                             220
                                             221      exit.
```

Figure 11-31. Partial listing of Sql01.CBL

The SQLCA expansion (from line 117) generates a large number of data items that you will not use for examples in this book. There are two exceptions: SQLCODE of line 121 and SQLSTATE of line 140. After execution of an SQL statement, both of these contain a code indicating the success or failure of the previously executed SQL statement as follows.

SQLCODE	Meaning
0	Statement ran without error
1	The statement ran, but a warning was generated. The nature of the warning is stored in SQLWARNING data items (not shown in the listing).
100	Data matching the query was not found or the end of the results set has been reached. No rows were processed.
Negative	The statement did not run due to an application, database, system, or network error.

The five-byte SQLSTATE variable was introduced in the SQL-92 standard. A value of 00000 means the previous SQL statement ran without error. For full details of SQLSTATE values, bring up the NetExpress online Help and search for SQLSTATE.

Required User-Inserted Code

Input Code

There are two elements of code you must insert into the CGI to complete this project: (1) code to make the input patron number available to the embedded SQL, and (2) code to prepare the SQL-returned data for output to the Web page. The former is accomplished by inserting the following statement immediately preceding The EXEC SQL statement (see Figure 11-31, line 178).

```
Move InPatronNumber to Patron-PatronNumber
```

Remember—InPatronNumber is the input form field; Patron-PatronNumber is the host variable defined by SQL.

Output Code

The output code of lines 204-219 checks the SQL-created data item SQLCODE to for a successful access of the database (a non-zero value means unsuccessful access—see the previous table). If the access is successful, page data items are set up using values returned by the SQL in the host variables. Notice that this code is inserted immediately following line 202.

You can now compile this program—correct any errors you encounter. When you have a clean compile, run the application. You will see that it works much the same as corresponding projects of earlier chapters.

Linking Tables and Accessing Multiple Rows.

Joining Two Tables

If you've studied the subprogram Lib-sub2.cbl, your know that it processes the two indexed files Patron.di and Book.di. When executed, the subprogram attempts to read the patron record for the designated patron number. If the record is found, the subprogram attempts to read records from the book file using the patron number as the secondary key value. Thus the two files are "linked" by virtue of program logic in the subprogram.

Relational database systems include a feature that allows you to "join" two tables based on a common field. The resulting database **join** is a **view** into the database that functions as if the data were from a single table. For instance, assume you defined a join to give you access to Patron and Book data for a designated patron, say patron 002. Then the view would look like Figure 11-32 in which each record (table row) consists of all fields (columns) from both tables. Consistent with the needs of a given application, you can select for the view only those fields pertinent to that application. If the designated record of the Patron table has no corresponding entries in the Book table (the patron has no books), the resulting view will be empty.

In this exercise you will use an SQL join that will allow you to access data from both the Patron and Book tables, thereby making available a selected patron and books checked out by the patron.

The SQL Cursor

The embedded SQL code of Sql01 returns a single row of data—that of the selected patron. For this exercise, you will need SQL to return one row from the table join for each book checked out by the patron. This action requires use of an SQL cursor. A **cursor** is a mechanism that enables you to fetch two or more rows of data, one row at a time. The cursor is so called because it indicates the current position in view (in the same way the screen cursor indicates the current position on the screen). As you will see in this exercise, NetExpress automatically inserts necessary cursor declaration code into your embedded SQL.

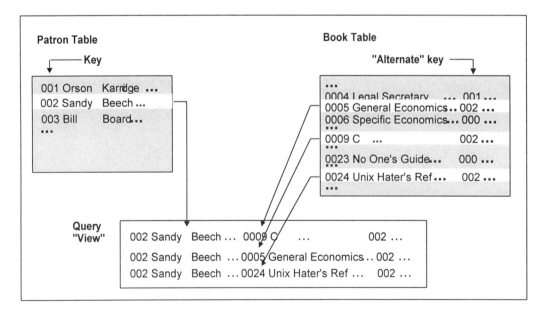

Figure 11-32. A view into two tables.

The Need for Two Queries

Figure 11-33 is a sample browser display for the application Sql02 (stored in the folder Proj1105). You can see that it displays data from the view in Figure 11-32. Notice that the name and address information is identical to that of the Sql01 project—you might surmise (correctly) that you could use the same SQL query to obtain this portion of the output as you did in Sql01. On the other hand, the book information can consist of one or more rows (three in this case). Therefore, you will need to use another query incorporating a cursor for this portion of the output.

Proj1105
Sql02

Creating the Queries

Generating the Query for Patron Data

As with the preceding project, the input and output pages and the basic CGI are stored as the application Sql02 in Proj1105-2 and are ready for you to create the query. The first of two queries you create will access patron data—it is identical to the query you created for Sql01. To get started, open this project (the project contents should be as shown in the window to the right) then proceed as follows—note that this is a repeat of the sequence you did for Sql01.

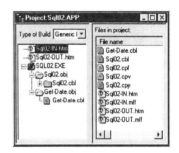

1. Click Tools/OpenESQL Assistant.
2. If your screen displays the previous query, click the Create New Query button ⓐ.
3. Double-click the data source name Library Application to display its table list.

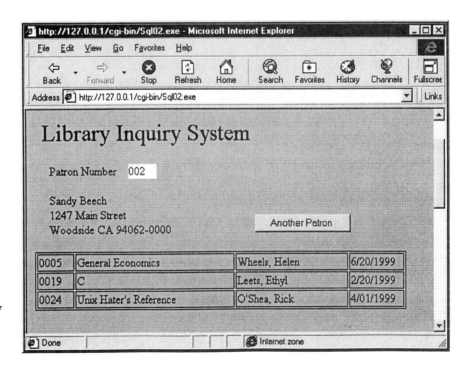

Figure 11-33.
Browser display for library system inquiry.

4. Double-click the Patron table icon.
5. From the resulting popup window, highlight SELECT (singleton).
6. Add the fields A.PatronNumber through A.Zip to the query .
7. Click the Search Criteria tab and insert the code:

> A.PatronNumber = :Patron-PatronNumber

8. Open the CGI Sql02.cbl.
9. Position the cursor immediately preceding the exit statement in the process-business-logic section.
10. Insert the query into your CGI; do not insert any auxiliary code.

Generating the Query for Book Data

You'll now create a second query, this to access the book data. You will also insert auxiliary code from this query that will suffice for both queries.

1. Click the New Query icon . The Assistant will list the available databases.
2. Double-click Library Application to list the tables contained in that database.
3. Double-click Patron.
4. From the resulting popup window, highlight SELECT (cursor) then click OK. Your query window will then look like Figure 11-34. (Your CSR number will probably be different.) Add A.PatronNumber to the query
5. Select the second table for this query by clicking the Book table icon in the OpenESQL Assistant window.

You will see the popup window of Figure 11-35. Notice that NetExpress automatically generates a join between this table and the patron table. To do this, NetExpress inspects the field list of each table searching for a field name common to both. In this example PatronNumber is the name of the patron table key field; it is also the name of the field we treat as the secondary key of the book table. Here you see how fields of one table are distinguished from fields of another table: by the prefix letter alias. The letter A designates the first table selected (Patron in this case) and B designates the second table selected (Book in this case). This is indeed the desired link between the two files. If you have an application in which the default is not the desired link, you must click No and type your own entry.

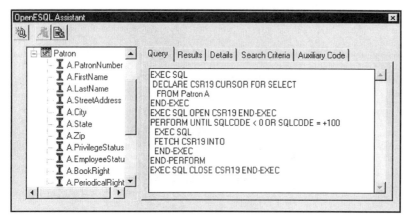

Figure 11-34.
Select query using a cursor.

Figure 11-35. Joining two tables.

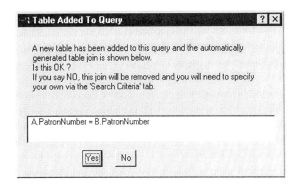

6. The display of Figure 11-35 is the desired criterion for establishing the join, so click the Yes button.

7. From the Book table column list, double-click the following to add them to the query.

    B.BookID
    B.BookTitle
    B.BookAuthor
    B.PatronNumber
    B.RemainingDays

You must now designate your search criteria, the same as you did with the previous project and with the patron query of this example. That is, you want to find rows of this table join in which the table-join patron number matches the user-input patron number.

8. Click the Search Criterion tab and you will see the following condition (establishing the relationship between the tables) already listed.

    A.PatronNumber = B.PatronNumber

9. You want the condition shown in Figure 11-36. You may need to expand the Target Type and select Host Variable. Make certain the AND radio button is selected. Click the insert button ▷ and the following code will be inserted into the right-most pane.

    A.PatronNumber = B.PatronNumber
    AND A.PatronNumber = :Patron-PatronNumber

Figure 11-36. Completing the search criteria.

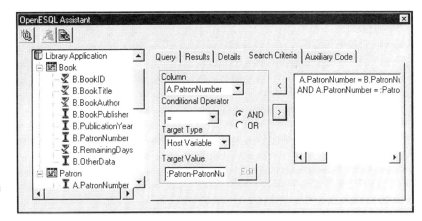

10. Click the Query tab; your query should look like Figure 11-37.

11. Insert this query's code into the CGI immediately preceding the `process-business-logic` section's exit statement (following the patron query code).

Inserting Auxiliary Code into the CGI

You must now insert into the CGI auxiliary code required by *both* of the inserted queries. This code will include both Working-Storage entries and procedural code to provide access to the two tables.

12. From Auxiliary code tab, insert the CONNECT and DISCONNECT statements in the CGI's main section as follows.

```
main section.
    perform process-form-input-data
    perform convert-input
    EXEC SQL
        CONNECT TO 'Library Application' USER 'admin'
    END-EXEC
    perform process-business-logic
    EXEC SQL
        DISCONNECT CURRENT
    END-EXEC
    perform sql02-out-cvt
    perform sql02-out-out
    exit program
    stop run.
```

When inserting declaration items from two or more tables, (the Auxiliary Code tab) it is easy to duplicate Working-Storage items thereby creating compiler errors. The following is a simple-minded method of making all the needed items available from

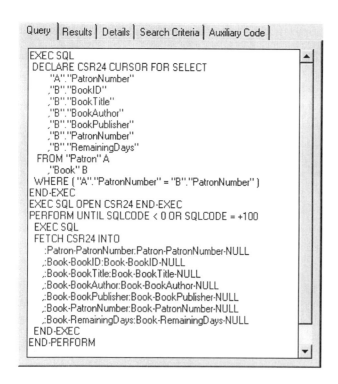

```
Query | Results | Details | Search Criteria | Auxiliary Code |

EXEC SQL
 DECLARE CSR24 CURSOR FOR SELECT
     "A"."PatronNumber"
    ,"B"."BookID"
    ,"B"."BookTitle"
    ,"B"."BookAuthor"
    ,"B"."BookPublisher"
    ,"B"."PatronNumber"
    ,"B"."RemainingDays"
  FROM "Patron" A
    ,"Book" B
  WHERE ( "A"."PatronNumber" = "B"."PatronNumber" )
END-EXEC
EXEC SQL OPEN CSR24 END-EXEC
PERFORM UNTIL SQLCODE < 0 OR SQLCODE = +100
  EXEC SQL
  FETCH CSR24 INTO
     :Patron-PatronNumber:Patron-PatronNumber-NULL
    ,:Book-BookID:Book-BookID-NULL
    ,:Book-BookTitle:Book-BookTitle-NULL
    ,:Book-BookAuthor:Book-BookAuthor-NULL
    ,:Book-BookPublisher:Book-BookPublisher-NULL
    ,:Book-PatronNumber:Book-PatronNumber-NULL
    ,:Book-RemainingDays:Book-RemainingDays-NULL
  END-EXEC
END-PERFORM
```

Figure 11-37.
Completed query for project Sql02.

the OpenESQL Assistant. You will add all fields that you need from Patron to the current query so that they will be included in the declaration items.

13. Add the fields A.PatronNumber through A.Zip to the query by double-clicking on each.
14. Reposition the cursor to the line after the following Working-Storage comment.

```
*> Enter additional working-storage items here
```

15. Select and insert the SQLCA Declarations code.
16. Select and insert the Host Variables Declaration code. Notice that two lines are inserted: one for each table.
17. Close the OpenESQL Assistant as you are finished with this portion of the exercise.
18. Enter this compiler directive *following* the existing directive.

```
$SET SQL(dbman=ODBC)
```

19. Compile the program to be certain you have no errors before entering user code.

User-Inserted Code

Relevant code from the completed CGI is shown in Figure 11-38. Here you see embedded SQL code for the first query (patron) at lines 253-276 and for the second query (books) at lines 279-303. To make your application functional, insert appropriate additional code as described here.

- The subscripted data item book-pointer is defined at line 100.
- Prior to executing the first query, appropriate data items are set to zero (lines 249 and 250) and the input data item value is moved to the SQL-defined data item (line 251.
- Following the first query, name and address information is prepared for the output form by the Cobol section set-up-name-address-lines (lines 320-338) which is performed from line 277. Do not make the mistake of inserting this section within the process-business-logic section. It is a separate section, one of two in this program
- The second query's code includes a Net Express generated inline Perform (lines 292-302) which is repeated for each row of the join view in which the input patron number is equal to the patron number of the selected view row. Because the host variables are simple data items (not subscripted) each row's data must be accessed within that loop. This is done by the Perform of line 301 (refer to the performed section of lines 306-318) which is programmer-inserted, not Net Express created.

Recall from an earlier chapter that book due dates are determined from a number-of-days field stored in the book file. The reason is to yield current dates when the program is run—otherwise, the date information will be outdated. The subprogram Get-Date converts the number-of-days to a date relative to the day you run the program.

```
      $set preprocess(htmlpp) endp                256          ,A.FirstName
      $SET SQL(dbman=ODBC)                         257          ,A.LastName
  1   IDENTIFICATION DIVISION.                     258          ,A.StreetAddress
  2       program-id. "Sql02".                     259          ,A.City
                                                   260          ,A.State
 10   DATA DIVISION.                               261          ,A.Zip
 11                                                262      INTO
 12   working-storage section.                     263          :Patron-PatronNumber
                                                   264                     :Patron-PatronNumber-NULL
 86       copy "Sql02.cpy".                        265          .:Patron-FirstName
 87       01 FormFields.                            266                     :Patron-FirstName-NULL
 88          03 BookAuthor      pic x(13) occurs 10. 267        .:Patron-LastName:Patron-LastName-NULL
 89          03 BookTitle       pic x(25) occurs 10. 268        .:Patron-StreetAddress
 90          03 serversidetext1 pic x(1) occurs 2.   269                   :Patron-StreetAddress-NULL
 91          03 BookID          pic x(4) occurs 10.  270        .:Patron-City:Patron-City-NULL
 92          03 InPatronNumber  pic x(3).            271        .:Patron-State:Patron-State-NULL
 93          03 DueDate         pic x(10) occurs 10. 272        .:Patron-Zip:Patron-Zip-NULL
 94          03 ssubmit         pic x(64).           273      FROM Patron A
 95          03 StreetAddress   pic x(20).           274      WHERE ( A.PatronNumber =
 96          03 CityStateZip    pic x(30).           275                     :Patron-PatronNumber )
 97          03 PatronName      pic x(23).           276    END-EXEC
 98                                                 277    Perform Set-up-name-address-lines
 99   *> Enter additional working-storage items here 278   EXEC SQL
100   01  book-pointer          pic 9(02).          279      DECLARE CSR19 CURSOR FOR SELECT
101                                                 280          A.PatronNumber
102   EXEC SQL INCLUDE SQLCA END-EXEC              281          ,B.BookID
                                                   282          ,B.BookTitle
126   EXEC SQL INCLUDE Patron END-EXEC            283          ,B.BookAuthor
                                                   284          ,B.PatronNumber
145   01  DCLPatron.                               285          ,B.RemainingDays
146       03 Patron-PatronNumber    PIC X(3).       286      FROM Patron A
147       03 Patron-FirstName       PIC X(10).      287          ,Book B
148       03 Patron-LastName        PIC X(12).      288      WHERE ( A.PatronNumber = B.PatronNumber )
149       03 Patron-StreetAddress   PIC X(20).      289      AND ( A.PatronNumber =
150       03 Patron-City            PIC X(14).      290                     :Patron-PatronNumber )
151       03 Patron-State           PIC X(2).       291    END-EXEC
152       03 Patron-Zip             PIC X(10).      292    EXEC SQL OPEN CSR19 END-EXEC
153       03 Patron-PrivilegeStatus PIC X(1).       293    PERFORM UNTIL SQLCODE < 0 OR SQLCODE = +100
154       03 Patron-EmployeeStatus  PIC X(1).       294      EXEC SQL
155       03 Patron-BookRight       PIC X(1).       295        FETCH CSR19 INTO
156       03 Patron-PeriodicalRight PIC X(1).       296          :Patron-PatronNumber
157       03 Patron-VideoRight      PIC X(1).       297                     :Patron-PatronNumber-NULL
158       03 Patron-Other           PIC X(20).      298        .:Book-BookID:Book-BookID-NULL
                                                   299        .:Book-BookTitle:Book-BookTitle-NULL
176   EXEC SQL INCLUDE Book END-EXEC              300        .:Book-BookAuthor:Book-BookAuthor-NULL
                                                   301        .:Book-RemainingDays:
190   01  DCLBook.                                 302                   Book-RemainingDays-NULL
191       03 Book-BookID          PIC X(4).         303      END-EXEC
192       03 Book-BookTitle       PIC X(25).        304      Perform Set-up-book-lines
193       03 Book-BookAuthor      PIC X(13).        305    END-PERFORM
194       03 Book-BookPublisher   PIC X(11).        306    EXEC SQL CLOSE CSR19 END-EXEC
195       03 Book-PublicationYear PIC X(4).         307    exit.
196       03 Book-PatronNumber    PIC X(3).      308 Set-up-book-lines section.
197       03 Book-RemainingDays   PIC X(3).      309    If SQLCODE = 0
198       03 Book-OtherData       PIC X(20).     310      Add 1 to book-pointer
                                                 311      Add 1 to c-BookData
212   PROCEDURE DIVISION.                         312      Move Book-BookId to BookID (book-pointer)
213                                               313      Move Book-BookAuthor
214   main section.                               314           to BookAuthor (book-pointer)
215       perform process-form-input-data         315      Move Book-BookTitle
216       perform convert-input                   316           to BookTitle (book-pointer)
217       EXEC SQL                                317      Call "Get-Date" using Book-RemainingDays
218           CONNECT TO 'Library Application'     318                   DueDate (book-pointer)
219                           USER 'admin'        319    End-If *>SQODE = 0
220       END-EXEC                                320    exit.
221       perform process-business-logic       321 Set-up-name-address-lines section.
222       EXEC SQL                                322    If SQLCODE = 0
223           DISCONNECT CURRENT                  323      String Patron-FirstName delimited by "  "
224       END-EXEC                                324                   "  "
225       perform sql02-out-cvt                   325           Patron-LastName
226       *> sql02-out                            326           into PatronName
227       perform sql02-out-out                   327      Move Patron-StreetAddress to StreetAddress
228       *> sql02-out                            328      Move spaces to CityStateZip
229       exit program                            329      String  Patron-City delimited by "  "
246       stop run.                               330                   "  "
247   process-business-logic section.             331           Patron-State
248   *> Add application business logic here.      332           "  "
249       Move 0 to c-ColumnHeads,                333           Patron-Zip
250               c-BookData, book-pointer         334           into CityStateZip
251       Move InPatronNumber to Patron-PatronNumber 335   Else
252                                               336      Move "Invalid patron number" to PatronName
253       EXEC SQL                                337    End-If *>SQLCODE = 0
254         SELECT                                338    Exit.
255             A.PatronNumber
```

Figure 11-38. Partial listing of Sql02.cbl.

Using the Application Wizard for an SQL Database

Using the Application Sql03

The next example of this chapter uses the Net Express Application Wizard to generate a basic project to access and update an SQL database. For an idea of what the wizard does for you, open and run the application Sql03 stored in the folder Proj1106. Your resulting browser screen will display name and address information for the first patron—see Figure 11-39. Notice the row of buttons at the bottom of the display—they provide the conventional database maintenance functions you commonly need. You can make needed changes to the current record and update it, or you can simply delete it from the database. For new record entry, you can clear the current record, type in a new one and insert it into the table.

> Proj1106
> Sql03

At the top of the screen, you see a row of buttons that provide you the ability to traverse records of the table—try each of these to see how it works.

Query Locate a designated record. For instance, enter 005 into the PatronNumber box and click Query. Your browser will display the record for this patron.

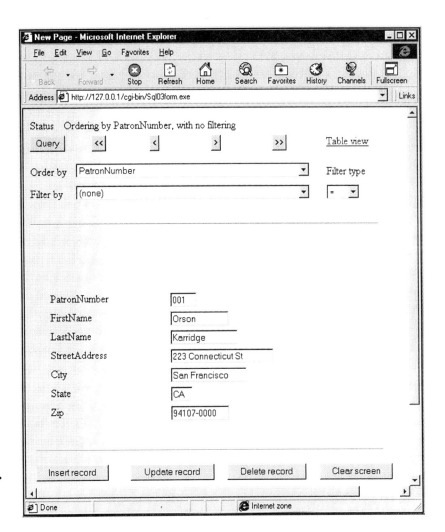

Figure 11-39.
Single-record display.

‹‹ Display the first record in the table.

‹ Display the record preceding the currently displayed record.

› Display the record following the currently displayed record.

›› Display the last record in the table.

You can change the sequence in which records are displayed by changing the **Order by** entry. For instance, expand the box and select City. Then click the **‹‹** button and you will see record 018 with the city Alameda displayed. Click the next-record button a few times and you will see that the records are displayed in sequence by the city entry.

You can also limit the display to only those records meeting a given criterion. For instance, assume you want only those records in which the patron's first name begins with the letter "T" or later in the alphabet.

1. Expand the **Filter by** box and select FirstName.
2. Expand the **Filter Type** box and select >= (greater than or equal to).
3. In the **FirstName** box (the Text Input control), type the letter T.
4. Click the Query button. The record 018 is the first you will see.
5. Successively click the next-record button and you will see four more before the first one is repeated. Remember, these are displayed in sequence by the city.
6. Change the **Order by** entry to FirstName, click the first-record button, then look at successive records. You will see them displayed in sequence by the first name.

The screen you are looking at displays a single record. For another view, click the first-record button then click on the Table view hyperlink (upper-right of your screen). Your browser will display the screen of Figure 11-40—notice that all records are displayed in first-name sequence and that the list includes only those with the first letter of the first name equal to or greater than the letter "T".

Click the Record view hyperlink to return to the single-record display. Change the **Order by** entry to PatronNumber and the **Filter by** entry to (none) as in Figure 11-39. Click the first-record button (to display record 001) then click the Table view hypertext link. Your browser will display the first 10 records in a table similar to that of Figure 11-40. Click the next-record **›** and the next group of ten records will be displayed.

This gives you a good feel for the functional aspects of this system. Let's see how simple it is to create the application.

Creating an SQL Application

In this exercise you will create a duplicate of the Sql03, the application you just completed investigating.

1. Create a new, empty project in a new folder; using any name that appeals to you, for instance, MySql.

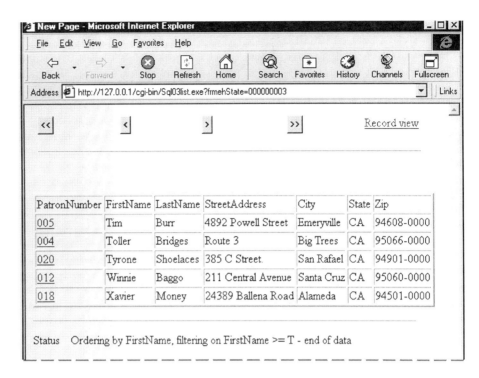

Figure 11-40. Table-form record display.

2. From the project window, click File/New/Internet Application.
3. In the Internet Application Wizard screen, select the SQL Database button then click Next.
4. In the ensuing Form Name and Title wizard screen, type the same name you used for the name of the project (for instance, MySql). For the title, type Library Inquiry.
5. Click Next and you will see the database selection window (Figure 11-21).
6. Expand the Library Application icon, expand the Patron table icon, then select the columns (fields) A.PatronNumber through A.Zip for this query.
7. Click Next and you will see the screen of Figure 11-41. Through the check boxes, you can select either single record display (Figure 11-39) or table view (Figure 11-40) or both.
8. Click Next and you see the screen of Figure 11-42 where you see that the user will have full capabilities to add, delete, and change records. To prohibit the user making any changes to the table, click the No radio button.
9. Click Next and you are presented with a verification screen. Click Finish and Net Express will build the application. Show patience as Net Express takes a while—there is much to be done.

When Net Express finishes, click the Rebuild icon; when the rebuild is complete, click Run. Your display should be exactly the same as the preceding Sql03.

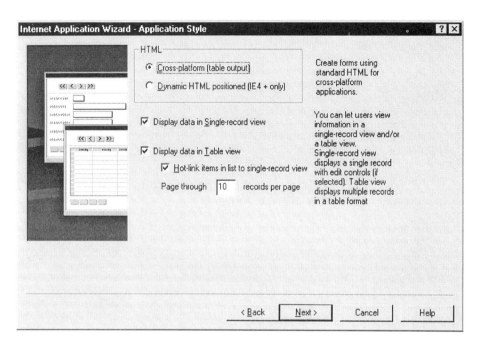

Figure 11-41.
Designating data
display form.

Modifying and Expanding a Wizard-Built SQL Application.

If you look at the list of files in the folder Proj1106, you will see the following components.

For display of a single record
Sql03form.cbl (the CGI; also listed are the copy files)
Sql03form.htm (the HTML page)
For the table view
Sql03list.cbl (the CGI; also listed are the copy files)
Sql03list.htm (the HTML page)

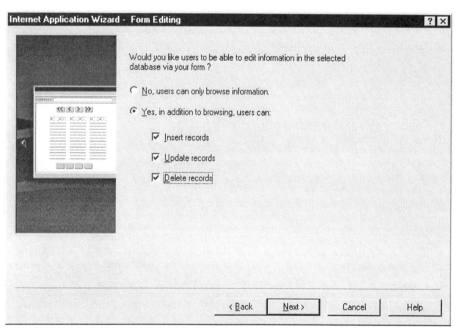

Figure 11-42.
Designating
allowable editing.

You can modify each of these just as if you had created them by the "conventional" means you've used in all the preceding examples. In fact, the folder Proj1107 contains the project Sql04 that provides controlled access to data in the patron and book tables of the library database. You see this application's component diagram in Figure 11-43.

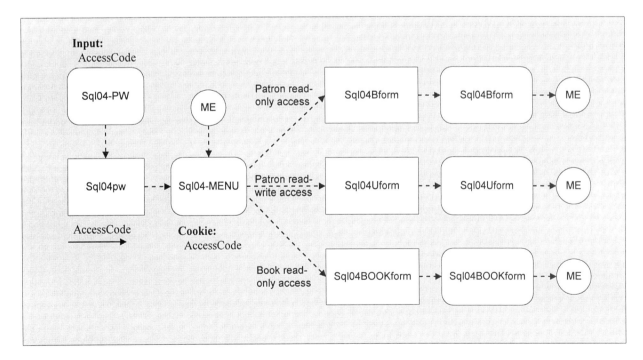

Proj1107
Sql04

- The input form Sql04-PW accept the user's code into a password control field. The value "SUPER" gives the user the right to update the patron file. Anything else restricts the user to read only.
- The CGI Sql04pw converts the input password to uppercase and stores it in a cookie. This cookie will be available throughout the run through the menu page Sql04MENU.
- Sql04MENU presents the user with the option of viewing patron data or book data.
- The sets of CGIs with the suffix "form" and the corresponding HTML pages were generated with the Application Wizard just as you did in the preceding exercise.

Before looking at this project's components, run the application to become familiar with how it works. Make a run entering "SUPER" for the access code; make another run without an access code entry.

Construction of this application involved the following basic steps, all with which you are familiar from previous exercises.

1. Using the application wizard, build the Sql04Bform components to provide browse (read only) access to the patron table.
2. Using the application wizard, build the Sql04Uform components to provide browse and update (read-write) access to the patron table.

Figure 11-43. Component diagram for the application Sql04.

3. Using the application wizard, build the Sql04BOOKform components to provide browse (read only) access to the book table.
4. Create Sql04-PW to accept the user's password entry.
5. Create Sql04-MENU to provide the user access to either the patron table or the book table.
6. Generate the CGI Sql04pw designating Sql04-PW as input and Sql04-MENU as output.

If you inspect each of the three wizard-generated pages (for instance, Sql04Bform) you will see that an Input Button has been inserted with an event returning control to Sql04-MENU. The only new element of this application is the event handler for the patron button of Sql04-MENU—it provides conditional transfer to either of two CGIs through a JavaScript if statement.

```
function inputbutton1_onclick_func()
{
if (AccessCode=="SUPER")
  {location.href="/cgi-bin/Sql04Uform.exe"}
else
  {location.href="/cgi-bin/Sql04Bform.exe"}
}
```

Notice the following about this.

- The test condition must be enclosed within parentheses.
- From the previous JavaScript examples, you might anticipate the need for something like
     document.form1.AccessCode.value
  to the left of the == operator. This is not needed (it is actually incorrect) as Net Express makes cookies directly available to JavaScript processing.
- The conditionally executed statement (or statements) must be enclosed within braces, the standard JavaScript technique for grouping.

You may find relatively basic use of the JavaScript if statement useful in creating versatile applications.

Summing Up

Project Summary

Proj1101 (Pat01) is relatively basic example application illustrating adding a record to the indexed file Patron.

Proj1102 (Pat02) uses a symmetric CGI in adding records to the indexed file patron. It includes a feature to display data from the preceding record as default data for selected fields of the next record to be entered.

Proj1103 (Pat03) is a basic example of a Web-oriented file maintenance system. The two basic options included in the application are record addition and record editing. This application is intended to give you an insight to setting up a multiple-component system with access to individual components through a main menu.

Proj1104 (Sql01) uses SQL to access and display data from the Patron table of the Library database.

Proj1105 (Sql02) features the SQL join in accessing data from two tables to produce output containing patron information and a list of books checked out to the patron. Two individual queries, one for patron data and one for book data, are the essence of this example.

Proj1106 (Sql03) was created using Net Express's feature to automatically generate an application using SQL. This example displays data in both individual record form and multiple-record table form. It includes record edit, insert, and delete capabilities.

Proj1107 (Sql04) illustrates creating an application by piecing together components generated by Net Express's automatic SQL based feature. It includes password protection for update capabilities to the Patron table.

General Summary

Relational databases store data in the form of tables. The Library database of this chapter includes the Patron table and the Book table, equivalent to the indexed files of previous chapters. Structured Query Language (SQL) is a commonly used language to access information from a relational database.

NetExpress includes a wizard, OpenSQL Assistant, to construct SQL queries and imbed them within Cobol CGI code. The Assistant generates host variables in the CGI program into which data is transferred from embedded SQL queries

The compiler directive

```
$SET SQL(dman-ODBC)
```

must be included in any CGI that uses embedded SQL.

The SQL join provides access to multiple tables of a database by using a common field to link those tables.

Examples of this chapter used the following JavaScript code in event handlers.

Set selected fields to spaces.

```
document.HTMLForm.FormCity.value = ""
document.HTMLForm.FormState.value = ""
document.HTMLForm.FormZip.value = ""
```

Conditionally transfer control to either of two CGIs.

```
if (AccessCode=="SUPER")
 {location.href="/cgi-bin/Sql04Uform.exe"}
else
 {location.href="/cgi-bin/Sql04Bform.exe"}
```

Assignment

11-1

The folder NE-progs includes the following three subprograms:

Book-sub1   Adds a record to the book file.
Book-sub2   Reads a record from the book file.
Book-sub3   Rewrites a record to the book file.

For this assignment you are to add another option to the project Pat03 (refer to Figure 11-9) for checking out a book to a patron as follows.

- Add a book-checkout option to the main menu.
- Accept the patron ID. If no such patron, display an appropriate message and return either to the input form to accept another patron number or to the main menu.
- Check the patron field books-out. If its value is equal to 10, the patron has checked out the maximum allowable number of books and must be denied. Display an appropriate error page and return either to the form to accept another patron number or to the main menu.
- For a valid patron under his/her limit, accept the desired book ID.
- Check to determine (1) if the book ID is valid and (2) whether or not the book is checked out. If the remaining-days field is zero, the book is available.
- Display appropriate error message pages for (1) invalid book ID and (2) book checked out. Give the user the option of returning to enter another book ID, another patron number, or to the main menu.
- For a successful transaction (checking the book out), increment the patron record's books-out field by 1 and set the book record's remaining-days field to 14.

Application Testing Notes:
Books 0006, 0007, 0013, 0021, and 0022 are available (not checked out).
Customer 001 currently has 7 books checked out.

11-2

For this assignment, you will use the following subprograms:

    Customer file
        Cust-sub2.cbl Reads a record from the file
    Order file
        Ord-sub1.cbl   Adds a record to the file

Prepare an application to create an order for a customer as follows:

1. Accept a customer number; verify that it is a valid number
2. Accept the customer's order. You can create this screen from the input page you prepared for Assignment 5-1. Note that the customer will not be entering the order number.
3. Verify to the customer her/his selections. Provide the customer the option to place the order or return to the order entry screen to make corrections.
4. Write an order record to the Order file. Obtain the order number from the first record of the order file using the same technique as used for this chapter's patron file example. (The key field value is 000—see the record definition and data listing in the Appendix.) Don't be concerned about the date fields.
5. Display an order-confirmation screen that includes the order number assigned to the order.

11-3
Create an application to access data from the Customer table of the Saddles database. (Note: You will first need to declare it as an ODBC data source.) Your application must accept a customer ID and display the customer name/address data. Display an appropriate message if the customer does not exist.

11-4
Create an application to access data from the Customer and Order tables of the Saddles database. (Note: You will first need to declare it as an ODBC data source.) Your application must accept a customer ID and display the customer name/address data and a list of orders placed by that customer. Order output must include the following:

Order ID
Saddle type—in the display, replace the saddle codes as follows.
    W Western
    E   English
    S   Spanish
Order date
Start date
Promised date
Scheduled date

For all dates, you will need to use the Get-Date.cbl subprogram to convert the number-of-days fields of the table into actual dates.

Data Files and Subprograms

Appendix Contents

About the Data Files 328
   Files in the NE-Data Folder 328
   Using the Data Files 329
Example Applications Files 330
   Data Files 330
      Patron file listing 330
      Patron record format 330
      Book file listing 331
      Book record format 331
   Subprograms 332
      Get-date.cbl 332
      Lib-sub0.cbl 332
      Lib-sub1.cbl 333
      Lib-sub2.cbl 334
      Lib-sub3.cbl 334
      Book-sub.cbl 336
      Book-sub1.cbl 337
      Book-sub2.cbl 338
      Book-sub3.cbl 338
      Pat-sub1.cbl 339
      Pat-sub2.cbl 340
      Pat-sub3.cbl 340
Assignment Files 341
   Data Files 341
      Customer record format 341
      Customer file listing 341
      Order record format 342
      Order file listing 342
   Subprograms 343
      Cus-sub0.cbl 343
      Cus-sub1.cbl 343
      Cus-sub2.cbl 344
      Cus-sub3.cbl 344
      Ord-sub1.cbl 347
      Ord-sub2.cbl 348

Appendix

Appendix Introduction

This appendix contains listings of all data files and subprograms required by
example applications and assignments of this book.

About the Data Files

Files in the NE-Data Folder

The folder **Elements-CWP\NE-data** contains the following data files for the example applications you will study and the assignments you will prepare.

Example applications
    Patron   Name/address file for library patrons.
    Book   Book data for books available to patrons.
Assignments
    Customer Customer file for horse equipment supplier.
    Order   Order data file for orders placed by customers.

If you check this folder, you will see files in sets of three, for instance:

PATRON.DI   The indexed data file. Its extension DI is user selected. For consistency in this book, all example indexed files of this use the extension DI (for Data-Indexed).

PATRON.IDX The index to the data file. The filename is the same as that of the data file; the extension IDX is set by Micro Focus.

PATRON.DAT The line sequential version of the indexed file. (Note: Micro Focus line sequential files are ordinary text files in which each record, or line, is terminated by the carriage return/line feed pair.

For some data file pairs, there is a duplicate with the suffix 2, for instance, PATRON.DI and PATRON2.DI. All file-processing subprograms that update a file operate on the duplicate, thereby preserving the original. If after a work session, you decide to restore the duplicate to its original contents you can do so through Windows Explorer. For instance, to restore PATRON, you would do the following.

1. Open the **Elements-CWP\NE-data** folder.
2. Delete both PATRON2.DI and PATRON2.IDX.
3. Copy and paste PATRON.DI and PATRON.IDX.
4. Rename the copies to PATRON2.DI and PATRON2.IDX.

If you move data files around, don't forget the index as you will receive an error upon attempting to open if the index is not in the same folder as the indexed data file.

Regarding the DAT file, it is included so that you can read it into a word processor and print it thereby giving you a hard copy for checking the output of your programs.

You will also find a Cobol file-conversion program corresponding to each set of data files. For instance, PAT-CVT.CBL converts the line sequential file to an indexed file (the result is a pair: data and index). You can use this if you wish to create your own data file or add records to the existing file.

Using the Data Files

Subprograms listed in this appendix access these indexed files. As with any Cobol program, file access requires an entry in the Select clause identifying the name of the file. Ordinarily, if the Select entry does not include a path, the system defaults to the current folder. For Web applications, you cannot count on this; *you must specify the full path or NetExpress probably will not find your file.* To this end, all file processing subprogram Select clauses include a full path, for instance:

```
Select Patron-File assign to disk
                  "c:\Elements-CWP\NE-data\patron.di"
```

If you load the data files per the instructions of the Chapter 0 you will be able to use the Cobol subprograms with no change. However, if you load the data files into another folder, you will need to change the Select entry accordingly.

Example Applications Files

Data Files

```
01  patron-record.
    10  pr-patron-number        pic x(03).
    10  pr-first-name           pic X(10).
    10  pr-last-key redefines
        pr-first-name           pic 9(03).
    10  pr-last-name            pic X(12).
    10  pr-street-address       pic X(20).
    10  pr-city                 pic X(14).
    10  pr-state                pic X(02).
    10  pr-zip                  pic X(10).
    10  pr-privilege-status     pic X(01).
    10  pr-employee-status      pic X(01).
    10  pr-book-right           pic X(01).
    10  pr-periodical-right     pic X(01).
    10  pr-video-right          pic X(01).
    10  pr-books-out            pic 9(02).
    10                          pic X(18).
```

Patron record format

```
000024
0010rson      Karridge    223 Connecticut St  San Francisco CA94107-0000GFYYY07
002Sandy      Beech       1247 Main Street    Woodside      CA94062-0000RFYNY03
003Bill       Board       1532 Bancroft Road  Berkeley      CA94703-0000RFYNN02
004Toller     Bridges     Route 3             Big Trees     CA95066-0000RPYNN01
005Tim        Burr        4892 Powell Street  Emeryville    CA94608-0000RPYNN01
006Justin     Case        349 Airport Way     Concord       CA94519-0000PNYNN02
007Ann        Chovie      2817 Laguna Street  Oakland       CA94602-0000PFYYY01
008Lee        Flett       3814 Marina Blvd.   San Francisco CA94123-0000RFYYY01
009Ima        Fox         137 Rengstorff Bl.  Santa Clara   CA95051-0000RFYYY01
010Frank      Furter      35 Crescent Circle  Orinda        CA94563-0000RFYYY00
011Anita      Hickey      4530 17th Street    San Francisco CA94114-0000RPYNY00
012Winnie     Baggo       211 Central Avenue  Santa Cruz    CA95060-0000GNYYY00
013Don        Key         453 Bayview Drive   Belvedere     CA94920-0000GNYYY00
014Ima        Knutt       1347 Sacramento     Berkeley      CA94702-0000RFYYN00
015Ann        Korridge    1523 Old Bayshore   Mountain View CA94043-0000RFYYN00
016Barry      Kuda        4237 Doppler Blvd.  Daly City     CA94014-0000RPYYY00
017Dee        Leete       125 Wharf Circle    Capitola      CA95010-0000PFYYY00
018Xavier     Money       24389 Ballena Road  Alameda       CA94501-0000PNYYN00
019Mike       Robe        2201 Pacific Ave.   San Francisco CA94115-0000RNNYN00
020Tyrone     Shoelaces   385 C Street.       San Rafael    CA94901-0000RFYYN00
021Jim        Shorts      15062 E. 14th St.   San Leandro   CA94578-0000GNYYY00
022Minnie     Skirts      531 Gray Peak Road  Belmont       CA94002-0000PPNNY00
023Art        Tillery     1987 Dallas Drive   Hayward       CA94545-0000GFYYY00
024Helen      Wheels      515 Bridgeport Ave  Sausalito     CA94965-0000RFYYY00
```

Patron file listing

```
01  book-record.
    10  br-book-id            pic x(04).
    10  br-book-title         pic X(25).
    10  br-last-key redefines
        br-book-title         pic 9(04).
    10  br-book-author        pic X(13).
    10  br-book-publisher     pic X(11).
    10  br-publication-year   pic X(04).
    10  br-patron-number      pic X(03).
    10  br-remaining-days     pic 9(02).
    10                        pic X(20).
```

Book record format

```
00000025
0001Business Law             Force, Gayle Legal Press198800107
0002Non-Business Law         Force, Gayle Legal Press199300500
0003Contract Law             Peace, WarrenLegal Press198800107
0004Legal Secretary ReferenceRobe, Mike   Legal Press199600114
0005General Economics        Wheels, HelenJim Beam    199400212
0006Specific Economics       Kerr, Ann    Jim Beam    198900000
0007Economics Today          Kerr, Ann    John Beam   198800000
0008Silicon Economics        Mite, Dina   Ayixa Press199700102
0009Starring Silicon Valley  Mite, Dina   Ayixa Press199500818
0010Introduction to Data ProcFlett, Lee   JP Publish.199600721
0011Computer Information Sys Key, Lee      JP Publish.199600321
0012Computers in Management  Key, Lee      JP Publish.199700414
0013The 123s of Computers    Zeen, Ben     JP Publish.199600000
0014The 456s of Laptops      Tory, Vic     JP Publish.199700911
0015Life Without Computers   Zapple, Adam Cobol Univ 199700115
0016The CORBA Standard       Yard, Bill    Ayixa Press199700811
0017Database Processing      Lesse, Moira Ayixa Press199500616
0018Object Technology        Beech, Sandy OT Tech     199600609
0019C                        Leets, Ethyl Ayixa Press199400200
0020Intro to Info Systems    Diss, John    DP Publ     199700312
0021Basic Programming        Seed, Lynn    JP Publish.199500000
0022Everyone's Guide to dBASEOlogy, ArchieDP Publ     198900000
0023No One's Guide to dBASE  Ology, ArchieJP Publish.198800103
0024Unix Hater's Reference   O'Shea, Rick Cobol Univ 199100204
0025The NEXT Step            Job, Anita    Ayixa Press199600117
```

Book file listing

Subprograms

```
 1  *> Subprogram Get-Date.
 2  *> Example applications involve dates e.g. due date
 3  *> for a book. Rather than include an actual date
 4  *> the number of days (from the current date)is used.
 5  *> This subprogram determines a date based on the day
 6  *> the program is run and the value in the number-of-
 7  *> days field. I do this so that the displayed
 8  *> output looks current. Otherwise, the data
 9  *> file would soon appear outdated.
10
11  Identification Division.
12      Program-id. Get-Date.
13
14  Data Division.
15    Working-Storage Section.
16      01  todays-date-info.
17          05  todays-date      pic 9(08).
18          05                   pic X(13).
19      01  due-date             pic 9(08).
20      01  due-day-count        pic 9(08).
21      01  ws-due-date.
22          05  ws-month         pic Z9.
23          05                   pic X(01) value "/".
24          05  ws-day           pic X(02).
25          05                   pic X(01) value "/".
26          05  ws-year          pic X(04).
27
28    Linkage Section.
29      01  ls-remaining-days    pic 9(03).
30      01  ls-due-date          pic X(10).
31
32  Procedure Division Using ls-remaining-days
33                            ls-due-date.
34      Move Function current-date to todays-date-info
35      Compute due-day-count =
36          function integer-of-date (todays-date)
37                              + ls-remaining-days
38      Compute due-date =
39          function date-of-integer (due-day-count)
40      Move due-date(1:4) to ws-year
41      Move due-date(5:2) to ws-month
42      Move due-date(7:2)  to ws-day
43      Move ws-due-date to ls-due-date
44          .
```

Get-date.cbl

```
 1  Identification Division.
 2  Program-ID. Lib-Sub0.
 3
 4  Data Division.
 5  Linkage Section.
 6  01  in-patron-number   pic X(03).
 7  01  patron-name        pic X(23).
 8
 9  Procedure Division using in-patron-number
10                           patron-name.
11      Evaluate in-patron-number
12        When "001"
13          Move "Orson Karridge" to patron-name
14        When "002"
15          Move "Sandy Beech" to patron-name
16        When "003"
17          Move "Bill Board" to patron-name
18        When other
19          Move low-values to patron-name
20      End-Evaluate
21          .
```

Lib-sub0.cbl

```
          $set sourceformat "free"               45  Linkage Section.
1  *>*****************************************     46    01  in-patron-number        pic X(03).
2  *> Library Application                         47    01  patron-info.
3  *> W. Price  9/28/97            LIB-SUB1.CBL    48      10  patron-name         pic X(23).
4  *> This subprogram provides read access to the 49      10  street-address      pic X(20).
5  *> following indexed file                      50      10  city-state-zip      pic X(28).
6  *>   PATRON.DI: Indexed by Patron Number; contains 51
7  *>     patron name, address data and other data.  52  Procedure Division Using in-patron-number
8  *> Subprogram parameters are:                  53                             patron-info.
9  *>   in-patron-number  Input key field value for 54
10 *>                     file read.               55    000-Main-module.
11 *>   patron-info       Output patron information. 56      Open Input Patron-File
12 *>*****************************************      57      Perform 200-process-user-request
13                                                 58      Close Patron-File
14 Identification Division.                        59      Exit program
15   Program-id. Library-Subprogram.               60        .
16                                                 61    200-process-user-request.
17 Environment Division.                           62      Move spaces to patron-info
18                                                 63      Move in-patron-number to pr-patron-number
19   Input-Output Section.                         64      Perform 800-read-patron-record
20   File-Control.                                 65      If patron-info NOT = low-values
21     Select Patron-File assign to disk           66        Perform 400-setup-patron-output
22       "c:\Elements-CWP\NE-data\patron.di"       67      End-if *>patron-info = low-values
23       organization is indexed                   68        .
24       access is random                          69    400-setup-patron-output.
25       record key is pr-patron-number.           70      Move spaces to patron-name
26                                                 71      String pr-first-name delimited by " "
27 Data Division.                                  72                                " "
28   File Section.                                 73            pr-last-name
29     FD  Patron-File.                            74            into patron-name
30       01  book-record.                          75      Move pr-street-address to street-address
31         10  br-book-id          pic x(04).      76      Move pr-city to city-with-spaces
32         10  br-book-title       pic X(25).      77      String city-with-spaces delimited by " "
33         10  br-last-key redefines              78                                " "
34             br-book-title       pic 9(04).      79            pr-state
35         10  br-book-author      pic X(13).      80                                " "
36         10  br-book-publisher   pic X(11).      81            pr-zip
37         10  br-publication-year pic X(04).      82            into city-state-zip
38         10  br-patron-number    pic X(03).      83        .
39         10  br-remaining-days   pic 9(02).      84    800-read-patron-record.
40         10                      pic X(20).      85      Read Patron-File
41                                                 86        Invalid key
42   Working-Storage Section.                      87          Move low-values to patron-info
43     01  city-with-spaces        pic X(16).      88      End-read
44                                                 89        .
```

Lib-sub1.cbl

```
                $set sourceformat "free"
 1  *>****************************************************
 2  *> Library Application
 3  *> W. Price  1/2/99              LIB-SUB2.CBL
 4  *> This subprogram provides read access to the
 5  *> following indexed file
 6  *>   PATRON.DI: Indexed by Patron Number; contains
 7  *>     patron name, address data and other data.
 8  *> Subprogram parameter is ls-patron-record
 9  *>     Input: ls-patron-number (record key)
10  *>     Output: ls-patron info.
11  *>           Set to low-values if record not found
12  *>****************************************************
13  Identification Division.
14    Program-id. LIB-SUB2.
15  Environment Division.
16    Input-Output Section.
17    File-Control.
18      Select Patron-File assign to disk
19          "c:\Elements-CWP\NE-data\patron.di"
20          organization is indexed
21          access is random
22          record key is pr-patron-number.
23
24  Data Division.
25    File Section.
26      FD  Patron-File.
27        01  patron-record.
28          10  pr-patron-number     pic x(03).
29          10  pr-first-name        pic X(10).
30          10  pr-last-key redefines
31              pr-first-name        pic 9(03).
32          10  pr-last-name         pic X(12).
33          10  pr-street-address    pic X(20).
34          10  pr-city              pic X(14).
35          10  pr-state             pic X(02).
36          10  pr-zip               pic X(10).
37          10  pr-privilege-status  pic X(01).
38          10  pr-employee-status   pic X(01).
39          10  pr-book-right        pic X(01).
40          10  pr-periodical-right  pic X(01).
41          10  pr-video-right       pic X(01).
42          10  pr-books-out         pic 9(02).
43          10                       pic X(18).
44    Linkage Section.
45        01  ls-patron-number       pic x(03).
46        01  ls-patron-info.
47          10  ls-first-name        pic X(10).
48          10  ls-last-name         pic X(12).
49          10  ls-street-address    pic X(20).
50          10  ls-city              pic X(14).
51          10  ls-state             pic X(02).
52          10  ls-zip               pic X(10).
53          10  ls-employee-status   pic X(1).
54
55  Procedure Division Using ls-patron-number
56                          Ls-patron-info.
57    000-Main-module.
58      Open Input Patron-File
59      Perform 200-process-user-request
60      Close Patron-File
61      Exit program
62      .
63    200-process-user-request.
64      Move ls-patron-number to pr-patron-number
65      Read Patron-File
66        Invalid key
67          Move low-values to ls-patron-info
68        Not invalid key
69          Move pr-first-name     to ls-first-name
70          Move pr-last-name      to ls-last-name
71          Move pr-street-address to ls-street-address
72          Move pr-city           to ls-city
73          Move pr-state          to ls-state
74          Move pr-zip            to ls-zip
75          Move pr-employee-status to ls-employee-status
76      End-read
77      .
```

Lib-sub2.cbl

```
                $set sourceformat "free"
 1  *>****************************************************
 2  *> Library Application
 3  *> W. Price  9/13/97             LIB-SUB3.CBL
 4  *> The subprogram accesses data from the following
 5  *> two data files.
 6  *>   PATRON.DI: Indexed by Patron Number; contains
 7  *>     patron name and address data.
 8  *>   BOOK.DI: Indexed by Book ID; contains book
 9  *>     title and other book information. If book is
10  *>     checked out, also includes Patron Number and
11  *>     due date. Patron number is secondary key.
12  *> The input parameter is the patron number
13  *> Output parameters are:
14  *>   Patron name and address data
15  *>   Count of number of books checked out
16  *>   Array containing book information
17  *>****************************************************
18
19  Identification Division.
20    Program-id. Library-Subprogram.
21
22    Environment Division.
23
24      Input-Output Section.
25      File-Control.
26        Select Patron-File assign to disk
27            "c:\Elements-CWP\NE-data\patron.di"
28            organization is indexed
29            access is random
30            record key is pr-patron-number.
31
32        Select Book-File assign to disk
33            "c:\Elements-CWP\NE-data\book.di"
34            organization is indexed
35            access is dynamic
36            record key is br-book-id
37            alternate key is br-patron-number
38              with duplicates.
39
40  Data Division.
41    File Section.
42      FD  Patron-File.
43        01  patron-record.
44          10  pr-patron-number     pic x(03).
45          10  pr-first-name        pic X(10).
46          10  pr-last-key redefines
47              pr-first-name        pic 9(03).
48          10  pr-last-name         pic X(12).
49          10  pr-street-address    pic X(20).
50          10  pr-city              pic X(14).
51          10  pr-state             pic X(02).
52          10  pr-zip               pic X(10).
53          10  pr-privilege-status  pic X(01).
54          10  pr-employee-status   pic X(01).
55          10  pr-book-right        pic X(01).
56          10  pr-periodical-right  pic X(01).
57          10  pr-video-right       pic X(01).
58          10  pr-books-out         pic 9(02).
59          10                       pic X(18).
60
61      FD  Book-File.
62        01  book-record.
63          10  br-book-id           pic x(04).
64          10  br-book-title        pic X(25).
65          10  br-last-key redefines
66              br-book-title        pic 9(04).
67          10  br-book-author       pic X(13).
68          10  br-book-publisher    pic X(11).
69          10  br-publication-year  pic X(04).
70          10  br-patron-number     pic X(03).
71          10  br-remaining-days    pic 9(02).
72          10                       pic X(20).
73
```

Lib-sub3.cbl (continued next page)

```
 74    Working-Storage Section.
 75      01  program-switches.
 76          10  end-of-file-sw      pic X(01).
 77              88  end-of-file          value "Y".
 78              88  not-end-of-file      value "N".
 79      01  book-pointer           pic 9(02).
 80
 81      01  todays-date-info.
 82          05  todays-date        pic 9(08).
 83          05                     pic X(13).
 84      01  due-date               pic 9(08).
 85      01  due-day-count          pic 9(08).
 86      01  ws-due-date.
 87          05  ws-month           pic Z9.
 88          05                     pic X(01) value "/".
 89          05  ws-day             pic X(02).
 90          05                     pic X(01) value "/".
 91          05  ws-year            pic X(04).
 92
 93    Linkage Section.
 94      01  ls-in-patron-number        pic X(03).
 95      01  ls-patron-info.
 96          05  ls-patron-name         pic X(23).
 97          05  ls-street-address      pic X(20).
 98          05  ls-city-state-zip      pic X(30).
 99      01  ls-book-counter            pic 9(02).
100      01  ls-book-info-array.
101          05  ls-book-info          occurs 10 times.
102              10  ls-book-id     pic X(04).
103              10  ls-book-title  pic X(25).
104              10  ls-book-author pic X(13).
105              10  ls-due-date    pic X(10).
106
107    Procedure Division Using ls-in-patron-number
108                               ls-patron-info
109                               ls-book-counter
110                               ls-book-info-array.
111
112    000-Main-module.
113        Perform 100-Open-Files
114        Perform 200-process-user-request
115        Perform 300-close-files
116        Exit program
117        .
118    100-Open-Files.
119        Open Input Patron-File
120                   Book-File
121        .
122
123    200-process-user-request.
124        Move spaces to ls-book-info-array
125        Move spaces to ls-patron-info
126        Move 0 to ls-book-counter
127        Move ls-in-patron-number to pr-patron-number
128        Perform 800-read-patron-record
129        If ls-patron-info NOT = low-value
130           Perform 850-string-patron-data
131           Perform 820-read-book-records
132        End-if
133        .
134
135    300-Close-files.
136        Close Patron-File
137              Book-File
138        .
```

```
139    400-set-up-book-info-line.
140        Move br-book-id to ls-book-id(ls-book-counter)
141        Move br-book-title
142                   to ls-book-title(ls-book-counter)
143        Move br-book-author
144                   to ls-book-author(ls-book-counter)
145    *> The input record includes due date as the
146    *> number of days from the date the program is
147    *> run. I do the following so that displayed
148    *> output looks current. Otherwise, the data
149    *> file would soon appear outdated.
150        Move Function current-date to todays-date-info
151        Compute due-day-count =
152              function integer-of-date (todays-date)
153                            + br-remaining-days
154        Compute due-date =
155              function date-of-integer (due-day-count)
156        Move due-date(1:4) to ws-year
157        Move due-date(5:2) to ws-month
158        Move due-date(7:2)  to ws-day
159        Move ws-due-date to ls-due-date (ls-book-counter)
160        .
161    800-read-patron-record.
162        Read Patron-File
163           Invalid key
164              Move low-values to ls-patron-info
165        End-read
166        .
167
168    820-read-book-records.
169        Move 0 to ls-book-counter
170        Move ls-in-patron-number to br-patron-number
171        Read Book-File key is br-patron-number
172           invalid key
173              Continue
174           not invalid key
175              Add 1 to ls-book-counter
176              Perform 400-set-up-book-info-line
177              Set not-end-of-file to true
178              Perform until end-of-file
179                 Read Book-File next
180                    at end
181                       Set end-of-file to true
182                    not at end
183                       If ls-in-patron-number = br-patron-number
184                          Add 1 to ls-book-counter
185                          Perform 400-set-up-book-info-line
186                       Else
187                          Set end-of-file to true
188                       End-If *>ls-in-patron-number ...
189                 End-Read *>Book-File next
190              End-Perform *>until end-of-file
191        End-Read *>Book-File
192        .
193    850-string-patron-data.
194        Move spaces to ls-patron-name
195        String pr-first-name delimited by "  "
196               "  "
197               pr-last-name
198               into ls-patron-name
199        Move pr-street-address to ls-street-address
200        Move spaces to ls-city-state-zip
201        String  pr-city delimited by "  "
202               "  "
203               pr-state
204               "  "
205               pr-zip
206               into ls-city-state-zip
207        .
```

Lib-sub3.cbl (continued from preceding page)

```
               $set sourceformat "free"
 1  *>*************************************************
 2  *> Library Application
 3  *> W. Price  5/23/98              BOOK-SUB.CBL
 4  *> The subprogram accesses data from the following
 5  *> two data files.
 6  *>   BOOK.DI: Indexed by Book ID; contains book
 7  *>     title and other book information. If book is
 8  *>     checked out, also includes Patron Number and
 9  *>     due date. Patron number is secondary key.
10  *>   PATRON.DI: Indexed by Patron Number; contains
11  *>     patron name and address data.
12  *> The input parameter is the book number
13  *> Output parameters are:
14  *>   Book information
15  *>   Name of patron name to whom the book is
16  *>   checked out and the due date
17  *>*************************************************
18
19  Identification Division.
20    Program-id. Book-Subprogram.
21
22    Environment Division.
23
24      Input-Output Section.
25      File-Control.
26        Select Patron-File assign to disk
27               "c:\Elements-CWP\NE-data\patron.di"
28               organization is indexed
29               access is random
30               record key is pr-patron-number.
31
32        Select Book-File assign to disk
33               "c:\Elements-CWP\NE-data\book.di"
34               organization is indexed
35               access is random
36               record key is br-book-id
37               alternate key is br-patron-number
38                 with duplicates.
39
40  Data Division.
41    File Section.
42      FD  Patron-File.
43        01  patron-record.
44            10  pr-patron-number       pic x(03).
45            10  pr-first-name          pic X(10).
46            10  pr-last-key redefines
47                pr-first-name          pic 9(03).
48            10  pr-last-name           pic X(12).
49            10  pr-street-address      pic X(20).
50            10  pr-city                pic X(14).
51            10  pr-state               pic X(02).
52            10  pr-zip                 pic X(10).
53            10  pr-privilege-status    pic X(01).
54            10  pr-employee-status     pic X(01).
55            10  pr-book-right          pic X(01).
56            10  pr-periodical-right    pic X(01).
57            10  pr-video-right         pic X(01).
58            10  pr-books-out           pic 9(02).
59            10                         pic X(18).
60
61      FD  Book-File.
62        01  book-record.
63            10  br-book-id             pic x(04).
64            10  br-book-title          pic X(25).
65            10  br-last-key redefines
66                br-book-title          pic 9(04).
67            10  br-book-author         pic X(13).
68            10  br-book-publisher      pic X(11).
69            10  br-publication-year    pic X(04).
70            10  br-patron-number       pic X(03).
71            10  br-remaining-days      pic 9(02).
72            10                         pic X(20).
73
 74  Working-Storage Section.
 75    01  program-switches.
 76        10  end-of-file-sw       pic X(01).
 77            88  end-of-file           value "Y".
 78            88  not-end-of-file       value "N".
 79    01  book-pointer             pic 9(02).
 80
 81    01  todays-date-info.
 82        05  todays-date          pic 9(08).
 83        05                       pic X(13).
 84    01  due-date                 pic 9(08).
 85    01  due-day-count            pic 9(08).
 86    01  ws-due-date.
 87        05  ws-month             pic Z9.
 88        05                       pic X(01) value "/".
 89        05  ws-day               pic X(02).
 90        05                       pic X(01) value "/".
 91        05  ws-year              pic X(04).
 92
 93  Linkage Section.
 94    01  in-book-id               pic X(04).
 95    01  book-info.
 96        10  ls-book-title         pic X(25).
 97        10  ls-book-author        pic X(13).
 98        10  ls-due-date           pic X(10).
 99        10  ls-book-publisher     pic X(11).
100        10  ls-publication-year   pic X(04).
101        10  ls-patron-name        pic X(23).
102
103  Procedure Division Using in-book-id
104                           book-info.
105
106  000-Main-module.
107    Perform 100-Open-Files
108    Perform 200-process-user-request
109    Perform 300-close-files
110    Exit program
111    .
112  100-Open-Files.
113    Open Input Patron-File
114               Book-File
115
116  200-process-user-request.
117    Move in-book-id to br-book-id
118    Perform 820-read-book-record
119    If book-info = low-value
120      Continue
121    Else
122      If pr-patron-number = "000"
123        Move low-values to ls-patron-name
124      Else
125        Perform 800-read-patron-record
126      End-If  *>pr-patron-number = "000"
127    End-if
128    .
129  300-Close-files.
130    Close Patron-File
131          Book-File
132    .
133  400-calculate-date.
134    *> The input record includes due date as the
135    *> number of days from the date the program is
136    *> run. I do the following so that displayed
137    *> output looks current. Otherwise, the data
138    *> file would soon appear outdated.
```

Book-sub.cbl

```
139      If br-patron-number = low-values                158      Not invalid key
140         Move spaces to ls-due-date                    159         Move spaces to ls-patron-name
141      Else                                             160         String pr-first-name delimited by "  "
142         Move Function current-date to todays-date-info 161                        "  "
143         Compute due-day-count =                       162                     pr-first-name
144             function integer-of-date (todays-date)    163                     into ls-patron-name
145                           + br-remaining-days         164      End-read
146         Compute due-date =                            165      .
147             function date-of-integer (due-day-count)  166   820-read-book-record.
148         Move due-date(1:4) to ws-year                 167      Read Book-File
149         Move due-date(5:2) to ws-month                168         invalid key
150         Move due-date(7:2)   to ws-day                169            Move low-values to book-info
151         Move ws-due-date to ls-due-date               170         not invalid key
152      End-If *>br-patron-number = low-values           171            Move br-book-title to ls-book-title
153      .                                                172            Move br-book-author to ls-book-author
154   800-read-patron-record.                             173            Move br-book-publisher to ls-book-publisher
155      Read Patron-File                                 174            Move br-publication-year
156         Invalid key                                   175                            to ls-publication-year
157            Move low-values to ls-patron-name          176            Move br-patron-number to pr-patron-number
                                                          177            Perform 400-calculate-date
                                                          178      End-Read *>Book-File
                                                          179      .
```

Book-sub (continued)

```
                    $set sourceformat "free"              52
 1  *>**********************************************       53  Procedure Division Using ls-book-record.
 2  *> Library Application                                 54
 3  *> W. Price  2/15/1999            BOOK-SUB1.CBL        55     000-Main-module.
 4  *> This subprogram provides for the addition of       56        Perform 100-Open-File
 5  *> records to the book file BOOK.DI.                   57        Perform 200-add-new-record
 6  *> Key field is Book ID                                58        Perform 300-close-files
 7  *> First record (key value 0000) contains the last    59        Exit program
 8  *> used key value in bytes 5-8 of that record.        60        .
 9  *> It is updated with each record addition.           61     100-Open-File.
10  *>**********************************************       62        Open I-O Book-File
11                                                         63
12  Identification Division.                               64        .
13     Program-id. Book-Add-Subprogram.                    65     200-add-new-record.
14                                                         66        Move "0000" to br-book-id
15     Environment Division.                               67        Perform 800-read-book-record
16                                                         68        Add 1 to br-last-key
17     Input-Output Section.                               69        Move br-last-key to ls-book-id
18     File-Control.                                       70        Move ls-book-record to book-record
19        Select Book-File assign to disk                  71        Perform 850-write-book-record
20            "c:\Elements-CWP\NE-data\book2.di"           72        If br-book-id not = low-value
21            organization is indexed                      73           Move spaces to book-record
22            access is random                             74           Move ls-book-id to br-last-key
23            record key is br-book-id                      75           Move "0000" to br-book-id
24            alternate key is br-patron-number            76           Perform 860-rewrite-book-record
25               with duplicates.                          77        End-If *>br-book-id  not = low-value
26                                                         78        .
27  Data Division.                                         79
28     File Section.                                       80     300-Close-files.
29        FD  Book-File.                                   81        Close Book-File
30           01  book-record.                              82        .
31              10   br-book-id          pic x(04).        83
32              10   br-book-title       pic X(25).        84     800-read-book-record.
33              10   br-last-key redefines                 85        Read Book-File
34                   br-book-title       pic 9(04).        86           Invalid key
35              10   br-book-author      pic X(13).        87              Move low-values to br-book-id
36              10   br-book-publisher   pic X(11).        88        End-read
37              10   br-publication-year pic X(04).        89        .
38              10   br-patron-number    pic X(03).        90     850-write-book-record.
39              10   br-remaining-days   pic 9(02).        91        Write book-record
40              10                       pic X(20).        92           Invalid key
41                                                         93              Move low-values to br-book-id
42     Linkage Section.                                    94        End-write
43        01  ls-book-record.                              95        .
44              10   ls-book-id          pic x(04).        96     860-rewrite-book-record.
45              10   ls-book-title       pic X(25).        97        Rewrite book-record
46              10   ls-book-author      pic X(13).        98           Invalid key
47              10   ls-book-publisher   pic X(11).        99              Move low-values to br-book-id
48              10   ls-publication-year pic X(04).       100        End-rewrite
49              10   ls-patron-number    pic X(03).       101        .
50              10   ls-remaining-days   pic 9(02).
51              10                       pic X(20).
```

Book-sub1.cbl

```
                  $set sourceformat "free"
 1 *>***********************************************
 2 *> Library Application
 3 *> W. Price  2/15/1999                    BOOK-SUB2.CBL
 4 *> This subprogram provides read access to the
 5 *> following indexed file
 6 *>    BOOK.DI: Indexed by Book Number; contains
 7 *>       book name, address data and other data.
 8 *> Subprogram parameter is ls-book-record
 9 *>       Input: ls-book-id (record key)
10 *>       Output: book record.
11 *>              Set to low-values if record not found
12 *>***********************************************
13
14 Identification Division.
15   Program-id. BOOK-SUB2.
16
17   Environment Division.
18
19     Input-Output Section.
20     File-Control.
21       Select Book-File assign to disk
22                "c:\Elements-CWP\NE-data\book2.di"
23                organization is indexed
24                access is random
25                record key is br-book-id
26                alternate key is br-patron-number
27                 with duplicates.
28
29 Data Division.
30   File Section.
31     FD  Book-File.
32       01  book-record.
33          10  br-book-id          pic x(04).
34          10  br-book-title        pic X(25).
35          10  br-last-key redefines
36              br-book-title        pic 9(04).
37          10  br-book-author       pic X(13).
38          10  br-book-publisher    pic X(11).
39          10  br-publication-year  pic X(04).
40          10  br-patron-number     pic X(03).
41          10  br-remaining-days    pic 9(02).
42          10                       pic X(20).
43
44   Linkage Section.
45       01  ls-book-record.
46          10  ls-book-id           pic x(04).
47          10  ls-book-title        pic X(25).
48          10  ls-book-author       pic X(13).
49          10  ls-book-publisher    pic X(11).
50          10  ls-publication-year  pic X(04).
51          10  ls-patron-number     pic X(03).
52          10  ls-remaining-days    pic 9(02).
53          10                       pic X(20).
54
55 Procedure Division Using ls-book-record.
56
57   000-Main-module.
58     Open Input Book-File
59     Perform 200-process-user-request
60     Close Book-File
61     Exit program
62
63   200-process-user-request.
64     Move ls-book-id to br-book-id
65     Read Book-File
66       Invalid key
67         Move low-values to ls-book-record
68       Not invalid key
69         Move book-record to ls-book-record
70     End-read
71       .
```

Book-sub2.cbl

```
                  $set sourceformat "free"
 1 *>***********************************************
 2 *> Library Application
 3 *> W. Price  2/15/1999                    BOOK-SUB3.CBL
 4 *> This subprogram provides rewrite access to the
 5 *> following indexed file
 6 *>    BOOK.DI: Indexed by Book Number; contains
 7 *>       book name, address data and other data.
 8 *> Subprogram parameters are:
 9 *>    book-record      Input book record.
10 *>    ls-book-id  Output key field value.
11 *>         Set to low-value for invalid file rewrite.
12 *>***********************************************
13
14 Identification Division.
15   Program-id. BOOK-SUB3.
16
17   Environment Division.
18
19     Input-Output Section.
20     File-Control.
21       Select Book-File assign to disk
22                "c:\Elements-CWP\NE-data\book2.di"
23                organization is indexed
24                access is random
25                record key is br-book-id
26                alternate key is br-patron-number
27                 with duplicates.
28
29 Data Division.
30   File Section.
31     FD  Book-File.
32       01  book-record.
33          10  br-book-id          pic x(04).
34          10  br-book-title        pic X(25).
35          10  br-last-key redefines
36              br-book-title        pic 9(04).
37          10  br-book-author       pic X(13).
38          10  br-book-publisher    pic X(11).
39          10  br-publication-year  pic X(04).
40          10  br-patron-number     pic X(03).
41          10  br-remaining-days    pic 9(02).
42          10                       pic X(20).
43
44   Linkage Section.
45       01  ls-book-record.
46          10  ls-book-id           pic x(04).
47          10  ls-book-title        pic X(25).
48          10  ls-book-author       pic X(13).
49          10  ls-book-publisher    pic X(11).
50          10  ls-publication-year  pic X(04).
51          10  ls-patron-number     pic X(03).
52          10  ls-remaining-days    pic 9(02).
53          10                       pic X(20).
54
55 Procedure Division Using ls-book-record.
56
57   000-Main-module.
58     Open I-O Book-File
59     Rewrite book-record from ls-book-record
60       Invalid key
61         Move low-values to ls-book-id
62     End-rewrite
63     Close Book-File
64     Exit program
65       .
```

Book-sub3.cbl

```
                    $set sourceformat "free"
 1 *>***********************************************
 2 *> Library Application
 3 *> W. Price  8/11/97                  PAT-SUB1.CBL
 4 *> This subprogram provides for the addition of
 5 *> records to the patron file PATRON.DI.
 6 *> Key field is Patron Number
 7 *> First record (key value 000) contains the last
 8 *> used key value in bytes 4-6 of that record.
 9 *> It is updated with each record addition.
10 *>***********************************************
11
12 Identification Division.
13    Program-id. Patron-Add-Subprogram.
14
15    Environment Division.
16
17       Input-Output Section.
18       File-Control.
19          Select Patron-File assign to disk
20                "c:\Elements-CWP\NE-data\patron2.di"
21                organization is indexed
22                access is random
23                record key is pr-patron-number.
24
25 Data Division.
26    File Section.
27       FD  Patron-File.
28          01   patron-record.
29                10   pr-patron-number      pic x(03).
30                10   pr-first-name         pic X(10).
31                10   pr-last-key redefines
32                     pr-first-name         pic 9(03).
33                10   pr-last-name          pic X(12).
34                10   pr-street-address     pic X(20).
35                10   pr-city               pic X(14).
36                10   pr-state              pic X(02).
37                10   pr-zip                pic X(10).
38                10   pr-privilege-status   pic X(01).
39                10   pr-employee-status    pic X(01).
40                10   pr-book-right         pic X(01).
41                10   pr-periodical-right   pic X(01).
42                10   pr-video-right        pic X(01).
43                10   pr-books-out          pic 9(02).
44                10                         pic X(18).
45
46    Linkage Section.
47       01   ls-patron-record.
48                10   ls-patron-number      pic x(03).
49                10   ls-first-name         pic X(10).
50                10   ls-last-name          pic X(12).
51                10   ls-street-address     pic X(20).
52                10   ls-city               pic X(14).
53                10   ls-state              pic X(02).
54                10   ls-zip                pic X(10).
55                10   ls-privilege-status   pic X(01).
56                10   ls-employee-status    pic X(01).
57                10   ls-book-right         pic X(01).
58                10   ls-periodical-right   pic X(01).
59                10   ls-video-right        pic X(01).
60                10   ls-books-out          pic 9(02).
61                10                         pic X(18).
62
63 Procedure Division Using ls-patron-record.
64
65    000-Main-module.
66       Perform 100-Open-File
67       Perform 200-add-new-record
68       Perform 300-close-files
69       Exit program
70    .
71    100-Open-File.
72       Open I-O Patron-File
73
74
75    200-add-new-record.
76       Move "000" to pr-patron-number
77       Perform 800-read-patron-record
78       Add 1 to pr-last-key
79       Move pr-last-key to ls-patron-number
80       Move ls-patron-record to patron-record
81       Perform 850-write-patron-record
82       If pr-patron-number  not = low-value
83          Move spaces to patron-record
84          Move ls-patron-number to pr-last-key
85          Move "000" to pr-patron-number
86          Perform 860-rewrite-patron-record
87       End-If *>pr-patron-number  not = low-value
88    .
89
90    300-Close-files.
91       Close Patron-File
92    .
93
94    800-read-patron-record.
95       Read Patron-File
96          Invalid key
97             Move low-values to pr-patron-number
98       End-read
99    .
100   850-write-patron-record.
101      Write patron-record
102         Invalid key
103            Move low-values to pr-patron-number
104      End-write
105   .
106   860-rewrite-patron-record.
107      Rewrite patron-record
108         Invalid key
109            Move low-values to pr-patron-number
110      End-rewrite
111   .
```

Pat-sub1.cbl

```
                $set sourceformat "free"
1  *>***********************************************
2  *> Library Application
3  *> W. Price  7/15/98               PAT-SUB2.CBL
4  *> This subprogram provides read access to the
5  *> following indexed file
6  *>   PATRON.DI: Indexed by Patron Number; contains
7  *>     patron name, address data and other data.
8  *> Subprogram parameter is ls-patron-record
9  *>     Input: ls-patron-number (record key)
10 *>     Output: patron record.
11 *>           Set to low-values if record not found
12 *>***********************************************
13
14 Identification Division.
15  Program-id. PAT-SUB2.
16
17  Environment Division.
18
19    Input-Output Section.
20    File-Control.
21     Select Patron-File assign to disk
22         "c:\Elements-CWP\NE-data\patron2.di"
23         organization is indexed
24         access is random
25         record key is pr-patron-number.
26
27 Data Division.
28   File Section.
29    FD  Patron-File.
30     01  patron-record.
31        10  pr-patron-number      pic x(03).
32        10  pr-first-name         pic X(10).
33        10  pr-last-key redefines
34            pr-first-name         pic 9(03).
35        10  pr-last-name          pic X(12).
36        10  pr-street-address     pic X(20).
37        10  pr-city               pic X(14).
38        10  pr-state              pic X(02).
39        10  pr-zip                pic X(10).
40        10  pr-privilege-status   pic X(01).
41        10  pr-employee-status    pic X(01).
42        10  pr-book-right         pic X(01).
43        10  pr-periodical-right   pic X(01).
44        10  pr-video-right        pic X(01).
45        10  pr-books-out          pic 9(02).
46        10                        pic X(18).
47
48    Linkage Section.
49     01  ls-patron-record.
50        10  ls-patron-number      pic x(03).
51        10  ls-first-name         pic X(10).
52        10  ls-last-name          pic X(12).
53        10  ls-street-address     pic X(20).
54        10  ls-city               pic X(14).
55        10  ls-state              pic X(02).
56        10  ls-zip                pic X(10).
57        10  ls-privilege-status   pic X(01).
58        10  ls-employee-status    pic X(01).
59        10  ls-book-right         pic X(01).
60        10  ls-periodical-right   pic X(01).
61        10  ls-video-right        pic X(01).
62        10  ls-books-out          pic 9(02).
63        10                        pic X(18).
64
65 Procedure Division Using ls-patron-record.
66
67  000-Main-module.
68    Open Input Patron-File
69    Perform 200-process-user-request
70    Close Patron-File
71    Exit program
72    .
73  200-process-user-request.
74    Move ls-patron-number to pr-patron-number
75    Read Patron-File
76     Invalid key
77       Move low-values to ls-patron-record
78     Not invalid key
79       Move patron-record to ls-patron-record
80    End-read
81    .
```

Pat-sub2.cbl

```
                $set sourceformat "free"
1  *>***********************************************
2  *> Library Application
3  *> W. Price  7/16/98               PAT-SUB3.CBL
4  *> This subprogram provides rewrite access to the
5  *> following indexed file
6  *>   PATRON.DI: Indexed by Patron Number; contains
7  *>     patron name, address data and other data.
8  *> Subprogram parameters are:
9  *>     ls-patron-number  Output key field value.
10 *>       Set to low-value for invalid file rewrite.
11 *>   patron-record     Input patron record.
12 *>***********************************************
13
14 Identification Division.
15  Program-id. PAT-SUB3.
16
17  Environment Division.
18
19    Input-Output Section.
20    File-Control.
21     Select Patron-File assign to disk
22         "c:\Elements-CWP\NE-data\patron2.di"
23         organization is indexed
24         access is random
25         record key is pr-patron-number.
26
27 Data Division.
28   File Section.
29    FD  Patron-File.
30     01  patron-record.
31        10  pr-patron-number      pic x(03).
32        10  pr-first-name         pic X(10).
33        10  pr-last-key redefines
34            pr-first-name         pic 9(03).
35        10  pr-last-name          pic X(12).
36        10  pr-street-address     pic X(20).
37        10  pr-city               pic X(14).
38        10  pr-state              pic X(02).
39        10  pr-zip                pic X(10).
40        10  pr-privilege-status   pic X(01).
41        10  pr-employee-status    pic X(01).
42        10  pr-book-right         pic X(01).
43        10  pr-periodical-right   pic X(01).
44        10  pr-video-right        pic X(01).
45        10  pr-books-out          pic 9(02).
46        10                        pic X(18).
47
48    Linkage Section.
49     01  ls-patron-record.
50        10  ls-patron-number      pic x(03).
51        10  ls-first-name         pic X(10).
52        10  ls-last-name          pic X(12).
53        10  ls-street-address     pic X(20).
54        10  ls-city               pic X(14).
55        10  ls-state              pic X(02).
56        10  ls-zip                pic X(10).
57        10  ls-privilege-status   pic X(01).
58        10  ls-employee-status    pic X(01).
59        10  ls-book-right         pic X(01).
60        10  ls-periodical-right   pic X(01).
61        10  ls-video-right        pic X(01).
62        10  ls-books-out          pic 9(02).
63        10                        pic X(18).
64
65 Procedure Division Using ls-patron-record.
66
67  000-Main-module.
68    Open I-O Patron-File
69    Rewrite patron-record from ls-patron-record
70     Invalid key
71       Move low-values to ls-patron-number
72    End-rewrite
73    Close Patron-File
74    Exit program
75    .
```

Pat-sub3.cbl

Assignment Files

Data Files

```
01  customer-record.
    10  cr-customer-id           pic x(04).
    10  cr-customer-first-name   pic X(12).
    10  cr-customer-last-name    pic X(12).
    10  cr-street-address        pic X(25).
    10  cr-city                  pic X(16).
    10  cr-state                 pic X(02).
    10  cr-zip                   pic X(10).
    10  cr-phone-number          pic X(12).
    10  cr-credit-rating         pic X(01).
    10  cr-credit-limit          pic 9(04).
    10  cr-current-balance       pic 9(04)V99.
    10                           pic X(10).
```

Customer record format

```
00001020
1001Fawn      Dew         588 Quail Run Road       Winona         WY82780-0000307-555-0993A6000000000
1002Adam      Zapple      21 Pinewood Way          San Francisco  CA94107-0000415-555-9861A5000000000
1003Rob       Burr        572 Pawnee Blvd.         Pine Ridge     SD57782-0000605-555-7025B3000125065
1004Xavier    Money       Bar None Ranch           Eureka         CA95501-0000707-555-6001A5000000000
1005Fern      Aksent      92A Sutter Road          Winona         WY82775-0000307-555-0074A5000000000
1006Dina      Sauer       33 Western Way           Beaumont       TX77703-0000409-555-0006B2500000000
1007Rudy      Baga        1 Country Road           Rock Springs   WY82901-0000307-555-0074A5000000000
1008Rob       Berry       1500 Washington Blvd.    Castle Rock    SD57791-0000605-555-6204A6000235750
1009Sandy     Eggo        P.O. Box 27              Winona         WY82775-0000307-555-9003A5000324512
1010Seymour   Kleerly     4310 Mesa Ave.           Winona         WY82775-0000307-555-6392A6000000000
1011Dee       Lite        Circle G Ranch           Salida         NE69388-0000308-555-1701A5000000000
1012Marsha    Mello       22 Mello Ranch Road      Salinas        CA93901-0000408-555-9448B3000131213
1013Don       Key         2443 Pine Street         Split Rock     WY82293-0000307-555-4495C0000078124
1014Archie    Ology       Route 22F                Redmond        OR97756-0000541-555-9936A4000000000
1015Rocky     Terraine    South Fork Ranch         Winnemuca      NV89445-0000702-555-8503B3000233122
1016Gary      Mander      238 Mesa Verde           Salida         NE69388-0000308-555-0145B2500187756
1017Vic       Tory        100 Circle West          Hailey         ID83333-0000208-555-0661C1000433120
1018Luke      Warmwater   199 Balen Court          Independence   MO63044-0000816-555-9907B3000000000
1019Eileen    Dover       Route 1 Box 345          Bridger        WY82755-0000307-555-6603A5000000000
1020Bill      Yard        P.O. Box 12              Buffalo Gap    TX79508-0000797-555-1997A6000343455
```

Customer file listing

```
01  order-record.
    10  or-order-id              pic X(03).
    10  or-customer-id           pic X(04).
    10  or-saddle-type           pic X(01).
    10  or-order-options.
        20  or-stirrup-covers-sw pic X(01).
        20  or-padded-seat-sw    pic X(01).
        20  or-leather-tooling   pic X(02).
        20  or-silver-ornaments  pic X(02).
    10  or-date-determination-fields.
        20  or-order-date-count  pic 9(03).
        20  or-start-date-count  pic 9(03).
        20  or-promised-date-count pic 9(03).
        20  or-scheduled-date-count pic 9(03).
    10                           pic X(20).
```

Order record format

```
000134
1011016SNNBRNO000160410405
1021018EYYNONO000160425425
1031004WNNHTBD015160415418
1041001EYYNONO030165410410
1051020SNNBBBA044170422430
1061019WNNCOBR060165430435
1071017WYNHTBA075165420430
1081014WYNBBBD080160432430
1091014SYNCUST090161433438
1101010WYYBBBD100160425410
1111017WYNNOBE110165430430
1121015WNYNOCU130170432430
1131011SYYBANO150190414414
1141012SNNBABE163160420430
1151008ENNBRNO180162410410
1161015WNYAUBE200164439448
1171009WNYNOBA210167434433
1181005SYNNOBA220165430425
1191018EYYBABR230160425430
1201020WYNBACU250165434435
1211006SYNBABO265155427430
1221019WYNBRBR280160430430
1231001ENNBANO285170420430
1241009SNYNOST300160425430
1251001WYNBBBE300160430435
1261010WYNHTCU310165436440
1271007WYYCOBE320160430430
1281006SYNBBBO333150420420
1291001WNNAUCU340160424427
1301016SNNCOST360160410410
1311004WYNCUST370160430430
1321008ENNCUNO380155425424
1331013WNNBABA390160440460
1341007WYYNONO400160430460
```

Order file listing

Subprograms

```
 1 Identification Division.              9 Procedure Division using ls-in-customer-ID
 2 Program-ID. Cus-Sub0.               10                      ls-customer-name.
 3                                      11    Evaluate ls-in-customer-ID
 4 Data Division.                       12       When "1001"
 5 Linkage Section.                     13          Move "Fawn Dew" to ls-customer-name
 6 01  ls-in-customer-ID  pic X(04).    14       When "1002"
 7 01  ls-customer-name   pic X(23).    15          Move "Adam Zapple" to ls-customer-name
 8                                      16       When "1003"
                                        17          Move "Rob Burr" to ls-customer-name
                                        18       When "1004"
                                        19          Move "Xavier Money" to ls-customer-name
                                        20       When other
                                        21          Move "No record for customer"
                                        22                      to ls-customer-name
                                        23    End-Evaluate
                                        24
```

Cus-sub0.cbl

```
                $set sourceformat "free"
 1 *>**********************************************  54      10  ls-credit-rating     pic X(01).
 2 *> Saddle Order Application                       55         88  credit-excellent   value "A".
 3 *> W. Price  3/1/99            CUS-SUB1.CBL        56         88  credit-limited     value "B".
 4 *> This subprogram provides read access to the    57         88  advance-pay-only   value "C".
 5 *> following indexed file                         58      10  ls-credit-limit      pic $$,$$9.
 6 *>   CUSTOMER.DI: Indexed by Customer ID; contains 59      10  ls-current-balance   pic $$,$$9.99.
 7 *>   customer name, address data and other data.  60
 8 *> Subprogram parameters are:                     61 Procedure Division Using ls-in-customer-id
 9 *>   in-customer-id  Input key field value for    62                       ls-customer-info.
10 *>                   file read.                    63
11 *>   customer-info      Output customer information. 64  000-Main-module.
12 *>**********************************************   65     Open Input Customer-File
13                                                    66     Perform 200-process-user-request
14 Identification Division.                           67     Close Customer-File
15    Program-id. Customer1-Subprogram.               68     Exit program
16                                                    69
17    Environment Division.                           70  200-process-user-request.
18                                                    71     If ls-in-customer-id = space
19       Input-Output Section.                        72        Move low-values to ls-customer-info
20       File-Control.                                73     Else
21          Select Customer-File assign to disk       74        Move spaces to ls-customer-info
22               "c:\Elements-CWP\NE-data\customer.di" 75        Move ls-in-customer-id to cr-customer-id
23               organization is indexed              76        Perform 800-read-customer-record
24               access is random                     77        If ls-customer-info NOT = low-values
25               record key is cr-customer-id.        78           Perform 400-setup-customer-output
26                                                    79        End-if *>customer-info = low-values
27 Data Division.                                     80     End-if
28    File Section.                                   81        .
29       FD  Customer-File.                           82  400-setup-customer-output.
30       01  customer-record.                         83     Move spaces to ls-customer-name
31          10  cr-customer-id    pic x(04).          84     String cr-customer-first-name delimited by " "
32          10  cr-customer-first-name  pic X(12).    85          " "
33          10  cr-customer-last-name   pic X(12).    86          cr-customer-last-name
34          10  cr-street-address       pic X(25).    87          into ls-customer-name
35          10  cr-city           pic X(16).          88     Move cr-street-address to ls-street-address
36          10  cr-state          pic X(02).          89     Move spaces to ls-city-state-zip
37          10  cr-zip            pic X(10).          90     String  cr-city delimited by " "
38          10  cr-phone-number   pic X(12).          91          " "
39          10  cr-credit-rating  pic X(01).          92          cr-state
40              88  credit-excellent  value "A".      93          " "
41              88  credit-limited    value "B".      94          cr-zip
42              88  advance-pay-only  value "C".      95          into ls-city-state-zip
43          10  cr-credit-limit   pic 9(04).          96     Move cr-phone-number    to ls-phone-number
44          10  cr-current-balance  pic 9(04)V99.     97     Move cr-credit-rating   to ls-credit-rating
45          10                    pic X(10).          98     Move cr-credit-limit    to ls-credit-limit
46                                                    99     Move cr-current-balance to ls-current-balance
47    Linkage Section.                               100        .
48       01  ls-in-customer-id    pic X(04).         101  800-read-customer-record.
49       01  ls-customer-info.                       102     Read Customer-File
50          10  ls-customer-name    pic X(23).       103        Invalid key
51          10  ls-street-address   pic X(20).       104        Move low-values to ls-customer-info
52          10  ls-city-state-zip   pic X(28).       105     End-read
53          10  ls-phone-number     pic X(12).       106
```

Cus-sub1.cbl

```
          $set sourceformat "free"
1  *>***********************************************
2  *> Saddle Order Application
3  *> W. Price  2/1/99              CUS-SUB2.CBL
4  *> This subprogram provides read access to the
5  *> following indexed file
6  *>    CUSTOMER.DI: Indexed by Customer ID; contains
7  *>       customer name, address data and other data.
8  *> Subprogram parameters are:
9  *>    in-customer-id  Input key field value for
10 *>                     file read.
11 *>    customer-info  Output customer information.
12 *>                    Name and address data is
13 *>                    returned as individual fields.
14 *>***********************************************
15
16 Identification Division.
17    Program-id. Customer2-Subprogram.
18
19    Environment Division.
20
21      Input-Output Section.
22      File-Control.
23        Select Customer-File assign to disk
24             "c:\Elements-CWP\NE-data\customer.di"
25             organization is indexed
26             access is random
27             record key is cr-customer-id.
28
29 Data Division.
30    File Section.
31      FD  Customer-File.
32      01  customer-record.
33          10  cr-customer-id          pic x(04).
34          10  cr-customer-first-name  pic X(12).
35          10  cr-customer-last-name   pic X(12).
36          10  cr-street-address       pic X(25).
37          10  cr-city                 pic X(16).
38          10  cr-state                pic X(02).
39          10  cr-zip                  pic X(10).
40          10  cr-phone-number         pic X(10).
41          10  cr-credit-rating        pic X(01).
42              88  credit-excellent      value "A".
43              88  credit-limited        value "B".
44              88  advance-pay-only      value "C".
45          10  cr-credit-limit         pic 9(04).
46          10  cr-current-balance      pic 9(04)V99.
47          10                          pic X(10).
48
49    Linkage Section.
50      01  ls-in-customer-id           pic X(04).
51      01  ls-customer-info.
52          10  ls-customer-id          pic x(04).
53          10  ls-customer-first-name  pic X(12).
54          10  ls-customer-last-name   pic X(12).
55          10  ls-street-address       pic X(25).
56          10  ls-city                 pic X(16).
57          10  ls-state                pic X(02).
58          10  ls-zip                  pic X(10).
59          10  ls-phone-number         pic X(12).
60          10  ls-credit-rating        pic X(01).
61              88  credit-excellent      value "A".
62              88  credit-limited        value "B".
63              88  advance-pay-only      value "C".
64          10  ls-credit-limit         pic $$,$$9.
65          10  ls-current-balance      pic $$,$$9.99.
66
67 Procedure Division Using ls-in-customer-id
68                          ls-customer-info.
69
70    000-Main-module.
71      Open Input Customer-File
72      Perform 200-process-user-request
73      Close Customer-File
74      Exit program
75      .
76    200-process-user-request.
77      If ls-in-customer-id = space
78        Move low-values to ls-customer-info
79      Else
80        Move spaces to ls-customer-info
81        Move ls-in-customer-id to cr-customer-id
82        Perform 800-read-customer-record
83        If ls-customer-info NOT = low-values
84          Perform 400-setup-customer-output
85        End-if *>customer-info = low-values
86      End-if
87      .
88    400-setup-customer-output.
89      Move cr-customer-first-name
90                        to ls-customer-first-name
91      Move cr-customer-last-name
92                        to ls-customer-last-name
93      Move cr-street-address    to ls-street-address
94      Move cr-city              to ls-city
95      Move cr-state             to ls-state
96      Move cr-zip               to ls-zip
97      Move cr-phone-number   to ls-phone-number
98      Move cr-credit-rating  to ls-credit-rating
99      Move cr-credit-limit   to ls-credit-limit
100     Move cr-current-balance to ls-current-balance
101     .
102   800-read-customer-record.
103     Read Customer-File
104       Invalid key
105       Move low-values to ls-customer-info
106     End-read
107     .
```

Cus-sub2.cbl

```
          $set sourceformat "free"
1  *>***********************************************
2  *> Saddle Order Application
3  *> W. Price  3/1/99              CUS-SUB3.CBL
4  *> Subprogram parameters are:
5  *>    in-customer-id  Input key field value for
6  *>                     file read.
7  *>    customer-info   Output customer information.
8  *> The subprogram accesses data from the following
9  *> two data files.
10 *>    CUSTOMER.DI: Indexed by Customer ID; contains
11 *>       customer name, address data and other data.
12 *>    ORDER.DI: Indexed by Order ID; contains order
13 *>    information.  Customer ID is secondary key.
14 *> The input parameter is the patron number
15 *> Output parameters are:
16 *>    Order name and address data
17 *>    Order count for customer
18 *>    Array containing order information
19 *>***********************************************
20
21 Identification Division.
22    Program-id. Customer3-Subprogram.
23
24    Environment Division.
25
26      Input-Output Section.
27      File-Control.
28        Select Customer-File assign to disk
29             "c:\Elements-CWP\NE-data\customer.di"
30             organization is indexed
31             access is random
32             record key is cr-customer-id.
33
34        Select Order-File assign to disk
35             "c:\Elements-CWP\NE-data\order.di"
36             organization is indexed
37             access is dynamic
38             record key is or-order-id
39             alternate key is or-customer-id
40               with duplicates.
```

Cus-sub3.cbl (1 of 3)

```
41
42 Data Division.
43    File Section.
44    FD  Customer-File.
45    01  customer-record.
46        10  cr-customer-id           pic x(04).
47        10  cr-customer-first-name   pic X(12).
48        10  cr-customer-last-name    pic X(12).
49        10  cr-street-address        pic X(25).
50        10  cr-city                  pic X(16).
51        10  cr-state                 pic X(02).
52        10  cr-zip                   pic X(10).
53        10  cr-phone-number          pic X(12).
54        10  cr-credit-rating         pic X(01).
55            88  credit-excellent       value "A".
56            88  credit-limited         value "B".
57            88  advance-pay-only       value "C".
58        10  cr-credit-limit          pic 9(04).
59        10  cr-current-balance       pic 9(04)V99.
60        10                           pic X(10).
61
62    FD  Order-File.
63    01  order-record.
64        10  or-order-id              pic x(03).
65        10  or-customer-id           pic x(04).
66        10  or-saddle-type           pic X(01).
67            88  type-western           value "W".
68            88  type-english           value "E".
69            88  type-spanish           value "S".
70        10  or-order-options.
71            20  or-stirrup-covers-sw   pic X(1).
72                88  stirrup-covers       value "Y".
73                88  no-stirrup-covers    value "N".
74            20  or-padded-seat-sw      pic X(1).
75                88  padded-seat          value "Y".
76                88  no-padded-seat       value "N".
77            20  or-leather-tooling     pic X(2).
78                88  tooling-none         value "NO".
79                88  tooling-basic        value "BA".
80                88  tooling-buffalo-bill value "BB".
81                88  tooling-coogan       value "CO".
82                88  tooling-aurilio      value "AU".
83                88  tooling-brush        value "BR".
84                88  tooling-horse-tail   value "HT".
85                88  tooling-custom       value "CU".
86            20  or-silver-ornaments    pic X(2).
87                88  silver-none          value "NO".
88                88  silver-beads         value "BE".
89                88  silver-bobbles       value "BO".
90                88  silver-bangles       value "BA".
91                88  silver-stars         value "ST".
92                88  silver-binary-digit  value "BD".
93                88  silver-custom        value "CU".
94        10  or-date-determination-fields.
95            20  or-order-date-count    pic 9(03).
96            20  or-start-date-count    pic 9(03).
97            20  or-promised-date-count pic 9(03).
98            20  or-scheduled-date-count pic 9(03).
99        10                           pic X(20).
100
101   Working-Storage Section.
102   01  program-switches.
103       10  end-of-file-sw           pic X(01).
104           88  end-of-file            value "Y".
105           88  not-end-of-file        value "N".
106   01  order-pointer                pic 9(02).
107
108   01  todays-date-info.
109       05  todays-date              pic 9(08).
110       05                           pic X(13).
111   01  the-date                     pic 9(08).
112   01  day-count                    pic 9(08).
113   01  ws-the-date.
114       05  ws-month                 pic Z9.
115       05                           pic X(01) value "/".
116       05  ws-day                   pic X(02).
117       05                           pic X(01) value "/".
118       05  ws-year                  pic X(04).
119

120 Linkage Section.
121    01  ls-in-customer-id           pic X(04).
122    01  ls-customer-info.
123        10  ls-customer-name         pic X(23).
124        10  ls-street-address        pic X(20).
125        10  ls-city-state-zip        pic X(28).
126        10  ls-phone-number          pic X(12).
127        10  ls-credit-rating         pic X(01).
128            88  credit-excellent       value "A".
129            88  credit-limited         value "B".
130            88  advance-pay-only       value "C".
131        10  ls-credit-limit          pic $$,$$9.
132        10  ls-current-balance       pic $$,$$9.99.
133
134    01  ls-order-counter            pic 9(02).
135    01  ls-order-info-array.
136        05  ls-order-info occurs 5 times.
137            10  ls-order-id            pic x(03).
138            10  ls-customer-id         pic x(04).
139            10  ls-saddle-type         pic X(07).
140            10  ls-order-options.
141                20  ls-stirrup-covers    pic X(3).
142                20  ls-padded-seat       pic X(3).
143                20  ls-leather-tooling   pic X(12).
144                20  ls-silver-ornaments  pic X(12).
145            10  ls-date-determination-fields.
146                20  ls-order-date        pic X(10).
147                20  ls-start-date        pic X(10).
148                20  ls-promised-date     pic X(10).
149                20  ls-scheduled-date    pic X(10).
150
151 Procedure Division Using ls-in-customer-id
152                           ls-customer-info
153                           ls-order-counter
154                           ls-order-info-array.
155
156 000-Main-module.
157     Open Input Customer-File
158                 Order-File
159     Perform 200-process-user-request
160     Close Customer-File
161           Order-File
162     Exit program
163     .
164 200-process-user-request.
165     Move spaces to ls-order-info-array
166     Move spaces to ls-customer-info
167     Move 0 to ls-order-counter
168     Move ls-in-customer-id to cr-customer-id
169     If ls-in-customer-id = space
170        Move low-values to ls-customer-info
171     Else
172        Perform 800-read-customer-record
173        If ls-customer-info = low-values
174           Continue
175        Else
176           Perform 400-setup-customer-output
177           Perform 820-read-order-records
178        End-if *>customer-info = low-values
179     End-if
180     .
181 400-setup-customer-output.
182     Move spaces to ls-customer-name
183     String cr-customer-first-name delimited by " "
184            " "
185            cr-customer-last-name
186            into ls-customer-name
187     Move cr-street-address to ls-street-address
188     Move spaces to ls-city-state-zip
189     String  cr-city delimited by " "
190             " "
191             cr-state
192             " "
193             cr-zip
194             into ls-city-state-zip
195     Move cr-phone-number   to ls-phone-number
196     Move cr-credit-rating  to ls-credit-rating
197     Move cr-credit-limit   to ls-credit-limit
198     Move cr-current-balance to ls-current-balance
199     .
```

Cus-sub3.cbl (2 of 3)

```
200   450-setup-order-output.
201     Move or-customer-id
202              to ls-customer-id (ls-order-counter)
203     Move or-order-id
204              to ls-order-id (ls-order-counter)
205     Evaluate True *>saddle type
206       When type-western
207         Move "Western"
208              to ls-saddle-type (ls-order-counter)
209       When type-english
210         Move "English"
211              to ls-saddle-type (ls-order-counter)
212       When type-spanish
213         Move "Spanish"
214              to ls-saddle-type (ls-order-counter)
215     End-evaluate *>True *>saddle type
216
217     Evaluate True *>stirrup covers
218       When stirrup-covers
219         Move "Yes"
220              to ls-stirrup-covers (ls-order-counter)
221       When no-stirrup-covers
222         Move "No"
223              to ls-stirrup-covers (ls-order-counter)
224     End-evaluate *>True *>stirrup covers
225
226     Evaluate True *>padded seat
227       When padded-seat
228         Move "Yes"
229              to ls-padded-seat (ls-order-counter)
230       When no-padded-seat
231         Move "No"
232              to ls-padded-seat (ls-order-counter)
233     End-evaluate *>True *>padded seat
234
235     Evaluate True *>tooling
236       When tooling-none
237         Move "None"
238              to ls-leather-tooling (ls-order-counter)
239       When tooling-basic
240         Move "Basic"
241              to ls-leather-tooling (ls-order-counter)
242       When tooling-buffalo-bill
243         Move "Buffalo Bill"
244              to ls-leather-tooling (ls-order-counter)
245       When tooling-coogan
246         Move "Coogan"
247              to ls-leather-tooling (ls-order-counter)
248       When tooling-aurilio
249         Move "Aurilio"
250              to ls-leather-tooling (ls-order-counter)
251       When tooling-brush
252         Move "Brush"
253              to ls-leather-tooling (ls-order-counter)
254       When tooling-horse-tail
255         Move "Horse Tail"
256              to ls-leather-tooling (ls-order-counter)
257       When tooling-custom
258         Move "Custom"
259              to ls-leather-tooling (ls-order-counter)
260     End-evaluate *>True *>tooling
261
262     Evaluate True *>silver ornaments
263       When silver-none
264         Move "None"
265              to ls-silver-ornaments (ls-order-counter)
266       When silver-beads
267         Move "Beads"
268              to ls-silver-ornaments (ls-order-counter)
269       When silver-bobbles
270         Move "Bobbles"
271              to ls-silver-ornaments (ls-order-counter)
272       When silver-bangles
273         Move "Bangles"
274              to ls-silver-ornaments (ls-order-counter)
275       When silver-stars
276         Move "Stars"
277              to ls-silver-ornaments (ls-order-counter)
278       When silver-binary-digit
279         Move "Binary Digit"
280              to ls-silver-ornaments (ls-order-counter)
281       When silver-custom
282         Move "Custom"
283              to ls-silver-ornaments (ls-order-counter)
284     End-evaluate *>True *>silver ornaments
285
286     Move or-order-date-count to day-count
287     Perform 500-compute-date
288     Move ws-the-date
289              to ls-order-date (ls-order-counter)
290
291     Add or-order-date-count, or-start-date-count
292                             giving day-count
293     Perform 500-compute-date
294     Move ws-the-date
295              to ls-start-date (ls-order-counter)
296
297     Add or-order-date-count, or-promised-date-count
298                             giving day-count
299     Perform 500-compute-date
300     Move ws-the-date
301              to ls-promised-date (ls-order-counter)
302
303     Add or-order-date-count, or-scheduled-date-count
304                             giving day-count
305     Perform 500-compute-date
306     Move ws-the-date
307              to ls-scheduled-date (ls-order-counter)
308   .
309   500-compute-date.
310   *> The input record includes due date as the
311   *> number of days from the date the program is
312   *> run. I do the following so that displayed
313   *> output looks current. Otherwise, the data
314   *> file would soon appear outdated.
315     Move Function current-date to todays-date-info
316     Compute day-count =
317              function integer-of-date (todays-date)
318                             + day-count - 400
319     Compute the-date =
320              function date-of-integer (day-count)
321     Move the-date(1:4) to ws-year
322     Move the-date(5:2) to ws-month
323     Move the-date(7:2) to ws-day
324   .
325   800-read-customer-record.
326     Read Customer-File
327       Invalid key
328       Move low-values to ls-customer-info
329     End-read
330
331   820-read-order-records.
332     Move 0 to ls-order-counter
333     Move  ls-in-customer-ID to or-customer-ID
334     Read Order-File key is or-customer-ID
335       invalid key
336         Continue
337       not invalid key
338         Add 1 to ls-order-counter
339         Perform 450-setup-order-output
340         Set not-end-of-file to true
341         Perform until end-of-file
342           Read Order-File next
343             at end
344               Set end-of-file to true
345             not at end
346               If ls-in-customer-ID = or-customer-ID
347                 Add 1 to ls-order-counter
348                 Perform 450-setup-order-output
349               Else
350                 Set end-of-file to true
351               End-If *>in-customer-ID ...
352           End-Read *>Order-File next
353         End-Perform *>until end-of-file
354     End-Read *>Order-File
355   .
```

Cus-sub3.cbl (3 of 3)

```
                $set sourceformat "free"                    46  Working-Storage Section.
 1 *>*******************************************       47    01  header-record.
 2 *> Saddle Order Application                          48        10  hr-order-id                  pic x(03).
 3 *> W. Price  3/1/99                  ORD-SUB1.CBL    49        10  hr-last-key                  pic 9(03).
 4 *> This subprogram provides for the addition of     50        10  hr-other                     pic X(40).
 5 *> records to the order file ORDER.DI.               51
 6 *> Key field is Order ID                             52  Linkage Section.
 7 *> First record (key value 000) contains the last   53    01  ls-order-info                    pic x(31).
 8 *> used key value in bytes 4-6 of that record.       54
 9 *> It is updated with each record addition.          55  Procedure Division Using  ls-order-info.
10 *>*******************************************       56
11                                                      57    000-Main-module.
12 Identification Division.                             58      Open I-O Order-File
13   Program-id. Order1-Subprogram.                     59      Perform 200-add-new-record
14                                                      60      Close Order-File
15    Environment Division.                             61      Exit program
16                                                      62        .
17     Input-Output Section.                            63    200-add-new-record.
18     File-Control.                                    64      Move "000" to or-order-id
19       Select Order-File assign to disk               65      Perform 800-read-order-record
20           "c:\Elements-CWP\NE-data\order.di"         66      Move order-record to header-record
21           organization is indexed                    67      Add 1 to hr-last-key
22           access is random                           68      Move hr-last-key to or-order-id
23           record key is or-order-id                  69      Move ls-order-info to order-record (4:)
24           alternate key is or-customer-id            70      Move "390160440460"
25             with duplicates.                         71                to or-date-determination-fields
26                                                      72      Perform 850-write-order-record
27 Data Division.                                       73      If or-order-id not = low-value
28   File Section.                                      74        Perform 860-rewrite-order-record
29     FD  Order-File.                                  75      End-If *>or-order-id not = low-value
30     01  order-record.                                76        .
31        10  or-order-id          pic x(03).           77    800-read-order-record.
32        10  or-customer-id       pic x(04).           78      Read Order-File
33        10  or-saddle-type       pic X(01).           79        Invalid key
34        10  or-order-options.                         80          Move low-values to ls-order-info
35           20  or-stirrup-covers-sw  pic X(1).        81      End-read
36           20  or-padded-seat-sw     pic X(1).        82        .
37           20  or-leather-tooling    pic X(2).        83    850-write-order-record.
38           20  or-silver-ornaments   pic X(2).        84      Write order-record
39        10  or-date-determination-fields.             85        Invalid key
40           20  or-order-date-count   pic 9(03).       86          Move low-values to or-order-id
41           20  or-start-date-count   pic 9(03).       87      End-write
42           20  or-promised-date-count pic 9(03).      88        .
43           20  or-scheduled-date-count pic 9(03).     89    860-rewrite-order-record.
44        10                          pic X(20).        90      Rewrite order-record from header-record
45                                                      91        Invalid key
                                                        92          Move low-values to or-order-id
                                                        93      End-rewrite
                                                        94        .
```

Ord-sub1.cbl

```
            $set sourceformat "free"
  1 *>*********************************************
  2 *> Saddle Order Application
  3 *> W. Price  3/1/99                  ORD-SUB2.CBL
  4 *> This subprogram provides read access to the
  5 *> following indexed file
  6 *>    ORDER.DI: Indexed by Order ID; contains
  7 *>       order number, customer ID, and other data.
  8 *> Subprogram parameters are:
  9 *>    in-order-ID  Input key field value for
 10 *>                      file read.
 11 *>    order-info       Output order information.
 12 *>*********************************************
 13
 14 Identification Division.
 15    Program-id. Order2-Subprogram.
 16
 17   Environment Division.
 18
 19      Input-Output Section.
 20      File-Control.
 21        Select Order-File assign to disk
 22             "c:\Elements-CWP\NE-data\order.di"
 23             organization is indexed
 24             access is random
 25             record key is or-order-id
 26             alternate key is or-customer-id
 27              with duplicates.
 28
 29 Data Division.
 30    File Section.
 31     FD  Order-File.
 32     01  order-record.
 33         10  or-order-id          pic x(03).
 34         10  or-customer-id       pic x(04).
 35         10  or-saddle-type       pic X(01).
 36            88  type-western      value "W".
 37            88  type-english      value "E".
 38            88  type-spanish      value "S".
 39         10  or-order-options.
 40            20  or-stirrup-covers-sw  pic X(1).
 41               88  stirrup-covers    value "Y".
 42               88  no-stirrup-covers value "N".
 43            20  or-padded-seat-sw  pic X(1).
 44               88  padded-seat       value "Y".
 45               88  no-padded-seat    value "N".
 46            20  or-leather-tooling  pic X(2).
 47               88  tooling-none      value "NO".
 48               88  tooling-basic     value "BA".
 49               88  tooling-buffalo-bill value "BB".
 50               88  tooling-coogan    value "CO".
 51               88  tooling-aurilio   value "AU".
 52               88  tooling-brush     value "BR".
 53               88  tooling-horse-tail value "HT".
 54               88  tooling-custom    value "CU".
 55            20  or-silver-ornaments  pic X(2).
 56               88  silver-none       value "NO".
 57               88  silver-beads      value "BE".
 58               88  silver-horseshoes value "BO".
 59               88  silver-rings      value "BA".
 60               88  silver-stars      value "ST".
 61               88  silver-binary-digit value "BD".
 62         10  or-date-determination-fields.
 63            20  or-order-date-count    pic 9(03).
 64            20  or-start-date-count    pic 9(03).
 65            20  or-promised-date-count pic 9(03).
 66            20  or-scheduled-date-count pic 9(03).
 67         10                          pic X(20).
 68

 69 Working-Storage Section.
 70
 71   01  todays-date-info.
 72       05  todays-date          pic 9(08).
 73       05                       pic X(13).
 74   01  the-date                 pic 9(08).
 75   01  day-count                pic 9(08).
 76   01  ws-the-date.
 77       05  ws-month             pic Z9.
 78       05                       pic X(01) value "/".
 79       05  ws-day               pic X(02).
 80       05                       pic X(01) value "/".
 81       05  ws-year              pic X(04).
 82
 83   Linkage Section.
 84   01  ls-in-order-ID           pic X(03).
 85   01  ls-order-info.
 86       10  ls-order-id              pic x(03).
 87       10  ls-customer-id           pic x(04).
 88       10  ls-saddle-type           pic X(07).
 89       10  ls-order-options.
 90          20  ls-stirrup-covers     pic X(3).
 91          20  ls-padded-seat        pic X(3).
 92          20  ls-leather-tooling    pic X(12).
 93          20  ls-silver-ornaments   pic X(12).
 94       10  ls-date-determination-fields.
 95          20  ls-order-date         pic X(10).
 96          20  ls-start-date         pic X(10).
 97          20  ls-promised-date      pic X(10).
 98          20  ls-scheduled-date     pic X(10).
 99
100 Procedure Division Using ls-in-order-ID
101                           ls-order-info.
102
103   000-Main-module.
104     Open Input Order-File
105     Perform 200-process-user-request
106     Close Order-File
107     Exit program
108
109   200-process-user-request.
110     Move spaces to ls-order-info
111     Move ls-in-order-ID to or-order-ID
112     Perform 800-read-order-record
113     If ls-order-info NOT = low-values
114        Perform 400-setup-order-output
115     End-if *>order-info = low-values
116       .
117   400-setup-order-output.
118     Move or-customer-id to ls-customer-id
119
120     Evaluate True *>saddle type
121        When type-western
122           Move "Western" to ls-saddle-type
123        When type-english
124           Move "English" to ls-saddle-type
125        When type-spanish
126           Move "Spanish" to ls-saddle-type
127     End-evaluate *>True *>saddle type
128
129     Evaluate True *>stirrup covers
130        When stirrup-covers
131          Move "Yes" to ls-stirrup-covers
132        When no-stirrup-covers
133          Move "No" to ls-stirrup-covers
134     End-evaluate *>True *>stirrup covers
135
```

Ord-sub2.cbl (1 of 2)

```
136   Evaluate True *>padded seat                 178
137     When padded-seat                          179   Move or-order-date-count to day-count
138       Move "Yes" to ls-padded-seat            180   Perform 500-compute-date
139     When no-padded-seat                       181   Move ws-the-date to ls-order-date
140       Move "No" to ls-padded-seat             182
141   End-evaluate *>True *>padded seat           183   Add or-order-date-count, or-start-date-count
142                                                184                             giving day-count
143   Evaluate True *>tooling                     185   Perform 500-compute-date
144     When tooling-none                         186   Move ws-the-date to ls-start-date
145       Move "None" to ls-leather-tooling       187
146     When tooling-basic                        188   Add or-order-date-count, or-promised-date-count
147       Move "Basic" to ls-leather-tooling      189                             giving day-count
148     When tooling-buffalo-bill                 190   Perform 500-compute-date
149     Move "Buffalo Bill" to ls-leather-tooling 191   Move ws-the-date to ls-promised-date
150     When tooling-coogan                       192
151       Move "Coogan" to ls-leather-tooling     193   Add or-order-date-count, or-scheduled-date-count
152     When tooling-aurilio                      194                             giving day-count
153       Move "Aurilio" to ls-leather-tooling    195   Perform 500-compute-date
154     When tooling-brush                        196   Move ws-the-date to ls-scheduled-date
155       Move "Brush" to ls-leather-tooling      197   .
156     When tooling-horse-tail                   198   500-compute-date.
157       Move "Horse Tail" to ls-leather-tooling 199   *> The input record includes due date as the
158     When tooling-custom                       200   *> number of days from the date the program is
159       Move "Custom" to ls-leather-tooling     201   *> run. I do the following so that displayed
160   End-evaluate *>True *>tooling               202   *> output looks current. Otherwise, the data
161                                                203   *> file would soon appear outdated.
162   Evaluate True *>silver ornaments            204   Move Function current-date to todays-date-info
163     When silver-none                          205   Compute day-count =
164       Move "None" to ls-silver-ornaments      206         function integer-of-date (todays-date)
165     When silver-beads                         207                             + day-count - 400
166       Move "Beads" to ls-silver-ornaments     208   Compute the-date =
167     When silver-bobbles                       209         function date-of-integer (day-count)
168       Move "Bobbles" to ls-silver-ornaments   210   Move the-date(1:4) to ws-year
169     When silver-bangles                       211   Move the-date(5:2) to ws-month
170       Move "Bangles" to ls-silver-ornaments   212   Move the-date(7:2) to ws-day
171     When silver-stars                         213
172       Move "Stars" to ls-silver-ornaments     214   .
173     When silver-binary-digit                  215   800-read-order-record.
174     Move "Binary Digit" to ls-silver-ornaments 216   Read Order-File
175     When silver-custom                        217     Invalid key
176       Move "Custom" to ls-silver-ornaments    218     Move low-values to ls-order-info
177   End-evaluate *>True *>silver ornaments      219   End-read
                                                   220   .
```

Ord-sub2.cbl (2 of 2)

Index

A

Accept statement 45, 47
   accessing Cookie with 263, 264
Access database management system 294-296
Alias 301
Alias 312
Aligning controls 111, 112
Animate 67, 68
Application file 12
Application Wizard 147, 148
   with SQL database 317-322
Asymmetric program 218
Attribute 60-62
   ID 61
   MaxLength 61
   Name 61, 62
   Size 61
   Title 61
   Value 61
Autofix, IDE 24

B

Back button 82
Background-Image property 196
Bar, Horizontal control 71
Bitmap file 195
BODY tag 38,
Book data file listing 331
Book file record format 331
Book file 166
Book-sub.cbl subprogram listing 336
Book-sub.cbl, subprogram 230, 231
Book-sub1.cbl subprogram listing 337
Book-sub2.cbl subprogram listing 338
Book-sub3.cbl subprogram listing 338
Borders project 197-200
Borders.cbl CGI listing 200
BR tag 38
Breakpoint 20-22
Browser back button 82
Browser 29, 30
Bug 6

C

CD, Examples Application 4, 5
CGI generation, saving CBL file 87
CGI 42, 43
CGI program
   creation of 64-66
   execution of 78, 79
   generated components 76-78
   Net Express generated 76-92
   symmetric 287-289
   user application code 79
CGI program description
   Pat02.cbl 288, 290
   Pat03write 293-295
   Sql02 315
   Sstate01sav.cbl 266-268
   Sstate02order 272-274
CGI program listing
   Borders.cbl CGI 200
   Cookie01a.cbl CGI 255

Cookie01b.cbl CGI 256
Cookie01d.cbl CGI 257
Cookie02code.cbl CGI 260
Cookie02get.cbl CGI 261
Lib06.cbl CGI 145
Lib07.cbl 148
Lib08.cbl CGI 155
Lib10.cbl CGI 171
Lib11.cbl CGI 177
Lib12.cbl CGI 180
Lib15.cbl CGI 223
Lib16.cbl CGI 229
Lib17.cbl CGI 233, 234
Ltr01.cbl CGI 113
Pat01.cbl CGI 286
Pat02.cbl CGI 289
Pat03write.cbl CGI 295
Sql01.cbl CGI 308
Sql02.cbl CGI 316
Sstate02find.cbl CGI 273
Sstate02order.cbl CGI 273
State01ret.cbl CGI 267
State01sav.cbl CGI 267
CGI.skl skeleton file 5
Cgi-bin folder 192
CGI-min.skl skeleton file 5, 65
CGI-nibi.skl skeleton file 5, 65
Check Box 100-104
   attribute, Checked 103
   attribute, Name 103
   attribute, Value 103
   CGI code 104
   creating 101
   HTML produced by 102
   initializing 212
Checked attribute, Check Box 103
Checked attribute, Radio Button 105
Client 28-30
Client/server 28-30, 36,37
Cloning an application 84-88
COBOLOccurs property 178, 180
COBOLPicture property 61, 64
Color display 129-133
Color icon 69
Column headings 117, 118
Common Gateway Interface 42, 43
Compile button 16
Compiler directive, sourceformat 22
Compiler directive, SQL 307
Compiler errors 18
Component diagram 219
   Cookie01 251
   Cookie02 258
   Cookie03 261
   Hidde03 249
   Hidden01 242
   Hidden02 246
   Lib 17 231
   Lib15 219
   Lib16 227
   Pat01 284
   Pat02 288

Pat03 291
Sql04 321
Sstate01 265
Sstate02 271
Connect statement, SQL 305, 306, 314, 315
Control tree 56
Control
   Check Box 100-104
   dominant 111
   Hidden Input , name display 244, 245
   Hidden Input 240-250
   Image 195-197
   Input Button 213
   Input Image 199, 200
   Input Password 246, 247
   insertion of 59, 60
   Radio Button 100, 105-109
   Reset Button 115
   Select 121-127
   Server-Side Text 63, 64
   Submit 62
   Table 115-120
   Table 173-176
   Text Input 60, 61
   Text Input, for output 71
   Text 58, 59
   TextArea 170
   Text Input, ReadOnly attribute 154
Controls, alignment of 111, 112
Controls, grouping of 110-111
Cookie, accessing with Accept 263, 264
Cookie 240
   CGI code 253-257
   Expiration date 262, 263
   inserting into a form 252, 253
   persistent 259-263
   retrieving 255-257
   with server-side file 269-273
Cookie01 project 251-257
Cookie01 project 258-261
Cookie01a.cbl CGI listing 255
Cookie01b.cbl CGI listing 256
Cookie01d.cbl CGI listing 257
Cookie02code.cbl CGI listing 260
Cookie02get.cbl CGI listing 261
Cookie03 project 260, 261
Cooperative computing 28
Copy file 284
   CPF 76-78
   CPV 77, 78
   CPY 76-78
   displaying 83
CPF copy file 76-78
CPV copy file 77, 78
CPY copy file 76-78
Cross-platform page 55
Cursor, SQL 310
Cus-sub2.cbl subprogram listing 344
Cus-sub3.cbl subprogram listing 344
Customer data file listing 341
Customer file record format 341

D

Data file listing
   Book 331
   Customer 341
   Order 342
   Patron 330

Data file, designating access to 329
Data validation 157-161
Database management system, Access 294-296
Database table 294-296
Database, relational 294
Debug folder 17, 192
Debug 19-22
Deploy Web application 9
DI file 92
Diagram, component 219
   (see also component diagram)
Disconnect statement, SQL 305, 306, 314, 315
Display statement 45
Domain name 33, 34
Dominant control 111
Duplicating a CGI 87, 88
Duplicating an application 84-88

E

Elements-CWP folder 4
Embedded HTML 47, 78, 79
Embedded SQL 296-309
end tag 39
Entry point, subprogram 266
Entry points, Sstate subprogram 276, 277
Error message 18, 19
ESQL (see Embedded SQL)
Event handler 204-213, 290
   creating Help window 205-208
   defined 204
   setting check boxes with 212
   setting radio buttons with 212
   setting values with 208-211
Event 204
Events01 project 206-208
Events02 project 208-211
Examples Application CD 4, 5
Existing application project 142-144
Expiration date, cookie 262, 263
External-form clause 43-47
   repeating data 178-180
Extranet 31

F

File access 90-93
File processing 284-295
   maintenance 290-295
   record addition 284-295
File (also see Data file listings)
   DI 92
   IDX 92
   image 195
Fix-attr.bat 5
Folder,
   cgi-bin 192
   debug 17, 192
   Elements-CWP 4, 53
   naming standard 4
   NE-Data 92, 328, 4, 5
   NE-Examples 4, 14, 53
   NE-Images 4, 193,194
   NE-Progs 4, 5
   NE-Utils 4
Fonts, IDE 24
Form Designer 56, 57
Form Express 147-157, 184-187
   application creation 149-151
   modifying HTML pages 152-157

FORM tag 38, 40, 41
Format tool bar 69
Free format 22, 23

G

Gateway program 30
Get-date.cbl subprogram listing 332
GIF file 195
Graphic, as hyperlink 203, 204
Graphics file 70, 71, 195
Graphics, adding to a page 195, 196
Grid size, changing 153
Grouping controls 110, 111

H

HEAD tag 38, 40
heading tag 38, 39
Help window, event handler 205-208
Hidden Input control 240-250
    CGI considerations 243-245
    name display 244,245
    toolbar icon 242
Hidden01 project 241-245
Hidden02 project 246, 247
Hidden03 project 249, 250
Horizontal Bar control 71
Host computer 33
Host variable 300
Hotspot 201
HTM file 66
HTML 29, 30, 37-41
    Page Wizard 55, 56
    tag (see tag, HTML)
HTTP 32
Hyperlink 201
    creating 201, 202
    graphic as 203, 204
Hypertext Markup Language (see HTML)
HyperText Transfer Protocol 32

I

Icon, project 6
ID attribute 61
IDE 12-15, 24
    autofix 24
    color 24
    fonts 24
Identified by phrase 44-47
ID Radio Button attribute 105
IDX file 92
If command, JavaScript 322
Image control 195-197
Image file 70, 71, 195
Input Button control 213
Input HTML tag 102
Input Image control 199, 200
Input page 57-62
Input Password control 246, 247
Input tag 38, 40, 41
INT file 15
Integrated Development Environment 12-15, 24
Interface, CGI 42
    ISAPI 42
    NSAPI 42

Internet 28, 29
    addressing 32
    Application Wizard 64-66
    protocol 32
    Server Application Program Interface 42
Intranet 31
ISAPI 42

J

JavaScript 157, 205, 207-213
    commands, if 322
    JavaScript, alert statement 207-208
    data validation functions 157-159
    setting check boxes with 212
    setting radio buttons with 212
    JavaScript, setting values with 208-211
Join, SQL 310
JPEG file 195
Justify text 112

L

Lib01 project 54-68
Lib02 project 79-83
Lib03 project 84
Lib04 project 88-90
Lib05 project 91-93
Lib06 project 142-146
Lib07 project 146, 147
Lib08 project 148-155
Lib09 project 156
Lib10 project 167-172
Lib11 project 172-178
Lib12 project 178-183
Lib13 project 184-187
Lib14 project 201, 202
Lib15 project 218-225
Lib16 project 226-229
Lib17 project 229-234
Lib01.cbl CGI 76-78
Lib03.cbl CGI 77, 88
Lib06.cbl CGI 145, 146
Lib07.cbl CGI 146, 147
Lib08.cbl CGI 155
Lib10.cbl CGI 171, 172
Lib11.cbl CGI 177,178
Lib12cbl CGI 177-182
Lib15.cbl CGI 221-224
Lib16.cbl CGI 228, 229
Lib17.cbl CGI 233, 234
Lib01.cbl CGI listing 77, 81
Lib05.cbl CGI listing 93
Lib06.cbl CGI listing 145
Lib07.cbl CGI listing 148
Lib08.cbl CGI listing 155
Lib10.cbl CGI listing 171
Lib11.cbl CGI listing 177
Lib12.cbl CGI listing 180
Lib15.cbl CGI listing 223
Lib16.cbl CGI listing 229
Lib17.cbl CGI listing 233, 234
Lib-cal1.cbl 12
Library inquiry application 34, 35, 52
Lib-sub0.cbl subprogram listing 332, 343
Lib-sub0.cbl subprogram 88, 89
Lib-sub1.cbl subprogram 91
    listing 333, 343

Lib-sub2.cbl subprogram 140-144
    listing 334
Lib-sub3.cbl subprogram 12, 16, 167-169
    listing 334
Ltr01 project 100, 109-111
Ltr01.cbl CGI listing 113

M
MaxLength attribute 61
MFF file 66
Microsoft Access 294
Multiple output forms 226-229
Multiple Submit buttons 229-234
    Name attribute 232
Multiple-screen input 247-258

N
Name
    attribute 61, 62
        Check Box 103
        HTML 62
        Radio Button attribute 105-109
Name/value pair 41
Naming convention 54
NE-Data folder 4, 5, 92, 328
NE-Examples folder 4, 14
NE-Images folder 4, 193, 194
NE-Progs folder 4, 5
NE-Utils folder 4
Net Express project 12
Net Express toolbar 15,16
Netscape Server Application Program Interface 42
NSAPI 42

O
ODBC 297, 298
    driver 297
Open Database Connectivity 297, 298
OpenESQL Assistant 299-316
Order data file listing 342
Order file record format 342
Ord-sub1.cbl subprogram listing 347
Ord-sub2.cbl subprogram listing 348
Output page 63, 64

P
P tag 38, 39
Page Element control, Horizontal Bar 71
Page Element 71
Page file, HTM 66
    MFF 66
Password (see Input Password control)
Pat01 project 284-286
Pat01.cbl CGI listing 286
Pat02 project 287-290
Pat02.cbl CGI listing 289
Pat02.cbl CGI program 288, 290
Pat03 project 290-295
Pat03write CGI program 293-295
Pat03write.cbl CGI listing 295
Pat1-sub subprogram 283
Pat2-sub subprogram 283
Pat3-sub subprogram 283
Patron file 166
    data listing 330
    record format 282, 330
Pat-sub1.cbl subprogram listing 339

Pat-sub2.cbl subprogram listing 340
Pat-sub3.cbl subprogram listing 340
Persistent cookie, 259-263
Positional form 57
Program stepping 18
Program (also see CGI program listings)
    asymmetric 218
    symmetric 218-223
Project creation 53-55
Project folders
    Proj0301 54, 55
    Proj0401 79
    Proj0402 84
    Proj0403 88-90
    Proj0404 91
    Proj0501 100, 109
    Proj0502 115
    Proj0503 121
    Proj0504 125
    Proj0505 130
    Proj0601 142
    Proj0602 146
    Proj0603 148
    Proj0701 167
    Proj0702 172
    Proj0703 178
    Proj0704 184
    Proj0801 197
    Proj0802 201
    Proj0803 206
    Proj0804 208
    Proj0901 218
    Proj0902 226
    Proj0903 229
    Proj1001 241
    Proj1002 246
    Proj1003 249
    Proj1004 251
    Proj1005 258
    Proj1006 260
    Proj1007 265
    Proj1008 270
    Proj1101 284
    Proj1102 287
    Proj1103 290
    Proj1104 299
    Proj1104 311
    Proj1106 317
    Proj1107 321
Project
    completed 66
    icon 6
    rom existing application 142-144
    Net Express 12
    screen 66
Projects
    Borders 197-200
    Cookie01 251-257
    Cookie02 258-261
    Cookie03 260, 261
    Events01 206-208
    Events02 208-211
    Hidden01 241-245
    Hidden02 246, 247
    Hidden03 249, 250
    Lib01 54-68
    Lib02 79-83

Lib03 84
Lib04 88-90
Lib05 91-93
Lib06 142-146
Lib07 146, 147
Lib08 148-155
Lib09 156
Lib10 167-172
Lib11 172-178
Lib12 178-183
Lib13 184-187
Lib14 201, 202
Lib15 218-225
Lib16 226-229
Lib17 229-234
Ltr01 100, 109-111
Pat01 284-286
Pat02 287-290
Pat03 290-295
Select01 121-125
Select02 125-129
Select03 130-134
Sql01 299-310
Sql02 311-316
Sql03 317-319
Sql04 321, 322
Sstate01 265-269
Sstate02 270-274
Table01 115-120
Table02 119, 120
Properties, COBOLOccurs 178-180
Property (see also Attribute)
    Background-Image 196
    COBOLPicture 61, 64
    style 69, 70
Property pane, Form Designer 57
Publish Web application 9

Q
Query, multiple 311-316
    simple 300-302

R
Radio Button 100, 105-109
    CGI user-inserted code 108
    initializing 212
    multiple groups 109, 110
    Net Express generated CGI code 107, 108
Radio Button attribute
    Checked 105
    ID 105
    Name 105-109
    Value 105-109
ReadOnly attribute, Text Input control 154
Rebuild 67, 68
Rebuild button 16, 17
Record format
    Book file 282, 331
    Customer file 341
    Order file 342
    Patron file 330
Relational database 294
Repeating data, External-Form 178-180
Repetition control, with Hidden Input 241, 242

Reset Button control 115
Run 67, 68
Run button 16, 17
Run Through button 20

S
Save-As command, HTML page 85
Script Assistant 204-208
Search criterion, SQL 302-304
Searching, string 133, 134
Security control
    with Cookie 258-261
    with Hidden Input 245-247
Select control 121-127
    properties 121, 124
    CGI user-inserted code 125
    CGI user-inserted code, multiple selection 128
    multiple selection 125, 126
    Select Options 122, 123
Select, SQL 302
Select01 project 121-125
Select02 project 125-129
Select02.cbl CGI program 128
Select03 project 130-134
Server 28-30
Server, Solo 67
Server-side file, using cookie with 269-273
Server-side program 30
Server-Side Text control 63, 64
Server-side-file records, removing 272, 274
Share, Web 192-194
Size attribute 61
Skeleton file
    CGI.skl 5
    CGI-min.skl 5
    CGI-nibi.skl 5, 221
Software update 6
Solo 67, 192
Source pool, adding files 90, 268, 269
Span 58, 59
Span HTML tag 102
Span, from Form Express 152, 153
SQL 296
    code, inserting into CGI 304-307, 314,31
    compiler directive 307
    Connect statement 305, 306, 314, 315
    cursor 310
    Disconnect statement 305, 306, 314, 315
    join 310
    Search criterion, 302-304
    Select 302
    view 310
    Working-Storage entries 307
Sql01 project 299-310
Sql01.cbl CGI listing 308
Sql02 CGI program 315
Sql02 project 311-316
Sql02.cbl CGI listing 316
Sql03 project 317-319
Sql04 project 321, 322
SRC Image entry 196
Sstate subprogram 264, 265
    entry points 276, 277
Sstate01 project 265-269

Sstate01sav.cbl CGI program 266-268
Sstate02 project 270-274
Sstate02find.cbl CGI listing 273
Sstate02order CGI program 272-274
Sstate02order.cbl CGI listing 273
State preservation 240
    server-side file 240, 264-274
    with cookie 240, 251-264
    with Hidden Input control 240-250
    with persistent cookie 259-263
State01ret.cbl CGI listing 267
State01sav.cbl CGI listing 267
Statelessness, Web 141, 142
Statement, SQL Connect 305, 306, 314, 315
    SQL Disconnect 305, 306, 314, 315
Step action 18-22
Step button 16
String search 133, 134
Structured Query Language 296
Style property 69, 70
    Background-Color 70
    Background-Image 70, 71
    Border-Style 70
    Border-Width 70
Submit button control 62
    multiple in a form 229-234
Subprogram
    adding to project 89, 90
    entry point 266
Subprogram listings
    Book-sub.cbl 336
    Book-sub1.cbl 337
    Book-sub2.cbl 338
    Book-sub3.cbl 338
    Cus-sub2.cbl 344
    Cus-sub3.cbl 344
    Get-date.cbl 332
    Lib-sub0.cbl 332
    Lib-sub0.cbl 343
    Lib-sub1.cbl 333
    Lib-sub1.cbl 343
    Lib-sub2.cbl 334
    Lib-sub3.cbl 334
    Ord-sub1.cbl 347
    Ord-sub2.cbl 348
    Pat-sub1.cbl 339
    Pat-sub2.cbl 340
    Pat-sub3.cbl 340
Subprograms
    Book-sub.cbl 230, 231
    Lib-sub0.cbl 88, 89
    Lib-sub1.cbl 91
    Lib-sub2.cbl 140-144
    Lib-sub3.cbl 12, 167-169
    Pat1-sub.cbl 283
    Pat2-sub.cbl 283
    Pat3-sub.cbl 283
    Sstate 264, 265
Subscripted data items
Symmetric CGI 218-223, 287-289

T
Table
    control 115-120, 173-176
    Data 116
    database 294-296
    inserting cells 117
    inserting controls into 118, 119
    Row 116
    search criterion, SQL 303-304
    type, VariableArray table 183
Table01 project 115-120
Table02 project 119, 120
Tag, HTML 37-41
    BODY 38,
    BR 38
    end 39
    FORM 38, 40, 41
    HEAD 38, 40
    heading 38, 39
    Input 38, 40, 41, 102
    P 38, 39
    TITLE 38, 39
Tag, Span, HTML 102
Template file
    CGI.skl 5
    CGI-min.skl 5
    CGI-nibi.skl 5, 221
Text control 58, 59
Text Input control 60, 61
    for output 71
    ReadOnly attribute 154
Text justification 112
TextArea control 170
TIF file 195
Title attribute 61
TITLE tag 38, 39
Tool bar, format 69
Toolbar, Net Express 15,16

U
Universal computer 28
Universal Resource Locator (see URL)
URL 33, 34

V
Validation, data 157-161
Value attribute 61
    Check Box 103
    Radio Button attribute 105-109
Variable, host 300
VariableArray table type 183
View, SQL 310

W
Web 28-31
Web application, deployment 9
    document 29
    page 29, 30
    server 30
    server, Solo 67
    share 192-194
    site 30
    as client server 36-37
    stateless nature 141, 142
WebSync 6-8
Wizard
    Application 147, 148
    HTML Page 55, 56
    Internet Application 64-66
World Wide Web 28-31
    (see also Web)

Other COBOL Books From Object-Z Publishing

Object-Z Publishing specializes in COBOL books to bring you tools that are critical to the rapidly changing computing landscape. For more information or to order any of the following, refer to our Web site **www.objectz.com**.

Elements of Object-Oriented COBOL, 1997, W. Price, ISBN 0-9655945-0-5
This pace-setting book presents the basic principles of object methodology as implemented with object-oriented features of the next COBOL standard. It includes a diskette with numerous example applications prepared with Micro Focus COBOL.

Elements of Micro Focus Dialog System, 1999, A. Lorents, SSBN 0-9655945-4-8
This book shows you how to develop Windows interfaces to Cobol programs using MERANT Micro Focus Dialog System. Numerous examples are presented in a tutorial format to facilitate self-study.

Available during 2000—check our Web site www.objectz.com.

COBOL 2000+, Procedural Features & Enhancements in the Next COBOL Standard, 2000, D. Schricker and E. Arranga, ISBN 0-9655945-5-6
Written by two outstanding figures in the world of COBOL (Schriker is the chair of X3J4, the COBOL technical committee) this lucid book gives you an insight, replete with examples, to the wide array of new features in the next Standard.

Basics of Merant/Micro Focus Interactive Development Environment (IDE), 2000, P. Mulchen and W. Price. A fully illustrated, example rich introduction to using the Merant/Micro Focus Interactive Development Environment. Written by people who know the ins and outs of the system.

Elements of Object-Oriented COBOL, Second Edition, 2000, W. Price, ISBN 0-9655945-6-4
Expands on the first edition including an introduction to abstract data types and a significant expansion of collection classes. An appendix is devoted to using Micro Focus Net Express for running applications.